DUTCH CALVINISM
IN MODERN AMERICA

DUTCH CALVINISM IN MODERN AMERICA

A HISTORY OF A CONSERVATIVE SUBCULTURE

James D. Bratt

WILLIAM B. EERDMANS PUBLISHING COMPANY
GRAND RAPIDS, MICHIGAN

Copyright © 1984 by Wm. B. Eerdmans Publishing Co.
255 Jefferson Ave. S.E., Grand Rapids, Mich. 49503
Printed in the United States of America

Library of Congress Cataloging in Publication Data:

Bratt, James D., 1949–
  Dutch Calvinism in modern America.

  Bibliography: p. 307.
  Includes index.
  1. Reformed Church—United States—History. 2. Dutch
—United States—Religion. 3. Calvinism—United States—
History. I. Title.
BX9495.B73 1984   285.7'73   84-13717

ISBN 0-8028-0009-2

To my grandparents

Henry Bratt
Emma Koning
Theunis Ribbens
Gertrude De Witt

Lions in the tribe of Judah

Contents

Preface   ix
Acknowledgments   xii
Illustrations   xiii

PART I: THE NETHERLANDIC BACKGROUND
Chapter 1   Secession and Its Tangents   3
Chapter 2   Abraham Kuyper and Neo-Calvinism   14

PART II: DUTCH, REFORMED, AND AMERICAN:
DEFINITIONS, 1900–1916
Chapter 3   Varieties of Reformed Experience   37
Chapter 4   Reconnoitering America   55
Chapter 5   Politics: Theory, Taste, and Trouble   67

PART III: WARS WITHOUT AND WITHIN, 1917–1928
Chapter 6   Dutch Americans and World War I   83
Chapter 7   Forming the Battle Lines, 1919–1920   93
Chapter 8   The Resolution, 1921–1928   105

PART IV: THE CONSOLIDATED COMMUNITY, 1928–1948
Chapter 9   A Religious Fortress   123
Chapter 10 Calvinists in a Darkening World   142

PART V: REBELLION AND REFRACTION
Chapter 11 Four Renegade Novelists   159

PART VI: AT HOME AND UNEASY, 1948–1970s
Chapter 12 Americanization Again, 1948–1963   187
Chapter 13 Evangelical and Ethnic, 1964–1970s   204

Appendix   222
Notes   225
Selected Bibliography   307
Index   325

Preface

In the past fifteen years, two blocs of Americans have been re-discovered—ethnics and evangelicals. This is a study of a group that belongs to both, but to neither (nor to "America" itself) altogether comfortably. That is the first anomaly. Another is the very persistence of a Dutch-American network late into the twentieth century. If any group should have "melted" into American society, it is these people with their northwest European origins, their nearly Anglo-Saxon lineage, their Protestant religion and Protestant ethic. And socially, in fact, the Dutch have adjusted quite well. By and large they are prosperous and patriotic, little troubled by the problems of the less fortunate.

But their *cultural* record tells a different story, one heavy with a sense of antagonism and displacement. Of southern and eastern Europeans, perhaps America's least regarded immigrants, such might be expected. Why do the same chords—reflexive hostility to a derisive establishment, and the feeling of being an embarrassment in a liberal, secular society—reverberate also through this "favored group's" experience?[1] And why the uneasiness with evangelicalism, which, after all, has also been "outcast" for much of this century and, in many of its sectors, shares specific religious roots (Reformed theology and a pietistic mode) with the Dutch?

In pursuit of these and other enigmas, this book explores the intellectual history of those communities established by the Dutch who immigrated to the United States between the 1840s and World War I. It describes the substance of their thought—the ideas, the opinions, the issues of consequence—but especially the mentalities that shaped it. Like much recent historiography (but also, I would argue, in better tune with the historical record), it gives particular emphasis to the lasting European influences upon the ethnic experience, to the ways in which the Dutch past persisted through and even helped promote changes in the new world.

This is also necessarily a work in religious history. For Dutch America, theology has supplied the terms, and the church and its subsidiaries have supplied the forum, of intellectual discourse. Their cultural record is hardly truncated on this account, however, for if there is one thing these people have insisted on, it is that religion includes all of life, that it stands as the source and judge of all other human activity.

ix

Consequently, the group has for decades applied the lens of its faith to American society and culture, to political events and social theories, to art, science, and scholarship.

Hence the political and social correlates of religious thought have a large place in what follows. It will be obvious that in these areas as elsewhere the Dutch were governed by decidedly "conservative" instincts. Without attempting a final definition of that term, I have sketched the philosophical and psychological patterns that describe conservativism in the Dutch case. I took pains—and some pleasure—in pointing out where these correlations deviate from the predictable. Where they do not and where I have disagreed with the conclusions they drew, I have generally accepted my subjects on their own terms, criticizing only failure to fulfill professed intentions.

The other central issue in this account is, inevitably, "Americanization." I have not tried to resolve the confusion that surrounds this word too, but I do offer certain corrective points. First, the term as traditionally used (i.e., with regard to cuisine, holiday customs, and manners of speech and dress) may touch only the surface of ethnic life, missing the complex interchanges that acculturation comprises. Second, "Americanization" transcends "the language question" with which it is too often identified. In the Dutch case, at least, the same cultural forces were at work before, during, and after the language change. Third, conflicts arose not only between the group and the larger society but also, and equally, within the community itself. Most important, the *object* of acculturation is at least as crucial as its *degree;* the question of how much a group has "Americanized" must always be paired with an inquiry as to which stream of American life—indeed, which "America"—it has joined.

Finally, for the Dutch as for others, "Americanization" also entailed "modernization."[2] There is no reason to explicate here either the phenomenon or the commentary it has bred, but the coincidence does in part account for my giving detailed exposition to certain arguments and attitudes below. These show not only newcomers assessing America, but a whole group struggling into modernity. I hope this book, therefore, will provide useful material for scholars interested in the latter sort of question. I also hope that the "educated laity" that Dutch Calvinism has produced in such abundance will appreciate this account of their history. To keep the presentation less cluttered for them, I have put most theoretical and group-comparative commentary in the notes.

Having said something of what this study *is,* I should like to clarify what it is *not.* It gives considerable attention to the social context of intellectual life, but it is not intended as a social history.* There already

---

* Basic denominational statistics that provide a backdrop to this study are provided in the Appendix, pp. 222–24.

exist two fine traditional works in that vein, and promising explorations of the group by "new" social historians are in progress.[3] In addition, I cover only the latter of the two principal eras of Dutch-American settlement. The immigration of the colonial era constituted quite a different movement, requiring separate treatment. The ties that did develop between the colonial and nineteenth-century communities I have treated only to the extent that they were significant for the later movement. Finally, within that later movement, I cover the twentieth-century phase more than the nineteenth-century phase, which means that I treat the descendants of immigrants as much as the immigrants themselves. I made this choice partly to rectify a common historiographical imbalance and partly to cross over the traditional watershed of the language question and examine ethnic life in its later stages.

Some closing words on terminology. With a few exceptions for purposes of style, I have designated the people and language of the Netherlands not as "Hollanders" and "Holland" but as "Dutch," to me the more accurate usage.* "Reformed" I have unavoidably had to use sometimes as the name of a specific denomination, other times as the designation for a larger tradition and community. I have tried to make clear in each case which sense applies. I also talk much of "Calvinism," another term defying precise definition, because my subjects themselves used—indeed took pride in—the name. What they meant by it, of course, was not exactly what John Calvin taught in sixteenth-century Geneva; nor was it the nebulous characterization assigned all sorts of psycho-social phenomena in the name of Max Weber. Rather, this type of "Calvinism" stemmed from one interpretation of Reformation thought as developed under particular national circumstances over several centuries. More specific explication is given in the appropriate places throughout the text. Finally, I have used "Dutch-American" and "Dutch Reformed in America" interchangably. As I realize only too well, many Dutch immigrants did not move into Dutch-American settlements at all, and some who did join the settlements did not join the Reformed denominations. But because this study concerns the enduring community, I have had to let these "outsiders" go. With that understanding, the two terms are equated for reasons of style and nuance.

---

* All translations from the Dutch are my own.

Acknowledgments

Of the many people who helped with this work, my gratitude goes first to Sydney E. Ahlstrom, who supervised it as a doctoral dissertation. His suggestions on structure and substance greatly aided my presentation; his encouragement and sympathy helped sustain me not only at the dissertation stage but through all my years in graduate school. It was a privilege then to work under such a model of humane learning, but it has been only later, in the trials of teaching, writing, revision, and rethinking on this and other subjects, that a full appreciation of his sensitivity in things scholarly and personal, stylistic and spiritual, could finally emerge. This book is a first and inadequate payment of my debt to him, a debt I am honored to share with many others.

David Brion Davis and Richard W. Fox also read this as a dissertation and gave valuable suggestions for revision. I am especially grateful to Professor Davis for his accommodation then and his gracious encouragement since. I am also indebted to several professors at Calvin College: to Ronald Wells, who turned me as an undergraduate toward American history; to George Marsden, who read large portions of this book at an early stage; to Herbert Brinks, who helped me greatly in my archival work and shared his knowledge of Dutch-American history in many rewarding conversations; and to Richard Mouw, who combined support and challenge as only he can do. Elton Bruins of Hope College very tactfully made me moderate some earlier statements. Any errors or offenses that remain are mine alone.

I have the researcher's perennial obligation to librarians, especially to the Inter-Library Loan staff at Sterling Memorial Library, Yale University; to Norman Kansfield of Western Theological Seminary; and to Peter De Klerk of Calvin Seminary. Special appreciation goes to Conrad Bult of Calvin College Library, who went the second mile in facilitating my research; to Jon Pott, T. A. Straayer, and Marlin Van Elderen at Eerdmans for patience and good counsel; and to Helen Caldrer who typed the final draft. Tina Bruinsma, my wife, did not type a word this time but went on to greater labors. The fruit of those I am happy to add to her unfailing patience, love, and good cheer as reasons for my deepest gratitude. Finally, of my many debts to my parents, Bert and Anita Ribbens Bratt, I can here redeem the first, their putting me in the line of those to whom this book is dedicated.

Illustrations

The illustrations listed below appear in a section between pages 146 and 147. The author and publisher wish to thank the following sources for their help in providing these materials and for permission to reproduce them here:

To Herbert Brinks and the Calvin College Heritage Hall Collection for photos marked *

To Tom Ozinga and the Calvin College Office of College Relations for the photo marked **

To Andrew Vander Zee and the Hope College archives for the photos marked †

To Elton Bruins of Western Theological Seminary for the photos marked ††

To the Christian Reformed Board of Publications for the photos marked ‡

To Great Commission Publications for the photo marked ‡‡

To Time-Life, Inc. for the photo marked §

To Margaret Vriend for the photo marked §§

To the *Reformed Journal* for the photos marked #

To New Brunswick Theological Seminary for the photo marked ##

[1] Hendrik de Cock*
[2] Hendrik P. Scholte*
[3] Albertus C. Van Raalte*
[4] Koene Vanden Bosch and wife*
[5] Abraham Kuyper*
[6] Caricature of Abraham Kuyper, ca. 1909*
[7] G. Groen van Prinsterer*
[8] Herman Bavinck*
[9] Lammert J. Hulst*
[10] John Van Lonkhuyzen*

[11] Johannes Groen*
[12] Geerhardus Vos*
[13] Henry Beets*
[14] Nicholas M. Steffens††
[15] Evert J. Blekkink††
[16] Gerrit Dubbink††
[17] Matthew Kolyn††
[18] Western Theological Seminary campus††
[19] Hope College campus†
[20] Gerrit Diekema

[21] Henry Geerlings*
[22] Klaas Kuiper family*
[23] Calvin Seminary faculty, 1916*
[24] Williams Street School*
[25] Theologische School te Grand
     Rapids*
[26] Franklin campus building,
     1917*
[27] Calvin Seminary students*
[28] Hope College students†
[29] Third Reformed Church
     McKinley memorial, 1901
[30] Third Reformed Church semi-
     centennial celebration, 1917
[31] Harry Bultema*
[32] Ralph Janssen*
[33] Herman Hoeksema*
[34] Henry Danhof*
[35] Louis Berkhof*
[36] Henry J. Kuiper‡
[37] R. B. Kuiper*
[38] E. J. Tanis*
[39] Clarence Bouma*
[40] Cecil De Boer*
[41] Henry J. Ryskamp*
[42] Bastian Kruithof††
[43] Western Theological Seminary
     faculty, 1939††

[44] Henry Zylstra*
[45] Henry Schultze*
[46] Arnold Mulder†
[47] David Cornel De Jong*
[48] Frederick Manfred*
[49] Peter De Vries§
[50] George Stob*
[51] Harry Boer*
[52] Cornelius Van Til‡‡
[53] Henry Van Til*
[54] William Harry Jellema*
[55] H. Evan Runner*
[56] Americans at the Free
     University§§
[57] Louis Benes††
[58] Peter Y. De Jong*
[59] John Vander Ploeg‡
[60] Lester De Koster‡
[61] Calvin Franklin campus
     Seminary building*
[62] Calvin Knollcrest campus
     Seminary building**
[63] Reformed Journal staff#
[64] Lewis Smedes#
[65] Howard Hageman##
[66] Robert Schuller†
[67] Amway Center for Free
     Enterprise

PART I

THE NETHERLANDIC
BACKGROUND

1

Secession and Its Tangents

Although the second wave of Dutch emigration to America began in 1846, accounts of it have typically begun with a religious event in 1834, the "secession" of two congregations from the National Reformed Church in the Netherlands. Today this historiographical instinct still seems sound, requiring amplification more than debunking. The popularity of the Secession (over 120 churches joined in the next two years alone) and the government's alarmed reaction to it intimated that this was no mere ecclesiastical quirk. Rather it constituted a forthright protest by the lower levels of Dutch society against some of the fundamental social and cultural developments of the nineteenth century. As these same trends made emigration certain, the Secession came to have a crucial influence in the process by which thousands of Netherlanders were transplanted into the United States.

At the same time the Secession continued a long line of dissent within the Dutch Reformed Church. Ever since the seventeenth century, small bands of the zealous had been gathering across the country for private devotionals designed to supplement what they regarded as the bland preachments of a church that tried to be as inclusive as possible. Unlike their descendants in the 1830s, however, these "conventicles" (*gezelschapen*) usually managed to work out an accommodation with the local church, making formal separation unnecessary. In some places, conventicles took over whole congregations. Thus there developed within the Church a party of the devout vocal on the national level and strong, sometimes dominant, on the local scene.[1]

Viewed more broadly, this movement represented the Dutch branch of European pietism.[2] Both followed the conventicle mode of organization and held the same general set of theological-behavioral imperatives. Simply stated, they wanted Christianity to be made full and deep. This entailed, first, a focus upon such themes as human inability and worthlessness and on Christ's death as the only source of salvation; but more, it entailed the vital, personal realization of such doctrines through heartfelt experience. The converted were then obliged to maintain ongoing intimacy with God through rigorous intro-spection and daily "spiritual exercises"; to "practice godliness," reject-ing "the things of the flesh and the world" and obeying "precisely" the law of God as recorded in Scripture; and throughout, to submit to the appraisal and admonition of their fellow "faithful."[3]

Besides such essentials, the Dutch exhibited two other pietist traits: internal diversity (with different conventicles following the emphases of different leaders)[4] and puritanical strictures regarding popular mores. *De fijnen* ("precisianists") abstained, often ostentatiously, from the sins they considered the most obvious violations of God's law—any "desecration" of the Sabbath, seasonal fairs (for being moral holidays), strong drink (for weakening the conscience), playing at cards or dice (for inducing careless living and reliance on evil forces), and theater attendance and dancing (for encouraging illicit sexuality).[5]

On other points, Dutch pietism diverged from the general Euro-pean movement, at least from its stereotype. It fostered few of the "excesses" that appeared in Germany—radical social arrangements, reformist passions, doctrinal eccentricities—perhaps because it was not forced into institutional (and ideological) separation.[6] Most important-ly, Dutch pietism from the start allied itself with the orthodox theology of the Established Church that pietists elsewhere so often regarded as their chief enemy. In the ongoing struggle in the Reformed Church between the party loyal to the strict, predestinarian Synod of Dort (1618–19) and the followers of Jacobus Arminius and Descartes, the more liberalized theology first won tolerance, then dominance, so that orthodoxy became less and less the prevailing opinion among the church elite. To hold their own, orthodox theologians turned to pietist conventicles for support. The latter, wary of the liberals' high esteem of reason and human potential, welcomed such overtures.[7]

Two of the leading figures in Dutch church history exemplify this fusion. Gijsbert Voetius (1589–1676) led the struggle of the old the-ology against the Cartesians, while William á Brakel (1635–1711) intended his three-volume *summa Redelijke Godsdienst* (in the eyes of one scholar the ablest synthesis of European pietist theology) to be an aid to devotion and holy living. Yet each endorsed the concerns of the other. Under the tutelage of these *oude schrijvers* ("ancient writers," or "the Fathers"), read for centuries in conventicles and family circles, it was the devout who promoted the catechetical training of the young, which the Church had let languish, and who insisted on both a learned and a converted ministry.[8] Dutch pietists disliked "cold, formal orthodoxy" just as much as their European brothers did, but they disliked the theology of "rationalism" and "humanism" even more and tried to turn a warm, vibrant orthodoxy against it.[9]

Understandably, these circles were not pleased with much that happened in the Netherlands in the era of the French Revolution. Long among the staunchest supporters of the House of Orange, they saw in the overthrow of the Statholder the triumph of their traditional enemy, the urban merchant oligarchy; similarly, in Revolutionary ideology they detected the old liberalism in more virulent form. But the Restoration brought no relief, only further decline, tinged with betrayal. For now Orange itself seemed to be furthering Revolutionary tendencies, as William I (he was now king, no longer statholder of a republic) cast himself as an enlightened autocrat and pushed forward the process of political centralization. Of special affront to the pious was his transformation in 1816 of the National Church into the State Department of Religion, just another civil institution ruled by a bureaucratic hierarchy. This completed the process that had begun to alienate them a century before, removing control of religious affairs from the local level and making the church more a promoter of social unity than a body of fervent believers.[10]

The economic hardships of the time compounded these grievances. The disruption of trade during the Napoleonic wars had badly damaged an already stagnant Dutch economy; the reign of William I saw accelerating decline, culminating in a general crisis between 1845 and 1850. During this slump the nation's elite improved its position by capturing a larger share of the national wealth and important posts and functions. The economic lot of rural commoners thus worsened just as their power in local affairs, including the ecclesiastical, declined. Moreover, as landholders moved from a paternalistic to a contractual mode of organization, many tenants and day-laborers lost their only form of economic security and anxiously surveyed the growing number of the drunken, the dissolute, and the permanent paupers who roamed the Dutch countryside at this time.[11]

Theologically, this stratification was mirrored in diverging religious sentiments. The more affluent leaned toward enlightened agnosticism or, more frequently, the comfortable theology of "the Groningen school."[12] The latter, in its pulpits and its aptly named periodical, *Truth in Love: A Theological Journal for Cultured Christians,* preached a "reasonable" brand of Romantic religion. Christ was less a bleeding Savior than a model of fully realized humanity; the end of religion was less salvation from sin than the achievement of virtue; the human heart was less a sin-blackened seat of evil in need of radical conversion than a trustworthy organ of discernment fit to replace doctrinal standards as the ultimate measure of religious truth. Understandably, the ideal of "right-thinking men" walking "the path of morality," especially as this was embodied by prosperous burghers, did not impress the struggling as the last word in religious wisdom. They turned instead to conventicles or "faithful" congregations of the National Church for the message of divine power, human frailty, and heartfelt conversion.[13]

In the 1830s, however, the customary conventicle arrangement broke down in many communities, first of all in Ulrum, Groningen, the parish of Hendrik de Cock. Dissatisfied with the Groningen theology in which he had been trained, de Cock had discovered in 1829 the works of Calvin and the Synod of Dort and began to sound their themes in his sermons. This attracted from surrounding parishes a considerable number of worshipers discontented with their own pastors. Before long de Cock was baptizing their children and attacking his clerical opposition as "wolves in the sheepfold of Christ," for both of which offenses he was suspended from his charge. But his congregation refused to accept the demotion and "seceded" from the National Church to "return" to the "true church," the earlier, "uncorrupted" form of that body. Several other ministers joined de Cock, by choice or coercion, as did a recent seminary graduate who was refused a post because of his association with these men.[14]

The scope of Seceder disaffection is evident in the extent of their complaints about all three areas of church life—doctrine, liturgy, and polity. They protested that the Church's weakening of the authority of the traditional confessional standards (part of the reorganization of 1816) was an invitation to heresy and anarchy. They decried the introduction of hymns into worship as another channel of heterodoxy— hymns being the words of man as opposed to psalms, the words of God. And they condemned the new polity of 1816, both in principle and for making these other changes possible.[15]

Such charges reverberate with the tones of disinheritance: a distant national elite had usurped local prerogatives, opened the Church to corruption, and made reform impossible. What the official documents suggest, the movement's constituents confirmed. Where the Secession took hold there were significant correlations between social status and ecclesiastical direction. The "big farmers," the local aristocracy, the "progressive" and "enlightened" elements of society ridiculed the movement; the hired hands, the poorer farmers, and the small tradesmen (but not the destitute) composed almost its entire membership.[16] The authorities did not miss the coincidence. Official provincial reports for 1836 described Seceder membership as "for the most part . . . from the lowest ranks," "uncultured," "the least significant," having "no man of name" among them. Individual leaders were variously described as "a maniac" and "a miserable" creature, and de Cock was labeled "the most dangerous man in society."[17] To so grave a threat the government responded sharply, outlawing Seceder meetings, imprisoning some of their pastors, quartering troops in their homes, and levying exorbitant fines upon individuals and congregations.[18] This policy ended in 1840 only after a new king had assumed the throne and the Seceders' contentment with solely a religious mode of protest had become evident.

The Secession, then, had a threefold set of natural sympathizers: those caught between an aggrandizing elite and a growing pauper class, many of the "faithful" in the National Church, and conventicles, which had come in face of the centralizing process to fear for their informal independence. In fact, many of the Secession's first churches were old conventicles in new guise. The tradition had always been strong around de Cock's Ulrum, for instance, and the disparity between the number of congregations and ministers at an early stage of the Secession—128 and 6—obviously shows the techniques of independent formation and self-sustenance at work.[19]

This very advantage, however, presented the Secession with its worst problem. The customs of diversity and local autonomy, crossed with the willful personalities characteristic of schismatic leadership, engendered major conflicts within the new band of churches as early as 1837. De Cock and Simon Van Velzen, envisioning a purified version of the National Church, stressed doctrinal orthodoxy and the authority of the new denomination's general synod, while Antonie Brummelkamp and Albertus Van Raalte left more power to the local congregation and emphasized experiential religion. Hendrik Scholte, in turn, had a strong millenarian strain in his preaching, advocated almost complete independence, gave little attention to doctrine per se but a great deal to the conversion experience, and wished to create pure churches by submitting prospective members to stringent tests of piety. The balance of power shifted from one year's synod to another as these three groups forged and broke alliances. The Scholtian and "Geldersche" parties (so named because Van Raalte and Brummelkamp worked out of that province) triumphed in 1837 on matters of polity, but the "Northern" school (de Cock and Van Velzen worked in Groningen and Friesland, the northernmost provinces of the Netherlands), with "Gelderland's" assistance, won a decisive victory in 1840 over Scholte's perfectionist, sectarian tendencies. The tension was reduced somewhat in 1846–47 when those who were most disaffected, led by Scholte and Van Raalte, emigrated to the United States. Most of the remaining diversity became harmonized after the churches established a seminary at Kampen in 1854. Under the instruction of a trained clergy the sons of the Secession took on a heavily "Northern" character, stressing confessional and synodical authority, though these were infused with enough piety to satisfy "Gelderland."[20]

The 1846–47 exodus was only the first instance of what for our

purposes was the Secession's most notable effect. The connection between Secession and emigration has received a great deal of attention—
from Dutch contemporaries, whom it often infuriated; from historians,
who have seized upon it as a clue to the entire emigration's meaning;
and from the emigrants' descendants, who have used it to prescribe for
the ethnic community a certain character and mission. In fact, the
connection has been too obvious. Scholars and spokesmen alike have
long exaggerated the Secessionist part of the emigration by concentrat-
ing almost exclusively on the group migrations between 1846 and 1856
led by Secessionist pastors, thereby coming to think that most immigrants were Seceders fleeing religious oppression. Unfortunately for
this view, substantial emigration from the Netherlands began not in the
years of religious persecution (1835–40) but a decade later, during a
severe agricultural depression brought on by the infamous potato
blight. For the rest of the century, emigration fluctuated with the business cycle, declining in general between 1850 and 1880 (the "cham-
pagne years" of Dutch agriculture), slumping particularly during the
American depressions of 1857 and 1873, and resurging from 1880 to
1900 in response to "the most severe and widespread crisis through
which modern European agriculture has passed."[21] In addition, less
than four percent of the pre-1880 emigrants cited religious reasons for
their departure, while over ninety percent declared an economic
motive.[22] In short, Dutch emigration generally conformed to the larger
European pattern: it was "a mass exodus of the rural poor."[23] Occupa-
tionally, three-fourths of the emigrants were farmers, day-laborers, or
small craftsmen. Few of them came from the pauper class, and even
fewer from the rich; the vast majority came from the lower and middle
ranks, and these from the countryside rather than the city.[24]

On the other hand, economic considerations do not fully explain
Dutch emigration either. If in aggregate it followed economic trends, its
internal composition showed a pronounced religious skewing.[25] Seceders were far more likely to leave the country than were members of any
other religious group. Between 1831 and 1877 they composed seventeen percent of all Dutch emigrants, despite the fact that in the terminal
year they represented no more than five percent of the total population—and that after four decades of persistent growth.[26] In the
province of Friesland, Seceders formed two percent of the population in
1849 and seven percent in 1879, but twenty-one percent of the emigrants between 1831 and 1877.[27] Figures for shorter periods are even
more striking. Between 1844 and 1857 almost ten percent of all Seceders left the Netherlands for America.[28] These represented thirty-five
percent of all Dutch Protestant emigrants—proportionally, more than
eight times the number of other Dutch Protestants. During one brief
period, 1846–49, they even constituted a strong majority (sixty-four
percent) of Protestant emigrants, and an even half of all Dutch emi-

grants, a remarkable achievement in light of their 2.3 and 1.3 percent shares of the respective populations.[29]

Obviously, the Secession would carry more weight in Dutch America than in the Netherlands. But its influence would be greater still because of two factors that statistics do not immediately reflect. Emigration appealed to the same socio-economic groups as the Secession, and so it also appealed to the Secession's natural sympathizers. Many National Church emigrants did not hesitate to migrate under Seceder auspices or to join Seceder congregations in Dutch America; indeed, some exhibited a religious zeal equal if not superior to the Seceders'. Secondly, the period of Seceder exodus, owing to its precedence and corporate nature, happened to be the most significant in the entire course of Dutch emigration. The Netherlands did not experience the sort of full-blown phases of "America fever" and "group migration" that were so pronounced in such nations as Ireland and Sweden. A miniature version of these did occur, however, among the Seceders.[30] In the early years Seceder ecclesiastical networks became the chief means of recruitment, communication, and financing for emigration. Seceder propaganda began to break down customary inhibitions against the move, and organized bodies of Seceders (at times large segments of existing congregations) migrated under the lead of Secessionist clergy.[31] Thus an "immigrant tradition" became established in Seceder circles, with momentous consequences.

The Dutch, like others, did not emigrate randomly but in chains of kin, neighbors, and associates. The Seceders' early cohesiveness made emigration easier and more appropriate for them than it seemed for others. Later stages of emigration followed this precedent, reflecting more the established religious distinctions than the differences among the economic strata of Dutch society. For the period of the largest emigration to the United States (1880–1917, when several times the 1830–79 total left) we can therefore project, in the absence of a statistical analysis, a disproportionately high rate of orthodox Calvinist participation, especially since the new church's share of the Dutch population would grow to ten percent.[32]

Seceder ideology brought this propensity to full measure. Since religious and patriotic identities were so intertwined, the step of secession implied more than withdrawal from a corrupt church; it bespoke separation from a fallen nation. Persecution of "the true Reformed" by their old defender, the House of Orange, confirmed this implication. If the Netherlands had turned its back on God, if henceforth he would have as his people not the nation as a whole but a faithful remnant within it, and if the apostate nation oppressed the faithful, then, the Seceders reasoned, they were free to leave for a land that, if not holy, was at least tolerant.[33]

These feelings were multiplied for those Seceders who lost out in the movement's internal struggles. By 1845 the parties led by Hendrik Scholte and A. C. Van Raalte had become, respectively, separated from and suspect within the larger group. They in turn gave up on the Secession: the quest to purify the church had not only failed to achieve its goal but had itself become part of the problem. Twice disillusioned, the outcasts of the outcast, these groups exhibited the strongest tendencies toward both doctrinal innovation and emigration. Thus the Dutch case came to resemble that of the English, the Scandinavians, and some Germans: the immigrant vanguard came from "the fringe" of extreme sectarians and "idealists."[34]

Finally, the economic forces that encouraged emigration had religious overtones as well. As the Weberian model would have it, the Seceders saw the moral, spiritual, and material as interdependent. Their apologias for emigration underscored the point. The "deplorable" material conditions of the Netherlands, they declared, at once constituted divine punishment of a faithless nation and made it impossible for faithful Christians to obey "the expressed will of God," namely, to provide for their families, contribute to charity, and aid "promotion of God's Kingdom." Economic stagnation had also led to "idleness," which "excited man's inward corruption" so that a "stream of social and civil pollution is flowing in the midst of us," endangering the moral well-being of the pious. Hence they sought "resort to a country where the work awaits the man, and not man the work" and where "God's beautiful creation is still ready to receive men" with the promise of wholesome environment, self-sufficiency, and religious opportunity.[35]

ARISTOCRATIC ALIENATION: THE REVEIL

The evangelical revival of Restoration Europe had an elite as well as a popular phase. Its Dutch manifestation was "the Reveil," which stemmed directly from currents in Switzerland and England and appealed most to the best born and educated.[36] The father of the Reveil in the Netherlands was William Bilderdijk (1756–1831), the foremost Dutch poet of the age. A classic exemplar of reactionary Romanticism, Bilderdijk despised rationalists, utilitarians, and revolutionaries of every sort and championed Orange, orthodoxy, and tradition. He paid for his sentiments—and was reinforced in them—by going into exile when the French took the Netherlands in 1795; yet he so valued stable order that he returned to serve Louis Bonaparte. Deprived by political intrigue of the university post he deserved, he began teaching small groups privately in Leiden, carrying on the cause there and in his endless writings.

After Bilderdijk's death, leadership of the Reveil fell to his most eminent protégés, particularly Isaac da Costa, a converted Jew and man of letters, and G. Groen van Prinsterer, secretary of the Cabinet and archivist of the royal records. They continued Bilderdijk's strategy of "elite conventiclism," meeting privately in one another's homes for Bible study, devotional exercises, and lectures on Dutch history, literature, and current social problems.[37] They also shared the older conventicles' theological posture, especially the reassertion of scriptural authority and stress upon the "salvation triad"—man's corruption, Christ's exclusive atonement, and experiential conversion.[38]

Not surprisingly, the Secession had direct ties with the Reveil. Hendrik P. Scholte was associated with its leaders already in his student days at Leiden, where he had formed a study cell of his own. This "Scholte Club," also known as "the da Costiaanen," included almost all of the Secession's early leaders, several of whom also attended da Costa's meetings occasionally.[39] Despite these contacts, the Reveil circle supported the Secession only partially. The aristocrats deplored the "tone" and "extremes" of the Secession and distrusted any agitation among the lower orders. Moreover, they disapproved of ecclesiastical schism as a step away from their ideal, the reestablishment of Reformed orthodoxy as the official national religion. Therefore they refused to join the Seceders even though they did work against the state's repressive measures.[40] The Seceders in turn decried the Reveil's loyalty to a "false church" but welcomed its legal assistance.

The longer-range significance of the Reveil for the Secession, as for the nation as a whole, lay in the realm of social and political attitudes. In fact its indignation at the new order in Dutch society had animated it all along. Far from being the much-touted "age of freedom and enlightenment," cried da Costa, it was a time of "slavery, superstition, idolatry, and darkness," "perverse," "abominable," and "impious."[41] The Reveilers' diagnosis of such horrors was forthright and similar to counterrevolutionary theory all over the Continent: the Netherlands had become infected in whole and in every part by the philosophy and practice of "the Revolution"; it could regain its health only by returning to Christ and History.[42]

By "the Revolution" the Reveilers meant more than the chain of events beginning in France in 1789. That had been just the political outbreak of a disease spiritual in essence. The real "Revolution" was the Enlightenment, the eighteenth century's substitution of reason for revelation as the source of truth, of human desire for divine law as the standard of ethics. Nor were these simply badly mistaken but genuine efforts to find truth and right; rather, they were deliberate, malicious attempts to defy God and cast mankind into the deepest misery. On this score, the Reveil allowed, the Revolution had succeeded all too well. The new science enslaved men to a modern form of superstition; the new art celebrated the depraved and ugly; the new philosophy fostered a hungering for intellectual and moral certainty that it could never satisfy and thereby led to immorality and despair.[43]

From the philosophical Revolution had proceeded the political, directly and inevitably; in Groen van Prinsterer's slogan, "unbelief" produced "revolution." The political Revolution too was perversely successful; it had cured none of the old problems but introduced many more.[44] Here the Reveil critique borrowed most clearly from such counterrevolutionary theorists as Burke, Haller, and Stahl. The Revolution had reduced society from a harmony of diverse parts to a chaos of disconnected fragments, had replaced the natural, unifying allegiance to king and country with the impersonal regulations of a centralized bureaucracy. Stability and dignity of rule had degenerated into a ceaseless rotation through office of greedy cliques, and the weak, having lost the protection of traditional rights and noblesse oblige, had become helpless before the ruthless ambition of the newly powerful. In sum, instead of its promised liberty and equality, the political Revolution had forged a new set of chains, created a new system of rank and privilege, and fostered perpetual dissatisfaction at all levels of society.[45]

The antidote to all this, Groen reiterated, was "the Gospel" and "History"—that is, the spirit of Christian love and the social ordinances implicit in divine law, and the nation's natural course of development, with which all innovations had to comply. Concretely, this meant restoring traditional communities, ranks, and orders with all their privileges and duties.[46] But above all the Reveil looked for the restoration of the consciousness of authority and obedience. This was its ruling passion, the nation's greatest need, the prerequisite to all further reforms, because this alone ensured tranquility and order.[47]

Reveil social philosophy proved flexible enough over the years to maintain its viability. It grew from Bilderdijk's reaction to Groen's constructive conservatism, and from absolute to constitutional monarchism. It accepted political and technological innovations such as extending the franchise and building railroads and factories. Whatever the value of its solutions, it certainly identified many of the baneful consequences of Europe's recent upheavals. But both its ideology and its strategy contained flaws that reflected badly on the movement and long haunted its political children in the National Church and Secession alike. Although the Reveilers espoused a program for reforming society, they directed most of their energy inward, preaching to the already converted, and seemed often to relish more the condemnation of evils than their correction. They were also self-righteous, blind to their perennial error of identifying anything they disliked as "Revolutionary." By their own standards, the essence—and evil—of "the Revolution" was not "democracy," "equality," or civil liberties, but "atheism"; yet they rarely hesitated to condemn the former without demonstrating its involvement with the latter.

It was left to a succeeding generation to correct some of these mistakes. Yet the reactionary strain never died out completely, persisting in particular among the Seceders, with whose traditionalism it could readily combine. The Reveil carried over to Dutch America, then, as germative political instinct. Both there and in the Netherlands, however, its theory was challenged by the emergence in the late nineteenth century of a new school of orthodoxy with quite another cultural vision.

2

Abraham Kuyper and Neo-Calvinism

The link between religious and social crises defined orthodoxy's fortunes for the rest of the nineteenth century. The middle decades, the last florescence of traditional Dutch agriculture, were marked by ecclesiastical calm; the Seceder church grew, but quietly. In the last third of the century, however, the long-overdue process of industrialization finally swept the nation. So did a spectacular revival of Calvinism.

"Neo-Calvinism," as it was named, drew off the Reveil, Secession, and Hervormde Kerk orthodox, but in the process transformed them beyond their imaginings—and, often, beyond their desire. The movement was nationwide in intent and comprehensive in scope, addressing every facet of national life with a coherent ideology and specific program. From 1870 to 1920 it held the Netherlands' attention, wrote much of its political and cultural agenda, and in the end reshaped some of its fundamental structures. Nor did its influence end at the national borders. Since these were exactly the decades of the heaviest Dutch emigration to the United States,[1] Neo-Calvinism was transported to the new world as well, with far-reaching consequences.

Dutch Neo-Calvinism was led—indeed personified—by one man, Abraham Kuyper (1837–1920).[2] More than anyone else (one can almost say more than everyone else put together), Kuyper defined the ideology of the movement—in over twenty thousand newspaper articles, in scores of pamphlets and speeches on controversial or celebratory occasions, and in multivolume treatises on theology, politics, education, science, and philosophy. He also led the battle for its practical implementation. He was editor for almost fifty years of two of the movement's newspapers, a political daily and religious weekly; cofounder of and professor at the Calvinistic Free University in Amsterdam; advocate of Christian elementary schools; leader of a huge

secession from the Hervormde Kerk and cofounder of a new denomination formed by the merger of this group with the earlier Secession;
promoter and defender of the Christian labor movement; head of the
Anti-Revolutionary political party for forty years; long-time member of
the national legislature and prime minister of the Netherlands for four
years.[3] Obviously, the ideas and career of such a figure cannot be
thoroughly treated in a few pages, so we shall review here only the
central themes of his thought, especially those which figured most in
Dutch America.

Since many, especially from the old Secession, suspected Kuyper of
being a corrupter of the Reformed tradition, it is best to begin by
showing how much he shared with them. First, he had experienced a
personal conversion profound enough to please the most demanding
pietist; better yet, this had won him away from the most dreaded heresy. Kuyper had been raised in a home of mild ethical Protestantism and
had become the protégé of the great modernist J. H. Scholten in his
studies at Leiden. But through a series of events—a "miraculous" find
of rare documents during his doctoral work, his reading a Christian
novel while seriously ill, confrontations with the staunch devotion of
his first parishioners, his attendance at a Moody revival in England—he
came to judge all forms of liberal Protestantism to be emotionally
inadequate and intellectually unsound.[4] He brought the convert's fervor to his "mission" (as he conceived it) of defending orthodoxy.

In the area of doctrine, Kuyper did as well as could be expected in a
movement whose every member considered himself a theologian. The
majority of the orthodox found him correct most of the time and tolera-
ble for the rest, and all applauded the vigor and persistence of his
attacks upon the "enemy." On the test of ethics he fared even better,
ritually decrying the "rising tide of worldliness," especially the three
cardinal sins of the pietist code—dancing, theater attendance, and gambling. In his political platform he advocated strict repression of public
vice.[5] And finally, Kuyper prized personal religious devotion, as he
showed by writing more than two thousand meditations which sounded the familiar themes—intimacy with God, the contrast of human
dependence and divine grace, and warnings against excessive "earthly
concerns."[6]

But above all it was Kuyper's relentless and resourceful champion-
ing of Calvinism that secured his reputation. For him, Calvinism was
not just another brand of Christianity but its highest, most systematic
and coherent expression.[7] Nor was Calvinism limited to things religious; it enveloped politics, economics, science, and art—in Kuyper's
favorite phrase, "every sphere of life." "Calvinism did not stop at a
church order, but expanded in a life-system . . . created a life-and-
world-view, and such a one as was, and still is, able to fit itself to the

needs of every stage of human development, in every department of life."[8] Equally glorious was its historical achievement. By destroying the medieval church's tyranny (Kuyper's dialectics claimed all of the Reformation for Calvinism), it could take credit for the development of modern European civilization and its finest fruits: progressive science and emancipated art; constitutional, republican government and civil liberties; thriving agriculture, commerce, and industry; and a purified family life. The moral of this history lesson was obvious: the Netherlands, and (Kuyper never being bashful) Europe itself, could return to glory only by returning to its Calvinistic soul.[9]

Such a resurrection constituted Kuyper's grand ideal and dictated the two central motives behind all his labor: to stir the orthodox from their passive isolation and to direct the ensuing passion against liberalism's political and cultural hegemony. The first aim required mobilization of what the elite of the time called "the backward element of the nation"—what Kuyper called *de kleine luyden,* "the small people"—the largely rural mass caught between the paupers and the prosperous and forming the stronghold of Reformed conviction.[10] Kuyper worked here ironically, availing himself of the possibilities created by liberal legislation and modern techniques.[11]

But organization would avail little without a change in consciousness. Advocacy of such a change became Kuyper's principal message to his followers; their resistance to it provoked the only occasions on which he turned his considerable capacity for satire upon his own flock. Quite simply, the Reformed needed to purge themselves of their "pietistic dualisms," their separation of Sunday from the workweek, of the spiritual from the physical—in theological terms, of nature from grace. Were they to be *Calvinists* again, they could no longer dismiss certain fields (scholarship, art, and politics) as inherently "worldly"; they had instead to recognize these and all occupations as Christian callings, and more generally they had to make engagement rather than withdrawal their paradigm of the Christian life. Theologically, redemption had to be resubordinated to creation, it being the start of the restoration of the world to its original perfection. As Kuyper put it forcefully in *Lectures on Calvinism,*

> The world after the fall is no lost planet, only destined now to afford the Church a place in which to continue her combats; and humanity is no aimless mass of people which only serves the purpose of giving birth to the elect. On the contrary, the world now . . . is the theater for the mighty works of God, and humanity remains a creation of His hand, which, apart from salvation, completes under this present dispensation here on earth, a mighty process, and in its historical development is to glorify the name of Almighty God.[12]

The other side of Kuyper's grand design, confronting liberalism, we shall examine later. Suffice it to say here that he insisted his followers' activity remain thoroughly Christian. While they addressed the problems of society without sanctimony or "spiritualizing," they needed to present distinctive solutions, to challenge rather than compromise with the world.

This did not dispel all doubts, however. Kuyper's enthusiasm for adapting rather than preserving tradition already worried some:

> what the descendants of the old Dutch Calvinists . . . have to do, is not to copy the past, as if Calvinism were a petrifaction, but to go back to the living root of the Calvinist plant, to clean and to water it, and so to cause it to bud and to blossom once more, now fully in accordance with our actual life in these modern times, and with the demands of the times to come.[13]

More disturbing was his vision of Christian cultural action. At best, skeptics claimed, this vision would divert believers' attention from central to peripheral concerns; at worst it would open the body of the faithful to fatal corruption. One could not enter "the world" without becoming "worldly," as Kuyper's own warnings (in their reading) acknowledged.

That Kuyper did not succumb to such fears stemmed in part from his confidence in the technique of analysis that he used. "Principial thinking," derived both from the Idealist philosophy of his student days and from his intuitive temper, formed the core of his defenses but also of his vision, his psychology, and his legacy. Its first premise was that the determinative forces of reality were not external or material but the ultimate commitment of the heart of man, his "life-principle." This principle harnessed the instincts and shaped ideas, actions, and environment—in that order. Similarly on a larger scale, every nation, every civilization was simply the elaboration of a principle or of the conflict of principles. Therefore history was explicable as the development of ruling ideas.[14]

Kuyper pressed these nineteenth-century commonplaces into a Calvinistic system by one crucial operation, declaring all fundamental principles to be religious, commitments to or defiance of God's will. From their response to God, every person and society—more or less consciously, with greater or lesser system—built an operative philosophy, a culture, a way of life. For Neo-Calvinists, therefore, every school of thought, all political and economic action, all human behavior whatsoever had religious roots and might be legitimately evaluated by religious criteria.

For decades "principial thinking" was the distinguishing characteristic of all Kuyperians both in Europe and America, although some later became disenchanted with the carelessness with which it could be applied. It certainly was abused by some who found in it a substitute for thinking, by many more who believed that identifying, by whatever mental gymnastics, a thinker's "starting point" or "standpoint" or "the spirit of the age" constituted the whole of intellectual activity. Other of its weaknesses were inherent: underestimation of the material forces of existence, imposition of a theistic scheme regardless of the milieu or intent of the materials, tendencies to create specious unities. According to those using this technique, for example, Rousseau, Marx, and Weber all ignored divine revelation and were thus principially "materialistic"; this meant they could be said to share essentially the same view of society. Voltaire and Kant, Schleiermacher and Nietzsche all "started from man" rather than "from God"; therefore they could be placed in a single religious line.

But the technique had commensurate value, especially for people emerging from a parochial social and intellectual past. It legitimized fresh, serious thinking about a wide range of concerns that their pietism had generally discouraged and made them wary of identifying the Christian faith with one element or another of its cultural context. A skilled practitioner like Kuyper could apply the technique with distinguished results—such as making keen analyses of the pretensions of liberal Protestantism and identifying the conservative as well as liberal progeny of the Enlightenment. Finally it enabled Neo-Calvinists to declare, to their everlasting credit, that reason was the servant of the heart; that no intellectual activity, including the natural sciences, was impartial or value-free or without presuppositions; and that every social organization operated according to and in the interests of an ideology—and this in an age when such contentions were consistently ignored or denied.

If principialism could be arbitrary, the principles Kuyper used to define Christian attitudes toward "the unbelieving world" seemed downright contradictory. The paradox served Kuyper's genius well but left Neo-Calvinism with ominous ideological strains.

On the one hand Kuyper proclaimed that there existed an "antithesis" between the church and the world. Although he never completed the metaphysical and anthropological background of this motif, he did intimate in this vein a complete and antagonistic dichotomy. The redeemed lived out of one principle—love for God—and everyone else lived out of the opposite, however it might be expressed. Between themselves the two groups comprised the entire human race; there was no one uncommitted, or committed to a third principle, and no middle ground on which to stand. Since they embodied two different principles, they had no task in common and neither reason nor opportunity to cooperate.[15]

Practical application, not theoretical elaboration, constituted

Kuyper's real interest in this theme. It offered him opportunities to indulge his considerable rhetorical powers, especially his penchant for militaristic imagery. Kuyper loved to portray ideological armies on the march, hearts united, banners flying, principial standards going on before. "Principle must hear witness against principle," he cried, "world-view against world-view, spirit against spirit." "Over against so mighty a life-movement [the variegated religion of unbelief] we can place with any prospect of success only the movement of an antithetical life." More important, the antithesis required separate Christian organizations in every field. "They who still have faith . . . must begin by drawing a boundary about themselves, that within this circle they might develop a *life of their own*. . . . Only in this way can they grow up for the combat that must be expected."[16] The Reformed applied themselves to this task with a vengeance, establishing within twenty years a Calvinistic university and elementary schools, Calvinistic newspapers, a Calvinistic political party and labor union, Calvinistic hospitals, social welfare agencies, trade associations, study groups, and a "purified" Reformed church.

Significantly, Kuyper's appeal to the antithesis peaked in the first half of his career, the period of institutional formation,[17] and declined in his later years, when Calvinists had to take their share of managing public life. The concept served a crucial strategic purpose: besides showing Reformed skeptics that cultural activity did not endanger purity of faith, it fortified group identity during a potentially threatening transition. Certainly it must have mobilized many Seceders, living as they did under the memory of separation. But its darker legacy was equally apparent: few doctrines could match the antithesis at fostering spiritual arrogance or abusing principial analysis.

As if to counter these flaws, Kuyper brought forth his second principle, the idea of common grace.[18] God's grace, this doctrine suggests, works not only upon the elect to the salvation of their souls but touches all men, all creation, by restraining the power of sin and by enabling knowledge and virtue to flower in the absence of true religion. To be sure, the two forms of grace are not equal. The grace enjoyed by the elect is "special," limited in scope, richer in essence, "spiritual" in object, eternal in reward; the other variety is "common," merely "earthly" and temporal, and its recipients are quite unable to perform "saving good" (i.e., perfect virtue in the eyes of God). Nonetheless, though "common," this is still real grace, God's deliberate favor to men; though not "saving," the good done by the heathen is still good, just as their knowledge, if imperfect, is still useful and true.

To sell so unsettling a theory to the Reformed, Kuyper first argued that it overcame problems of logic and fact in their theology. Common grace reconciled the doctrine of total depravity with the presence of good among the unconverted, at the same time reaffirming God's sovereignty by making that good the fruit of divine grace rather than of human effort.[19] For the more educated, the concept resolved a dilemma that had perplexed them since their gymnasium days: how could the beauty of the classics be defended in the face of theological strictures against the corruption of natural man? Now both Bible and Confession declared that Plato, Vergil, and all the rest merited study and respect. More generally, the doctrine gave orthodox rebuttal to those who pressed the antithesis or parochial pietism so far as to deny the obvious virtue and wisdom among non-Christians and thus bring down ridicule upon the faith.

In fact, common grace came to be the linchpin for the entire transformation of consciousness Kuyper was trying to effect.[20] Common *grace* honored earthly existence by describing it in the worthiest terms of the orthodox vocabulary. It encouraged the redeemed to respect the good remaining in the world and to strive to augment it. Even more, it made many elements of human culture—institutions such as the law and the community, artistic and technical ability, academic disciplines, and scientific methods—not just products but *means* of grace, instruments whereby God restrained sin and enabled men to try to develop creation as he had originally designed. Finally, it legitimized a certain amount of cooperation between the redeemed and unbelievers on the grounds that to some extent they shared a sense of the good and therefore a common purpose.

Precisely these implications alarmed the more suspicious. In effect, the doctrine served to catalyze the opponents of cultural engagement just as much as the proponents. Nor was the idea without problems of internal logic. When speaking "from common grace," Kuyper seemed susceptible to the very sort of error he exposed so tellingly among his liberal enemies—namely, the facile identification of Christianity with one piece or another of European civilization.[21] It would seem, however, that Kuyper had little choice. Having mobilized the Reformed under the banner of antithesis, he had to direct them toward responsible public activity on a national scale, and this required a check on self-righteousness and the development of a sense of general public good that their organizations could serve. Both of these common grace provided admirably.[22]

Still, the first purpose for drawing the orthodox into the public arena remained protest and opposition. Besides militaristic imagery, an antagonistic tone and confrontational strategy marked Kuyper's public language through his entire career. Ideologically he started with the Reveil tradition; in fact, he cast himself as Groen's anointed successor. But here again he so worked to adapt rather than replicate, and so freely borrowed from other sources as to transform this legacy into an inspired critique of modern life.[23]

Like Groen, Kuyper assigned enormous influence to "the Revolution"; it received his primary attention and determined by its very structure the shape of his reply. "The Revolution" had worked on two levels—most dramatically on the socio-political level, but more fundamentally (according to principial method) on the cultural-philosophical level—with remarkable parallels between the two in matters of motive, means, and consequence. Hence, the corresponding levels of Kuyper's commentary mirrored each other too.

Of first importance was tracing the Revolutionary spirit through the maze of ideas. Kuyper pursued this task with a principial analysis bordering on legerdemain. It says much about his mind that he could perceive a simple unity in all the varieties of this—*especially* this—century of European thought. It says even more that the names he assigned—"Humanism," making man the center and measure of reality; "Pantheism," identifying man and nature with God; "Materialism," denying the reality of the spiritual and nonempirical—were to him functionally equivalent. In any case, he saw the same spirit producing the Idealistic philosophy and Romantic art of the early century and the positivistic science and Realism that supplanted them. In his own day, Kuyper said, this principle took the form of the evolutionary hypothesis, the reigning dogma in the sciences and humanities alike. Over in religion, its latest expression was "Modernism" (i.e., advanced liberal Protestantism), a different faith entirely from the Christianity in which it cloaked itself, and, for all its spiritual vocabulary, nothing more than an unusually confident, thoroughgoing materialism trimmed with ethical sentiment.[24]

According to Kuyper, proponents of the liberal world view in all its forms claimed that it had been established by science as indisputably and universally true and ridiculed its opposition as primitive and ignorant. More than anything else this smugness triggered Kuyper's rage. The liberals' boasts about their tolerance were blatantly hypocritical: they dismissed orthodoxy's objections to their theories as "intolerance" that they need not tolerate. Their principial imperialism stifled intellectual diversity and creativity—all biologists had to be evolutionary, all geologists uniformitarian, all philosophy nonrevelational.[25] Even more striking was the liberals' naivete, their failure to see that their thinking served unproven and unprovable assumptions, that they operated by faith just like the people they scorned. It was this faith, for example, far more than the existing factual data, that explained the popularity of Darwin's theory of evolution, Kuyper declared. Darwin himself knew that the evidence for his theory was fragmentary in the natural sciences and worse in the realm of the spirit.

> But as he [Darwin] later added, this did not shake *my belief* in the Evolution-theory. . . . We are dealing here not with a compelling, concisely proven thesis, but with a hypothesis supported by gravely

defective induction, whose wide popularity finds its basis *not* in indisputable facts, far less in complete *evidence,* but in a general mood of the spirit; because Darwin's theory offers our learned and cultured circles exactly the sort of solution to the world-problem that corresponds to their deepest sympathies.[26]

As with evolution, so with every other part of the liberal intellectual system.

This world view not only *was* less but had achieved less than it claimed. It had failed to create the nobler man it had promised; it had succeeded only in wasting the treasure of earlier ages. Under its hegemony people were denied fulfillment of their strongest instincts—the hope of immortality, the yearning for comfort and moral certainty—and offered more of what had troubled them to begin with—the specter of a remorseless, inescapably material existence. Already barren, life was next stripped of its moral foundations and social harmony, since the denial of any transcendent source of authority reduced ethical standards to the will of the strong. Modernism could not even fulfill its raison d'être—to be "scientifically" founded and utterly "realistic"—for few things more flagrantly contradicted the hard facts of reality than its postulates about God's love, man's goodness, and the diminishment of evil. As more of its adherents came to realize this, Kuyper declared in surveying his own setting, there settled upon the elite and common folk alike "a gray dusk" of skepticism, distrust, and weariness. Europe was succumbing to "spiritual atrophy."[27]

The medicine prescribed for this disease was familiar—a resurgence of the Christian faith, now in the transmitting institutions of culture (the university and the church). Inasmuch as the problem was philosophical, a new "starting point" was all-important. Actually, the "new" should be the old, the "principle" that had been "thrown off" a century before: belief in God, reliance on his revelation, acknowledgment of human sinfulness, and responsibility to divine law.[28] Thence would flow true scholarship, pure art, sound religion. Kuyper had few illusions about the readiness of the European mind to adopt his solution. Yet since Christians had the only answer, they were to proclaim it nonetheless. God demanded obedience, not success.[29]

Kuyper thus envisioned for his nation a pluralistic culture, the followers of each faith—first the Calvinists, but the Modernists, Arminians, and Catholics as well—founding separate institutions for religion and education and elaborating their world views therein. Simple honesty, not to mention hope for progress, demanded such a structure. And perhaps out of the ensuing ideological combat, Kuyper hoped, the superiority of Calvinism would become apparent, converting some and blessing the culture as a whole to the extent that the latter approached its vision.[30]

Turning to politics, Kuyper like so many of his contemporaries looked back a century to 1789 for the baseline of modernity and, as in his cultural critique, rooted all the intervening regimes, no matter how disparate, in a single and mistaken "principle." But now he introduced new sources of judgment: not just God's scriptural Word but also his "ordinances" (the normative structures of life) and history (the place where these unfolded) were binding.[31]

The political "Revolution" erred, therefore, in its "Humanism" but equally in its thinking to build society *de novo*. The vanity—in both senses of the word—of such an enterprise seemed to Kuyper only too fitting for the Revolution's natural constituency, the urban bourgeoisie. Their political philosophy was equally appropriate.

> The French Revolution . . . tried to build up an artificial authority based on the free will of the individual. . . . [It] destroyed that organic tissue, broke those social bonds, and finally, in its work of atomistic trifling, had nothing left but the monotonous self-seeking individual, asserting his own self-sufficiency.

The consequences were dire but also ironic, for now as rulers the bourgeoisie were trapped by the very engine of their power.

> The French Revolution, and so, too, present day Liberalism, is anti-social and the social need which now disturbs Europe is the evil fruit of the individualism which was enthroned with the French Revolution.[32]

Unable to endure fragmentation, in other words, Europeans were turning to the authoritarian and communal solutions offered by radicals Left and Right. But since these shared the mistaken "starting point" of the "moderates," their programs would not solve the problem. They would not discipline but crush freedom, not restore individuals to natural communities but impose artificial collectivities upon them.[33]

Those who took comfort from the apparent absence of such threats from their own countries deluded themselves, warned Kuyper, because the Revolution had corrupted Europe's whole political ethos. Here again he applied interchangeable designations—"secularization," the negative phase, destroying the old; and "materialization," the positive, supplying a replacement. In principle, once the exchange was effected there was nothing to forestall the worst consequences. Even (perhaps *especially*) liberal regimes could see these well advanced in their very midst if they cared to look: money and power were fixed as the standards of social worth; the poor were deprived of their protection (custom and religion) against the aggression of the rich; the ruthless were rewarded; violence, hatred, and inequity were spreading; and the value and meaning of human life were everywhere degraded.[34]

One of Kuyper's greatest achievements lay in his thorough application of this critique, not least because he had to cut through arbitrary reactionary patterns embedded in Dutch Reformed attitudes. Orthodox instincts branded as "revolutionary" any and all manifestations of the democratic and egalitarian spirit, and conversely, they were quick to favor proposals for stronger authority, stricter order, and defense of privilege and property. But Kuyper laid bare the conservative and aristocratic sides of the Revolution as well. To him, *all* the nonreligious parties—radicals and conservatives, liberals and socialists, monarchists and anarchists—were branches of the same tree, fed from the same root: the belief in human autonomy.[35] The purest revolutionaries, Kuyper insisted, were presently the foremost defenders of law, order, and private property, for the moving forces of the Revolution, competitive individualism and materialism, had their ultimate incarnation in capitalism. Socialism, in turn, represented nothing more than the final destination at which liberal capitalism would arrive if it followed its principles to their logical conclusion.[36] Thus for Kuyper a "radical" system was more consistent and honest, if not more beneficial, than its "moderate" rival. Christians forced to choose among parties of Revolutionary heritage were certainly not automatically right in supporting conservatives against radicals.

This was only the first sign of Kuyper's radical sympathies. As there were varieties of revolutionary politics, so there were aristocratic and democratic tendencies among the Anti-Revolutionaries. Kuyper pushed for the latter, even to the point of splitting the party. In those instances where he warned against socialism and the "dangers" of democracy, he was objecting not to their egalitarian vision or attacks upon privilege but to the functional atheism of their philosophy and the artificiality of their proposed arrangements.[37] At the same time, the most zealous of the radical Dutch socialists, Domela Nieuwenhuis, valued him as an ally against conservatives and liberals alike. "I have thought many times that at bottom we do not stand so far from each other," he wrote Kuyper. "There are whole sections of your writings that I can take over, and indeed which I have used in my speeches."[38] From the start of his career to the end, Kuyper cast himself as the champion of "the small people," both to appeal to that bedrock of Calvinist loyalty and to assert the rights of the voiceless.[39]

Kuyper's radicalism peaked in his deliverances on industrial economics, *the* social question of the time. In this vein he presented nineteenth-century history as one long tale of oppression and duplicity by merchants, industrialists, and financiers and their political front-men, the liberals and conservatives. With traditional restraints abolished by the French Revolution, the bourgeoisie had first ground the poor to dust and then refused them any extension of their own precious liberty, equality, and prosperity.[40] As the beginning of a counterattack, Kuyper condemned laissez-faire political economy, defended labor's right to organize, and advocated an industrial insurance system, the abolition of woman and child labor, and interventionist measures to relieve poverty.

This point also saw the climax of Kuyper's criticism of his own constituents. They damned radical movements as revolutionary, he lamented, yet supported an order just as revolutionary and grossly unfair besides. They idolized private property instead of seeing it as a secondary right, "hobbling in the rear" far behind "the righteous demand" for social justice. They praised the rich despite the fact that Christ, the prophets before him, and the apostles after had "invariably [spoken] *against* those who were powerful and living in luxury, and *for* the suffering and oppressed." And elsewhere he wrote, "How completely different things would be in Christendom if the preaching of Christ were also *our* message, and if the basic principles of His kingdom had not been cut off from and made foreign to our social life by over-spiritualization." Apathy among Christians concerning the claims of social justice stood as their greatest sin and shame, not least for causing many to lose their faith and giving Revolutionary movements easy credit. Correcting this situation, Kuyper declared, entailed nothing more than obedience to God's law, but that demanded from Calvinists an end to their pietistic slumbers and to their automatic identification of "Christian" with "conservative."[41]

Kuyper's political scheme did allow Calvinists to cooperate temporarily, after careful consideration, with one or another Revolutionary party. He favored more, however, a tactic he actually used to put Calvinists in the government—coalition with the Catholics, another (though "impure") Christian party. But these were secondary matters. His first concern was to present the nation with a positive, thorough, and distinctly Christian political witness, and this required an independent philosophy, a practical program, and a separate party. Kuyper wanted the Reformed not to place themselves at one point or another on the secular spectrum but to create, as it were, an entirely new spectrum, or, in the natural imagery he preferred, to grow as an entirely different tree fed from a distinct principial root.[42]

The first principle of his philosophy pointed to the first step of reform. By insisting that the nation's health rested on its "acknowledgement of God's sovereignty, also in political affairs," Kuyper meant to revive the religious consciousness of the national mind. A restored spiritual ethos provided the only ties that could harmonize individuals and groups without enslaving them. Only divine authority could check human power; only the transcendent realm gave hope to the oppressed, sound standards of value for public conduct, and dignity to human life.[43]

Kuyper's leading idea was fully as plausible as that of his opponents; certainly it was sound in terms of social psychology. But it raised one troubling question that Kuyper never resolved: What place would the secular have in the reformed nation? How could Kuyper simultaneously assert, as he did, pluralistic tolerance and spiritualized politics? If a large part of the nation should refuse to acknowledge divine sovereignty, what basis would there be for the Anti-Revolutionaries to work with them in public life? In addition, this idea, like any other, was open to abuses that were not long in materializing. Kuyperians often reduced "the sovereignty of God" to a slogan, a magic wand with which to dismiss or distort opposing ideas, a panacea that allowed them to dream that if only people professed correct principles, poverty, disorder, and oppression would cease.

One mistake Kuyper did *not* make, though, was just to rehearse principles. A renewed soul required a healthy body, and Kuyper spent many volumes drawing its blueprint. Consciously based upon Scripture and "creation ordinances," the plan drew heavily upon normative (to Calvinistic eyes) Dutch history for details.[44]

In Anti-Revolutionary theory, the basic unit of society was the family. It alone among social institutions had its origins before the Fall and in the explicit ordinance of God. The home contained every type of relationship found in society and taught all the skills and duties needed there. Thus its rights took precedence over those of any other institution, and its defense constituted the first concern of sound government.[45]

Besides being a microcosm, the family was also the seed of society, for the latter had come into being through the simple extension of numbers beyond a single dwelling. But as society evolved it came to express ever more elaborately the innate diversity of human interests. People clustered together out of loyalty to a common region, religion, or custom. Loose networks bound together those sharing a broad field of endeavor (e.g., agriculture, commerce, scholarship), while stronger alliances united specialists within each field. Ranks and orders grew up because of the unequal distribution of talents among men. Finally people founded institutions expressly for the better exercise of specific functions: the university for scholarship, the church for religion, the guild for crafts. Kuyper never tired of celebrating this diversity; indeed, a profusion of distinctions was to him the hallmark of a healthy society, the "natural," "spontaneous" result of a "free course of development."[46] As implied by the label he gave his theory—"sphere sovereignty"—Kuyper wished each functional, occupational, and geographic unit to have independence from external imposition. (He simply assumed that a high degree of harmony and equity naturally existed among them.) In such "organic" communities he also saw an alternative to the twin demons of Revolution, atomism and collectivism.

They provided an authentic sense of identity, a social location between the individual and the mass, and a source of firm but manageable discipline.[47]

In sharp contrast, the state was "artificial" and "mechanical," ordained by God only in consequence of man's fall into sin. It was imposed upon but completely distinct from "free, organic society" and had only negative functions. It might legitimately maintain order, provide for defense, and try to correct imbalances within and among the various "spheres," but should never be allowed to take the initiative in society, lest it stifle it. Kuyper's state had potent authority but few powers and fewer activities. It was the final guardian of society's order but also the worst threat to its liberty. It was to be feared, in both senses of the term.[48]

Naturally liberalism emerged guilty on this point also. While eroding the basis of legitimacy, it had multiplied the state's concerns. In effect, it fostered disorder which it then sought to check through regimentation. Inevitably, the social spheres had become corrupted, turned from their original purposes into governmental agencies, their vitality ebbing with their independence. Since its program would only multiply intrusions, political liberalism offered nothing but the prospect of a thoroughly rationalized and stagnant society.[49]

In contrast the Anti-Revolutionaries supported measures they thought would strengthen organic groups and restore diversity: the household franchise, local initiative, a decentralized regime, occupational or functional representation in one house of the national legislature, equal support for all (not just the secularized) school systems, and voluntary welfare and social reform movements. But for Kuyper, these measures awaited something more profound, a spontaneous upsurge of the elemental Calvinism and latent power of "the small people." In addition to renewing the religious ethos of national life, their triumph would sweep away the intrusive, artificial mechanisms of state and allow the natural forces of social life to flow freely again.[50]

The revival of "the small people" would redeem society from its sins of regimentation and stagnation. It was this vision as much as his theism (for him the two were intimately intertwined) that impelled Kuyper throughout his career, appearing in his first major address, "Uniformity, the Curse of Modern Life" (1869), and in his last, "The Small People" (1917). It also molded his argument against liberal culture, bringing us full circle. Modern thinkers, too, had begun by dismissing the wisdom which the community had built up through centuries of concrete experience, had destroyed, as it were, the organic harmony of knowledge. Then they tried to reorder the fragments in vast monistic systems spun out of abstract speculation. These gave no place to the detailed and unique; they ridiculed divergent schools of thought;

and they induced artificial regularity—all the prerequisites for final suffocation. But soon, Kuyper predicted, the "instincts" of "the folk-consciousness" would reassert themselves, overwhelm monistic intellectualism, and revitalize cultural life.[51]

In retrospect it is obvious that Kuyper's critique encapsulated the previous century of Dutch Calvinist experience. From their position of a claimed monopoly on intelligence, the learned and polished had ridiculed the orthodox, and liberal governments had pursued policies harmful to their interests; hence Kuyper's suspicion of the state and his animus against prevailing systems of thought. His praise of faith and instinct, of traditional communities and decentralized society, reflected the values of the lower-middle level of the countryside and smaller cities where Calvinism thrived. This perspective enabled Kuyper to perceive much that his contemporaries missed and to make acute appraisals of the course his society was taking. In seeing how much a person's heart and social position affected his intellect, Kuyper worked as an unwitting pioneer in the sociology of knowledge. He knew the price exacted by the rise of the urban industrial order and knew which groups had paid it. He also sensed the growing alienation and loneliness this order was inflicting upon its inhabitants. Finally, he foresaw the regimentation common to mass society and the possibilities for oppression inherent in the modern state.

But some of his mistakes proved to be nearly as influential as his successes. First of all, it was hardly appropriate for one who practiced principial analysis the way Kuyper could to complain about the penchant of liberalism for monism. It is also puzzling that one so conscious of human depravity could praise almost without qualification the "free" and "natural" development of social institutions and instinctively frown upon restraints. Perhaps still imbued with the very pietism he criticized, Kuyper often forgot that groups as well as individuals could be corrupt, that "natural" social forces (e.g., the Industrial Revolution) could cause immense damage. He missed some of the rich possibilities for critical realism that his theology offered. He was equally imperceptive in his postulate of severe opposition between "the state" and "society." Although he gave evidence of knowing better, his instincts led him to minimize the possibility of society using the state as an instrument for its own ends. This attitude would reduce some of Kuyper's constituents to ideological absurdity in later years when it became evident (in light of corporate business's dynamics of centralization and homogenization) that his negative, regulatory state could not maintain the type of society he wanted. Finally, his naivete about the means of overcoming entrenched power is remarkable, especially in view of his many decades in professional politics. Certain interests might once have been aided by "artificial" means but had long since become most "naturally" entrenched; how then could the traditional harmony Kuyper extolled be restored without the forceful, remedial state action he deplored? On "the social question" in particular, Kuyper's inability to resolve this difficulty led many—followers and enemies alike—to mistake him for an apologist for the strong and the status quo. His suspicion of the state and unfounded confidence in "natural, organic" forces prevented him from translating his denunciations of ravaging capitalism into adequate restraints on its power.

So bold a proposal as Kuyper's inevitably generated controversy among the Reformed. Since the resulting factionalization recurred in Dutch America, we shall explore it in detail later, pausing here to sketch only some of its major features.

One Dutch-American party comprised those descendants of the earlier Secession most loyal to that movement's original idea of separation for the preservation of purity. Uneasy with Kuyper's political radicalism, more uneasy with parts of his theology, and most uneasy with his cultural activism, they burst into open opposition in 1892 when their denomination merged with the "sorrowing churches" (named the "Doleantie," from the Dutch word for *mourning*—i.e., the mother church's apostasy) that Kuyper had led out of the Hervormde Kerk in 1886.[52] Now facing the "corruption" of their own body, the dissidents pursued three courses of action: they forced yet another schism, they mounted a guard for orthodoxy in the merged church, and, in a few important cases, they emigrated to the United States. This split in particular, then, had strong reverberations in Dutch America.

A larger but less cohesive group stood in the traditions of the Reveil and the evangelical party within the Hervormde Kerk. Although it had come to accept the state's giving only preference rather than sanction to the Reformed faith, this group held doggedly to the vision of a national church. Its members were sympathetic to orthodoxy but more concerned with having a general Protestantism aggressively asserted against all "foreign" creeds—most pointedly, the very Catholicism Kuyper was cooperating with politically—as normative for the entire nation. Thus they appealed not to the Confessions "strictly taken," as had the Secessionists and Kuyper, but to the simple "spirit of the gospel." Socially they cherished the unity and discipline made possible by the inclusive network and norms of a broad church and figured prominently in the group that aligned orthodoxy with political conservatism.[53]

Naturally this party found much to fear in Kuyper's program—his radical spirit, his contempt for mere conservatism, his separatist strategy and refusal to subordinate ideological differences to "practical cooperation," and, most fundamentally, his vision of social and cultural pluralism. Their opposition, similar to that of the old Seceders (but for the opposite reason), began to swell in the wake of Kuyper's 1886 church split and climaxed in the 1890s.[54] On the political front, Kuyper's speeches on the social question, his coalition with the Catholics, and his support of franchise extension prompted a large segment of the Anti-Revolutionary party to secede and form a separate, forthrightly conservative party. Recalling Groen, they described it as "Christian-Historical," as distinct from Kuyper's description of his own party as "Christian-Democratic." Shortly thereafter the scene shifted to academia as Kuyper purged the Free University of those who asserted the "starting point" of scholarly endeavor to be "the teachings of the Bible" as interpreted by the individual, rather than "the principles of Calvinism" systematically elaborated.[55]

The third great controversy did not materialize until after Kuyper's death but did stem from the fundamental ambiguity he left between common grace and antithesis. Already during his lifetime a divergence had opened as various followers emphasized one theme at the expense of the other. Foremost in this movement stood Herman Bavinck, Kuyper's contemporary (1854–1921) and his only intellectual peer among the Reformed.[56]

Bavinck had been born into a quintessential Secessionist household (his father was one of the movement's first ministers and theological professors), and he always retained its deep sense of piety and orthodoxy. But like Kuyper, he also excelled at the University of Leiden and participated in the most sophisticated intellectual discussions of his time. Throughout his career—twenty years as professor at the Secessionist seminary at Kampen and twenty as professor at the Free University—he sought to reconcile these two loyalties, both for his own sake and for that of the Reformed community.

Bavinck was another of Neo-Calvinism's Renaissance men, a scholar in theology, philosophy, education, and psychology; an essayist on problems intellectual (theory of science and art) and social (feminism and war); and a member of the Anti-Revolutionary party's central committee and of Parliament. He shared Kuyper's principial psychology and underscored the major themes of his critique: the baneful workings of "the Revolution" both social and intellectual, the fragmentation of thought wrought by the secular attitude, the monistic systems in which it sought a new unity, and the philosophical materialism it blithely assumed. Even more of his work involved elaboration of the alternative Kuyper had proposed—Christian theism as the only adequate explanation and guarantor of order in nature, certainty in knowledge, and security in society.[57] True to his heritage, he made his lasting scholarly achievement a comprehensive and sophisticated presentation of Reformed orthodoxy, the four-volume *Gereformeerde Dogmatiek*.

Yet to this task he brought a spirit quite different from Kuyper's, one that made him a model for the next generation of Dutch Reformed intellectuals both in the Netherlands and in the United States. Tolerant, genial, irenic, he never caricatured an opponent or impugned his motives but tried to give him all the credit he deserved. Often described as the Aristotle to Kuyper's Plato, Bavinck was inductive and empirical and displayed less confidence in any type of analysis that presented man's thinking as determined by deduction from fixed principle. "Principle" to Bavinck meant less a hard idea than the general spirit with which people struggled to order their world and solve specific problems. Human thought systems were for him rather fragile; developing, not complete; having relative, not absolute value.[58]

Befitting this style, Bavinck worked most tellingly in developing the idea of common grace. It was he, in fact, who recalled the Reformed community's attention to it in 1894, six years before Kuyper's publication.[59] To his Secessionist brothers he announced its necessity in unmistakable terms: their "pietistic" alternative was heresy—

> the love of the separated, closed community; the avoidance of art, science, culture and all good things of the earthly life and the denial of the calling which we have in home, society, and state; these are always fruits, not of the healthy Reformation but of the sickly Anabaptist plant.[60]

Common grace also served well Bavinck's purposes as a mediating intellectual. With it he could postulate a large area of reason common to men of all faiths, find much value in non-Christian cultures and contemporary thought, and justify his apologetic approach. Thus, while he did criticize modernist science and religion—the former for avoiding ultimate questions, the latter for its unsatisfying answers—he implied that in the end they were more incomplete than wrong.[61] Finally he was confident to the point of naivete regarding the ability of Christianity to act as a leaven in society to influence it subtly for good.[62]

By 1900, then, the orthodox Reformed in the Netherlands had become lodged in three camps: (1) a "broad church" group (Reveil and Hervormde Kerk evangelicals) holding to a pre-Enlightenment model of irenic, generally conservative Protestantism normative for the whole nation; (2) "post-Enlightenment Reformed sectarians" (the old Seceders), vigilant for orthodoxy among themselves and content to let the rest of the world go; and (3) "post-Enlightenment Calvinists" (the Neo-Calvinists), aiming to join the scope of the first with the intensity of the second in order to create a magnificent third that would transfigure Dutch life altogether.

Obviously Kuyper did not represent all three, but he did influence them all, as a catalyst and an unavoidable standard of measure if in no other way. For generations the Reformed would define themselves by the selections they made from his system or by their agreement or disagreement with that system as a whole. Nor could anyone better defend his own position than by demonstrating that it fulfilled the mandates Kuyper had drawn.

Whatever the disagreements, no one in the Reformed circle could remain unmoved by so monumental an achievement. Kuyper uncannily reflected almost every turn of Reformed character while infusing that character with a new spirit and sense of purpose. Expressed with his eloquence, Calvinism shone with more beauty, vitality, and import than its believers had ever imagined it could. And above all Kuyper proved infectious. Years after his death people would still be quick— too quick—to boast of their allegiance to "Calvinism," eager to extract from it solutions to all the world's problems, confident that such could easily be done. Hence the remarkable (if, to a later time, somewhat amusing) scope of Reformed ambition among its enthusiastic adherents, and their passion for making deep study and bold pronouncements about almost everything on earth. It would not be uncommon, for instance, for even the most mundane Reformed periodicals, in America as well as the Netherlands, to carry essays in the history of philosophy or geopolitical, world-historical interpretations of current events. If Kuyper's American followers could not aspire to his level of practical achievement, they redoubled their belief that the world (especially their new world) could be conclusively understood if it were only first thought through from the correct "starting point." Thus they set out on what became a perennial mission, "applying Calvinistic principles to every sphere of life."

Finally, Kuyper offered the Reformed a new conception of society quite befitting their modern condition. To be sure, pluralism represented a chastening for them. They could no longer think of themselves as being the "real" nation, but only a part of it. They were encouraged to assert their faith but had to accept, even respect, the other ideological sectors of society. Gone was the dream of reinstituting archaic sanctions, group symbols, that certain "tone" upon the country.

But pluralism also served them as a means to remarkable growth, even triumph. If the whole nation no longer served their faith, neither did it any longer command their undivided loyalty. The religious community stood beside and often above the nation and thrived as a result. Moreover, under Kuyper's leadership the Calvinists, in coalition with the Catholics, decisively transformed the structure of Dutch society as a whole so that for the first half of the twentieth century it was vertically stratified (in Dutch idiom, "pillarized") along religious lines. Just as Kuyper had proposed, the adherents of the various world views created separate communities, each defined in terms of its ideology and each having a complete set of institutions.[63] For the Dutch who were emigrating to the United States in record numbers during these years, this model would play a major part in shaping their new lives. So would the memory of the passionate struggle in the Netherlands in which the Reformed community had been so dramatically transformed.

PART II

DUTCH, REFORMED, AND AMERICAN: DEFINITIONS, 1900–1916

3

Varieties of Reformed Experience

As economic factors determined the contours of Dutch emigration, religion stamped its composition and the character of the subculture that it produced.[1] For Dutch Americans religion has been *the* medium of culture, and thus also of acculturation; the many issues, divisions, and changes of both have consistently registered in religious terms. Why this was so is a matter of conjecture. Certainly the appeal of religious fervor and emigration to the same social strata in the Netherlands was crucial. Then too, the modest size of the Dutch-American community precluded a pluriform institutional structure like those, for example, of Italian, Jewish, and Black Americans; the Dutch had to concentrate all their resources in a single network. Finally, some have claimed extraordinary religiosity to be inherent in Dutch character, a view that in light of the Netherlands' cultural system of the past century cannot be casually dismissed.[2]

But whatever the reasons, there can be little doubt that religion has indeed had this role. Those communities established by religious groups proved to be the foundation of the enduring ethnic subculture. Of the dozen projects based solely on economic considerations, run by scrupulous leaders, and launched with good intentions, few survived even one generation; the success rate was poorer yet for the notorious schemes of assorted Dutch land speculators. Few settlements went long without a church, and few became churched without being church-run. If most of a community's inhabitants were not devout to begin with, they soon either converted, became silent and moved to its fringes, or they left, disgusted at their proselytizers. Thus the proverb, "no church, no kolonie," was borne out in fact; those individuals and settlements lacking a religious confirmation of ethnic identity have mostly melted away without significant trace.[3] As congregations became the heart of each locality, so denominations have been the networks binding together the Dutch communities across the country, and church-related colleges and periodicals have provided the main forums of intellectual activity.

Religion also showed itself stronger than ethnicity, technically defined. From the start, "Dutch" America incorporated immigrants from East Frisia and Bentheim, both across the German border. That border had hardly existed religiously, since Dutch-originated pietism, conventicle chains, and even the 1834 Secession had spread readily across it. The Reformed from these provinces entered the same immigrant network as the Dutch and joined their churches in the new world, though maintaining their ethnic-linguistic independence for decades.[4]

Of course it was not religion in general but the orthodox Reformed type that was determinative.[5] The more devout held decisive roles at both ends of the migration process—in the Netherlands, as we have seen, and in the United States, where the communities that turned out to be most influential were those established in the 1840s and '50s by groups of Seceders (often led by Seceder pastors). These settlements spawned almost all the other Dutch communities in America and served as magnets and processing points for later immigrants.[6] Finally, even though Seceders constituted a minority of all Dutch immigrants, they had three striking advantages: the lion's share of ethnic leadership during the formative years, thousands of orthodox allies among immigrants of Hervormde Kerk background, and an intense ideology that could dominate the milder, less cohesive views of the majority.[7]

Even so, the Seceders could not remain untouched by the influx of different types in the later waves of immigrants. On the one hand, so many of these seemed (to old Seceder eyes) to come for purely economic reasons, diluting the character of the churches. On the other, the coincidence of mass immigration with the Neo-Calvinist revival in the Netherlands infused the community with an orthodoxy just as intense as the Secession's but of a quite different spirit. Moreover, this diversity compounded a major *internal* disjunction; within a decade of its founding, Dutch America had split into two denominations.

The leader of the western Michigan settlement, Albertus Van Raalte, had encouraged his "Kolonie," and by extension the other settlements, to enter into ecclesiastical union with the church established by the Dutch immigrants of the colonial era. This, the Reformed Church in America (RCA), had given Van Raalte considerable moral and financial support in his transplantation. He in turn found its blend of orthodoxy and pronounced piety congenial to his own disposition, that of the "Geldersche," or experiential school of the Secession.[8] Van Raalte had never absorbed the Seceders' separatist spirit either. Rather than having left the Hervormde Kerk, he had been prevented from joining it, the authorities having suspected him of associating with other Secessionist leaders.[9] Thus Van Raalte did not instinctively fear union; in fact, he saw the RCA alliance as particularly beneficial, a way to save the Kolonie from poverty, isolation, and backwardness.

But many in Michigan opposed the merger, questioning the doctrinal and liturgical purity of "the East." They complained that the Reformed Church used hymns in worship just like the State Church in the Netherlands (and with the same possibilities for Arminian corruption), that it practiced open communion, that it neglected catechetical training for the young and catechism preaching for adults, and—worst of all—that it doubted the validity of the Secession in the Netherlands. Soon the entire Kolonie was embroiled in debate over the dissenters' charges and Van Raalte's reliability, a debate that gave vent to all the animosity created both by Van Raalte's monopoly of power and by differences in the settlers' provincial origins and religious affinities.[10] The conflict demonstrated that the Seceders had no monopoly on the passion for orthodoxy. It was the Seceder Van Raalte who proposed union, while many of the dissenters were of Hervormde-Kerk background.[11] In any case, the dispute climaxed in 1857 when four congregations broke from Van Raalte and "the East" to (shades of 1834) "return to the standpoint of the fathers."[12]

The new sect's early years were dismal—its numbers few, its clergy erratic, its existence at all times precarious. But in the 1880s its perpetuation was guaranteed by another schism in the RCA, this time over Freemasonry. Hostility toward Masonry had long been present in the western Dutch enclaves, but in 1880 the RCA's four western classes petitioned the General Synod to declare church and lodge membership incompatible. When the Synod refused, many midwestern congregations broke their old fellowship and joined with the Seceders of 1857. More important, the Seceder church in the Netherlands officially condemned the RCA action and recommended that its emigrants affiliate with the dissenters upon settling in America.[13]

Thus at the very beginning of the largest wave of Dutch emigration to the United States, the smaller sect—the Christian Reformed Church (CRC), as it came to be known—received an endorsement that helped bring a majority of the immigrants into its fold.[14] By this time certain salient features were also emerging on each side. The Reformed held the place of the "established" church in the community: more genial and tolerant, connected to an American institution of long standing, and tending to absorb the less fervent of the later immigrants. The Christian Reformed, in turn, prided themselves on strictness of creed and code. They looked to European "fathers" for guidance and retained the Dutch language longer, increasing their attractiveness to new immigrants on both counts. Intellectually, the CRC was more rigorous, more

creative (having no American ally to rely on), and far more produc-
tive.[15]

By now, major paths of Netherlandic influence were also marked
out. Of the two Seceder factions that had led immigration, the more
radical, Hendrik Scholte's, was the shorter lived. Scholte was so fiercely
independent, and his followers so dependent upon him, that his death in
1868 led to the demise of his church as well. Thereafter, members of the
Iowa colony joined either the CRC or, as Pella dissenters had already
done in 1856, Van Raalte and the RCA. Thus the Seceder strain most
like "typical American" evangelicalism (Scholte was millennial, experiential, and biblicistic, with antipathies toward ecclesiastical authority
and the Confessions) had the least enduring influence.[16] The more
moderate Van Raalte left a deeper mark. But his church changed too. In
the 1857 split, loyalists and dissenters were identical in Netherlandic
church background: fifty-five percent Hervormde, forty-five percent
Seceder. But from that year to 1880, as the Seceder percentage of immigrants fell fourteen percentage points (to thirty-one percent), the share
coming to the RCA fell twenty-five points (to twenty percent), while the
CRC share fell only six points (to thirty-eight percent). Leadership
sources differed even more. The CRC clergy ordained between 1857
and 1900 was one hundred percent of Seceder background, compared
to just twenty-six percent of those ordained by the western RCA.[17]
More important, the third Seceder faction was becoming prominent.
This confessional-synodical school had been underrepresented in the
initial migration but gained influence as "Northern" immigration began in earnest in the late 1860s.[18] Its rise in influence coincided with
CRC growth, with the result that the denomination developed a permanent confessionalist cast. Again, leadership origins are more striking
still: four out of five of the CRC clergy ordained in the nineteenth
century had northern Netherlandic background.[19] Thus the most traditional and least "American" type had the greatest impact.

While debates over the denominational schism continued for decades, the problem of Americanization soon overshadowed it. The sheer
number and power of "the Americans," the apparent inevitability that
immigrant children would adopt "American ways," the rapidity with
which urbanization and improved communications were reducing
rural isolation (the subculture's primary defense)—all seemed gravely
foreboding for the cause of Dutch identity in the new land. Hence the
tone of apprehension that colored so much of the community's discussions in this era.

Because it received the lion's share of the immigrants after 1880,
the Christian Reformed Church addressed the problem at greater
length and with more pain. Its first thorough treatments of "Americanization" appeared around the turn of the century; by World War I

the issue had become a cliche.[20] Some ministers denounced any adaptation whatsoever as the fruit of a sinful pride that would bring ill-disguised heresies into the church and destroy ethnic identity.[21] But these lost the battle early, and their ever-decreasing numbers had to be content with merely slowing the pace of retreat or denouncing this or that American institution. By World War I most of the community would take the view if not the forceful tone of Barend Klaas Kuiper, one of the keenest students of the problem:

> We are quickly changing from Hollanders to Americans. This process of Americanization by itself is not in the least a problem. It is a process that cannot and may not be held back. We shall become Americans and we must become Americans. It is an irresistible, moral duty.[22]

The Dutch also agreed on what "Americanization" theoretically ought to be. They all believed that sooner or later the "Dutch Reformed" had to become "American Reformed"—that is, that nationality had to be sacrificed to religion. True, some insisted that *real* "Reformed-ness" required certain "Dutch" traits, if not the language itself. But even they agreed on the priorities.

This meant, however, that Americanization also entailed great danger, as even its advocates warned. "This danger does not consist in the fact that in the long run our original national character will disappear," wrote B. K. Kuiper. "That must be. The danger is this, that our people will also lose their Reformed character. And that must not be." The only defense against such an eventuality, he wrote elsewhere, was the development of "Calvinistic consciousness."[23] Others used the same formula with somewhat different terms: Americanization required a deepening of piety and confessional loyalty.[24] A Christian Reformed historian even read this argument into the past to justify the Secession of 1857:

> Our great and peculiar duty and calling here was and is . . . to become more and more what God in his providence in the past had designed us to be as a Calvinistic people. . . . To reach this purpose . . . we had no right to be benevolently assimilated. . . . Christian isolation therefore was a duty, isolation to develop ourselves quietly and without undue haste, to become firmly settled as to our principles . . . until we are prepared enough, strong enough, to cast us with body and soul and all our previous Calvinism as a world-and-life view as well as a religious system, into the arena of American religious and political and social life.[25]

Such rhetoric reveals another Dutch conviction: Americanization would be a two-way, not a one-way street. As the inaugural article of the community's foremost journal declared: "We are not and will not be a pretty piece of paper upon which America can write whatever it pleases."[26] Acculturation was to entail not the eradication but the reassertion of old values in a new context. Nor did this confidence spring from illusion. The stream of Dutch immigration reached its high-water mark in these years, adding thousands to the group's numbers (see Appendix). More than a dozen Dutch periodicals appeared daily, weekly, or monthly, and each issue was sure to report the organization of new congregations or the construction of more elaborate edifices by established ones. The Dutch even maintained a range of ancillary in-stitutions in this era—mutual-aid societies, real estate companies and banks, recreation centers, political and labor clubs—and the de-nominations made plans to build private schools, a mental hospital, a tuberculosis sanitarium, and to expand their colleges. With such evi-dence of God's favor there was cause for bright dreams. "America" was strong and demanded recognition, but the Dutch were thriving and could grant recognition at least partly on their own terms.

Another strength was the near unanimity of the Dutch-American pulpit. In view of all the disputation we will be considering in what follows, this becomes as important as it is striking. The sermon was still, after all, the community's most potent literary form: the center of its collective rite, the official pronouncement of its leadership, the favorite genre of its publishing houses.[27] That the sermons of these years, what-ever their source, sounded the same themes bespeaks the common core of Dutch-American loyalties. That these themes were overwhelmingly those of orthodox Reformed pietism argues the continuity of the group's heritage.

But if "pietistic," which sort of pietism? The pulpit assumed the elementary, that sin was pervasive and salvation essential, and typically concluded with a *toepassing,* the "application" that pressed the eternal question hard upon the listener's heart. Rather than building out from this center, however, most ministers kept a tight orbit about it. They did not wish to address specific circumstances but to paint and repaint the metaphysical given, that all men everywhere were lost and helpless, enemies of God. The great disparity appeared in nearly every sermon: God, magnificent as Creator and Redeemer, as unfolder of history and embodiment of all virtue; man as having at best only the appearance of goodness, for the rest a capacity for evil ("righteousness as filthy rags" was one favorite image) matched only by powerlessness to change ("clay awaiting the potter"). Happily, the pulpit made no self-righteous exception for the elect, even after salvation: "God's people are poor and miserable in themselves, poor in virtue, poor in strength, poor in every respect."[28]

Only divine condescension of enormous proportions could bridge the gap. Accordingly, Dutch-American piety focused on God's mercy, endless and abounding; on Christ's self-humiliation and suffering (Lenten sermons were among the favorites); and on the utter dependence of the redeemed. A certain passivity and individualism therefore marked the normative "holy life." Cultivation of private intimacy with God; hostility to the lusts of the flesh and lures of the world; direction of good works toward the temporary and remedial; and persistent anticipation of one's heavenly destiny, where peace and repose, "eternal and untroubled rest await you"—rarely did ideals besides these emerge.[29]

Life viewed from the Dutch pulpit and pew was not, then, the energetic, optimistic, progressive thing so familiar to American Protestantism. Rather, a cyclical quality prevailed, for the believer no less than for the worldly, in his spiritual life as well as his public. He could not fully understand or control these cycles, nor were their limits loose or fluid. The Dutch pastoral ethic was not one of perfectionism but of penitence, of tribulation, or according to the titles of the sermons themselves, of pilgrimage: "The Character and Bliss of the Pilgrim to God's Zion," "Foreigners and Fatherland." The believer had duties in the world—in general, testifying with word *and* life for the Lord and against sin; in particular, being a diligent parent, a dependable worker, an obedient citizen. But daily life was to be regarded under eternal truth, which meant that believers would never conquer the sin in themselves or in the world. If this made them somber, at least it spared them self-delusion.[30]

Variations in the sermonic literature involved emphasis more than substance. An occasional Neo-Calvinistic voice declared that under the Lordship of Christ "all the earth" belonged to the faithful, but just as soon warned the faithful not to become earthly. The English language sermons from the RCA showed a somewhat stronger change, shading toward the moderate, mild, and joyful.[31]

But the pulpit achieved its harmony only by skirting the most nagging issue: "Americanization." Agreeing to become "American Reformed" had been easy; defining exactly what "Reformed" and "American" meant was far more difficult. In sum, the intellectual history of Dutch America between 1900 and 1916 is the story of debate over these concepts, a debate carried on by four factions divided by their different perceptions and definitions of the terms.[32]

THE FOUR MENTALITIES

The moderation of some RCA pulpits became much more pronounced in the *Leader,* the English periodical of the RCA "West." The paper's name reflected its self-image as much as its influence; the voice of "the better element" in the Dutch community, it addressed the respectable citizen in a refined tone.

The *Leader*'s chief contributors—Evert J. Blekkink, Gerrit H. Dubbink, Matthew Kolyn, and William Moerdyke—had the same origins and career pattern. They were born in or immigrated very young to the pioneer Dutch settlements in the Midwest, attended Hope College and an RCA seminary, held several pastorates in that denomination, and by 1907, the year of the *Leader*'s founding, were situated in western Michigan either as professors at Western Seminary or as pastors of prestigious churches.[33] Befitting their tenure in the United States, they looked to colonial America, not the nineteenth-century Netherlands, as the heroic epoch of the Dutch Reformed experience and recounted on all occasions the Reformed Church's honorable role in American history.

This institutional connection figured large in the character as well as the rate of the *Leader* circle's Americanization. The most potent influence was educational. From the start, professors trained in the RCA "East" dominated the Hope College and Western Seminary faculties, and many of the West's ministers received their degrees at the East's New Brunswick Seminary.[34] Assimilating into the RCA East also meant verging on the American Protestant mainstream. The East had long cooperated with the American evangelical alliance that had led the great nineteenth-century movements for domestic revivalism, foreign missions, and social reform. So powerful had this alliance proven that it had assumed many functions of an established church: its behavioral pattern constituted official morality, and its rhetoric and ideas—what one historian calls "a pan-Protestant ideology"—served as a principal unifying force for the nation as a whole.[35]

Before assigning "the West" entirely to "American" influence, however, we should note how neatly their development followed imperatives from their own ethnic past. As their share of new immigrants decreased, they were both forced and free to pursue the Eastern connection. As the immigrants they did attract hailed more and more from Hervormde Kerk background, they could well gravitate toward the "National Church" of America. And as their Seceder origins were of the experiential-moralist ("Geldersche") strain, they could approve of revivalist-reform evangelicalism out of rather than in spite of their Netherlandic heritage. In fact, the *Leader* circle came to resemble most closely the Reveil-evangelical party in the Hervormde Kerk: moralistic, genteel, willing to submerge strict "Reformed-ness" in general Protestantism in order to spread that faith over the entire nation.[36]

The *Leader*, then, was the voice of normative Americanism in the Dutch community. Appropriately, it showed hostility toward both Catholicism and the CRC's Christian school movement, sometimes in the same breath. Touched with the millennial optimism of the time, the *Leader* perceived the world as being less locked in a fundamental tension with the church than flailing in the latter stages of a struggle that Christianity was sure to win. Declared a Blekkink editorial entitled "The World is Growing Better,"

> Christian civilization is marching forward and the world is growing better morally. There is a rising tide of goodness in the earth. . . . Every department of human life is increasingly and favorably affected by the gospel of Christ. . . . The kingdom of righteousness is majestically moving forward to the establishment of the new heaven and the new earth.[37]

Not that Christianity's triumph would offend non-Christian peoples. "The Master's teachings" represented mankind's grandest ideals, the truth that all men pursue. Following Jesus was no less a matter of "uplift" than of conversion:

> To be for man in the highest sense is to have the spirit of the Master. It is to look at man from the standpoint of what he may become by the grace of God. . . . Christ enriched humanity . . . [and] sowed the earth's acreage with seed-thoughts that the centuries are gradually and magnificently maturing into the harvest of a world-wide Christian civilization.[38]

The *Leader* applied this cheerfulness to the individual believer too. Christianity "produces a personality which is strengthened, enriched, elevated and liberated."[39] Dependence on a loving Father should develop from appreciation of divine goodness, not from fear of the world. Thus, such meditations as "The Joy of Prayer," "The Forward Look," and "Religious Certainty" dotted *Leader* columns, and with every change of the seasons its readers could expect sentimental illustrations of God's care in the form of analogies from nature: "Autumn," "The Sower," or "Fruit Trees."

The piety of joy mattered greatly, for it induced a life of service: "more joy and happiness will be experienced and more work accomplished if Christians view things from a bright and hopeful standpoint."[40] And service was *the* end of religion. The *Leader*'s Christian was always busy harvesting in the Lord's fields, as a businessman bringing the gospel of honesty to commerce, or as a citizen supporting those statesmen who ruled the nation according to "moral and religious principles," such as "the good of all" and "the spirit of true democracy."[41] But the highest service remained "religious work," preferably in cooperation with other American Christians in the YMCA, Sunday School federations, and especially foreign missions. Indeed, for the RCA the latter represented both the pinnacle of dedication and the proof of the denomination's excellence. Did not Hope College send proportionately more missionaries to China, India, and Arabia than any other school in America?[42]

The *Leader* asserted Reformed identity only on theological grounds strictly defined. It consistently affirmed the Reformed Confessions and decried liberal heresies—"the so-called new theology, . . . the evolutionary theory and method of goodness, . . . the socialistic idea of salvation by the mass instead of the individual, . . . the preacher who is still endeavoring by the wisdom of man, instead of the power of God, to save the lost."[43] Against such errors, however, it often urged the tenets of "general" rather than "Reformed" orthodoxy: divine revelation, scriptural authority, substitutionary atonement, and the resurrection.

Nicholas Steffens, the senior professor at Western Seminary and the only one trained in the Netherlands, urged a more confessional strategy. Not accidentally, his outlook was considerably less rosy than that of his colleagues. "Do you call our age a grand age? You are right, but it is also grand in the ruthless destruction of everything that is dear to a Christian heart," he stated. He also sounded Neo-Calvinist themes, assailing "Revolutionary" atheism and pleading for a comprehensive Christian world view: "Our principles have either to be upheld or abandoned. . . . Calvinism has to be rehabilitated in all its pristine vigor and glory. . . . Let us return to Dordt and Westminster in order that we may begin an era of progressive Calvinistic theology."[44]

But his was the only hint of Neo-Calvinism in the Reformed Church. ("Even our own paper," Steffens wrote Abraham Kuyper, "is in the hands of a clique which seeks to prevent me from expressing and defending Reformed principles.")[45] Its leaders had little use for principial analysis of "the spirit of the age" or for any other Kuyperian tool. Instead they used general categories and terminology. Hence, they could make little systematic criticism of American Protestantism, or of Protestant America. Nor did they have Neo-Calvinism's sense of the corporate or of a distinctively Christian cultural program. They are best described as outgoing pietists who hoped to lift individuals to a higher moral plane and thereby to lead society toward broadly defined virtues.

In contrast to such serenity, the other parties emerged out of sharp debate. Given Dutch America's preoccupation in this era with defining itself *vis-à-vis* its environment, this debate came to focus on the relationship of "the church" to "the world." But it began in that traditional seedbed of Calvinistic dispute, the doctrine of predestination.

The quarrel began already in the 1880s and continued full force into the new century. At first, the issue involved the timing of election. The infralapsarians, representing the Secessionist line, maintained that God performed election after the fall of man, while supralapsarians, the Neo-Calvinists, reversed the sequence, indeed, placed election before creation itself.[46] Soon the argument moved to the process of salvation. The "Supras" maintained that the elect were redeemed at birth, that

The Four Mentalities of the Dutch-American Community

	Seceders / Pietists "Infras"	Neo-Calvinists / Kuyperians "Supras"
Outgoing Optimistic	Reformed Church "West" The *Leader* Evert Blekkink Henry Geerlings	Positive Calvinists The *Banner* B. K. Kuiper Johannes Groen/Henry Beets
Defensive Introverted	Confessionalists *De Gereformeerde Amerikaan* Foppe Ten Hoor L. J. Hulst	Antithetical Calvinists *De Gids—De Calvinist* Klaas Schoolland John Van Lonkhuyzen

infant baptism assumed regeneration to have already taken place, that a "conversion experience" was not the moment of "rebirth," but only the instant in which one became aware of a previously accomplished fact. Therefore, the instruments of the church—preaching and sacraments—did not induce but simply confirmed regeneration. The Kuyperians argued this interpretation as sounder scripturally and more fruitful ecclesiastically. It placed the emphasis where, for the Calvinist, it belonged—on God's sovereign control rather than on man's reception. It released the laity from perpetual (and selfish) worry over the state of their souls, and the pulpit from the emotionalism and repetition needed to spark conversions. God's people were free to pursue the more pressing task of applying Christ's teachings to realms outside the church.

The Supras spent most of their time explaining these innovations to a cautious audience. Doctrinally, their cause languished after the CRC Synod of 1906 declared infralapsarianism the traditional Reformed and more thoroughly scriptural position.[47] Here and throughout the controversy, the Infras held the initiative and pursued it aggressively. They had at their service the community's leading journal, *De Gereformeerde Amerikaan,* and counted in their number the most highly respected ministers in the Dutch community. Two of these were prestigious sons of the Secession, Hendrik Van Hoogen and Hendericus Beuker, both of whom had studied at Kampen Seminary under Hendrik de Cock's own son and had been called to important posts in America after long service in the Netherlands.[48] Two others, Lammert J. Hulst and Foppe M. Ten Hoor, were more vocal and longer-lived and hence led the Infra retort.

Hulst's credentials were impressive. Born in 1825 to parents active in conventicles, he could even in the twentieth century recall the holy days of 1834. As a child and young pastor, he had agonized over his standing with God before finally experiencing a conversion of extraordinary force. After immigrating to Michigan, he became one of the foremost ministers in the community and bolstered the struggling CRC by leading the exodus from the Reformed Church during the Masonic controversy.[49] Active well into his eighties, Hulst was at once denominational patriarch and savior, a weighty antagonist for whomever he opposed.

Ten Hoor shared this religious pedigree but established his reputation in the Netherlands rather than in America. An 1880 graduate of Kampen, Ten Hoor had for fifteen years led the anti-Kuyperian forces among the heirs of the Secession, writing books against Kuyper's doctrine of the church and contributing to an anti-Doleantie periodical. Imported in 1896 to a bastion of conservatism on Grand Rapids' southeast side,[50] Ten Hoor continued his battle as cofounder and editor of De Gereformeerde Amerikaan (established in 1897) and, after 1900, as occupant of the CRC's most prestigious intellectual post, the chair of Systematic Theology at the Theological School in Grand Rapids.

Hulst applied himself to the doctrinal specifics in question, Ten Hoor to theological method; both grounded their arguments in the pietistic tradition.[51] Hulst held that regeneration occurred in time rather than eternity, in the human heart rather than the mind of God, and that it was not presupposed at baptism but had to be experienced later in life. Kuyperians could think otherwise, Ten Hoor declared, only because they had departed from the true Reformed line. Orthodox Reformed thinkers had always bound themselves to Scripture as interpreted by the church in the Reformed Confessions, but Neo-Calvinists abstracted from the Bible one idea, the sovereignty of God, and transformed it into an authoritative principle to which they made the Confessions submit. Such "conceit" (Hulst's label) partook of all too current an error—the elevation of the individual over the collective, of modern speculation over traditional wisdom.[52] The consequences could only be deleterious. First, an incorrect "starting point" (the two had no quarrel with this element of Kuyper) would undermine the whole edifice of truth. Second, piety itself would die. As Neo-Calvinism's doctrine must destroy earnest self-examination, so its intellectualism would dampen the fires of vital faith. "Away with such a dreaming philosophy. . . . Away with such human speculation which corrupts God's work instead of promoting it."[53]

Fueling this anger was a matter of group politics. In the Netherlands, the Kuyperians were seen as trying to subordinate the Secessionist Kampen Seminary to the Neo-Calvinistic Free University, a move that would remove theological education from direct ecclesiastical control. A similar movement was alive in Dutch-American circles with regard to the Grand Rapids Theological School. As foremost professor there, Ten Hoor thus had institutional as well as ideo-logical reason for wrath. Theology was "the queen of the sciences," he maintained, not an ordinary discipline to be integrated into the univer-sity curriculum and there criticized by its purported equals.[54] Ten Hoor's invocation of this medievalism was not an instance of nostalgia but a step in keeping with the elevation by pietism of things "spiritual" over things "natural."

But beneath the institutional maneuvers, and beneath the the-ological argumentation as well, lay contrary cultural concepts. Against those of Kuyper, the Infras rallied those of the Secession. Hulst, for example, rendered the history of the church as a simple story of declen-sion: every church followed the Roman Catholic path, succumbing to the seductions of power and wealth, thereby forfeiting purity of faith. How ominous then did Kuyper's "Christian" cultural activism appear.

> Does not experience teach what fruit is produced whenever preach-ers concern themselves with worldly affairs? Their religious tasks are neglected; their preaching and their intercourse with church mem-bers become worldly. . . . The people go much more gladly to public entertainments than to church. Above all, the youth rave about worldly play. . . . Truly, now is no time to put the emphasis on general grace and to reject particular grace.[55]

Ten Hoor drew the contrast more invidiously, suggesting that Kuyper's movement was of the rich and respectable, led by the intellectual elite, aimed at worldly glory, whereas

> the Secession emerged from the spiritual life, born out of the need of the soul. . . . It was a reformation of poor, lost sinners who felt the need of redemption through Christ and who fled from the dead churches of Rationalism in the Reformed Church. . . . It was a refor-mation of the foolish, the weak, the ignoble, accounted nothing according to the world . . . [and opposed by] all that is rich and learned and mighty.[56]

If Reformed people wished to remain God's people, they had to remain, as Ten Hoor put it in the title of one of his sermons, "The Worthless of the World."[57] Indeed, they had to glory in the fact and resist any alteration thereof.

Over against Neo-Calvinism Ten Hoor always posited the official Confessions and the works of Reformed theologians of *de bloemtijd,* "the period of florescence." The seventeenth rather than the nine-teenth was for him the definitive century of Reformed theology; *its* thinkers had the time-tested truths for every age.[58] Indeed, for Ten Hoor the Reformed standards constituted Truth itself, above which the mind could not stand and beyond which it had no reason to go.

In less sophisticated form, such were the sentiments of the largest group of Dutch Americans, Reformed and Christian Reformed alike. Thus they can aptly be labeled "Confessionalists."[59] As they narrowed all intellectual effort toward traditional doctrine, so they tended to confine social concern to the ecclesiastical sphere strictly defined. Hence, Ten Hoor saw spiritual renewal and confessional loyalty as the essence of Americanization and derided as stupid illusions all Neo-Calvinistic attempts to create Christian political organizations.[60] When forced to react to the extraecclesiastical world, the Confessionalists usually produced weak, unsystematic analyses. In evaluating "America," they operated from an automatic traditionalism, an instinctive though not absolute or principial loyalty to Dutch models, and a concern for the effects it would have on personal piety and "purity." They shared hostility to Kuyperianism with the *Leader* circle but had none of that group's confidence regarding the outside world. Thus they qualify as inward-looking pietists.

Kuyperians in America were not only opposed from without but divided within. While sharing the Neo-Calvinistic hallmarks—supralapsarian theology, principial method, and Christian cultural activism—they split over the polarity in Kuyper's thought and so produced contrary conceptions of "Calvinism." One group, the "positive Calvinists," concentrated on the conciliatory and reformist aspects of his system; the other followed "the antithesis."

The two most prominent "Antitheticals" had come under Kuyper's spell in the Netherlands. John Van Lonkhuyzen was a student and family friend of Kuyper who arrived with great fanfare in Grand Rapids in 1911 to become pastor of a large west-side congregation.[61] His collaborator, Klaas Schoolland, had been born into a Secessionist family but soon moved to the Kuyperian cause. He emigrated in 1891 under less auspicious circumstances—for "reasons of health" following a nervous collapse induced by academic strain. Whether blessed by America's climate or aroused by its depravity, he soon recovered his powers sufficiently to begin the great labor of duplicating Kuyper's triumphs in his adopted land. Professor of Classical Languages at Calvin College, founder of a Calvinist political club in Grand Rapids, and voluminous contributor to the weekly newspaper *De Gids* ("The Guide," later incorporated into *De Calvinist*), Schoolland led all in rigorous principial thinking.

Schoolland's adaptation, however, worked subtle but critical changes in Kuyper's system. Where Kuyper developed principles out of concrete situations and toward practical effects, Schoolland spun his in abstraction and remained exclusively theoretical. Kuyper mixed several strains; Schoolland saw little besides the antithesis. His series on the subject in the weekly *Calvinist* ran for ninety installments. Moreover, Schoolland made the antithesis absolute:

No neutral ground exists. There is no middle ground between God's Kingdom and the kingdom of Satan. . . . The wisdom of man stands opposed to the wisdom of God. The will of man directly opposes the will of God. These two theses can be developed and broadened and applied in relationship to every facet and activity of human life. From them nothing is excluded.[62]

True to Kuyper, Schoolland never translated this dichotomy into a pietistic conflict between the spiritual and the material, and therefore never urged his readers to forsake the world. Instead, as God would restore his creation rather than destroy, so they were to build the Kingdom of God within the world. Since complete restoration would occur only in eternity, however, the redeemed might never hope for success (as "the world" defined it) on earth. Particularly in America, they were not to fall under the illusion of "progress" or think that enlarging the fund of "general good" was true service of God. Rather, Calvinists should construct a holy community within and against the larger society and a system of thought that defied prevalent philosophies. Christian cultural witness existed to condemn "the world," not to save it.

Naturally, Schoolland wanted separate Calvinistic organizations everywhere, but his rationale varied from time to time according to conditions. Sometimes separation was the best means of guarding the elect's purity, and other times it was the most efficient way to develop the Reformed community fully—but always it was a matter of principle and served to strengthen antithetical consciousness. "Through them [separate organizations] we shall become more conscious of our position over against the world, the unbelieving world."[63]

Of the entire Antithetical program, the separatist corollary aroused the most controversy. Sooner or later everyone had to decide whether or not to support the Christian labor union, political party, and weekly newspaper. Whenever faced with objections appealing to "unique American conditions," Schoolland would reply on the level of principle. Principles possessed universal validity and applied in Grand Rapids as surely as they did in Amsterdam, for nowhere in the world could the children of God and the children of Satan cooperate. "In our *isolation*," Schoolland repeated after Groen van Prinsterer, "and in our *independent action* lie our strength and our prospects for the future."[64]

More than any other faction, the Antitheticals distrusted things American and adhered to Dutch examples. This did not issue, however, from hostility to America in particular but from hostility toward "the world" in general. America happened to be the world at hand, the Netherlands the place where Calvinists had most fully developed antidotes. So it was the Antithetical Calvinists who subjected "America" to the most searching critiques, though in a somewhat obscure Continental guise. They also led the resistance to language change, fearing the loss of communication with their European model.[65] But in defining Americanization, they showed a striking similarity to their sometimes Confessionalist opponents. They too wished to Americanize by cultivating a set of ideas, only substituting Antithetical principles for the Confessions.

In fact, Confessionalists and Antitheticals had more than this in common. Foppe Ten Hoor could use Kuyperian rhetoric. The Reformed thinker's "two-fold starting point," he once declared, was the antithesis and principialism. John Van Lonkhuyzen, in turn, demanded strict confessional allegiance.[66] More important, the two parties shared the same generative instinct, a fear of "the world," and a corresponding focus of attention upon the small body of the redeemed. Both scorned the thought of improving the world. Both directed their energies inward, to build up the faithful whether in piety alone or in piety conjoined to the socio-cultural aspects of life. Van Lonkhuyzen spoke for both in a sage contrast of their mentalities with that of the *Leader:*

> If you are satisfied with it [Christianity] as it is today then [foreign] missions is your great task, but if not, if you desire a deeper rather than a broader Christianity, then you must combat the influence of anti-Christian thought. By thus fighting the evils within, we can do more for the coming of God's Kingdom than by any amount of missions work.[67]

The other brand of Neo-Calvinists shared the Antitheticals' institutional concern. "Deeper Christianity" and strong community alike required a full range of Reformed organizations in which the faithful could be nurtured from the cradle to the grave. Such, in fact, was the burden of the entire positive Calvinist party. It lay at the heart of their statement on Americanization, Barend Klaas Kuiper's *Ons Opmaken en Bouwen,* the most thorough analysis of the subject to appear in Dutch-American circles. And it was personified by the party's clerical leaders. Johannes Groen ministered to the largest congregation in the CRC and championed the cause of separate Christian schools; Henry Beets sold one ecclesiastical organization after another (missions, a college, an English-language periodical) to a wary constituency.[68]

But positive Calvinist advocacy had a different purpose: not to shelter the elect from the world but to prepare them to go out and transform it. "Of such churches as ours," declared Groen a bit grandly, "our land has great need; therein lies the hope of our nation."[69] Christian action in political and economic affairs should not just witness against "the world's" folly but try to correct it, he maintained, just as Christian education should not only be different from but better—as education—than its secular counterpart.

Through all this the influence of Kuyper was clear. The whole purpose of institution building, said B. K. Kuiper, was the development of a "Calvinistic world-and-life view." In the inaugural issue of the CRC's English-language weekly, Beets proclaimed his love for Calvinism as "a comprehensive life-and-world view," for "its massive logic, its stupendous grandeur, its sublime conceptions, its vast compass. . . . It is the purest, most comprehensive conception of the great, vital truths of the infallible Word of God."[70] That they stood on the common-grace side of Kuyper was equally clear. For them, the human race contained not two but three classes of people: the positively Christian, the positively anti-Christian, and the great neutral mass, susceptible to pressure from either side but having ideals to which Christians could appeal. The Dutch, therefore, were called to join other American Christians to press their witness as forcefully as possible to those standing on middle ground, to show them by their own standards the superiority of Christian to non-Christian culture. True Neo-Calvinists, this party hoped to give a distinctive Christian testimony in "every sphere of life," but unlike the Antitheticals they did not insist on doing this through separate organizations. Separatism was a matter of tactics, not principle.

Under such an attitude toward "the world," the American portion thereof could shine more favorably. Again, life histories confirmed disposition.[71] Johannes Groen was one of the few prominent CRC ministers of this era to have been born in America, whereas Beets and Kuiper, though natives of the Netherlands, arrived in the United States while in their teens and there had formative experiences—Kuiper's being the higher learning of the University of Chicago, and Beets's being a religious conversion in a small Secessionist town in Kansas. Over there in the Netherlands, said Beets, "no one spoke to us about our soul. Here consecrated people *did*. Here some of us came to the light and the burden of our heart rolled away—do you wonder that we *love* the land wherein we found *spiritual* life and light?" All three urged faster rather than slower language change. Groen became entangled in endless controversy because he approved of certain "American" institutions. Beets was downright cosmopolitan, building bridges to other denominations and serving the English-speaking section of the CRC in critical offices.[72]

On certain points, this party gravitated toward the RCA optimists. Beets spent increasing amounts of time and energy agitating for foreign missions, and positive Calvinist pulpits voiced some of the happy piety familiar to the *Leader*.[73] Neo-Calvinist rigor, however, kept such similarities to a minimum. More numerous were connections with the inward-looking groups. These Calvinists did not exaggerate the power of evil in the world, but neither did they minimize it; they used Kuyper's technique of principial analysis; and they were adamant confessionally.

If Groen advocated bold innovation, he also praised "The Old Paths" of Reformed theology. Calvinistic action might save America but only if it bound itself to the principles of Scripture with childlike faith.[74]

These connections, and others mentioned above, should caution us against absolutizing factional differences. Parties there were, but within a community. Later, debate would explode into full-scale polemic, but even then it would be debate over definitions of common loyalties. At this stage it was quite possible to straddle categories, as one Christian Reformed theologian demonstrated. Louis Berkhof, child immigrant to America and graduate of Calvin and Princeton Seminaries, taught theology at the Grand Rapids school from 1906 until 1944, a sure sign of confessional orthodoxy. But he was also an accomplished practitioner of the fine art of applying Calvinistic principles to topics of the day; by 1916 he had written *Christendom en Leven*, *The Church and Social Problems*, and *The Christian Laborer in the Industrial Struggle*. Together these form a composite picture of the Dutch-American mind of the time.

Already here Berkhof showed the agility that would enable him alone to survive the tests of strife and time. Christ came to save souls *and* society, he argued; redemption applied to the physical as well as to the spiritual; the redeemed would find perfection only in eternity but had to apply their principles "in all spheres" of this world. Berkhof displayed the full line of Kuyperian wares, condemning "Revolutionary individualism" and Modernism, affirming the cultural mandate and the importance of principle. With one group of Neo-Calvinists he could call for a witness that improved the world; with the other, the necessity of separate organization. And with the Confessionalists he declared that knowledge of doctrine was the highest good, preaching to lost souls was the primary task, the circle of believers was the first object of concern, and deepening of piety was the crux of Americanization.[75]

Factional coexistence gave the discourse of this period a repetitive air. Reiteration rather than development or compromise seemed the concern of all; yet no group could push to a decisive triumph. The generative mentalities are still crucial to study, however, since *they*, more than and independently of country of birth, age of immigration, or even language, signified which views a person and ultimately the community would hold. Moreover, though first theological they were not finally that; they shaped political and social attitudes as well, and so endowed the community with tensions throughout the full spectrum of its concerns.

4

Reconnoitering America

The Dutch could attribute some of their arguments in these years to their differing dispositions. But since their assessments of America, as much as their piety, stemmed from a common base, another factor was also at work—a deep ambivalence toward the new land itself. On the one hand, everyone heard America praised. Sometimes this merely served to preface a longer discourse bewailing American vice; sometimes it continued without qualification. But at "pioneer" reunions or political rallies, on the 4th of July or "Dutch-American Day" at the state or county fair, someone was bound to hold forth on the wonders of the new land and its special significance for Hollanders.

These portrayals recalled Abraham Kuyper's own, with their praise for America's freedom and cohesion, gratitude for its abundance and opportunity, and high claims for Dutch "contributions" to its history. Then came the nub of the issue, characterization of America as a "Christian country." Time and again Dutch Americans asserted (accurately) that the United States had not experienced the revolutionary explosion that had rocked Europe and (less accurately) that it had therefore not suffered a deluge of Revolutionary ideas but grown in an unbroken line from its Calvinistic sources. If some "elements" in its society exhibited non-Christian traits, at bottom America's ethos and institutions were nevertheless "Christian." And so the United States was *heel anders*, "entirely different" from Europe. Claimed positive Calvinist Edward J. Tanis,

> American politics have never been of the atheistic revolutionary
> character as has been true even of the Netherlands. Practically all our
> presidents were Christian men. . . . For the Christianity and Chris-
> tian political principles of men like McKinley, Harrison, Garfield,
> Grant, we are bound to have the deepest respect. The Netherlands

with all her "Calvinistische Politiek" has never produced stauncher Christian statesmen. . . . These men were Christian not only in their personal lives but also in the performance of their political duties.[1]

Publishers joined this enterprise, adding to instruction in the new world's ways (their ostensible purpose) tributes to its virtues. Henry Beets's lives of Lincoln and McKinley are typical of the genre. He wrote, said the preface of his first biography, to awaken "our people" to their duties and opportunities as citizens; nothing else he had done was more important, to his mind.[2]

Beets's choice of the biographical mode suited his conception of America well: it was *the* land of the individual, giving each person all the opportunities he needed, all the rewards he deserved. While some Americans measured these rewards solely by wealth and status, Beets admitted, America's ultimate standard was moral excellence. In Beets's biographies, his heroes came from poor but honest stock; both Lincoln and McKinley were presented as having worked hard, led pure lives, and even in political office always followed conscience, never external pressures.[3] Corruption and demagoguery only hindered political success in America, Beets insisted. Lincoln and McKinley were carried to the White House by keeping clean reputations and calling the nation to noble purposes. That both were carried untimely out of office gave him no pause; assassination was tamed into an allegory of supreme self-sacrifice.

In applying these tales for his Dutch readers, Beets consciously turned to Horatio Alger. Unlike Thomas Lincoln, he warned, Hollanders ought not to succumb to wanderlust or neglect the spiritual when choosing a vocation, but like son Abraham, they ought to pursue one task at a time, always striving to do their best.[4] If Beets replaced Alger's "luck" with Providence, the traditional "pluck" remained intact, along with such other familiar virtues as piety, thrift, and obedience.

Such portraits could only encourage Dutch aspiration. If America demanded nothing but the old ways, if it were basically Christian and offered liberty and prosperity too, then Americanization would hardly be difficult or dangerous. As one pastor (Ame Vennema) declared on the semicentennial of Van Raalte's arrival in America, the Dutch immigrant "is indeed, in all but externals, an American before he crossed the sea." And so in rhetoric typical of the time, the melting pot took on a holy aura. "Rather would God bless this land with one great nation . . . a nation that can assimilate the most varied peoples . . . gradually blending these [into] the greatest and strongest people of the world. . . . Every part of the globe must furnish its quota to form a constituent part of a new people, who will feel but little thrill at the sight of a foreign flag, but who all in ardent patriotism will salute the star spangled banner."[5]

This assessment, however, represented the final opinion only of the *Leader* circle and some positive Calvinists. Elsewhere praise led to cautions, and cautions to warnings that American culture threatened the very core of the community's existence. From the inward-looking parties one might expect such complaints as Foppe Ten Hoor's: "The American circles with which our people have the most contact, exert in general a very pernicious influence. . . . Dangers threaten us as a Reformed church from all sides." But even positive Calvinist B. K. Kuiper could describe the community's situation in America in the gloomiest terms:

> The overwhelmingly great majority of our fellow-citizens are indifferent or in part even antagonistic to these principles [of the Reformed]. Almost all educational institutions from the highest to the lowest; almost the entire press, daily newspapers as well as periodicals, not only the secular but the religious as well; our courts, our legislatures, organized politics and social life, the pulpits themselves; and therefore almost all public opinion stands arrayed in battle-order against the small circle that yet holds tooth and nail to the Reformed world-and-life conception.[6]

Apparently, America was not so *heel anders* after all. Its vague Christianity could neither satisfy those seeking a "full-orbed" witness nor check the growing anti-Christian forces in the land. The only thing it could do was seduce "the rising generation" away from a rich to a shallow faith. Therefore the Dutch felt compelled to adjust to America slowly and with great caution, now criticizing themselves, now their environment.

This mood was deepened by the ethnic factor. For all the agreement that nationality ought to be submerged into religion, celebrations of "distinctively Dutch" traits persisted well past World War I. Was not "Dutchness," somehow, an ineradicable part of true "Reformedness"?[7] Many disagreed on paper, but few demurred entirely in their hearts or manners.

Interestingly, it was the stalwart of the Confessions, Foppe Ten Hoor, who gave this nationalistic approach its fullest reading.[8] Equally striking, given the rest of his thought, were his premises: religion followed national character, and national character geography. Thus, the Netherlands had a moderate climate and terrain; its people were not given to extremes. As the nation was small, so was each person's portion, so he became a jealous guardian and thorough worker. Mentally, the Dutchman was always moderate in style, skeptical of radical notions, determined to penetrate to an idea's roots and unravel all its implications. Boundaries, principles, the theoretical plane—such constituted the Dutch spiritual insignia. But now some of these people had settled in America, Ten Hoor continued, a land *heel anders* indeed.

Desert and jungle, sunshine and snow, plains and mountains all made this a land of extreme contrasts. With abundance everywhere Americans worked swiftly, moved often, and regarded surface appearances alone. In spirit they were broad but shallow, careless of distinctions, concerned with consequence rather than principle.

To the obvious question about adjustment to so foreign a culture, Ten Hoor gave different replies at different times. When he first addressed the problem, in 1898, he advocated a crossbreeding of Dutch and American traits to produce a superior hybrid: "America too has her characteristic qualities, and these must pass over into us and grow up with our Dutch peculiarities into a new whole."[9] More than just the duty of people who had chosen a new fatherland, this blending would help rid the Dutch of their characteristic defects—complacency, abstraction, and narrowness of vision. A few years later, however, Ten Hoor was describing America with much more suspicion. His denunciations at this time (1901) of things English indicate the cause of his change of heart; the Boer War had shown him what happened to a Dutch remnant living in an Anglo-Saxon Babylon. Now the sharp contrast between Englishman and Hollander redounded all to the latter's credit. As a *handelsvolk*, "a nation of shopkeepers," the English could neither transcend utilitarian calculation nor cease their mindless activism long enough to examine the deeper nature of things. From such a people, declared Ten Hoor, the Dutch need adopt nothing: 'We have not come to America to Anglicize but to Americanize."[10]

Precisely what constituted this difference Ten Hoor never made clear, for at this juncture he re-formed his battle line, leaving the plain of national character for the high ground of religious principle.[11] There, presumably, Dutch character would shine to best advantage. For their part, the English, both old world and new, followed Christ to enhance their own welfare—to obtain bliss in heaven, peace of mind on earth, and divine sanction for their petty desires. The Dutch, by contrast, as true Calvinists, sought first God's glory and obedience to his will. The English created *een zeer druk Christendom*, "a very busy Christianity," asking only "What must I *do?*" But "the scripturally sound Christian asks: 'What must I be and then do?' . . ." Since "external life-activity depends upon inner life-strength," the Dutch obviously shone the better of the two.[12] Finally, English superficiality caught up with them in religion as everywhere else. Unable to plumb Scripture for rich and systematic doctrine, they could not stand firm before doubt or rise above the emotions of the moment. How unlike the "deep" Dutch, thorough in knowledge, keen in argument, stalwart for the truth.

Ten Hoor's survey sounded almost every theme of Dutch commentary. Indeed, some of these became cliches. Who did not see that America's mind was *oppervlakkig*, "superficial," its polity "individualistic," its typical citizen "very broad but not deep," asking always and only "Does it pay?"[13] Because religion stood at the heart of the community's fortunes, the Dutch gave America's soul the closest scrutiny. Their conclusions fit Ten Hoor's mode of analysis: America was "Methodistic" (i.e., Anglo-derived). Undoubtedly the Dutch usage distorted much in the Methodist tradition, strictly considered, but they had in mind not so much the denominations that went by this name as a theological-cultural perspective, an easy evangelicalism, that had infused *many* churches—and indeed the "American spirit" itself.[14]

"Methodism" came into play on levels high and low. To diehards of Dutchness, it connoted the use of organs, choirs, and even the English language in worship; to those of confessional memory, it showed in the "spirit of Remonstrantism" of most American churches; to the principially acute it betrayed Humanism in a Protestant guise.[15] But all agreed on its salient features: doctrinal indifference, passion for "programs," impulsive innovation. Evangelicals replaced catechism with Sunday School, Bible study with prayer meetings, doctrinal sermons with topical discourses. Having sacrificed the intellectual in Christianity, they had to resort to the emotions of the ignorant—revivals— or to the tastes of the respectable—"sound organization" pleasing the businessman and "social service" pleasing his wife. In each case they imitated "the world," whether of mass entertainment, of big business with its mergers and boards, or of charities with their assorted benevolences.

The Reformed were determined, of course, to find a theological source for such errors. Neo-Calvinists pointed to the substitution of individualistic for covenantal (i.e., corporate) theology, or of preventive for positive concepts of redemption (consider, for instance, Dwight Moody's famous lifeboat metaphor). Foppe Ten Hoor drove back to "starting points"—in the Methodist case, subjectivity.

> There are many people in Christendom who will not let go of I-sovereignty, and still wish to remain Christians. . . . They make a god resembling themselves, an anthropological god—a god whom they do not serve but which serves them. Thus their religion is not theological but anthropological.[16]

From there, Ten Hoor could broaden his critique to link "Methodism" with "mysticism" and "Modernism." The first, by looking to the "inner light," placed personal experience over biblical teaching and so conceived of God, truth, and morality however it pleased. Further, it reduced the vast distance between God and man, equating certain human capacities with the divine. Modernists played the intellectualist version of the game. They not only challenged divine authority in religion—substituting "science" as the mystics had substituted "feeling" for Scripture—but also humanized the object of religion. "Theology thus becomes the knowledge of Christian or even of human religion and is no longer the knowledge of God. . . . It becomes anthropological and subjective."[17] To these principial connections B. K. Kuiper added those of habit. It was theological apathy that fed all these movements, for by failing to teach orthodoxy, "Methodism" could not keep heresy from taking hold. "Methodism actually, effectually, and almost inevitably must so become a powerful ally of Modernism."[18]

The long series of articles devoted to these "errors" indicates the gravity of the threat Dutch leaders saw in them. Modernism might now reside only in distant universities, but it was there capturing the minds of the future. Mystical tendencies already lay within the Reformed community (Ten Hoor's very first series in *De Gereformeerde Amerikaan* was devoted to this problem), and Methodism surrounded it. Nicholas Steffens saw these developments building all too close to home: "*We are on the road* toward those circumstances which you are now opposing," he wrote Abraham Kuyper in reference to his own Reformed Church;

> the modern and irenic spirit is rising. And if one wants to speak against it [Steffens referred to his own experience], he finds the columns of the papers closed to him. . . .
> . . . And our Holland people are going under in the maelstrom. . . . We still have true Reformed people in our communities, but what can the poor sheep do when they find themselves in the hands of leaders . . . who think about nothing but Synodical and practical matters?[19]

Steffens's solution was drastic: "Sometimes I wonder if leaders in the Netherlands shouldn't direct emigration elsewhere."[20] But most turned to the defenses their various mentalities dictated. With Ten Hoor and most pulpits, Louis Berkhof advocated a vigorous assertion of traditional Reformed spirituality, especially submission of emotion to reason and reason to Scripture, so that "our children shall be of a different spirit than that which rules our land."[21] Henry Beets agreed, but for a more positive reason: "the less we lay stress on them [Reformed principles], and the more we are carried away by the superficial religion which abounds in our land, the more we shall miss our high calling as a leaven and a salt."[22] B. K. Kuiper urged both sides of the Neo-Calvinist strategy. To "Methodists," susceptible to reform, Calvinists ought to show from history how a religion aiming at God's glory produces more benefits for mankind than one directed toward human happiness. But to Modernists the Reformed witness should be more defiant:

> As long as we are not agreed as to starting point all further discussion

must necessarily be futile. All that we can do is to place our orthodox views, if possible a complete world-and-life-view, over against his, and show that it follows just as logically and cogently from our fundamental principles, as his view from his principles.[23]

Both tactics, Kuiper added, required strengthening of the Reformed body—confessionally, as Ten Hoor had said, but also institutionally. Nothing would avail without an educational system that produced leaders to teach and defend the Reformed tradition.

The Antitheticals, the least mollified, alternated between the grim and the satiric. Klaas Schoolland saw the United States as a modern Laodicea, neither hot nor cold but contemptibly lukewarm. Its people gave Christ lip service and its leaders dressed in Christian garb, but this was "general, external religiosity, an idle form which covers deadly indifference."[24] Only principial consciousness could pierce such facades. John Van Lonkhuyzen seemed less apprehensive. With a keen (perhaps "American") eye for profits, he selected Billy Sunday's 1915 Michigan crusade for the basis of a book-length analysis of American religion. Sunday, Van Lonkhuyzen decided, was good for America but bad for Christianity. He induced "Methodists" to take what for them was the first step toward religious vitality, an emotional realization of sin; he was a good "icebreaker" in this Arctic of "indifferentism and materialism." But to break this ice he had to commercialize religion, make man the initiator and measure of religious experience, and reduce Christian ethics to business "success" or external proprieties. His lack of dignity insulted God and made Christianity a laughingstock. Besides, Sunday's message reflected the worst weaknesses of American culture. It was superficial, for he preached not against Sin, but against sins, "especially those few which head the Methodist list of sins, and lets lie the other sins which are not so prominent." It was individualistic; the "souls" Sunday managed to save rarely became incorporated into the institutions of faith. Nor was this "icebreaker" clearing the way for "the full fleet" of Christian thought and action. In short, Van Lonkhuyzen implied, the Reformed should cultivate a deep, enduring faith; for America, something else would have to do.[25]

Van Lonkhuyzen's conclusions represented the opinion of much of the Dutch community. Only in 1916 did a Christian Reformed dissent emerge, and that from the pen of Henry Beets. Earlier Beets had agreed with his colleagues, but after witnessing the 1915 Michigan crusade he praised Sunday for his "general" orthodoxy and for attacking the sins of *all* social classes. Sunday gave Americans the shaking they needed, Beets believed; he might employ unusual means but was addressing an unusual (read *heel anders*) situation.[26]

In contrast, the progressive party in the Reformed Church praised Sunday from the start and on every point. According to *Leader* "Current Events" editor Henry Geerlings, Sunday made "religion" the talk of the town wherever he campaigned; he brought many "to Christ." Surely these were "good things." Equally admirable was the fact that each campaign was efficiently organized, "a perfect piece of machinery." As for "the contagion that infects the throng and moves it with a common impulse," Geerlings had no doubt that any reasonable man would identify the "unseen reality behind it all" as God's hand.[27] The same attitude emerged regarding other movements on the American religious scene. "Men and Religion Forward," the Laymen's Missionary Movement, the Federal Council of Churches, and the YMCA all advanced "religion" and "Christ's work" and so deserved the support of "decent men." With the world getting better and Christianity aiding the process, the *Leader* felt little need for analytic rigor.

Turning to secular affairs, the Dutch showed no "pietistic" muting of concern. Rather, propelled by immediate need no less than by Kuyper's example, they sought to analyze socio-political America with as much care and with as Reformed a sensibility as they had employed in analyzing its religion. Their basic ambivalence also remained. They hoped to determine their future deliberately but feared that America, by its power or seductive novelty, would sweep them away. And they found America's much-heralded virtues fundamentally linked with its most grievous faults—its prosperity with greed, its freedom with disorder.

By 1900, the lament over "materialism" was old and widespread among the Dutch (having, of course, venerable antecedents among the pious of all ages). Already in 1883 a member of the original Van Raalte expedition had bewailed its rise:

> When I reflect upon our spiritual condition in those early days . . . shame comes to my face as I think about the present. . . . Alas! how things have changed; but they have not become better. Our fields indeed have been cleared and we have gone forward in material matters, but we have lost much of our early earnestness and piety.[28]

Speakers at the Semicentennial of 1896 repeated this theme. According to one, as the pioneers' piety had flowered in the wilderness, so the sons' was withering in the present comfort. Two pastors—both, notably, from the RCA—perceived God's blessing in the pioneers' agricultural failures. "The Lord wanted to test the people, teach them that there are treasures which neither beetle nor grasshopper can ever destroy." "But what would have been the aspect of things if these people had become rich quickly? . . . In all probability, the Lord would have forgotten them."[29]

In the new century, therefore, antimaterialism would be the common property of all Dutch-American factions. The Antithetical Calvinists focused on the principial materialism of American thought. *De Gereformeerde Amerikaan* feared the effect the American pursuit of wealth would have on traditional devotion. In its customary vague and sweeping tone it cried,

> Our youth live in a world which has been almost completely seized by Materialism. American life today is characterized by a rush after material things. People want gold. They want goods. They want pleasure. ["Men wil geld. Men wil goed. Men wil genot."] . . . For many of our nation the dollar is the idol before which they bow.[30]

Positive Calvinists, in discussing Americanization, cautioned that the economic motive of most Dutch immigrants, legitimate in itself, threatened to destroy their spiritual life in the new land. Then too, "the materialistic spirit of the age" might extinguish "all consideration for the intellectual, artistic, and spiritual development of our nationality in America."[31]

Even the Reformed Church progressives joined this chorus, faulting the age for being enamored of the physical and natural. The *Leader* was confident, however, that people would soon "regain their balance" and return to poetry, philosophy, and theology—the "deeper" part of life.[32] The other parties did not anticipate so automatic a solution. The Neo-Calvinists hoped to foster cultural development through Christian higher education, but the Confessionalists could do no more than reassert, a bit desperately, pietist formulas:

> The spiritual stands above the material and must first be sought. . . . How foolish it is to give your heart to the things of the world! It is just dust. ["Het is slechts stof."] It can make no one really happy. . . . But he who first and above all else seeks the spiritual and heavenly and eternal shall be truly happy in life and in death and for eternity.[33]

Many maintained that the only menace worse than materialism was licentiousness, because of its particular potential for corrupting the young. "Worldliness," it seemed, infected most every aspect of American society. Denunciations of the same formed the common denominator of the community's social thought, just as pietism, where this critique originated, did for religion. Between pulpit and press, the Dutch saw a "thousand and one forms" of pollution: "Theaters and vaudettes. Intoxication in saloons and card-playing. Dance-halls and clubhouses. Autorides and immorality. Excursions on the Sabbath"; and, more generally, all violations of Puritan mores, any form of gambling or erotic display, anything associated with drunkenness, Sabbath-desecration, and even implicit challenges to sobriety and good order.[34]

Of all these sins, the Dutch focused especially on those that were located in specifiable "dens of iniquity" and threatened sexual purity. Thus, dancing and theater attendance drew the strongest ire. Could anyone witness "the flushed faces, the glazed eyes, the short breath" of waltzing couples, asked Henry Beets, and still call the dance innocent? Were not the messages of film and theater "degrading, polluting, ruining souls and bodies and poisoning the minds of men?" Likewise the Dutch condemned saloons, where drunkenness and secrecy weakened inhibitions, and "autorides," which removed *de jongen* from the parental gaze.[35]

Such strictures carried over quickly into local politics. In its commentary on the Grand Rapids scene, for instance, *De Gids* downplayed the usual party labels; the real issue lay between the forces of propriety and "the open town element." In the political off season *De Gids* kept up a weekly expose of one sin spot or another, adding "private clubs" and "rooming houses" to the conventional list. But when elections drew near, it hammered home its principle of selection. Until the complete eradication of "pestholes" became feasible, the Dutch should support those candidates pledged to the most stringent possible enforcement of regulatory statutes.[36]

"Public morality," however, could be magnified into a broader critique. On this score the Dutch community joined the protests that filled the Progressive Era, awakened, in fact, by an episode of corruption that had given Grand Rapids nationwide notoriety. In the "water scandal" of 1900–1905, certain entrepreneurs had bribed the mayor, fourteen aldermen, a state senator, the city attorney, and the managing editors of the three leading newspapers to support a grossly inflated bond issue for a pipeline to Lake Michigan.[37] This, on top of alleged payoffs by saloon owners to local policemen and administrators, fired even stolid Hollanders to action. The political club Fas et Jus became their voice, municipal honesty their major theme. The first plank of the society's platform called for "strictest honesty," "true economy," and "highest efficiency in local government"; another demanded stern supervision of public works to eliminate graft.[38]

But corruption was not only local or official. Along with many of their contemporaries, the Dutch were outraged by the graft and manipulation of public welfare by industrial and commercial corporations. The epitome was Wall Street speculation and the government's collusion therein. In the wake of the panic of 1907 *De Gereformeerde Amerikaan* snapped,

> How nice for Wall Street that the administration of this land, from one political party as well as the other, is so partial on its behalf. Wall Street speculates and loses millions of dollars. Should a panic then

ensue, the keeper of the nation's treasury does not hesitate to inter-
vene. . . . This is a godless practice that must be stopped.[39]

The notes of Henry Beets's 1899 Fourth of July oration showed a fear of
great wealth per se, not only when ill-begotten: "The *Demon of Money* . . . is like a gigantic *Octopus,* stretching forth his terrible arms over
our *ballot boxes* and *legislative halls,* and crushing with them our
farmers and common laborers."[40] But Klaas Schoolland had the most
penetrating insight, decrying the nation's whole course of development
under industrial capitalism. Not only did "bad" corporations make
and use their money dishonestly but the normal operations of "good"
corporations also had the most pernicious effects. By consolidating
finance and industry, corporate leaders had gained control of the entire
economy and could sacrifice the interests of laborers and small businessmen at will. By manipulating the press, they excited the public to
support the imperial adventures abroad and the further consolidation
at home that were required for the attainment of their ends. Thus they
infected the entire nation with their lust for wealth and empire. "Is this
great, worldly development really so necessary?" asked Schoolland.
"We doubt it very much."[41]

The very fear of oligarchy, however, made Dutch Americans wary
of characteristic Progressive reforms. The Grand Rapids Dutch, for
instance, contributed sizably to the defeat of a reform of the city charter
in 1912. A classic Progressive document, written by lawyers and businessmen and endorsed by Progressivism's national voice (the *Outlook*
of New York City), the proposal transferred power from a board of
aldermen dependent on partisan ward clubs to a managerial elite that
would administer the city's affairs "efficiently," according to "business
methods." While a few Dutchmen—notably, the college professors—
supported the charter, most agreed with attorney Dorr Kuizema that
"the new charter was drafted under the supervision of the big men of
the city and seeks to ban the small man's influence from government."
The objection fit the Progressive movement as a whole.

> The most wonderful thing of all is, that where men speak so much of
> returning government to the hands of the people, they use just those
> means that remove it as much as possible from their hands. And with
> this removal and centralization comes governmental high-handed-
> ness and interference, without the necessary opportunities and
> power of parrying these.[42]

Progressivism's alternate solution, direct democracy, was equally
troubling. Increasing popular power would bring either chaos or majority tyranny, Kuizema concluded. Schoolland time and again denounced popular sovereignty for being a principle that replaced obedi-

ence to God with blind allegiance to passion. B. K. Kuiper put it in principial language: Progressivism was "humanistic," making man the measure and end of politics.[43]

Thus, American reform returned most Dutch newcomers to their original quandary. Now fearing plutocracy, now democracy; cooperating with "the better element" of Grand Rapids but not too much; faulting Progressivism after trenchant analysis but tolerating, through silence, evils it (and they) had earlier denounced—the Dutch swerved between acuity and inconsistency, affection and suspicion. But perhaps only such an approach was appropriate to the ambiguity of the new land itself.

5

Politics: Theory, Taste, and Trouble

The longer the Dutch were in America, the more pressing yet less tenable their ambivalence became. Increasingly, politics proved the flashpoint. As the Progressive movement accelerated in the 1910s toward its climax in the American entry into World War I, it forced one burning issue after another on the attention of the Dutch. They responded from overlapping but conflicting political models. And so were multiplied confusion, zeal, and controversy.

The first model, one more of taste than of theory, came from the *Leader*. As the voice of the RCA's self-styled "progressives," it endorsed the larger movement with few exceptions (those being its occasionally "radical" notions) and with eager anticipation of its triumph.[1] The *Leader* had fewer immigrants to orient, and therefore worked on framing a conception of America to which people of "better sense"—the newcomers' children, perhaps—might aspire.

Concerning the question of first moment, the *Leader* felt little need to sift out the "Revolutionary" from the "Calvinistic" in the American character. Its typical historical survey, for instance, made no reference to the Puritans and their declension or to Deism and the Founding Fathers. It looked instead at certain American heroes—Washington, William Penn, the delegates to the Constitutional Convention—and declared them to have been "generally speaking, Christian men."[2] As for individuals, so for the nation.

That settled, the *Leader* turned to the exciting present, trusting its commentary to a man perfectly suited to the job, Henry Geerlings. Geerlings made as strong a statement by what he was as by anything he wrote. He had the right pedigree, being a descendant of the Van Raalte immigration and a graduate of Hope College. He had the right tone—genteel, sunny, and of the strictest propriety. And he had all the right offices: fifty years an employee of the Holland (Michigan) State Bank, forty-two years a member of the city's board of education, five times its mayor, director of its Chamber of Commerce, county supervisor, president of the local library board, health board, and the Michigan State Sunday School Convention. Geerlings incarnated success, respectability, and service.[3]

He generally filled his "Current Events" page in the *Leader* along four lines. First, descriptions, sometimes reverent, sometimes proud, of an example of "progress" in the technology of transportation, communication, manufacturing, or medicine. Here adjectives such as *faster, new, more,* and *efficient* reigned, always meaning "better" and usually indicating that mankind, led by American genius, had taken another step toward the millennium. Another week he would feature a heroic endeavor, whether Perry at the Pole or Pershing in Mexico. Or he might display his political acumen, speculating about the chances of various contenders at the coming conventions. But above all came "business" and his diagnosis of the prospects for "next season." Generally, of course, business was "fundamentally sound," but even in times of trouble he argued that the American people maintained "a wonderful kind of capital unimpaired—the spirit of determination, faith in themselves and in their fellow men, and ability to put defeat behind them and to make even of the elements of the present failure material on which to build better and stronger than ever."[4] Even vices prompted good cheer, since these aroused "good men" to moral passion and service. "Evil" steeled a man's character, provoking him to shun his ease and display the ultimate virtues—courage, hope, decency. Moral action in turn proved the value of religion. As Geerlings's coeditor stated,

> There is nothing that is so powerful in shaping society as the quiet, modest appeals to the right. *Piety is power.* In business, in politics, in social life . . . we need the man above all others, who is not a silent partner in the great firm of Goodness and Company, but one who sees the right and has the courage to speak for it unfalteringly.[5]

Accordingly, the *Leader* could direct political participation by the most elementary standards. "The call of the Christian today is to get into politics and . . . to vote for those that seem to him most likely to serve the cause of righteousness." American evils demanded not refined theories but simple fundamentals—the Ten Commandments, the Sermon on the Mount, the Golden Rule. These were not exclusively Christian but the platform on which all "lovers of righteousness" could stand; nor were they a set of unlikely ideals but rather America's sure destiny. "We are confident that the nation which is superior in moral life, righteous in dealing with matters at home and abroad, faithful to the fundamental principles of divine revelation, will in the end lead them all."[6]

The *Leader* could find abundant confirmation of its faith. The best evidence stood at the very apex of American politics in the person of Theodore Roosevelt. Crusader against corruption, and champion of sound business, moral vigor, and social order, Roosevelt epitomized *Leader* ideals. Nicely, he added colonial Dutch ancestry to the bargain. At the end of Roosevelt's presidency, Evert Blekkink looked back with "a feeling of profound gratitude to the God of nations. . . . Materially, socially, politically, morally, intellectually, and religiously, he [Roosevelt] has been a wonderfully potent, uplifting and inspiring factor in the nation. There is not a sphere of human life and activity in the Republic which does not feel his influence for good."[7]

Locally the shining knight was Gerrit John Diekema. Born in Holland, Michigan, in 1859 (another son of the founders), a graduate of Hope College, and a prominent local lawyer, Diekema best fit the *Leader* profile. Yet he achieved a measure of political success that proved his appeal to all parts of the community—twice he was mayor of Holland, three terms a state representative, four years a member of Congress. In his congressional campaigns Diekema was endorsed by every Dutch-American notable and periodical in western Michigan, including the Neo-Calvinist *Gids*. Such support resulted from his standing foursquare on the fundamentals of Dutch-American practical politics. He was an ardent Republican (nine years the chairman of the state Central Committee), he assailed public vice and corruption in high places, and he championed the cause of business. His three great tenets as a legislator were key articles of the ethnic social creed: temperance guaranteed civic order, honesty in government and business ensured fair competition, and a high tariff enhanced "general" (i.e., business) prosperity. Together, Diekema believed, these principles would sustain the milieu that had made his own career possible, one where ambition implied opportunity and material success implied moral rectitude. To this end Diekema pressed a contradictory conception of the state, celebrating the glories of laissez-faire while demanding that government support business and suppress vice.[8]

But Diekema's real distinction lay in his ability to set nascent immigrant patriotism to the florid oratory of the time. In his remarks at a memorial service for McKinley, for example, he lauded the late president as "the brightest star . . . the most fragrant flower . . . the most democratic ruler of the freest people on earth"; then, perhaps as the strain of the moment took over, he heralded him as "the Gladstone of the twentieth century," a statesman impervious to class or partisan pressures. Diekema even encroached on holy ground, characterizing

McKinley's assassination as a "reenactment of Golgatha" consummated by the martyr's transfiguration and ascension into heaven—there, presumably, to keep watch over the course of American progress. As to one mode of that progress, Diekema shared McKinley's concept of American imperialism. "Providence ordains that we must help Cuba," he intoned. "We are fighting for principles and God in heaven is on our side."[9]

No Hollander publicly protested these remarks as blasphemous. In fact, few publicly criticized Diekema on anything. Yet it did not take an astute Kuyperian to sense a deficiency in all of Diekema's "eloquence." The *Leader*'s political vision—and the community's operative values—stand indicted by their own standards in the conclusion of an historian who compared Diekema to a contemporary senator and governor from Michigan: "it is impossible to read the public addresses delivered by William Alden Smith, Fred Warner, and Diekema, and, from the principles espoused and positions endorsed, state that one man of this trio came from a Dutch immigrant community."[10]

What could be more at odds with this than Neo-Calvinist theory? In tone and structure the contrast never diminished and the potential for substantive conflict would eventually be fully realized. Yet just as *De Gids* endorsed Diekema, so the pietists found congenial much of the system Klaas Schoolland propounded week by week in its pages.

It was a mark of Dutch America's ties to its European past, but also of the limitations of its creativity, that this system simply plagiarized Abraham Kuyper. Here, as with the antithesis, Schoolland began with a discourse on principialism in general and Calvinistic principles in particular, then followed with a discussion of the family, society, state, and education (in that order), all interlaced with the sacred words of the Kuyperian vocabulary: *organic, terrain, sovereignty.*[11]

Schoolland dwelled long on his "starting point," the sovereignty of God:

> We feel again, and with new strength, the absolute significance of the sovereignty of God, which we Reformed always put in the foreground, for all of life, in church and state, in home and society, and for all spheres of life . . . in all activities of life.[12]

But he never went beyond reassertions of this idea (and associated denunciations of "popular sovereignty") either to resolve the ambiguity of his "root principle" or to show its practical significance. Did "sovereignty" mean that God was in fact controlling every event in history, or that mankind was obliged to obey his laws and violated them to its own harm? Would universal human allegiance to this idea really cause urban immorality to disappear and transform labor/capital tension into loving cooperation? To both questions Schoolland would

have responded with a quick affirmative followed by yet another declaration that the principle of divine sovereignty was indeed beautiful,
comprehensive, and of great import for all areas of life. Despite this
insufficiency, many joined Schoolland in repeating his precious principle, the supralapsarians—so emphatic in stressing God's sovereignty in
their theology—naturally drawn to the idea itself, and the other parties
taking comfort in the sanctions it posited amid the American hubbub.

Following Anti-Revolutionary lines, Schoolland next moved to the
family: "All of human society proceeds from family life." So emphatic
was his concern here that his might be more accurately labeled a theory
of the family than of politics or society. In fact, adoring the family was a
favorite Dutch-American pastime. Henry Beets's presidential biographies supplied practical (and sentimental) illustrations, and Louis
Berkhof devoted one of his social essays entirely to a glorification of
motherhood, but B. K. Kuiper surpassed all with this paean:

> The Home! Wonderful creation of God! Wonderful in its simplicity!
> Wonderful in the complicated relationships among its component
> parts, so simple in themselves! As for the individual the proceeds of
> life are from the heart, so for society are the proceeds of life from the
> Home. The Family is Society in germ.[13]

Kuyperian rhetoric flourished especially at the next step, the
state/society contrast. Society grew "naturally" and "organically"
from Creation; its "free, spontaneous, and intuitive life" ought not to
be unduly restricted.[14] The state, on the other hand, was "artificial,"
imposed in response to sin. Of all the places where he could do so,
Schoolland went beyond Kuyper here, unconditionally opposing expansion of state power, in fact associating "state" and "sin" so often as
to make the two equivalent. But this only heightened the curious Anti-
Revolutionary contradiction. The state was always suspect, yet was
ordained by God and reflected the father's role in the family. It had
negative functions but supreme—and supremely important—authority.[15] Practical applications were no more consistent. Theaters, saloons,
and dance halls, though growing as naturally as possible, somehow did
not qualify as products of "spontaneous development" in "the social
sphere" but merited repression by the state. As to regulatory law, when
applied to protect the public health or prevent disruptions in family life
it was legitimate, but when directed against business or the patriarchal
family it became "intolerable interference" on the "terrain of free
society."

It was only when he applied his cherished antithesis to political
action that Schoolland antagonized his fellows. To be sure, he admitted, politics was *the* arena of common grace, but there as everywhere Christians had to act as recipients of special grace. Living as they

did "out of different principles," the redeemed and reprobate could not work toward the same ends, by the same means, or for the same reasons. Therefore, it was a matter of principle to form a separate Christian party and carry out separate Christian action.[16]

But that "action" was woefully slow in coming. For all De Gids's calls for Calvinistic participation in politics, Fas et Jus remained a debating society, its priorities reflected in the publication dates of its major documents: its Calvinistic principles of government appeared in 1905, its program for municipal action in 1913. Its political successes seemed almost accidental, surprising members and opponents alike. Despite "urgent, pressing social problems," then, the Antitheticals' "action" remained at the level of consciousness-raising among the righteous, which only served to start the cycle of theory all over again.[17]

If the pietists at the Leader scorned these practical shortcomings, the Confessionalists decried its principial obsession. Foppe Ten Hoor gave some token of this animus when he devoted no less eminent an occasion than his swan song in De Gereformeerde Amerikaan to derision of separate political organization: "A Dutch Calvinist political party in America! How is it possible that people can imagine such a fantasy? . . . We must let go of [this] illusion . . . the sooner the better." But his failure even to try to venture an alternative implied an unhappy choice of conclusions. Either (1) the majestic Reformed tradition had nothing to say about politics, or (2) one of the established American parties could serve adequately as a vehicle for its witness, or (3) the Reformed were to construct in theory a set of political principles deduced from the Confessions, but in practice were merely to complain about violations of these, abstain from political action whenever possible in favor of nurturing piety, and participate when necessary in an individualistic, haphazard way. The third option, of course, most clearly sums up Ten Hoor's stance.[18] A Confessionalist colleague succinctly expressed the attitude it fostered: "Let us earnestly beseech God, my readers, that we do not sink into these sinful practices!"[19] Should the Reformed response be more positive, its boundaries would still be narrow. Louis Berkhof, for example, called Calvinists to be concerned in principle with every problem in modern society but to concentrate in practice on cleaning the church's house and preaching to men's souls.[20]

Positive Calvinists such as Henry Beets faulted all three options, then fell toward each. With the Leader, Beets spoke of undefined "forces for good" in American politics. With the Antitheticals he called for "a Moses to lead us out of the wilderness . . . in these critical social times" by articulating "fundamental principles" and a "final solution." And with the Confessionalists, he called for prayers for the president because of the added temptations of his office: exposure to profanity and pressure to join a lodge, to attend the theater, or to travel on Sunday.[21]

All this might have continued as gentlemanly discussion were it not for the intrusion of specific issues from the outside world. The first of these seemed initially to offer another occasion for agreement. As local option campaigns swept Michigan annually between 1908 and 1916, the temperance crusade caught up the entire community. The "saloon" provided an inviting target because it stood at the center of the manifold vice that Dutch America abhorred: its wares made the common man dissolute, its bribes made the public official corrupt. All agreed that the saloon damaged the family, wasted wages, increased taxes, fostered disrespect for the church, ruined men's bodies, corrupted their minds, and led their souls to hell. Much of the time it seemed the parties rivaled each other merely in the degree of revulsion in their rhetoric.[22]

But as *the* emblem of American Protestantism, Prohibition won its strongest support from the Reformed Church progressives. It even induced a curious change in their mental patterns. On this cause the *Leader* took on a Neo-Calvinistic tone, speaking in terms of antithesis and absolutes. "Neutrality on this question is treason to Christ," thundered Evert Blekkink. Total eradication was the only antidote adequate for the saloon's dangers. Absolute evils must be stamped out absolutely; half-measures were no measures at all.[23] Most Confessionalists and positive Calvinists also came down on God's side at election time, but only after equally unusual arguments. Here *De Gereformeerde Amerikaan* showed none of its customary fatalism about the presence of evil in the world. Gone too were its traditional fears of expanding state power and cooperation with the unredeemed. The *Banner* addressed the latter tactic with words seldom heard in Christian Reformed circles: "The fact that advocates of a certain reform movement do not share our world-and-life-view is not necessarily an objection to the movement." Equally novel (and unrepeated) was its attempt to explain away another denominational cliche—namely, that sin came from the heart, not from the environment: "We do not believe in conversion through environment, yet we all believe that a moral environment is better than an immoral one."[24]

The major break in Dutch unanimity appeared in *De Gids*. One of its editors, Ate Dijkstra, a Grand Rapids businessman and alderman, had been castigating the saloon for years in his column on municipal affairs. He now urged Dutch voters to deal with "booze" as they would with fire or cancer—absolutely. His coeditor, Klaas Schoolland, was second to none in abhorring the tavern: "the greatest, most shameful disgrace of America. . . . Away with such a pesthole, such a gateway to hell!" But he saw in local option the specter of even worse evils—

arbitrary popular sovereignty and humanism. Schoolland, at least, stood fast on his political principles. For him Prohibition constituted a dangerous intrusion of the state into the social sphere: "it strikes at personal life, the free life of home and society." Then too, saloons were one thing, drinking another. Clearly liquor was not evil in itself, so its use ought not to be totally forbidden. He sent his readers to the polls with a different cry: "Let us uphold our Christian and political and personal rights and freedoms and protect them against all ungodly and pernicious encroachments." Lest anyone think he defended liberty out of "typically American" sentiment, he showed otherwise. Free moral choice was essential to human nature, he argued, and (the redeemed choosing good, the reprobate evil) to the full development of the antithesis.[25]

Such thinking aroused scorn and sorrow. Truly, said Henry Beets, Schoolland's was a deplorable stand that shamed the CRC in its rival's eyes.[26] To the *Leader*, it demonstrated how men who had not lived long in America's pure atmosphere clung to "foreign" ideas and hampered the forces of uplift.

The era's "social question" prompted even more divisiveness. The *Leader* allowed that "reasonable" labor unions might be a "force for good" as long as they restrained their demands, but many Confessionalists and Antitheticals deemed union and church membership incompatible. This judgment followed from two premises: American unions were socialistic, and socialism was revolutionary atheism. Here pietists and Kuyperians alike practiced principial analysis and in an inflammatory way. Socialism became first and last a religious movement, aimed at the eradication of Christianity and the deification of man. To perceive it as a system of economic thought, a critique of the present order, or a vision of a more just society betrayed superficial thinking. "Sound thinking" showed its many dangers. Socialism "ignored sin" and practiced moral environmentalism. Socialism was ruthlessly materialistic in philosophical tenets as well as practical goals, and so had no place for the spiritual. "The Moloch of Socialism" would destroy the family and create a leviathan state that would crush "free social life." Quite naturally, therefore, "it is not possible for a true Christian to be a true Socialist. The Christian-Socialist is to us an impossible person. The antithesis between true Christianity and true Socialism is to us totally implacable."[27]

Significantly, the Dutch subjected no other American institution to so suspicion-laden a scrutiny. Yet they should not be dismissed as callous reactionaries, for in counterpoint to this theme and from the same groups came genuine sympathy for the laborer. "Our sympathy is with the simple but frequently poor workingman," declared Klaas Schoolland. "The sympathy of our Saviour . . . was—and is—always with the poor and oppressed." To those who attributed workers' misery to their sin, factory-worker-turned-minister Jacob Manni replied,

> Truly, in our land are found many causes which must bring about a spirit of discontent. Above all these are the great privileges that capitalists have above the workers and the consequence of their proud self-exaltation. . . . The one thing that can be said of them is, that at the cost of others or by the sweatdrops of the working classes they have built up their capital.

Among the most grievous abuses cited by this critic were long hours, unsafe conditions, child labor, and the exposure of working women to "immorality." The harshest reproach came from Louis Berkhof, who borrowed Kuyper's argument in *Christianity and the Class Struggle:* capitalism arose from Revolutionary humanism; its individualism, selfishness, and merciless exploitation had produced not only filth and slums, tortured bodies and minds, but a torn society and meaningless labor.[28]

When these two attitudes mixed, the Dutch could be double-minded: "truly, Christians must be earnestly concerned with the Social Question and seek measures of betterment for the working class," but none of these measures might be "in defiance of a single divine ordinance."[29] When the two clashed, however, as they did during the 1911 furniture workers' strike in Grand Rapids, principle defeated sympathy. According to Schoolland, the union's very existence and especially its use of the strike excited tension between labor and management, encouraging selfishness and class hatred. The union placed material above spiritual considerations, human will over divine law, and—most improbably, in view of Schoolland's social theory—violated the principle of free development in social life. "This all lies on the line of the Revolution," Schoolland decided; it stood condemned by the Christian principles of altruism, cooperation, and love of neighbor. Notably, Schoolland never introduced these particular Christian principles into the discussion of any other problem. Nor did he bring them to bear in this case upon the manufacturers or consider the possibility that management had first committed the very sins he attributed to the union. Nor did he ponder the basis and the implications of his tacit support of management's cause. The principialist as reactionary could condone the errors of the mighty but not of the lowly.[30]

As an alternative to "godless" labor, the Antitheticals and Confessionalists advocated a separate Christian union. The course they wished it to follow was well suited to their defensive, submissive inclinations. Capitalist exploitation, it was amazingly maintained, required protection from socialist defilement first, and then promotion of employer-employee cooperation. The biblical injunction to love neighbor was translated for workers into an injunction to respect authority, or, in the preachers' pet phrase, to place one's duties above one's rights. It was hoped that management would do likewise. But that could hardly be enjoined, since strikes were relegated to the most extreme resort.[31]

On this issue it was the positive Kuyperians who came out in dissent. Well before the furniture strike one of their number had removed socialism from principial condemnation. While some of its extreme partisans might be anti-Christian, it was argued, socialism was not primarily a religion; and while some of its programs might be impractical, Christians had at least to listen to its critique of capitalism. Dorr Kuizema, whose concern for "the small man" had turned him against Progressivism, contradicted Schoolland in *De Calvinist* (often writing on the facing page) by supporting the workers in the 1911 strike. He did so partly for mundane reasons (laborers ought to work fewer hours in order to have more time for "the higher things of life") and partly out of a deeper critique. Workers should not have to endure a regime in which they were an atomistic mass, helpless before the employers' whims, deprived of their freedom and self-respect. As for principial analysts pronouncing judgment from on high, Kuizema had an overdue cautionary note:

> Changing circumstances cause alterations in [social] relationships and make it difficult to apply principles. . . . To find objective principles must always be our goal, but these are not always so obvious. Mature experience must also be considered, and the books of history opened, in order to understand the relation correctly. Then a sound application becomes possible.[32]

Johannes Groen opted for *more* principle—but the principle of common grace rather than antithesis. The laws of social development came from Creation, he argued, not Redemption; the antithesis was spiritual and need not be reflected in all temporal activity; the redeemed might operate in "the social sphere" according to natural law. Thus Christians could—indeed, *should*—cooperate with unbelievers on a "neutral terrain," the better to establish justice in society. Since in Groen's estimation the activities of most American labor unions did precisely that (by promoting equity and solidarity), the Reformed should join them. Christian workers might legitimately form a distinct caucus within a union to give a sharper witness to Christ's higher teachings, but they should not organize a counterunion unless the only existing union was clearly anti-Christian. Doing otherwise would disrupt the organic unity of society.[33]

Groen's conclusions, not to mention his invocation of the holy vocabulary—*organic, solidarity, terrain*—brought angry retorts from the Antitheticals.[34] But he suffered worse for his statements on the third pressing issue of the time, women's suffrage. The 1913 Michigan referendum on this question drew no opinion from the *Leader* but nearly unanimous opposition from Christian Reformed spokesmen. Considering Anti-Revolutionary social theory, this was natural. Society reflected the home, where, according to God's eternal ordinance, the husband ruled; how then could women possibly share in the governance of public life? Klaas Schoolland denounced the idea as "godless" and "unnatural," a defiance of divine and human law sure to "bring down misery upon thousands of homes." Louis Berkhof worked by condescension. Women, who already ruled the world as mothers, could not seriously wish to sacrifice real for illusory power. There could be only one explanation for so curious a phenomenon—the suffrage movement must be infected by the dread principle of "Revolution." And so it was. Feminist agitators wished to make the individual, rather than the family, the basic unit of society. Naturally "Revolutionary" chaos would ensue.[35] So instructed, the Dutch males of Michigan overwhelmingly repudiated the idea at the polls.

Groen alone broke denominational ranks. In a speech (he did not try this in a sermon) to his parishioners, he declared that the Bible made single women (those not under patriarchal authority) equal to men and that Reformed principles gave married women the "right to assist in regulating" everything that pertained to family life. Groen also invoked the *heel anders* argument: individualism in Europe might bear a Revolutionary connotation, but not in America:

> The Declaration of Independence and the Constitution of the United States are Christian documents which support a form of government not inconsistent with Christianity, and these documents are strongly individualistic. To say that individualism is revolutionary and anarchistic is making a serious indictment against our nation.[36]

The storm that ensued was literally violent. At Calvin Seminary, Berkhof presented an hour-long refutation of this "antibiblical" stance so "fraught with dire consequences for the future." Kuyperians both Antithetical (e.g., John Van Lonkhuyzen) and positive (e.g., B. K. Kuiper) called Groen's ideas "a subversion of the Creation ordinances of God." An open letter opposing Groen's speech appeared in the Grand Rapids *Evening Press*, signed by all but three of the Christian Reformed ministers in Grand Rapids. Finally, a public meeting was held at which Foppe Ten Hoor's successor at the Oakdale Park church waxed "very bitter in his opposition," exciting one member of the audience to cry out, "What shall be done with one who publicly denies God's holy ordinance?"[37] Two things, apparently. First, Groen had to defend himself before his ecclesiastical peers, which he did ably. Second, those offended had to take action themselves. One of his parishioners, said to be deranged and continually quarreling with his wife, met Groen walking along Eastern Avenue and shot him. Though the attack was not fatal, it did lead to a nervous breakdown that brought Groen's controversial career to a premature end.

His suffrage speech, then, brought the positive Calvinist Groen violent opposition, official vindication, and personal defeat—a mirror, in retrospect, of the immediate past and future of Dutch America as a whole. For by 1916 the positive Calvinists seemed destined to carry the day. In that year Michigan voted dry, and the CRC Synod gave its moral support to the forces of Prohibition, refused to condemn women's suffrage, and declared that church members might belong to secular labor unions (separate organization was better but not a matter of principle).

The fledgling Christian Labor Alliance in Grand Rapids never recovered from this blow. Nor did Fas et Jus long survive its failure to meet its pledge of electing a full slate of candidates in the 1915 and 1916 Grand Rapids elections; in fact, it had to struggle just to make the nominations.[38] Their separate organizations dying and their principles officially rebuffed, the Antitheticals in 1918 suffered the final indignity of seeing their journal, *De Calvinist,* pass into unfriendly hands and be renamed, with distressingly irenic spirit, the *Christian Journal.* The Confessionalists absorbed a similar blow—*De Gereformeerde Amerikaan* ceased publication in 1916.

Understandably, the positive Calvinists turned toward the American world with growing confidence. Johannes Groen's baptism of American individualism and the Declaration of Independence occurred in 1913. In 1914 Henry Beets and B. K. Kuiper issued the boldest calls yet for "Americanization." The year after, Edward J. Tanis proclaimed his "deep respect" for the great Christian statesmanship of Ulysses Grant, Benjamin Harrison, and William McKinley. The year after that, Beets endorsed Billy Sunday. The RCA *Leader* and general press alike took notice and ventured the hope that the CRC "progressives" might soon bring the whole denomination into the light.

But the opposing factions were still strong and soon to receive harsh vindication from "America" itself. For one, "the coming generation" had voices of its own. On the very night (April 5, 1917) that Groen "went over to the world" by addressing a secular labor union in Grand Rapids, the young preacher who would soon replace him at Eastern Avenue Christian Reformed Church and attempt a denominational purge of the common grace ideology concluded a lecture entitled "Social Christianity and Calvinism" with the cry of the antithesis: "Let this, above all in the particularly humanistic age in which we live, be our guiding principle: We work not for results regardless of methods and means. And practice may never dominate principle!"[39]

As it happened, the next morning the United States House of Representatives passed a declaration of war upon Germany, thereby inaugurating an era in which the Dutch, and many other ethnics, would learn some startling lessons about their new homeland. Out of the education, factional strife would rise to its bitter climax.

PART III

WARS WITHOUT AND WITHIN, 1917–1928

[1]   [2]

THE LEGACY OF 1834

Hendrik de Cock [1] and Hendrik P. Scholte [2] catalyzed the Secession of 1834. Later, Scholte and Albertus C. Van Raalte [3] led the Seceder emigration to America. Koene Vanden Bosch [4] (pictured here with his wife) was a founding minister of the True/Christian Reformed Church that broke with Van Raalte.

[3]   [4]

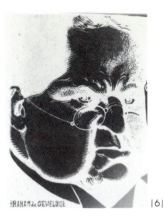

[5]

ᴮᴿᴬᴴᴬᴹ de GEWELDIGE

[6]

FOUNDERS OF NEO-CALVINISM

Abraham Kuyper [5], seen here in mid career, was awesome to his followers and awful to his enemies, as his famous 1909 caricature [6] suggests. G. Groen van Prinsterer [7] was Kuyper's principal antecedent; Herman Bavinck [8] was his great contemporary.

[7]

[8]

CRC EMINENCES PRIOR TO WORLD WAR I

Lammert J. Hulst [9] carried on the Seceder tradition against Kuyper's followers in America. John Van Lonkhuyzen [10] was leader of the Antitheticals. Johannes Groen [11], Geerhardus Vos [12], and Henry Beets [13] were the pulpiteer, scholar, and publicist, respectively, of positive Calvinism.

|14| |15|

THE RCA PROFESSORIATE PRIOR TO WORLD WAR I

Western Theological Seminary had as its poles the somewhat Neo-Calvinistic Nicholas Steffens [14] and the lion of American Protestant Progressivism, Evert J. Blekkink [15]. Gerrit Dubbink [16] and Matthew Kolyn [17] fell in between.

|16| |17|

THE RCA EDUCATIONAL MILIEU

The rather stark environs of Western Seminary in the early twentieth century [18] contrast with the idealized rendering of Hope College in the latter 1800s [19]. The print intimates "progress" — Van Raalte's "howling wilderness" had become academic "groves" — but masks the financial struggle these buildings represent.

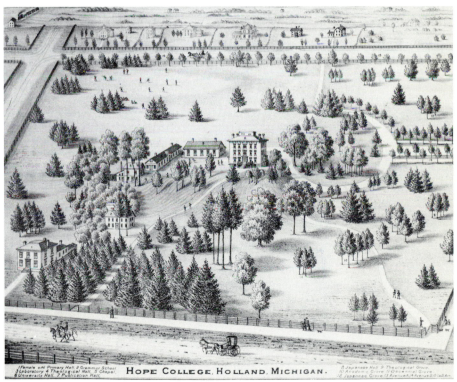

HOPE COLLEGE, HOLLAND, MICHIGAN.

[20]

RCA STATESMANSHIP

Gerrit J. Diekema [20] (third from right) is feted in 1930 as U.S. ambassador to the Netherlands. Diekema's term, though not this table, was vexed by the spread of the Depression across the Atlantic, in part as a result of the trade policies he had long championed. Henry Geerlings [21], Diekema's counterpart on the local (Holland, Michigan) scene, sits in genial retirement.

[21]

A CRC DYNASTY, CA. 1910   The Reverend and Mrs. Klaas Kuiper (seated right and left) and family, one of Dutch America's outstanding intellectual clans. Klaas championed the cause of Calvin College and Seminary, where sons Herman (far left) and "B. K." (far right) would teach and "R. B." (behind his father) would preside.

CALVIN COLLEGE AND SEMINARY FACULTY, 1916

As a decade of strife was about to explode, the combatants posed in rank. Bottom row, from left: F. M. Ten Hoor (first), Klaas Schoolland (third), Louis Berkhof (fourth), Samuel Volbeda (fifth), William Heyns (sixth). Second row, from left: H. J. Van Andel, Jacob Vanden Bosch, B. K. Kuiper, Ralph Janssen.

|24| |25|

THE CRC EDUCATIONAL MILIEU

CRC theological education progressed through three sites in Grand Rapids: the top floor of the Williams Street Christian School [24], ca. 1880; the building on Madison and Franklin [25], ca. 1900; and the Franklin Street campus [26], ca. 1920.

|26|

|27|

ETHNICITY AND AMERICANISM

On the verge of World War I, Calvin seminarians [27] could indulge in mock celebrations of the worldliness they would some years later be decrying, but Hope College students formed a military corps for more immediate crusading [28].

|28|

THE EFFORT TO AMERICANIZE

Third Reformed Church in Holland, Michigan, home to much of the RCA elite, was proud to be the flagship of Americanism. The sanctuary was draped for mourning after the death of William McKinley in 1901 [29], and for histrionic patriotism on the occasion of its semicentennial celebration in the war year of 1917 [30]. Naysayers decried this example at their peril.

|31|

|32|

FOUR HERETICS

CRC figures demoted or expelled in the battles of the 1920s included Harry Bultema [31] (a later photo), Ralph Janssen [32], Herman Hoeksema [33], and Henry Danhof [34]. B. K. Kuiper (see photo [22]) was another victim.

|33|

|34|

|35| |36|

FOUR WINNERS

*Louis Berkhof [35] and Henry J. Kuiper [36] (a later photo) dominated the
CRC for the next generation. R. B. Kuiper [37] symbolized the community's
link with conservative Presbyterians, while Edward J. Tanis [38] became the
popular voice of Neo-Calvinism.*

|37| |38|

|39|

|40|

NEO-CALVINISM AMERICANIZED

Abraham Kuyper's legacy was passed along largely through the semi-scholarly Calvin Forum, *edited by Clarence Bouma [39] and, in the 1950s, by Cecil De Boer [40]. Henry J. Ryskamp [41] wrote on socio-economic affairs, Bastian Kruithof [42] (a later photo) on religion and culture.*

|41|

|42|

WESTERN SEMINARY FACULTY, 1939 *This group linked the 1910s, when Evert Blekkink (seated right) was appointed, to the 1970s, when Lester Kuyper (standing left) retired. Its leading lights at the time were Albertus Pieters (seated left), John R. Mulder (standing center), and Simon Blocker (standing second from right).*

INTELLECTUALS AT PLAY

Henry Zylstra [44], Harvard Ph.D. in literature, shows his South Dakota pedigree at a Calvin College field day, 1940. Calvin President Henry Schultze [45] was no mean hitter, but his generation would find the younger group's pitch in the early '50s tough to handle.

|45|

6

Dutch Americans and World War I

The "progressive" tide had risen in Dutch America not by internal dynamics alone but under outside pressure, and that pressure took on an ominous new quality with the beginning of World War I. The moment when the war came home, therefore, deserves a close look.

That moment was May 1915, when the Germans sank the British liner (and on this trip, apparently, munitions carrier) *Lusitania* at the cost of some one hundred American lives. While the American press generally denounced the action, some Dutch Americans placed blame on the United States. John Van Lonkhuyzen, writing in the CRC's Dutch-language periodical, *De Wachter*, protested that the United States' commercial support of the Entente made such an incident likely, that President Wilson compounded the dangers of false neutrality with the belligerence of his protest to Berlin, and that Americans, especially the press, were irresponsible in blindly supporting Wilson's policy and prejudiced in attacking Germany. As the title of Van Lonkhuyzen's editorial put it, the nation was "Playing with Fire," bringing itself to the brink of unjust participation in the war. Putting words into practice, Van Lonkhuyzen, along with R. B. Kuiper—pastor, be it noted, of an English-speaking church—began circulating among Hollanders on Grand Rapids' west side a petition calling for an embargo on arms sales to all belligerents, a fair investigation of the *Lusitania* incident, and a fuller presentation of the German side of the submarine question.[1]

The Grand Rapids *News* led the response of the good Americans of the city, damning Van Lonkhuyzen as "a busy-body alien," "an interloper, a meddler and a spreader of distrust, discontent and sedition." It also called for his deportation and for "good Hollanders" to purge their ranks of such treason. Quick to heed, many of the Dutch condemned Van Lonkhuyzen in the *News*'s columns (though he too protested his loyalty there), while the Michigan courts taught the community something about freedom of speech by twice rejecting Van Lonkhuyzen's suit for damages from libel.[2]

This episode sketched the basic traits of Dutch-American experience during World War I. In terms of external relations, the war induced a conflict far more severe than common ethnic tension. Internally, it polarized the celebrators of pure Americanism and those somehow more "Dutch." The former established their credentials by attacking the latter who (*vide* Van Lonkhuyzen) increasingly were associated with the Antithetical position. Those in between hurried to profess patriotism more ardently and to prove it by hastening their "Americanization."

Despite its portents, Dutch Americans at first had been little stirred by the war. The midwestern leaders of the RCA should at least have been troubled since one of their number only three years before had announced the imminent demise of militarism. "It seems impossible that the Satanic principle of the highway robber, that might makes right . . . can much longer be respected and accepted in the adjustment of difficulties among nations." Rather, mankind was about to create an era of permanent peace: "We can do it if we will." When war nonetheless broke out these men attributed it to the primitive state of European morals and intelligence, so numbed by autocracy, greed, and national pride. In words he would forget three years later, Matthew Kolyn stated that he hoped the masses would resist the taxation and conscription required to carry on the conflict. Meanwhile, the *Leader* concluded, Christians should pray that Europe might soon come to its senses and that America might remain far above the fray, a beacon of peace, hope, and higher ideals.[3]

Yet the *Leader* had no problem justifying in the same breath the United States' use of arms to defend certain of these ideals ("humanity" and "civilization") against the depredations of irresponsible Mexicans. "The American people united, casting aside partisanship and prejudice . . . will stand behind President Wilson in his resolute purpose to uphold the dignity and security of this country" by sending American troops into Mexico, Henry Geerlings proclaimed.[4] So it came as no surprise that Germany's purported insults to American honor (the *Lusitania*, the Zimmerman note), to the rule of law (unrestricted submarine warfare), and to humanity ("the rape of Belgium") caused the *Leader* by 1916 to forget its distress with "the awful carnage of war." By the time of America's entry, it had elevated the war to the plane of pure ideology, making American participation inevitable.

> Germany is the world champion of armed tyranny and reaction, the United States of liberty and progress. The world could not go on without these two meeting in battle. They represent antagonistic ideas and systems which cannot both endure.[5]

Over the next months, the *Leader* kept pace with mainstream Protestant opinion in America, rising to a frenzy of patriotism that cast the conflict (again sounding Neo-Calvinistic) in terms of absolutes and antithesis. This was not only a just but a holy war, fought for "the principles of religious and economic freedom which Jesus Christ taught."

> On the one side we behold Christian civilization, the divine right of the people, democracy and religious liberty. On the other we have German Kultur, the divine right of kings, autocracy and super-stitious fear.
> . . . In a final baptism of blood and death, God will avenge upon Germany, foremost exponent of militarism and alone guilty of a sanctioned and ordered system of horrors and atrocities . . . the wrongs of Belgium, and of France, and of America, and of the whole world.[6]

Christian Reformed leaders also greeted the outbreak of war in Europe with anger at the high and pity for the lowly. But having never proclaimed the imminence of perpetual peace, they did not search for a single villain. Instead they saw the war as sad confirmation of Calvinism's teachings of total depravity and divine punishment for national sins—namely, Belgian atrocities in the Congo, Russian pogroms against the Jews, English imperialism, German Higher Criticism, and French atheism and licentiousness.[7] As the war proceeded, the Christian Reformed judged its participants with less one-sidedness than did their RCA cousins but with one momentous difference—to many of them, England was the culprit.

Henry Beets showed why by reading 1914 Europe under the memory of the Boer War. Britain was again extending its power, he maintained, this time in a conspiracy to contain German growth.[8] As pro-British sentiment intensified in the United States, however, Beets lapsed silent on the issue and let his more defensive compatriots defy public opinion. That they did, their fervor growing as American entry drew nearer. Klaas Schoolland supported Van Lonkhuyzen's petition campaign, ridiculed the United States' pretensions of neutrality, and, despite all the principal sanctity of law, declared the *Lusitania* sinking a justifiable act of war. Columnists in *De Wachter* strove throughout 1915 and 1916 to neutralize the British propaganda that filled American dailies by giving much space to pro-German accounts.[9]

Their campaign—and courage—peaked in the early months of 1917. John Van Lonkhuyzen sneered at the hypocrisy of American policymakers who loaned the Entente two billion dollars but demanded that Germany regard the United States as neutral, who applied the standards of the law of the seas against the Germans but not against the English, who insisted on their "rights" while professing love for the peace which such insistence would destroy. Meanwhile, Schoolland

published for Dutch readers the theory of an East Coast, WASP, cap-
italist-elite conspiracy to force American intervention. *These* "hyphenated Americans" (Schoolland returned the patriots' sting), having long
before entered Cecil Rhodes's scheme of conducting imperialism by
strategic investment, had tied American credit to the Entente cause.
This made perpetuation of the war and eventual German defeat the
bases of domestic prosperity. But now events had caught up with America the greedy, Schoolland warned. Its people would have to choose
either war and prosperity or peace with stagnation. Since they would
unhestitatingly pick the former, Americans should regard their soon-to-
be-slain sons as sacrifices for the national sin of avarice, not as martyrs
in a Christian cause. Indeed, the sordidness of its motives and its allies
should prove once and for all that America was not a Christian country.
To perfect his insolence, Schoolland called the Zimmerman note a
justifiable move by an encircled Germany; to show his desperation, he,
the scourge of "popular sovereignty," demanded that the government
hold a plebiscite before declaring war.[10]

With America's official entrance into the conflict, however, this
dissidence subsided. Some could only pray for God's mercy on all
involved; others criticized the stated purposes of the war—to end war,
to spread democracy—as unrealistic. Henry Beets's editorial of April
19, 1917, sounded the principal CRC themes. War might be an instrument of God's providence, might sometimes be necessary (he cited the
hoary examples of the American Revolution and the Dutch against
Spain), and might prompt noble conduct, but it always remained a
"dreadful calamity," especially for the common people who suffered
most from it. Since Congress had decided the question on behalf of all
the people, the citizenry should be quiet and obedient, praying for an
end to "this unspeakably horrid war" and leaving responsibility to
those in power.[11]

To true patriots in and outside the community, such declarations
were too formal, too tepid, and too late. "In this grave hour," with
righteousness locked in a death struggle with darkness, loyalty ought
not to be reluctant and dutiful but eagerly volunteered.[12] Nor did the
patriotism of May 1917 atone for the criticisms of March. And so there
descended on the denomination in general and on the Antithetical Calvinists in particular a storm of bitter hostility.

The *Leader* led the way with articles in December 1916 ominously
entitled "The Church Hyphen." Here all the clashes of cultural outlook, the denominational rivalries, the pent-up wrath of "the better
sort" of Hollanders could burst forth. Was it any mistake, asked the
Leader, that "disloyalty" correlated with ethnic identity and Neo-Calvinism? Not at all, for while the immigrants of 1847 had come for
spiritual purposes and had seen that their destiny, as decreed by God

and common sense, was assimilation into the grand new American race, the "later" immigrants (i.e., those of Kuyper's era) had come out of mercenary motives and refused to become fully American in language or mind. Huddled in their ethnic enclaves, blinded by their "foreign importations" (i.e., Neo-Calvinism), they could not see that Providence had made America the most Calvinistic of all nations. In the Netherlands, "God's sovereignty" was a call to battle; in America—the writer apparently not aware of his whole meaning—it was "a vapid platitude." In normal times, this stubbornness might be tolerated, but in a national emergency it was treasonous, even satanic, and should be repressed by law or, if need be, eugenics.[13]

In the ensuing months these arguments were repeated and refined, adding only the rhetorical touches of "solid American" propaganda. Neo-Calvinism, and particularly the Christian school system, came to be characterized as "militaristic," "Prussian in character and spirit," opposed "to everything that under God has made and preserved America to be the land of the free." Abraham Kuyper, for accepting the congratulations of the German government on his eightieth birthday, was "willing to be numbered among the baby-killers of the central powers" and therefore with the enemies of humanity and Christ. Moreover, his "detestable influence" had made "the average Dutch settlement in America . . . a hotbed of disloyalty."[14]

It was patriots outside the Dutch community, interestingly, who added a theological tack. The Grand Rapids *News* criticized the CRC's doctrinal conservatism as well as its "foreign philosophy." Since it held up "the old, the discarded, the obsolete, the dead, against the hope of the future, [i.e.,] the principles of liberty," it was no wonder that the denomination contained "wagging alien tongues" guilty of "high treason" and "sedition." The foremost liberal pulpit in Grand Rapids linked orthodoxy not just to disloyalty but to ignorance in general. The Christian Reformed were "un-American," "parochial," and "behind the times" because of their adherence to biblical infallibility, Calvin's bloody theology, and separate Christian schools.[15]

Other critics focused on political allegiance alone. The most vociferous of these, the *Michigan Tradesman,* a Grand Rapids weekly for operators of small businesses, complained that "the Christian Reformed churches harbor many preachers who are not loyal to the American flag. . . . Calvin College is a hotbed of treason." The *Tradesman* advocated mere imprisonment or deportation for the offending clerics but more severe measures for the rest. "The professors who are conceded to be anti-American should be stood up against a wall and shot. There is no proper place for them in this land of the free."[16]

Of course, the loyalty issue became most volatile when politics and religion crossed. This occurred most dramatically in February 1918, when Herman Hoeksema, the young minister of (again) an English-speaking Christian Reformed church in Holland, Michigan, and resident champion of Antithetical Calvinism, refused to allow the American flag in the sanctuary during worship. At this "the best element" in the city felt "aggrieved and somewhat humiliated" and they counterattacked with their most illustrious representative, Gerrit J. Diekema. His lecture must have satisfied even the most ardent patriot, as it condemned the ruthless Hun, unspeakable Turk, and grasping Hapsburg; praised American soldiers as "the bravest and manliest boys the air, the earth, and the sea have ever seen"; and cast the war in sacred, apocalyptic terms. In this final conflict between freedom and tyranny, God was using the United States to "give birth to the universal brotherhood of man and . . . usher in the promised reign of the Prince of Peace." Since "the flag stands for all that is pure and noble and good," and since the cause of Christ and country were the same, Diekema concluded that Hoeksema's act approximated treason. The Netherlands-born and -educated minister of Holland's Hope Reformed Church, Peter P. Cheff, raised the rhetorical ante still higher, characterizing Hoeksema's behavior as "positively criminal," and suggesting that support for the war effort constituted no less than the highest form of religious devotion.[17]

Hoeksema responded by turning to Calvinism, the Constitution, and personal insult. Since Cheff and Diekema appeared to be incapable of sound thinking, he declared, a constructive discussion was impossible; he would have to content himself with showing that "it is very well possible to be fully as loyal and truly patriotic as those that make it their business to advertise their patriotism at every opportunity." He also challenged them to prove their charges of treason in court, where "no high phrases, just *facts*" mattered. The facts were, Hoeksema continued, that he had condemned Germany already in 1914, that he believed America to be on the right side in a just war, but that neither this nor any other reason could ever justify measures of unsound principle. The flag might stand in the church during nonecclesiastical ceremonies but not during worship, for then God's people acted as part of a universal institution and might not declare national loyalty. To put the church in service of a nation corrupted its essence and threatened civil and religious liberty. Moreover, it abetted the decline of spirituality that was killing the church all over America, not least in the RCA churches of Holland, Michigan.[18]

This retaliation only excited further reproach, above all from the *Michigan Tradesman*. Any preacher who barred the flag from his church was a "Bolsheviki" who had "forfeited his right to exist among decent people and voluntarily made himself an object of disgust and suspicion." Such conduct resulted "directly" from "pro-German propaganda," aroused "joy in Berlin," and constituted treason. "Every churchman who cannot tolerate the sight of the American flag in his church is a fit subject for deportation or the firing squad." To similar threats Hoeksema reacted with an interesting display of his own Americanization. He took to carrying a pistol and, walking home one dark night in Holland, actually threatened to use it upon some would-be assailants.[19]

But not all Hollanders escaped unscathed. A Grand Rapids Central High School teacher who by birth and marriage belonged to two of the foremost Dutch families in Michigan was removed from her post for having published anti-British articles in 1916. A group of vigilantes in the same city perpetrated "paint raids" by night upon the homes of men of suspect loyalty. One victim, the prominent Christian Reformed publisher J. B. Hulst, awoke April 2, 1918, to find the colors of the German flag painted on his porch along with the slogans "Be an American" and "Buy a Liberty Bond." Too late he protested that he had indeed done so, three times in fact, for a total of $150.[20] Painting and "flagging" became popular sports in the rural districts of Michigan and Iowa, where Dutch farmers repeatedly found yellow stripes smeared on their barns and unrequested American flags hanging in their church sanctuaries.

The most grievous trial afflicted the Christian Reformed congregation of Peoria, Iowa. Like all impure Americans in that state, this group felt the severe restrictions imposed by its vigilant governor and legislature: no meetings, including church services, might be conducted in a foreign language unless (the authorities later conceded) full English translations had been sent them in advance. But this congregation had the added misfortunes of Dutch neighbors eager to prove their patriotism, American neighbors unable to distinguish between "Dutch" and "Deutsch," and a minister, J. J. Weersing, who not only refused to allow the flag in the sanctuary but also disparaged the government's request that pastors designate certain Sundays for the Red Cross, YMCA, and Liberty Loan. Federal marshals warned Weersing and five elders that his conduct smacked of treason, while the Pella *Weekblad*, in the name of the respectable Dutch of the area, censured him for not seeing in "this hour of crisis" his sacred duty to crush autocracy. Soon after, Weersing and the teacher at the local Christian school were forced to leave town, pursued by a band of several hundred patriots. Some of these, dissatisfied with both official and vigilante measures, took the final step of burning both the church and the school.[21]

To these attacks and others like them, Christian Reformed leaders responded by pleading with outsiders for understanding and with insiders for more fervent patriotism. Positive Calvinists led the way. Henry Beets enlightened critics as to the differences between being anti-British and pro-German and documented the CRC's support of

America's war effort. But in the same article he summoned his readers to dedicate "our manhood, our honor, our property and our sons at her [the United States'] shrine . . . wholeheartedly and promptly and liberally, trusting in the integrity of Congress . . . and honoring as our leader the President." Beets also took to the stump for the Liberty Loan, telling Dutch audiences that God, conscience, and patriotism alike demanded "devotion to our boys" and admiration for the nobility of American purpose. Woe to America should Germany triumph! Beets warned; the Kaiser would "bleed us to death with taxes and humiliate us as deep as Hades." Edward J. Tanis sermonized against all "slackers" and "pacifists" and emphasized that the institutional church's neutrality did not reduce the individual Christian's obligation to support the nation's cause.[22]

After a year of total war, even Klaas Schoolland changed his mind. Now Germany seemed to him "the greatest and most dangerous imperialistic power of all ages." Since America fought in simple self-defense, Schoolland argued, "let us show ourselves to be genuine Americans, true patriots, loyal citizens."[23] Patriotism became informally adopted into the denominational order when the CRC Synod of 1918 met in a hall bedecked with American flags, sent President Wilson a telegram declaring its support "in this righteous cause," and even joined the notoriously "liberal" Federal Council of Churches of Christ in America in order to facilitate its own ministrations in army camps.

Even this tide of Americanism, however, followed the contours of inherited mentalities. On the one hand the positive Calvinists led the war party in the CRC, but on the other they never approached the extremist pitch of RCA voices. The Antitheticals turned upon this very rhetorical excess, and with familiar weapons. By its very nature propaganda followed the erroneous principles of popular sovereignty and Humanism; how much more did its substance in the present case (the war to "Save Humanity," to spread "Democracy")?[24] The Confessionalists responded with protective pietism. Current events gained significance as allegories of spiritual realities. Soldiers might be risking and taking lives, but the *real* dangers and moral problems of army life involved profanity and sexual vice. Millions might have died in Europe and millions more been made desolate, but in the deepening of personal piety lay the true meaning of the war.[25]

The most striking evidence of persistence appeared in discussions of Americanization itself. Naturally, these increased in number and vigor during the war, but they altered nothing in the established formulas. The most thorough treatment, an oration by the young Clarence Bouma on Labor Day 1917—"Be an American!"—repeated in more urgent tones exactly what B. K. Kuiper and Foppe Ten Hoor had said years before: Dutch Americans should neither despise nor excessively praise their heritage but "combine gradually and carefully" the best Dutch with the best American traits to produce a superior hybrid, an "up-to-date, vital, American" Calvinism. The president of the patriotic 1918 Christian Reformed Synod agreed that the times had forced the church to enter fully into American life, but as "a leaven" and always holding firmly to the Confessions. Every analyst of acculturation recognized, joyfully or not, that "these serious times" demanded a faster pace of adjustment, but they all insisted most upon retaining the Reformed heritage.[26]

All their sorting out of loyalties limited Dutch-American creativity in what was perhaps the more profound task of searching out the war's meaning. Certain ideas drew unanimous assent. Henry Beets defined one in response to the attacks of Grand Rapids' liberals. What did the war show more clearly than the utter realism, the perfect "up-to-date-ness" of Calvinistic orthodoxy and the inadequacy of liberalism's "milk-and-water pabulum"? Matthew Kolyn had said the same for the RCA a year before:

> The present world war spells SIN in letters so large that all the world can read it. . . . What of those "generous impulses" of which we heard so much? What of that "native goodness" that needs only a little improvement and discipline to make of human nature all that can be desired? What of the effects of civilization, education and culture?[27]

Yet the enthusiastic also saw "a good side" to the war. For *De Wachter*, conversions among soldiers, a renewed consciousness of the seriousness of life, and stronger social unity showed how God used evil to produce good. Beets listed the triumph of temperance, increase in prayer, the uplift of "the Southern Negro," but above all the war's revelation of America's capacity for idealism and sacrifice rather than mere money and pleasure. Furthermore, the war's cultural "amalgamation . . . has brought us nearer to the goal of having not alone one country and one flag, but one language and one American spirit as well."[28]

A third common idea presented more difficulty. No one doubted that God had sent this "smelting fire" to punish the nations for their sins, but no one seemed able to demonstrate the precise workings thereof. B. K. Kuiper, for instance, opened his history *De Groote Oorlog* ("The Great War") by declaring that the conflict "was written in the Book of God's eternal counsel," far beyond the will of man, and that God guided its development according to his own design[29]—and yet in none of the remaining 370 pages did Kuiper ruminate upon that design or show how one event or another might have fulfilled it. Political choices and individual heroics, collective morale and economic forces composed the stuff of Kuiper's account, leaving the reader to wonder how God fit into it all.

Likewise with the idea of war as a scourge: time and again pulpit and press pointed to vice in France, to Rationalism in Germany, and to tyranny in Russia as the sores God was lancing with the sword. But rarely could they connect the instrument to the object of wrath. The Czar might fall in military defeat, but what did German Higher Criticism or French syphilis have to do with the cause or course of the war? Germany might recognize defeat as retribution for power-lust, but would the Entente nations see the same in victory? And on the American side, how did the formation of armies, of all things, correct the sins of swearing, Sabbath-breaking, and fornication, of "birth control, . . . sex perversion, the attempt to wipe out sex distinction, etc., etc.," for which God was chastening America?[30] Usually the assertion served as its own, and only, proof.

But as to more immediate meanings there was less mystery. The war years were the watershed for Dutch America. For the RCA optimists they marked the peak of the Progressive-Protestant crusade, a peak that led to a descent that, as it turned out, was swift and steep. For the rest, the war settled "the language question" beyond all doubt, but it only intensified the deeper issues of Americanization. Under wartime stress the Dutch had heightened their sense of themselves, of the surrounding society, and of the tension between them, leading them into the 1920s under pressure to define these three once and for all. And there was one more legacy. The fear and hysteria that colored national discourse in wartime passed over undiluted into the community's postwar disputes, augmenting the bitterness inevitable to any struggle so conclusive, especially one initiated from without.[31]

7

Forming the Battle Lines, 1919–1920

That the war had brought a great turning the Dutch saw not only for themselves but for the whole world. The unparalleled scale of the war, the fall of three empires, and the revolution, civil war, and new nations that came in their wake; the conference at Versailles and its proposed League of Nations; labor strife, inflation, and the specter of radicalism at home—all were breathlessly described in the Dutch press and, taken together, created an aura of the awesome and momentous. "This is a period of transition such as the race has never known," said Henry Geerlings. "Old systems are crumbling. Old institutions are passing away. Habits and traditions no longer bind. . . . Yesterday the agony of world war; today the consciousness that human society is being born again." And from the opposite end of the spectrum came a similar opinion:

> Our time is a period of transition . . . of unrest, change and perplex-
> ity. There seem to be no abiding realities, no eternal verities. . . .
> Things seem to change as you are considering them. All things seem
> to have lost their acknowledged and historical significance. . . . We
> are moving and admittedly we are moving fast.[1]

But when it came to assessing this movement, the full diversity of Dutch-American thinking reasserted itself, especially as wartime conformity waned. Thus the postlude to the war without became a prelude to the climactic conflict within.

Among Confessional pietists, a spirit of foreboding prevailed. The sermons Ymen P. De Jong, former associate editor of *De Gereformeerde Amerikaan*, preached around the end of the war found little cause for hope in current events—for that matter, little of *fundamental* import at all. As during the war, De Jong weighed the latest tumult of the nations in "spiritual" scales and pronounced it merely "earthly." A consequent parochialism also persisted. On Armistice Sunday, De Jong reviewed chiefly the emotional trials of his own flock; regarding the postwar influenza epidemic, which killed eighteen million people worldwide, the feature that he chose to note was the local government's decision to prohibit church services for two weeks—a health measure he regarded as ominous repression.[2] In short, with Europe and America in turmoil, De Jong pointed his people to piety as usual: more humility, more dependence on God, more suspicion of worldly affairs.

Since positive Calvinists usually took the opposite tack, it is noteworthy that this mood touched them too. B. K. Kuiper's "Calvinist searchlight" on current affairs fell in 1918 on the specter of the four horsemen of the Apocalypse.[3] History would end in a cataclysm of war, famine, and disease—a scenario *forecast* (not, we may note, *inaugurated*) by the Great War. His younger brother was bolder. Now in his second English-speaking (i.e., allegedly "progressive" and "American") charge, R. B. Kuiper preached a series of sermons that declared "the last days" to be at hand.[4] Notably, R. B. adduced the very evidence so fascinating to Protestant conservatives in America: the "Christian" (British) conquest of Palestine and Jewish migration thereto, the persecution of (Christian) Armenians in (Muslim) Turkey, the resurgence of religious cults, the first demonstrations of the flapper generation. He also shared their essential outlook: Christ would not come symbolically, as liberalism thought, in a general increase of love and peace, but physically, catastrophically, and on the heels of awful developments.[5]

Here was the old scourge from the Netherlands, Protestant liberalism, at last fully registering upon the Dutch in the American context. Both Kuipers directed their commentaries against it, especially its evolutionary optimism and trust in the tokens of "civilization." Democracy and prosperity, science, education, and technology all might bring "progress," B. K. Kuiper noted, but as Scripture and recent events showed, they also multiplied the human capacity for evil. Some of these, R. B. added, paved the way for the global consolidation of power that would mark the advent of the Antichrist and of his reign of terror upon the elect. More directly, Modernism was leading the great apostasy of the church, a cardinal feature of the last days, since it lay the ideological foundations for Antichrist.[6]

What then were the faithful to do? B. K. Kuiper suggested certain attitudes, and his "American" brother caricatured them. Thus defense of orthodoxy became militant vigilance. Skeptical caution toward modern developments approached pure reaction (democracy, science, and social reform became guilty by association). And sober obedience gave way to saccharine resignation: "the Christian strolls through this cemetery [the impending world-order], posture erect, head lifted, face beaming."[7]

The Kuipers had not addressed their subject out of the blue. By war's end, apocalyptic premillennialism was the rage of Dutch-American conversation. In 1918 their publishers deemed it profitable to print Dutch editions of the English millenarian works, *666: The Number of Man* by Philip Mauro and *Signs of the Times* by Robert Haldeman. But they had a voice of their own too in Harry Bultema, a CRC minister who in 1917 published *Maranatha! Eene Studie over de Onvervulde Profetie*.[8]

Bultema too saw great portents in current events: "Surely these are solemn days, so full of terror, at the same time the birth-throes of a new dispensation." And like his pietistic colleagues he perceived the days to be evil.

> If we look about us and take as our measuring-rod the high demands of a righteous God, then it is scarcely possible to paint with too dark colors. Whole denominations are totally modernistic. . . . On each terrain of life men live in brazen defiance of God's holy ordinances. The children of our time themselves in these times of distress are as frivolous as the generation of Noah and Lot. Young men think of little else than games and sport and dancing and drink.

Since history was degeneration, postmillennial visions were ludicrous:

> To expect in light-hearted optimism that this world will become better as its culture increases is thoroughly unBiblical. There is nothing in heaven or on earth that will make this world better. . . . At his return Christ will find no converted world, as Post-Millennialism dreams, but instead a world matured in evil.[9]

Finally, Bultema joined his colleagues in regarding liberal Protestantism as the spearhead of the enemy—for reducing the gospel of salvation to that of culture, for denying the central tenets of Christianity, for subjecting Scripture to rationalistic critique.[10]

But Bultema also turned his ire toward the Reformed tradition:

> Many well-meaning Christians have condemned the fervent anticipation of the future of the Lord as fanaticism or onesidedness. This common mistake has had the result that today in Reformed circles there is little preached or written regarding the return of Christ. While the whole world stands in fire and flames, we still discuss "the doctrine of baptism" and people seem to have no desire to know about the coming of the Lord.[11]

Reformed apathy toward prophecy was misleading in itself, Bultema maintained, since most of Scripture was prophetical and most prophecy still unfulfilled. In these momentous times, however, it constituted criminal neglect. But even when they did study prophecy, he argued, Reformed thinkers used a misleading—in fact, heretical—method. Their "spiritual-symbolic" interpretation abused language and defied scriptural authority as blatantly as did Higher Criticism. Rather, believers should expect literal fulfillment of prophecy.[12]

With these admonitions, Bultema proceeded to a detailed outline of the final days: resurrections and raptures, the restoration of Palestine to the Jews and the thousand-year reign of Christ at Jerusalem, the great tribulation and final judgment, through all of which the Jews played a major role. This enabled him to link his work to contemporary events (Zionism), but it also indicated a critical theological point, a dispensational concept of Scripture and history. The Jews formed a part of God's chosen people distinct from the church with a destiny and path to salvation all their own. "Israel," in fact, was God's chief instrument on earth; its was a temporal calling, a material reward.[13]

Bultema's scenario did not dwell so much on the horrors of the final days as on the peace and privileges Christ would bring the faithful. While the great tribulation unfolded on earth, they would enjoy Christ's company in the air and later return with him to rule the world. But these blessings had a price. In contrast to the Jews, the church had only a "heavenly" calling, to be pursued by "spiritual" means and rewarded in eternity. The church's earthly lot was suffering: "The more faithful she is the greater will be her oppression. For the more obedient she is to her glorious Head, the more the world will hate and persecute her." Therefore, Bultema concluded, "in our troubled days" the faithful should study prophecy, draw comfort from contemplating their eternal reward, and, most of all, give up their Christian cultural dream.

> To defend the honor of God on each terrain of life is a phrase much heard in right-thinking circles and is held forth by believers to be their precious calling; yet, for the Church in this dispensation it shall remain more a symbol of hope than a beautiful reality.[14]

Obviously, in *Maranatha!* the Dutch had another wholesale attack on the Kuyperian program. But they also faced what they had long anticipated, a challenge to the Reformed heritage arising from the American environment. Dispensational premillennialism constituted a (some would say *the*) pillar of American Fundamentalist theology.[15] Contemporary events had enhanced its credibility, while wartime pressure made it all the more attractive to Dutchmen looking for a genuine "American" type of thought. Thus Bultema marked out one avenue for Dutch acculturation—allegiance to an extreme pietistic vision, in alliance with a vast body of conservative Protestants largely of Anglo-Saxon background.

Some positive Calvinists at first praised the book, since its British sources and American possibilities appealed to their patriotic enthusiasm. But for the rest, and soon for them too, *Maranatha!* roused alarm. The Antitheticals led here as in the other war controversies. John Van Lonkhuyzen started with scorn—the book was "a dream, a fantasy, a fiction"—but quickly hit the heart of the issue. *Maranatha!* corrupted the Reformed tradition with the worst elements of American theology, he warned—"Methodistic" assumptions and "Anabaptist" conclusions. It talked of heaven but not of earth, of the soul but not the body; it reduced God's majestic work in history to the salvation and comfort of scattered individuals. This "spiritualizing" encouraged passive "dreaming about the future" at the expense of the positive action to which Christians were called. The book's popularity implied that the Dutch were falling into Americanization of the worst sort: "Here lie hidden principles which will have an influence on all our Christian action. Influence for evil. Precisely as they have had in the American world."[16]

The Confessionalists responded at greater length but on a narrower scale. Both Louis Berkhof and Y. P. De Jong (the latter in three hundred pages) criticized premillennialism's doctrinal positions without once examining its cultural implications. For both, the movement erred chiefly in demanding literal fulfillment of all prophecy and in ignoring its historical and rhetorical setting. In addition and quite "in the spirit of the times," premillennialists ignored the church's historical confessions, thus dodging the test of time and experience to which all doctrine had to submit, and arrogantly claimed that they alone were right and that the church had for nineteen centuries been wrong. From these faults, it was argued, proceeded all the rest.[17] The truth, by contrast, lay in traditional Reformed orthodoxy. Besides defending the figurative mode of interpretation—the "ideal, spiritual, eternal significance" of the prophecy was what mattered, rather than its "natural historical sense"—De Jong postulated (with frequent appeals to Kuyper and Bavinck) the "organic unity" of salvation history. God's revelation did not radically change from one "dispensation" to the next, nor did his plan of salvation, the nature of his Kingdom, the role of his Son, or the calling of his people. Through all history God had offered the same hope to, demanded the same obedience from, and exercised the same command over one united people.[18]

Bultema's dispensationalism became the critical point, especially his conception of Israel and the church as two peoples of God and his denial that Christ was king of the church ("Christ is King only of Israel"). Nor did the critics accept his "clarification" that Christ was "Head," though not "King," of the church. With "unrest in the churches" over his book, Bultema had to submit to ecclesiastical investigation. The CRC Synod of 1918 found time between its patriotic singing and resolutions to declare his statements on the two contested points to be in conflict with the Confessions and directed his consistory to admonish him properly.[19] But the Synodical committee acted so tactlessly that Bultema, most of his congregation, and scattered sympathizers left the denomination.

Significantly, the official response to the "*Maranatha* question" covered the narrowest of grounds and only the most obvious deviations. The deeper impulses of premillennialism—its supernaturalism, otherworldliness, cataclysmic view of history, and implied passivity—drew not warnings but praise. R. B. Kuiper's sermons, delivered *after* the Synodical decision, shared the premillennialists' pessimism and envisioned an alliance between the Reformed and these erring cousins against the modernist enemy. Berkhof praised their sense of scriptural authority and impending catastrophe. No less a personage than the president of the 1918 Synod proclaimed their cardinal conviction in closing the meeting: "Brethren, the Lord is coming! Everything indicates it. The signs of the times tell us it is so. Even the thundering cannon on the battlefield speak of it."[20] Hence from this "Americanizing" Synod came an inkling of the direction that Americanization might take: toward militant evangelicalism, restrained by strict Confessionalism.

But equally evident among the Dutch was the contrary (and more familiar) type of Americanism—that "progressive" spirit that had risen to full height in the war and now seemed destined to sweep the world. Out of the rubble of war, Progressives assured themselves, would rise a nobler civilization of freedom, prosperity, and brotherhood. Some of the Dutch picked up this idiom—"reconstruction," "cooperation"—and its grand confidence: "He who believes in a God beholds the advance of mankind."[21]

The *Banner* offered such sentiments intermittently; the *Leader,* more often.[22] But two new journals emerged—and in telling fashion—to lead the cause. The Antithetical *Calvinist* was bought out in August 1918 by the *Christian Journal*, which proceeded to dance on its predecessor's grave: principialism gave way to "broader" views and an upbeat tone. And in spring 1919, *Religion and Culture* appeared to replace *De Gereformeerde Amerikaan* as the community's scholarly organ. It set to work demoting Confessionalism and raising the community's "cultural level." At least, such was the intention: *Religion and Culture* wished to address "scientific" and "literary" as well as religious topics and invited original fiction and poetry from aspiring Dutch-American artists.[23]

Such had been a positive Calvinist aim from the start, and the mentality's ideological roots remained strong. *Religion and Culture* stressed that its analysis would proceed from a distinctively Reformed perspective, and B. K. Kuiper filled the *Christian Journal*'s inaugural statement with familiar themes—"the broad terrain of social life," "sound Christian standpoint."[24] Kuiper's successor as editor, Henry J. G. Van Andel, had come to the States in 1909 at the age of twenty-seven and, as Professor of Dutch Studies at Calvin College, did much to refresh the community's consciousness of Netherlandic developments, particularly the later, "common grace" phase of Herman Bavinck's thought.[25]

Van Andel articulated the *Journal*'s core perspective in terms of wartime dramatics. "We Dutch Reformed are living through a crisis" —Americanization. Yet the dangers of that crisis diminished in the face of its opportunities: "the whole church, the whole nation, the whole world lie open for our group." On either count, the times demanded harmonization of traditional diversities—between pietists and activists, Infras and Supras, the CRC and the RCA.[26] On the denominational score, Van Andel spoke in good faith: the *Journal*'s third principal voice was the rising star of the RCA, John Kuizenga, the new editor of the *Leader*, long a professor at Hope College and Western Seminary, and an advocate of reformist Calvinism.[27] But otherwise the *Journal* was not so ingenuous. For it became clear that certain parties were more worthy than others; specifically, that the Antitheticals and Confessionalists should defer to the positive Calvinists. In fact, much of the *Journal*'s work turned out to be a critique of these two parties, separately and as it linked them together.

The Bultema case had been decided just two months before the *Journal*'s founding, so its editors began with attacks on "excessive pietism." These followed established Kuyperian lines: from erroneous theological principles—otherworldliness, individualism, and a disregard for God's general grace and revelation—had come an enfeebled Christianity. Pietism had no calling beyond saving souls or maintaining pure doctrine, no sense of collective sin or a cultural mandate, no concern for intellectual disciplines besides theology or for social areas outside the church; in fact, it consigned all this to the devil and preached that it was a Christian duty to neglect it. There could be no doubt, said B. K. Kuiper, that this tendency had caused much of the superficiality of American Protestantism and that (as with *Maranatha!*) it had "already broken through here and there among us. And it is well worth pondering whether this spirit shall not work itself into us more deeply in the future."[28]

But the *Journal*'s chief innovation lay in connecting this tendency with that of the Antitheticals, signalling a major realignment in the Dutch community. For forty years "Kuyperians" had been identified in contradistinction to "pietists"; now the *Journal*'s editorial board brought together the outgoing parties from both sides, and its critique linked the two defensive groups. "It is typical that some Christians try to portray ours as the blackest of all times and in this connection preach of a constant development of evil in order to convince us that the Antichrist stands at the door," H. J. Van Andel declared with eyes on the Antithesis as well as *Maranatha!* "This conception is neither biblical nor historical. It is simply the product of an erring fantasy."[29]

"Separatism," as they labeled the Antithetical school, cost the contributors to the *Journal* considerable effort, partly because it shared the Neo-Calvinist heritage and partly because it had the ideological sophistication pietism lacked. Of their analyses, B. K. Kuiper's was the kindest, a poignant review offering a conclusion of (for that time) rare candor. Twenty years of Neo-Calvinist ideals, aspirations, and labor, he said, demonstrated the courage of men like Schoolland and Van Lonkhuyzen, but had "not exerted the least influence on the practical course of things. . . . Our influence on the political and social terrain has been exactly nothing." The pietists had fed this failure by their cultural apathy and by sharing the separatists' false idea of holiness (i.e., proscribing association with non-Christians). The first was "an error," Kuiper said; the second, "a mirage." What was needed was well-considered but effective practicality.[30]

Precisely, Van Andel agreed. The Antitheticals' problem involved their mental habits. They were cold and humorless, sterile in their eighteenth-century logic, oppressive with their party line, and arrogant for assuming that their principles described all reality for all time.

> It is dishonorable to use these men [Calvin, Kuyper, etc.] as popes, speaking ex cathedra. And it is a grave error to believe that all truth can be established through deduction. . . . It is naive to think that world problems can be clarified and solved if only men think like the Reformed.[31]

John Kuizenga combined these objections in bringing the attack to its peak (in his series "Principieel and Principieelitis"). This "scholastic rationalism parading as the true and only orthodoxy" crushed both the simple man's faith and the intellectual's freedom. But worse than its principialism was the principle it championed. The antithesis fostered "fanaticism" by ignoring all the good that remained in nature and society; it fostered "antinomianism" by despising natural and civil law as the rule of sin; and it promoted a "mad mysticism" by judging the world according to a "spiritual" dichotomy. These, in turn, rendered the common believer helpless to the lures of extreme millennialism.[32] And so, the *Journal* concluded, separatists completed their ironic circle: arch-Calvinists become "Anabaptist," feeding the "pietistic dualism" their movement was born to oppose.

The *Journal* posed its alternative by simple reversals: against mille-

narian escapism, engagement; against separate organization, cooperation (as Kuizenga described it, with all "social reformers," "as far as
possible," "in every good cause"); against "theology only," the pursuit
of all disciplines and appreciation of all creation. As to methodology,
today's "wind is fresh and blows from the direction of self-conscious
and independent examination," Van Andel proclaimed. Therefore,
conveniently, the Americanizing community should look to those "independent thinkers" who would develop rather than slavishly imitate
principles or, for that matter, Confessions. Finally, over against the
antithesis, the *Journal* raised the idea of common grace, and not in the
tacit manner typical before the war but overtly, deliberately, and to the
exclusion—even the ridicule—of its counterpart.[33]

One source of this model was the old idea of "Amerika als heel
anders." B. K. Kuiper allowed this guardedly, Kuizenga with enthusiasm. "How different [from the Netherlands] is the opportunity of the
Church in America because America has so largely been Christianized."[34] But the men of the *Journal* turned just as much as their opponents to "old country" sources. They consciously appropriated the
Kuyper of common grace (the Kuyper of the antithesis was naive and
hyperbolic) but valued Herman Bavinck even more. *Religion and
Culture* extended and deepened this commitment. From Bavinck were
derived the intuitive methodology and cooperative strategy, the glow-
ing implications of common grace, the hopeful glimpse of a bright new
age.[35]

The spring of 1919, with the founding of *Religion and Culture* and
the *Journal*'s three-part attack on its rivals, marked the high tide of the
positive Calvinists. Like their Antithetical brothers, though, once they
had declared their principles, criticized their opponents, and proclaimed the way of the future, all abstractly, there remained little to do
but to repeat themselves. Perhaps for this reason B. K. Kuiper of the
grand prospectus resigned his editorship in August 1919 to head a
normal institute for Christian school teachers. That this was for *Christian* schools implied limits on the cooperative strategy, limits Kuiper
had noted from the start. Where "there are no higher, no specifically
Christian principles involved . . . there is no reason to live and work
separately," but "where such . . . principles are involved, cooperation
in one and the same organization is not possible." Interestingly, principle and pragmatic considerations coincided. The community's "practical experience" demonstrated that separatism worked in education
but not in politics or labor. Kuiper also came to dour conclusions about
the results of "cooperation" elsewhere: it had either failed as badly as
separatism or produced a "superficial, vague and general Christianity
that is unworthy of the name."[36]

Furthermore, the world developing out of the war hardly lived up to the optimists' hopes. The machinations of Versailles and industrial strikes did not give much evidence of a new era of harmony, nor did inflation, unemployment, or rural depression augur well for prosperity. By late 1919 all the Dutch had written off the purported goal of the war, the League of Nations ("Worse than a vanity of vanities," Kuiper stormed; Wilson at Versailles "did what he could. And that was not much"), and advocated that America leave its European seducers to their sordid ways.[37]

On the domestic front, the entire Dutch community fell under the spell of the Red Scare. Though no one became as virulent as the *Leader*'s Henry Geerlings, who cheered every measure taken against "the mad dogs of humanity," no one doubted that "Bolshevism" was threatening America and should be firmly repressed.[38] To the particular dismay of the RCA, a new wave of debauchery swept the country in the wake of that great triumph of Good, Prohibition. More menacing to the CRC were the proposals (culminating in statewide referenda in Michigan and Iowa) to outlaw private and parochial schools. By the end of 1919 the most hopeful voices could do no better than describe the world situation as a stand-off between "confusion, bitter struggles, widespread unrest" on the one hand and "the strong, the pure and the true" on the other.[39]

More was involved than passing moods, however. The "progressive" parties had an enormous ideological stake in the war's "promises" and were discredited as these proved false. The parties reproached during the war had much to repay and they were not slow to do so. Already at the founding of the *Christian Journal* they had attacked. The Armistice, said D. H. Kromminga, marked the dawn of the age of Antichrist, not of progress; true Christians were called to combat, not "cooperation." In this "last hour" political and social concerns were the special temptation of the church. Thus the *Journal* was serving "poison" in "attractive dishes": "No one that loves the Church of Christ, no one that loves the Lord Jesus, can stand idly by and see the bride of his Lord degraded to the position of handmaid for cleaning up the dirt of this world."[40]

Herman Hoeksema, combat trained in the flag controversy of a year before, now "declared war" on the *Journal*'s "pseudo-Calvinism," which "would really have us mingle with the world . . . adopt the principles and methods of the world and deny our own."[41] With Schoolland in journalistic retirement following the demise of *De Calvinist*, Hoeksema became the leader of the party and took up the fight in the periodical traditionally belonging to its opponents. The Synod of 1918 had awarded him the doctrinal column in the *Banner* for his writing of the report against Bultema, and at the start of his tenure he fulfilled their expectations, beginning a survey of Old Testament history in an effort to correct millennialist misconceptions of the Kingdom of God. But somewhere in this exotic tale of Cain and Abel, Enoch, Jubal, and Tubal-cain, Hoeksema shifted his animus to the positive Calvinists, leaving the "unity of God's people of all ages" for the lessons of antithesis.[42]

Early history, according to Hoeksema, was nothing but the story of two distinct lines developing within the human race out of God's decision of election and reprobation. It showed that the two, though sharing the same talents and milieu, operated according to diametrically opposed "spiritual principles." Therefore they stood in an absolutely different moral light in the eyes of God, were always moving toward contradictory ends, and had nothing of significance in common. It was folly to hope that the reprobate might gradually be won over to the cause of God, for God worked in history to develop both his Kingdom and that of darkness to the full realization of their principles and enmity. The moral of the story was plain: God called the elect at every point to grow in loyalty to him and in hatred for sin and to nurture conflict, emphasize disparity, and above all forsake attempts, at once trivial and treasonous, to cooperate with unbelievers for an allegedly "natural" good.

Setting biblical history aside for the moment, Hoeksema went to the source of the Neo-Calvinist division by attacking the doctrine of common grace directly. Since "objectively speaking," "it is an inconceivability that God can show any grace at all [except] in the blood of Christ Jesus," and since "subjectively considered," "there is no receptivity in the heart of natural man for the grace of God in any sense," there could be no such thing as common grace. What seemed to be a divine blessing to the reprobate was actually a curse, for the recipient would necessarily use it for evil, thereby furthering his own damnation. Nor was there any such thing as "natural good," but only good measured by God's perfect justice. Since unbelievers could not meet that standard (as they did not participate in Christ's atonement), all they did was sin. And if general grace and general goodness did not exist, the elect had no grounds for cooperating with sinners in any cause. Thus Hoeksema issued more than a theological challenge when he finally voiced what the Antitheticals had long felt: "This 'common grace' idea we deny."[43]

A colleague of Hoeksema, Henry Danhof, repeated these themes in more richly symbolic circumstances—when he was called to substitute for the stricken Johannes Groen as principal speaker at a Christian Reformed ministers' conference in June 1919. Lecturing on the covenant of grace, Danhof turned that traditional Reformed concept into the engine of historical-antithetical development. He also showed the Antitheticals' ambivalence toward extreme millennialism. The antithesis developed "organically," thus mandating the earthly cultural task, but its full realization was nigh, the Antichrist imminent. Doing grim justice to both schools, he called the elect to prepare for the suffering of the last days, and not (as Bultema had said) for raptured bliss.[44]

Hoeksema had drawn the connection more explicitly a year before. If forced to choose between the *Christian Journal* and Bultema's millennialism, he theorized, he would take the latter without hesitation, even though he had recently written the official proscription of it.[45] Thus, whatever their differences, the Antitheticals and pietists did stand united, as the *Journal* had perceived, before a common enemy and in profound pessimism toward contemporary civilization.

If by the end of 1918 the day of Americanization was at hand, then by the end of 1920 the stage was set for its discordant enactment. In the wake of the war all the factions in the community had reasserted themselves in starker contrast than ever before; their generative principles had been abstracted from the realm of concrete issues and stood in naked confrontation. And in the process the definitive lines for the struggle had emerged as the defensive parties joined across the pietist/Kuyperian divide for the decisive battle.

8

The Resolution, 1921–1928

The process begun by World War I now culminated with three major events. There were two more heresy trials (besides the Bultema episode) in which the community settled its theological divisions, and there was an official pronouncement on ethics by which it defined its enduring unity. At issue in each case was the doctrine of common grace, which, positively or negatively, defined the various streams of the Dutch Reformed tradition and, as the theory relating "the people of God" to "the world," constituted the prime theological metaphor for the question of acculturation.

The first phase of the conflict centered on Ralph Janssen, Professor of Old Testament at Calvin Seminary. Born in America (in 1874, into a Christian Reformed farm family outside Holland, Michigan), influenced as a youth by Johannes Groen, and a graduate of the University of Chicago and the Free University of Amsterdam, Janssen had long been a champion of positive Calvinism. His Kuyperian concept of theology as a science had earlier alarmed Foppe Ten Hoor,[1] but beginning in 1918 complaints of greater gravity drew him into fiercer battle. Suspecting that he had become infected with "Higher Criticism," Janssen's fellow professors twice asked the Curatorium (Board of Trustees) to investigate his teaching, only to see him upheld and themselves reprimanded. Upon appeal, the Christian Reformed Synod of 1920 revoked the reprimand but still denied their charges, whereupon the professors, who had so often fretted about the ideas of "popular sovereignty" in American politics, appealed directly to "our people" via a broadside, "Further Enlightenment concerning the Janssen Case."[2]

Relying on students' notes of his lectures, the four professors accused Janssen of errors great in number and variety but mostly falling into three categories. First, he diminished the special character of God's actions in history by explaining ("explaining away" in their eyes) Old Testament miracles in terms of natural phenomena (the walls of Jericho fell in an earthquake, the sun "standing still" for Joshua was really a solar eclipse, and so on). Similarly, he denied the special character of God's people by interpreting Israel's religious history as only a gradual development toward monotheism and reflective of political-factional strife. Second, Janssen implicitly challenged Scripture's divine inspiration by teaching the documentary hypothesis, challenged its distinctiveness by emphasizing the similarities between Old Testament books and contemporary literature, challenged its unity by neglecting the contribution of each book to God's plan of salvation, and challenged its infallibility by subjecting it to critical analysis. Third, all these errors stemmed from the fundamental error of exalting reason and experience over Scripture. This mistaken "starting point" (here again Ten Hoor's old complaint) reflected Janssen's conception of theology as just another science "searching" for the truth without preconceptions.

Significantly, this criticism could usually document only the "appearance" of impropriety. Janssen sometimes used methods "similar" to those of "modern science"; "in effect" or "implicitly," his teaching "tended" toward the conclusions of "higher criticism."

> We see in Dr. Janssen's instruction a rationalistic tendency emerging [which] perhaps unconsciously, more or less places reason above God's Word, a tendency which gives more importance to the demands and assertions of modern science than to the direct witness of Holy Scripture. . . . These facts are significant in themselves, but also are so many straws which tell us which way the wind blows.[3]

To justify such methods, the professors, Confessionalists all, concluded their tract with a bit of antithetical thinking bound to appeal to the historical loyalties and current fears of Hollanders. Like the seventeenth-century struggle against Arminian "Rationalism," so the present conflict with "Modernism" was part of the eternal battle of "faith" and "unbelief." Against the principle of "worldly reason," it was argued, believers should assert an infallible Bible as a matter of faith; against the naturalism of "science," they should assert the supernatural, the miraculous, the unique in God's acts. And in their own circle, the professors concluded, "our people" should attack even the first signs of the rationalist disease, knowing that their entire faith, their future as a group, and (no less) their eternal salvation were hanging in the balance.[4]

Once more, as in the Bultema case, an "American" influence was showing, only this time on the side of the prosecution. A high view of biblical authority characterized all branches of the emerging Fundamentalist coalition, but none more than the one with which the Dutch had most contact, Princeton orthodoxy. The CRC's leading light, Geerhardus Vos, had left to join the Princeton faculty twenty-five years before, and many of the community's brightest sons had since followed him there for their graduate training. All those years and more, Princeton had been battling liberal theology, especially its Higher-Critical interpretations of the Bible; Vos had been hired, in fact, at a critical stage in that struggle. Now, in the wake of World War I, the conflict reached its crisis—at Princeton and, with great fervor and fanfare, in the American world at large. No doubt the Janssen case owed something to this example, as the prosecution's allusions and tactics made clear. But it owed even more to postwar cultural dynamics. It was less an imitation than a parallel, for the prosecution also spoke out of Dutch Reformed confessionalism (as witness its appeal to the Arminian controversy), and the defense was not only willing to meet it there but to cast the issue into terms even more distinctly the community's own.[5]

In any case, at the same time the professors were publishing their pamphlet, Herman Hoeksema was spreading the controversy through his *Banner* column. For all his intellectual renown, however, he raised only the level of emotion and self-righteousness. "There is no bitterness or jealousy in my heart," he explained. "It is the love of our church and of the truth, it is the glory of God and His Word that prompts me."[6] As a result there developed, as the denomination's official proceedings quaintly put it, "unrest in the churches." "Uproar" would have been more accurate. Eight of the denomination's thirteen classes asked that the case be reopened, and some leaders even proposed the radical step of convening Synod a year early to deal with it. In June 1921 the Curatorium satisfied the belligerents, though hardly due process, by giving Janssen a year's "vacation" from teaching.

Sensing which way *this* wind was blowing, Janssen worked hard but not always wisely in his own defense. In pamphlets published in February and June 1922 he refuted his opponents' charges seriatim, giving his own version of his teaching, defending it according to Scripture and the Confessions, and—most impressively—offering abundant corroboration from the works of indisputably orthodox scholars. Notably, it was the "moderate," "American" party in this struggle that appealed (and at great length) to traditional Dutch sources. Kuyper, Bavinck, and others, declared Janssen, used the documentary hypothesis and archaeological evidence, saw theology as a progressive science, and insisted that Scripture be interpreted free from dogmatic prejudice. Moreover, they never said that God's revelation and miracles had to be supernatural in means as well as in end and intent, but always allowed for mediation through nature, culture, or the individual mind. All this and nothing more he had said, Janssen concluded; therefore, he stood "in the Reformed tradition and in the line of our best Reformed theologians both past and present."[7]

Not content with this, however, Janssen turned the charge of heresy back upon his critics, accusing them of denying common grace and of thereby placing themselves outside the Reformed tradition. Herman Hoeksema, of course, stood first in line here, but, borrowing a page from the *Christian Journal*, Janssen put the Confessionalists right behind:

> Truly the question can no longer be avoided but must be pressed in our present crisis. . . . What is the relation . . . between the denial of Common Grace by Rev. H. Hoeksema . . . and the unReformed presentation of the doctrine of Grace of Prof. Ten Hoor? . . . We believe that the source of the evil of the denial of Common Grace, and the evil of the Anabaptist inclination, lies in our School, lies in the instruction of Prof. Ten Hoor, lies also in the instruction of the other three Professors.[8]

In his own case, Janssen argued, their removal of God's grace from the natural and common had forced his critics to denigrate man's residual abilities and misconceive the nature of miracles, revelation, and science.

However accurate, Janssen's counteroffensive did not help his cause. In the most widely read debate—Hoeksema vs. Janssen in the *Banner*, 1920–21—the antagonists became so embroiled in debate about the importance and confessional authority of common grace that Janssen never came to show how Hoeksema's "heresy" affected his conclusions about Janssen's teaching. When the *Banner* peremptorily closed its columns to the controversy, its readers were left with the impression that Janssen had avoided the "real" issue in order to hide his errors. Even when Janssen did show the connection, he rather unwisely cast the dispute in antithetical terms. In this ultimate "crisis," the "Anabaptist" and the "truly Reformed" stood opposed at every point; one must be right, the other thrown out.[9]

The opposition sustained at least one of Janssen's points, for their next pamphlet had joint Confessional-Antithetical authorship, the Confessional group consisting of the four professors and two preachers (Y. P. De Jong and Henry J. Kuiper) and the Antithetical group consisting of two other preachers (Hoeksema and Henry Danhof)—together known as "the four and four." The tract also brought the debate to its ethical nadir: it provided no new evidence but did serve up more invective and more of the same dubious tactics. But here and in Janssen's reply, one issue did receive new emphasis: the question of Israel's relationship with surrounding cultures. According to the "four and four," God's people borrowed nothing from their neighbors, especially in religion, but received the one true faith *in toto* by means of a special revelation. They also attained, by special grace, a moral level far beyond the capacities of the heathen. Thus the Old Testament taught that "Israel" should nurture its distinctiveness and its special link with God as a witness against its neighbors. To Janssen, since God used social patterns and the laws of nature to direct his people, "Israel" had much in common with surrounding cultures and could learn much of value from them. The implications for the Dutch-American "Israel" were clear.[10]

Party lines held firm throughout the dispute with only one exception: the Antithetical John Van Lonkhuyzen joined B. K. Kuiper and Johannes Groen in support of Janssen, probably out of respect for his Neo-Calvinist scholarship. *Religion and Culture* offered monthly support but by way of an overconfident—or despairing—strategy. Sometimes addressing the case directly, declaring " 'search for the truth' vs. 'possession of the truth' " a false dilemma and defending Janssen's orthodoxy "on all fundamentals," it usually settled for implication, issuing noble generalities for its readers to apply to "The Situation." Thus it advocated "progressive" orthodoxy, called for a brotherly spirit in discussions, and "deplored . . . the presence of a form of *religious fanaticism*" among "certain elements" in the denomination.[11]

But in debating by inference, *Religion and Culture* soon met its match in the *Witness,* founded by the "four and four" late in 1921 to prosecute their case monthly.[12] There Herman Hoeksema declared himself ready "to sound the alarm at the first sign of danger" from the "enemies [who] surround the church," while Louis Berkhof fearfully considered the relation of orthodoxy to Americanization: "We must mount our guard on principle if we do not want to be swallowed up in the stream and therewith . . . lose our identity." The *Witness* could also become specific, however, as in Henry Danhof's immediately notorious article "Faith in the Spade," which belittled archaeology, science, and even general revelation. More ominously, an unsigned article in the inaugural issue warned, "The roots of our present woes lie in our Seminary. . . . Professors of Theology occupy the most strategic positions in the ranks of the Church militant. . . . Pollute a stream at its source and all its waters will be contaminated."[13]

With anti-Janssen attacks at their peak, the CRC Synod convened in June 1922.[14] Receiving two briefs from the "Janssen Investigating Committee"—the majority report being signed by three of the "four preachers" and pronouncing Janssen's teaching "unReformed," and the minority report being signed by Van Lonkhuyzen and two others and recommending further study of the matter—the Synod summoned Janssen to defend himself in person. But Janssen refused, complaining bitterly of procedural errors made in his case. (B. K. Kuiper found no fewer than twenty-four, some of them of the gravest severity.)[15] Rejecting this protest, Synod moved toward a decision with Herman Hoeksema providing an apt conclusion to the entire two-year prosecution. Responding to Van Lonkhuyzen's plea that Synod show Christian love in its voting, Hoeksema took the floor to quote from Psalm 139: "Do I not hate them, O Lord, that hate thee? I hate them with perfect hatred: They are become as mine enemies." Synod then deposed Janssen for heresy and insubordination.[16]

A year before Synod's action, *Religion and Culture* had warned that "no one can ignore the law of Christian love except at a terrible cost"; "orthodoxy degenerated into sheer suspiciousness . . . becomes a source of untold mischief." At the same time, John Kuizenga had prophesied that the coming "travesty of justice" against Janssen would be "a Banquo's ghost that will not down until justice is done."[17] Both were right, and Herman Hoeksema would soon learn that the sword of hatred cut more ways than one.

Failing to establish his orthodoxy upon appeal, Janssen's supporters adopted the second part of his strategy, attacking "Anabaptists" for denying common grace. These, said Van Andel one month after the Synod's decision, constituted "The Foe within the Gates," and John Kuizenga issued the appropriate declaration of war: "We ought to tear up by the roots the various forms of Separatism, Dualism, Pietism, Anabaptism—the whole brood whose tendency is to tear Redemption loose from Creation [and] shrink down theology to mere Christology."[18]

The "Pietists" (Confessionalists), suddenly uncomfortable, cut their Antithetical ("Anabaptist") associates off from the *Witness* staff in late 1922. Since the 1922 Synod had removed Hoeksema from his *Banner* post, the Antitheticals faced the onslaught without ally or outlet. Their pamphleteering was weighty but overmatched by the opposition: a two-year campaign by *Religion and Culture*, John Kuizenga's declarations in the *Leader*, and the pamphlets of Jan Karel Van Baalen, a recent arrival from the Netherlands and—of no little help to his prestige—a blood relative of Van Raalte.[19]

Most of the debate was composed of conflicting exegeses of Scripture, the Confessions, and Reformed theology from Calvin to Bavinck, which we need not recount here. In essence, Hoeksema and Danhof claimed that most of these sources offered no evidence for common grace and much against it, that only a few theologians taught it and did so erroneously, and that the doctrine was at most heretical and at least trivial. Their opponents maintained the opposite, that common grace was "the fountainhead of Reformed thought," and that denying it was "against Reformed theology, against our Confession, against the Holy Scripture," and intolerable in a Reformed denomination.[20]

For the rest, the two sides picked up their earlier (1919) debate over the premises and implications of antithetical thinking. Both sides

agreed that the "starting point" was God's act of election and reprobation, but Hoeksema and Danhof elaborated the consequences of this
decision as "absolute" and "organic." It is difficult to interpret their
obsession with the point because they put it to so many different uses (in
fact, *all* they did, Van Baalen parodied, was chant "organic, *organic,*
ORGANIC!!!"), but it usually seemed to offer a means to dismiss the
virtue of the unregenerate and to define the direction of history. The
"principle" of sin spread to every unbeliever, corrupting "the seed"
from which his person and behavior grew. From eternity mankind
divided into two absolutely different races, each maturing toward a
perfect realization of its principle.[21]

The organic-antithetical idea had a few simple but important consequences. First, in a phrase that came to haunt Hoeksema, it was
"utterly inconceivable" that God could show any favor to the reprobate. Second, those things usually seen as common gifts from God—a
man's talents, for instance, and the bounties of nature—were blessings
only to the elect but curses to the reprobate since they were merely
means to spiritual ends. Third, the reprobate could not do any good in
any sense of the term. "So-called 'civic righteousness'" (loving one's
family, rescuing a drowning man, punishing murder) was motivated in
their case not by love of God but by selfish desires—to enhance one's
reputation, say, or to promote mutual security. Worse, it cloaked evil as
"good" and maintained a social order that allowed it to mature. Thus,
"this civic good remains sin before God. All that is not from belief, that
arises from the impulse of the natural heart is always and only evil."
Although individual sinners did not commit every sin, they did sin
absolutely as much as they could in their place in the organic development of things. The culmination of this logic was for Hoeksema quite
plain:

> All that is in the world, and all that has ever been instituted in the
> world, is for the friends of God. In that consciousness we are not
> afraid either to say very emphatically that we are *the* people. . . . We
> say that we know it all and we only know it. We tell all the world
> boldly that they must listen to us. . . . Do you not see, dear reader,
> that this fundamental thought is inspiring, and that it becomes more
> inspiring as you grasp its truth more clearly?[22]

To Hoeksema's opponents, however, the thought was abhorrent.
Thundered Van Baalen,

> And so did Rev. Danhof come to say openly at a classical meeting
> that the marriage between two non-Christians can be nothing more
> than bestiality and the sort of love which devils have for each other!!
> This is nonsense. It conflicts with Scripture and experience.

Was Hector's love for Andromache bestial or demonic? Did classical culture find no truth and Renaissance art no beauty? Was there no moral difference between one who murdered and one who refrained out of respect for his fellowman? Rising from common sense to Scripture, what about Paul's speech at Athens, Pharaoh's daughter saving the infant Moses, Solomon's cooperation with King Hiram of Tyre, the divine institution of the state—did these not show that God favored *all* men with blessings *as blessings*, that he did restrain the development of sin, that the unsaved could perform real (though not "saving") righteousness, discover truth that the redeemed could use, and cooperate with believers in certain natural aspects of life?[23]

Here the positive Calvinists pressed home most effectively their charge of "Anabaptism." In reducing all grace to "saving" grace, in denying all worth to the unsaved world, in so insisting on the separation of "the holy," and in his individualistic innovations beyond the Confessional consensus, Hoeksema adopted the principles and consequences of the Anabaptist line. Further, he committed the very sin he had seen in Janssen. For how could he pronounce "inconceivable" that which filled Scripture unless he placed the authority of his own reason above that of the Word? Hoeksema ignored any biblical evidence that contradicted the image of the God of wrath dear to his heart, Van Baalen said. He created a "single-track" theology where the Bible laid out a "double-track" theology; he resolved a paradox left standing by Scripture because it offended his sense of rationality.[24]

This was only the first of several role reversals in this phase of the conflict. Hoeksema, who had refused to be "sidetracked" by the introduction of common grace into the Janssen case, now insisted that common grace had indeed been the issue there and that all opponents of Janssen should join him in denying it. Hoeksema also complained that he was being tried for his alleged "tendencies" and "inclinations" and defended himself, as had Janssen, by strict exegesis of the Confessions. Meanwhile, his erstwhile allies on the *Witness* adopted the tactics *Religion and Culture* had used before: Hoeksema and Danhof were sound on the fundamentals of general orthodoxy, and common grace was merely an academic tangent in Reformed theology; therefore, this "interesting debate" ought to be conducted fairly, calmly, and in good order. Now *Religion and Culture* took the bellicose, precisianist line, insisting that the church adhere to "the specific things in Calvinism" and, if need be, sacrifice peace to a vigorous prosecution of heresy.[25]

Most interesting is the fact that in this case the Confessional and Antithetical parties prided themselves on having modified "Dutch" theology to fit the unique character of America, while the positive Calvinists, continuing their appeal to Dutch authorities, reached the point of ridiculing "American" innovations. "For us the word of a Kuyper or a Bavinck is of more significance than that of an American

Christian Reformed preacher or professor," Van Baalen declared, adding satirically,

> I hope that all those on the other side of the ocean who take an interest in our condition will, since the appearance of *Van Zonde en Genade,* express themselves with a little more respect whenever our young men "struggle" . . . to develop in a few magazine articles a new life-conception that is far better than the broad work of Father Kuyper. If Netherlanders do not do this I am afraid that they will reap bitter fruits organically because of it.

Hoeksema *did* appeal to Kuyper, but solely to his "organic-antithetical" side. For the Kuyper of *Gemeene Gratie,* he had only scorn. The doctrine was "worthless," "unReformed," and, in view of Kuyper's other teachings, "illogical," "impossible," "inexplicable."[26]

The two sides, in short, brought to full consciousness the selective adaptation from their heritage that lay at the base of Dutch-American divisions. Both recognized the present controversy as the climax of a decade of turmoil involving those divisions. And both realized the stakes of the struggle: "Americanization" of "the deeper sort." The war had "hasten[ed] the inevitable process of Americanization," said Hoeksema and Danhof, and made the relationship of God's people to the world the issue of the day. In this situation, the road to destruction was paved with common grace, for it was "nothing other than the theory for conformity to the world" and would "certainly paralyze all real Christian action and bring a tidal wave of worldliness over the churches."[27] For the *Witness,* "the many dangers" threatening the Dutch in their new land could best be met by keeping the antithesis prominent and common grace subordinate. Van Baalen reversed that relation and brought this line of analysis to the clearest light:

> Do people really still believe that the unavoidable Americanization is nothing other than a language question? No, it goes much deeper. . . . Whoever believes that we can remain outside the world . . . by urging our young people to embrace the Anabaptist error is badly mistaken. It is exactly the opposite. If we understand with our children that God in His Common Grace has left much good in the world, and that even a Christian, yes especially a Christian *as a child of the Lord,* can and may be thankful for it, then our coming generation . . . shall maintain our precious Calvinism. . . . Along the line of the Anabaptist error, through the denial of the good that God gives to his creatures, we shall within a few decades die of spiritual anemia.[28]

Against this background, the Christian Reformed Synod met in June 1924 to deal with the case. At the recommendation of a study committee composed of Confessionalists and positive Calvinists, it de-

cided that Scripture, the Confessions, and the best Reformed theologians did teach God's favor toward all men and not just the elect,
divine restraint of sin through the positive operation of grace, and the
unregenerate's "civic righteousness," which counted neither as sin nor
as "saving good" but as good nonetheless. Concerning these "three
points," Synod judged that "various expressions in the writings of the
Reverends H. Danhof and H. Hoeksema cannot very well be reconciled
with what Scripture and the Confessions teach us" and ordered "both
brothers to hold to the standpoint of our Confession."[29] Far from
doing so, however, the two established their own weekly in order to
criticize the Synodical decision; there and in the pulpit they reaffirmed
their position, whereupon their classes instituted proceedings against
them that led to their ouster from the denomination.

In the light of these events, the 1924 Synod gained the reputation of
being the "common grace Synod," implying a "progressive" Americanization. But its other actions tell quite another story. Before addressing the doctrinal controversy, the Synod voted to withdraw from the
Federal Council of Churches in protest of the "liberalism" "strongly in
evidence" there. Closer to home, the Synod rejected all appeals against
its deposition of Janssen with such vigor that the prime appellant,
Quirinus Breen, "one of the church's most promising young ministers,"
resigned his office.[30] Even its statements on common grace made major
concessions to Hoeksema and Danhof's motives and "Reformed" (not
just "general") orthodoxy.

> On the other hand Synod declares that they . . . intended to do
> nothing else but teach and defend Reformed doctrines, the teaching
> of Scripture and of our Confessions. . . . It cannot be denied that, in
> the fundamental truths . . . they are Reformed. . . .

The Synod also hinted of "one-sidedness" on their opponents' part and
praised the pair's "warnings against conformity to the world," to
which the "misuse" of common grace would lead.[31]

Clearly the Synod's words reflected Confessionalist rather than
positive Calvinist thinking. Common grace was tangential, not fundamental to Reformed thought; it had more potential for danger than for
progress; it did have, almost unfortunately, scriptural warrant, but its
denial hardly menaced the church's welfare as had Janssen's teaching;
"the brethren" should discuss it "prudently, moderately, and modest-
ly."[32]

The commentaries issued in the wake of the case confirmed this
tendency. A few voices, usually academics, gave common grace Kuyper's original purpose—to validate culture, integrate it with faith, and
uphold at once non-Christian achievement and Christianity's final
claims. But more common was a narrow, negative tack: common grace
was free from Arminianism, upheld total depravity, and had evan-

gelistic, not cultural value (it made possible preaching the gospel to the unconverted).[33] As a token of the latter line's preponderance, *Religion and Culture* was swallowed by the *Witness* in the 1925 merger of the two into the *Reformed Herald*.[34]

All this does not imply, however, that the majority saw no broader cultural issues involved in the case; the Synod's closing words on the matter spelled them out graphically. Given everything else it could have said, especially in the context of common grace, the Synod's "Witness to the Churches" demonstrated most remarkably the extent of the Confessionalist-pietist triumph. Recalling the admonitions of "Dr. Kuyper," "Dr. Bavinck," and "history" concerning "all one-sided uses and thus misuses of the doctrine of Common Grace," the Synod warned,

> If we observe the spiritual tendencies of the present time, we cannot deny that there exists much more danger of world conformity than of world-flight. The liberal theology of the present time actually wishes to eradicate the boundary between the church and the world. Many are searching more and more for the great task of the church in social life. The idea of a spiritual-moral antithesis is weakening in large measure in the consciousness of many, and gives way to a vague feeling of general brotherhood. . . . The doctrine of special grace in Christ is more and more driven to the background. . . . Through the press and through all sorts of inventions and discoveries, that in themselves should be valued as gifts of God, a great part of the sinful world is intruding into our Christian homes.
>
> Against all these and more pernicious influences, which press upon us from all sides, there is a crying necessity that the church mount a guard on principle; that she, along with her adherence to the above-mentioned [three] points, also fight tooth and nail for the spiritual-moral antithesis. . . . Without ceasing may she hold fast to the principle that God's people is a special people, living from its own root, the root of faith. . . . And with holy seriousness may she call . . . her people and especially her youth not to be conformed to the world.[35]

This "Witness to the Churches" stands as the seminal document in Dutch Americanization for revealing how the community resolved its inherited tensions and for identifying the two external enemies—the "liberal theology of the present time" and the "intruding sinful world" —that would dominate its attention for the next forty years. Since it will be most convenient to examine its response to the first in the next chapter, suffice it to say here that in the '20s *all* groups denounced "Modernism," the Confessionalists no more firmly than the positive Calvinists or the RCA optimists.[36] In fact, the ablest critique came from the latter, a token of the CRC's internal preoccupation in the era but more importantly of the RCA's dawning concerns about the very basis of its acculturation.

The America with which the RCA West had cast its lot some thirty years before had been—and was to have remained—Protestant. But the 1920s' Modernist-Fundamentalist spectacle raised doubts about that Protestantism's orthodoxy (upon which the entire West insisted) and even more about its hegemony. The practical realm was more worrisome still, and precisely when it should have been less. Already in the wake of the Great War, the *Leader* had noticed some portents—"Bolshevik conspiracies" and temporary unsettledness. But over time "immorality" increased. Everything from flappers and jazz to spending sprees and stock speculation signaled a swing in "the public tone" from the disciplined to the frenzied and overheated. Worse, the *Leader* could neither explain the switch nor do anything about it. Perhaps this double loss of control—of its own explanatory categories and of Protestant norms over American life—accounted for its increasing episodes of rage. Two late-'20s emblems of the challenge drew particular heat. The presidential candidacy of a Catholic prompted an editorial series enumerating "Fifty Reasons Why Al Smith Should NOT Be President." And challenges to Prohibition brought forth hysteria. Those who voted dry, declared Henry Geerlings,

> represent the property owners, the large group of taxpayers and the settled citizenry of the nation. They are law respecting and law abiding. [But those] who are driving against the dry regime have eaten of the spawn of the darkest blood of hell, and have become victims of a diabolical depravity that unfits them for fellowship with free and intelligent men.[37]

The Christian Reformed had less a stake to lose than one to make, but their making it in the '20s atmosphere had long-lasting repercussions. The second enemy named in the 1924 resolution, "worldliness," demanded an immediate response, and what better way to make it than by official declaration? Agitation for such increased after 1925 in a flood of sermons, articles, official appeals, and no fewer than three books on the subject, representing positive Calvinist as well as Confessionalist voices. The 1928 Synod obliged by proscribing three specific "worldly amusements."[38]

The process spoke to Americanization in several ways. The three sins specified—gambling, dancing, and the theater—constituted the old "negative trinity" of Reformed-conventicle mores; Dutch America was thus consciously perpetuating its European past. But at the same time it established links to conservative Protestants neither Dutch nor Reformed. The three sins had long aroused pietists everywhere—in America, particularly the "holiness" stream of the Fundamentalist coalition. Large portions of the Christian Reformed rationale were simple plagiarism of Fundamentalist authors, and the latters' "legalistic ethics," nature-grace dualism, and resignation of the world (or certain parts thereof) to the devil—all quite contrary to Calvinist norms—permeated the 1928 Synodical declaration.[39]

The Synod showed the depth of its concern by establishing a truly remarkable set of principles for Christian conduct. It began with traditional formulas: believers have "Christian liberty," which may not be restricted by lists of regulations; recreation and entertainment are legitimate needs. But it then imposed qualifications that rendered these principles meaningless. God's children must always subordinate "the physical to the spiritual," it said, "the temporal to the eternal." Moreover, Christian liberty ends at the line of offense to others, and that line was drawn narrowly. A Christian's pleasure might not entail the slightest violation of God's law, in spirit or letter, not even by implication; nor might it give "aid and comfort" to an institution whose "general influence" was evil; nor might believers associate even indirectly with people of bad tendencies.[40]

If consistently followed, these qualifying principles would have torn up the community's whole way of life. At most they enjoined radical separation from society; at least they rendered problematic the payment of taxes, the performance of military service, and employment by an unbelieving employer or any existing corporation. But the Christian Reformed applied them only to the three symbolic sins, thereby profiling their own values. Under gambling they included all games of chance, almost any use of cards or dice, and, occasionally, the grosser forms of business speculation. They condemned it in theory for denying God's sovereignty and defying providence, and more concretely for undermining a rational, frugal mode of life: "When we enter upon the way of chance we quit the line of ordinary reason and the regular order of life. . . . The appointed way of living is not by chance but by industrious labor and by reasonable computations and calculations."[41]

Dancing and movie-going engaged greater passion because they symbolized all the decadence of the age and stemmed from the worst (by this estimate) of all sins, sexual licentiousness. "Progressive" Calvinists seemed especially worried. *Religion and Culture* had attacked Whitman and Freud as well as the flappers, and Henry Beets warned that movies "are striking at the very basic cornerstone of American life and strength . . . because what they show and teach destroys the *sanctity of marriage* and of the *family*, and makes light of *personal purity*, being subtly and insidiously and intentionally *sensual*."[42] For these two sins the Synod accordingly resorted to its more rarefied "principles of conduct." Dancing, "fundamentally immoral" "because it nourishes forbidden lusts," was proscribed even in its "most innocent" forms since these might whet the appetite for stronger stuff; similarly the theater, with "its unblushing, disgusting display of sex." Those who saw the average movie or play by that very fact violated the commandment concerning adultery. Those who attended "innocent" plays or movies supported an industry generally given over to evil, endorsed the conduct of stage and screen personnel, and developed a habit that would weaken their powers of moral discrimination and lead them to attend wicked shows too.[43]

The Synod showed its earnestness not only by insisting on strict enforcement of its prohibitions but by removing B. K. Kuiper from his position as Professor of Church History at Calvin Seminary. Kuiper had attended movies and apologized loquaciously but inadequately for his sin. Thus the definitive era of Americanization ended with the demise of one of its earliest and best advocates.[44]

The year 1928 saw several other portentous changes as well. Former *Religion and Culture* editor Edward J. Tuuk fell victim to the nervous exhaustion that ended his career, John Van Lonkhuyzen gave up his American ministry and returned to the Netherlands, and Henry Beets ended his twenty-four-year editorship of the *Banner* and was replaced by Henry J. Kuiper, who began a twenty-eight-year term of his own. Taken with the events of 1924 (the death of Johannes Groen, the passing of Foppe Ten Hoor to emeritus status, and the purge of Herman Hoeksema and Henry Danhof), 1928 marked the completion of a generational change in CRC leadership that reflected the developments of the decade: the decisive shift from Dutch to English in language, the demise of Antithetical Neo-Calvinism as a distinct mentality, the decline of the positive Calvinists, and the return to dominance by the pietists.[45]

For creativity and bitter strife, the postwar decade has no equal in Dutch-American history. This distinction did not derive from either the intellectual superiority or moral deficiency of its participants but from the pressures of the time—the demand for acculturation, the need to agree on fundamentals in order to keep acculturation from taking away too much. Thus the positive Calvinists came to grief at the very time they should have been victorious. In 1916 these "progressives" seemed likely to gain the most from Americanization. But dramatically in 1922 and subtly in 1924 the community repudiated their philosophy, reducing them by 1928 to a minority bereft of their old voices and following the pietists' lead.

So also the defeat of Antithetical Calvinism was not as total as it might appear. Although the community rejected their most extreme positions, it confirmed their fundamental impulse. The antithesis was transformed from a principle into an instinct, quite in keeping with old pietist habits, and defensiveness became the CRC's cardinal trait, the basis of any coalitions with outside groups. The demise of the Antitheticals did involve losses, however. Surpassing all in theoretical rigor and sophistication, the Antitheticals also had an independence of mind that gave them superior judgment on many social issues—the rise of American corporate capitalism, Progressivism, Prohibition, and American participation in World War I. These virtues, to an unfortunately large degree, the community let pass while keeping their more noxious corollaries—self-righteousness, overgeneralization, and a reactionary impulse (for instance, regarding labor unions).

Finally, in this decisive decade of Americanization, the issue traditionally deemed most important, the choice of language, played a secondary role. As the "Americanizers" Johannes Groen and B. K. Kuiper carried on in Dutch, so the pastors of English-speaking congregations, Herman Hoeksema and R. B. Kuiper, could agitate against the extremes of wartime patriotism while the Netherlands-born and -educated Peter Cheff preached such chauvinism. As the "forward-looking" Ralph Janssen, H. J. Van Andel, and J. K. Van Baalen appealed most (in Dutch and English) to old-world sources, so the real winner of this era, the American-born and -educated, English-speaking Henry J. Kuiper, rose to the top through his vigilance for orthodoxy and holiness, by thus sounding an old alarm in a new tongue.[46]

PART IV

THE CONSOLIDATED COMMUNITY, 1928–1948

9

A Religious Fortress

After so constant and fierce a conflict, a moment of peace must have seemed only the eye of the hurricane. In fact, however, the 1930s turned out to be the calm after the storm. Strife turned so completely to stasis, ideological argument to so ritual a repetition of fixed formulas, that the new-found harmony had to be considered forced as well as natural. The suasions were primarily psychological: the 1920s had soured everyone on intellectual bloodletting for years to come. No one would break the peace or let anyone else try. And when caution and vigilance did not suffice, official sanctions were quickly applied.

The new era lived under other shadows as well. The settlement of the "language question," while removing a source of friction, signaled other worries. Dutch immigration died in the '20s along with the language, and the earlier immigrants' ties to the Netherlands were weakening as well.[1] Three prime means of ethnic fortification were thus lost at once, with the result that the community increasingly came to conceive of itself as small, isolated, and vulnerable, cut off from outside reinforcements, and apparently doomed by the course of history.

But history seemed to be dooming the "outside world" too. The Great Depression and Second World War lent the '30s and '40s an air of grim emergency that the Dutch took as a corroboration of their own. Consequently the outstanding feature of this era was its tone of fear, stronger than that of the prewar period and devoid of its balancing optimism. "There are so many indubitable proofs of a downward trend at the present time," said Louis Berkhof in an epitaph to the period, "that these disquieting thoughts cannot be set aside so light-heartedly."[2]

In response to all this there developed a garrison mentality, expressed alternately in strident and in doleful terms, leading variously to aggressive sorties, genteel lament, and resigned withdrawal, and touched with more than a little paranoia. Little hoping to change the world, Dutch Americans concentrated on maintaining purity and cohesion distinct from it. As H. J. Kuiper, preeminent Christian Reformed spokesman, put it,

> We shall have to fight and work much harder than we have done in the past twenty years if we are going to preserve [our heritage]. The forces that tend to obliterate . . . our distinctiveness are becoming stronger and more numerous. Unless we retrace our steps and dedicate ourselves anew . . . to the development of everything included in our Calvinistic heritage, we shall soon go the way of so many denominations . . . whose glory has now departed.[3]

Some of that heritage was already gone; the community in this period made much less explicit use of the examples and elaborate intellectual systems of its European background. These might have faded anyway, but the recent theological strife had given them an additional unpleasant connotation. So it was that "terrain," "organic," "the Revolution," and a dozen other terms largely disappeared from the Dutch-American vocabulary. But if traditional terminology was gone, inherited instincts were as vital as ever. There was little talk of "principle," but principial psychology molded most Christian Reformed thinking. So also with "common grace" and "antithesis." Continuity thus involved some devolution—from full to fragmentary knowledge, from conscious to habitual use—which tended to impair both theoretical sophistication and specific analysis.

The urge to interpret the world suffered no such diminution, however. The new situation might even have made it stronger. Three ethnic publishing houses were kept busy in the cause.[4] Both their oldest genre and their newest—the sermon and the popular religious novel (which first came into prominence in this era), respectively—conveyed operative self-conceptions and official norms. More topical works addressed certain branches of doctrine, a piece of American religious history, or social and cultural issues. The ethnic press treated these in yet more detail even though in the 1930s only religious journals remained, and these had to struggle against the financial difficulties of the Depression.

The RCA West, with its relatively less intense membership, had the most trouble. In 1933 the Depression forever silenced its Dutch-language paper, *De Hope,* and forced the *Leader* to amalgamate with the periodical serving the denomination's eastern section. Although the name of the hybrid, the *Christian Intelligencer-Leader,* mirrored the sometimes awkward alliance on which the RCA was founded, the new paper soon demonstrated a typical resolution of differences: it made a symbolic gesture (changing its name after some years to the *Church Herald*) and awarded the editorship to western pastors and professors.[5] For this reason and because of the West's overwhelming share of its circulation, the new paper differed little from the *Leader* in its independent days.[6] Still dominant was a moderate, genial pietism concerned with, in ascending order, doctrinal orthodoxy, personal religious experience, and moral probity. But the insecurity of the time noticeably modified the paper's inherited optimism. America appeared less inclined than ever to obey a stern morality, and a moralistic message no longer seemed adequate to internal needs either. Troubled by a fading identity, the West twice vetoed mergers with Presbyterian denominations and even questioned its ecumenical emblem, membership in the Federal Council of Churches. Campaigns for doctrinal education, orthodoxy, and "Reformed consciousness" appeared here as in the CRC.[7]

The CRC's pronouncements, however, made such disquiet seem like the fondest confidence. The *Banner* in this era was an alarm ringing through twenty years of night. A traditional feature of the Christian Reformed, this cry received its strident and persistent qualities from the personality of the man who edited the *Banner* for twenty-eight years, Henry J. Kuiper. Indeed, as his tenure lengthened it became increasingly difficult to distinguish between the man, the periodical, and the group they served. No one else in Dutch-American history stood so aptly for the character of the people and the times. Born in Grand Rapids in 1885 (thus by birth and seniority more "American" than most of his compatriots), educated among worldlings in the public school system there, ordained at a younger age (twenty-one) than anyone else in CRC history, Kuiper had risen through the wars of the '20s as a leading prosecutor of Ralph Janssen, B. K. Kuiper, and encroachments of worldliness. In his years of greatest power, Kuiper made the *Banner* stronger than it had ever been or ever would be—*the* authority on all matters of truth and morals, a voice whose every word was to be eagerly awaited, treasured, and—most of all—heeded.[8]

In his inaugural editorial Kuiper stated that he would direct the *Banner* down the path of progressive conservatism; two months later he criticized some of his readers for excessive resistance to change.[9] These proved to be the first and last occasions such sentiments came from his pen, for Kuiper soon began his move to the trenches of nearly pure reaction. As far as he was concerned, any change except a return to the literal usages of the past marked a step in the wrong direction. Worse, both internal decay and external assault seemed continuous and inevitable: the Reformed people's own carelessness and mistaken charity endangered their heritage while the outside world, thoroughly yet somehow ever increasingly corrupt, plotted ceaselessly to crush the faithful.

Kuiper's labors constituted an aggressive reassertion of the pietist-Confessionalist mentality best articulated by his professor at Calvin Seminary, Foppe M. Ten Hoor. Though Kuiper did occasionally praise Abraham Kuyper, this amounted to lip service. The part of the Dutch past he treasured was not "Calvinism" but Reformed theology; so also his prescription for the future:

> True conservatism FOR US, a Reformed people, lies in holding fast to our precious REFORMED heritage; and true progressiveness in advancing in our theology and in our spiritual and ecclesiastical life along REFORMED lines. . . . Our only hope . . . lies in a more pronounced distinctiveness.[10]

Kuiper's cultural analysis followed the pietist pattern too. But if the CRC thus had a Confessionalist regime, it allowed Neo-Calvinist variations. The most popular appeared in the *Banner*'s column for political and social commentary, authored by the young star of the old positive Calvinist school, Edward J. Tanis. Also American-born and -educated, Tanis lost much of his prewar regard for American institutions in the debacle of the 1920s, but he still labored to overcome his group's provincialism regarding the larger developments of their society. To this end, significantly, he turned to Dutch resources, presenting a modified Kuyperian outlook, a fair acquaintance with Dutch Neo-Calvinism's interwar adaptations, and a dedication to its extraecclesiastical mandates. All these were colored, however, by the pessimistic, defensive tones of the time.[11]

The Kuyperian cause gained momentum with the founding in 1935 of the *Calvin Forum*. Largely written by Christian Reformed academics, the *Forum* would bring Americanized Neo-Calvinism to its classic form.[12] This included above all the presuppositionalist method of critique and a venerable calling; as its inaugural issue declared, the *Forum* intended to "take the whole sweep of human thought and culture into its purview. . . . Calvinism is a matter of an all-inclusive world-and-life view."[13] Thus it reviewed art and literature, world and national politics, education and science, social trends and problems, as well as theology and philosophy. It also managed to harness the contrary impulses that had split Neo-Calvinism in the past. It did not endorse automatic antithesis or principial separation, yet its mood was pessimistic, its tone combative, its ruling concern the ubiquitous threats of secularistic culture. Common grace existed, but total depravity was more obvious. Finally, the *Forum* tried to practice the old formula of submerging ethnicity in religion—this by establishing connections with Calvinists elsewhere. Besides steady references to the history and programs of Dutch Neo-Calvinism, it promoted international Calvinistic conferences and Calvinistic study groups throughout the United States, and regularly published newsletters from Calvinists in Hungary, Great Britain, South Africa, Australia, Indonesia, and India.

The larger community regarded this strategy with more ambivalence. Some countenanced the passing of ethnic identity entirely as long as the vital elements of religion endured. One popular novel, set among the Dutch in Iowa, casually accepted ethnic intermarriage and the "American" modification of Dutch names—in general, a vigorous boiling of the melting pot.[14] But it scorned flippancy, easy wealth, and all other deviations from a stern Protestant ethic. Since, presumably, moral character lay at the heart of both America and the Dutch immigrant purpose, assimilation mattered little provided virtue remained strong. Another romance recorded the anguish of a Dutch covenant maiden torn between a dashing "man of the world" and a bumbling Dutch-born seminarian.[15] "Vera" eventually married the "outsider," as had two of her siblings, but only after he had "come to the Lord."

While it provoked little dissent, most Dutch-Americans worked this formula to a far more restrictive conclusion. The recurrent calls to "maintain our distinctiveness" never addressed anything but religious matters; yet the pattern of doctrine and mores such distinctiveness required was so particular that it entailed ethnic distinctiveness as well.[16] Conversely, religion once more served as the medium for the broadest social and cultural analysis. "America" and "American Protestantism" remained interchangeable.

By the 1930s, however, that analysis proceeded along less ethnic, more purely theological lines. The single force the Reformed had seen before—"Anglo-Saxon Methodism"—had since divided into two: "Fundamentalism" and "Modernism."[17] Since the Reformed stressed the doctrinal component of religion, it is not surprising that these movements came to monopolize their attention. It was regrettable nonetheless, inasmuch as it perpetuated their ignorance of the wide variety in American Protestantism (including, in the most relevant instance, other immigrant traditions) and made their thinking formulaic, their alternatives depressing.

That formula was established in the early '30s and reiterated constantly over the next twenty years. Fundamentalists were "brethren in Christ"; Modernists were "enemies of the Cross."

> The "opponent" to the right is our fellow-believer; the opponent to the left is on the side of the anti-Christ and cannot be recognized as a believer at all. We hope to sit . . . with the Lutheran, the Dispensationalist, Baptist, Arminian, and other orthodox believers, but not with those who deny the Christ of God and repudiate his redemptive work for sinners.[18]

Understandably, Modernism so conceived would arouse concern.

But the dimensions and passion of that concern were startling. Modernism simply dominated the intellectual agenda in this, a circle devoid of its actual presence. Such was one consequence of the symbolic use of religious phenomena. Modernism represented a mounting trend across the entire spectrum of American culture and so accorded well with the community's sense of encirclement and parlous times.

Liberal theology had taken center stage in Dutch-American consciousness in the 1920s with the Scopes trial and bitter doctrinal battles in the major denominations. The RCA, more closely attuned to the American scene, had reacted to these events quickly and well, thanks to John Kuizenga's abilities. The CRC had not been so up-to-date, owing to its internal preoccupations, so its systematic response did not begin until the 1930s.[19] Once launched, however, it soared, for the Christian Reformed had in H. J. Kuiper a superior capacity for vituperation, in Louis Berkhof the reigning voice of orthodoxy, and in the *Calvin Forum* the space required for lengthy exposition. Their vigilance compensated for the RCA's decreased fervor after Kuizenga's departure for Princeton Seminary.

Ironically, Princeton figured prominently in that episode in "the outside world" which most caught Dutch attention, the battle in the northern Presbyterian Church during the late '20s and '30s. Dutch Americans had long valued that denomination as the sole representative of orthodox Calvinism in mainstream Protestantism and so championed the cause of its conservative party and especially its leader, J. Gresham Machen. The "Orthodox Presbyterian" secession woke familiar instincts in the CRC, which contributed to the new church's Westminster Seminary a considerable amount of money and two professors, Cornelius Van Til and R. B. Kuiper.[20] The RCA's response was just as typical. Two of their most eminent figures—Kuizenga and Samuel Zwemer—stepped into the new Princeton faculty (thus contradicting the Fundamentalist principle of separation), there to uphold the moderate conservative position. The reciprocal effects were more subtle and telling. The RCA made of the incident another tie to broad church Protestantism, while the CRC experienced it as its first major "post-Americanized" event, a paradigm for understanding the stakes and the struggle in the new land.[21]

But the new land's battle was simply that of the old. Machen was cited right next to Kuyper (not entirely a compatible arrangement)[22] in an argument that largely repeated what Kuyper had said some seventy years before. The conclusion was fixed at the start. Supposedly bringing Christianity to a higher stage of development, liberal theology actually "denies just those things which historic Christianity has always claimed as its heart-truths"; therefore, it "has forfeited its right to the name 'Christian.' "[23] Within so diametric an opposition, the possibility of discussion, or even of mutual respect, vanished from the outset. The Reformed argument, like the liberal perhaps, served as a means of internal fortification.[24]

Today that argument serves best to register the profile of Reformed belief. The most insistent charge concerned authority. As they had condemned "Methodism" before the war, they now condemned Modernism as the ultimately "man-centered" faith, not bound by the Word but proceeding from the willful mind. The other preeminent theme involved the nature of man; their scorn for Modernism's belief in innate goodness and evolutionary progress reflected the Reformed axiom of human fallibility. From these two proceeded the rest. Appealing to the prosperous and powerful, Modernism taught the inviolability of the present world and normal process; thus it denied the transcendent, supernatural, and miraculous which for the Reformed longing constituted the heart of Christianity. The liberals stressed ethics and social reform; the Reformed subordinated these to metaphysics and internal redemption. In their conceptions of religion, the Modernists displayed their primordial confidence; the Reformed, their anxiety. The former saw Christianity as a general spirit, a body of myths and motifs capable of infinite mutation; the latter saw Christianity as a finite, irreducible set of beliefs the same through all the ages. The liberal preferred flux and ambiguity; the Reformed preferred permanence and certainty.

Thus far "principle against principle"; next the Reformed dissected liberal theology *vis-à-vis* its self-image. "It boasts of its modernity," said Louis Berkhof, "but as a matter of fact is nothing but a concoction of ancient errors dressed up according to the latest fashion."[25] As to the "science" that Modernists so dutifully followed, it was said that it had changed so radically in the last century that it was hardly any sure authority. Against liberalism's vaunted pragmatism, the Dutch recalled Kuyper's presuppositional psychology: all action grew out of conviction, and so the Modernist bromide "Deeds, not creeds" was at once both foolish and duplicitous, being itself an article of faith. In fact, all of Modernism's labors evinced a creed, unwritten but fully as real as that of orthodoxy.[26]

Most of all, the Reformed argued, liberalism had failed where it claimed its greatest strength—in its "realism." Its demythologizing left it unable to "satisfy the deepest needs of the soul."[27] Moreover, its conception of a God who loves but does not judge and its presumption that human nature is essentially benign provided an inadequate basis for explaining the contemporary world. "World events the last five years proclaim trumpet-tongued that God is not mocked," declared Western Seminary Professor Simon Blocker from the middle of the Depression. "Never has the universal sinfulness of human nature received more striking illustration than in the era now ended. . . ." Ten years later *Church Herald* editor Louis Benes could add World War II to the balance: "If ever in history there were a time to accept the fact of man's depravity, his insufficiency, and his utter need of God's intervention . . . it were now."[28]

Finally, the Reformed impugned the enemy's character and motives. Like Kuyper, they had long felt the sting of urbane condescension for common folk, particularly as cloaked in claims of tolerance. They responded in kind, discussing Modernism as they would a dread disease spread by unknown forces and killing all it touched, or as the roaring lion that St. Peter saw roaming the earth, seeking whom it might devour. Its favorite tactics, it was maintained, were hypocrisy and deviousness.

> [Modernism] retains the appearance of Christianity while having very little in common with it. It uses several of the old familiar terms, but pours into them a different content. . . . By this dubious practice it has ensnared many unsophisticated souls in its net.
> . . . The real protagonists of this new religion can only be described as wolves in sheep's clothing.[29]

Such reasoning sidestepped certain unsettling questions. Not once in all their deliberations did the Reformed seriously try to explain the appeal of liberalism, the problems it addressed, the questions it answered, the conditions favorable to its spread. Nor did they consider whether orthodoxy had inadequacies that liberals met or at least exploited. They could explain the movement only in terms of the perversity of the human spirit or the wiles of the devil.

To repeat, the novelty of the Reformed polemic in this period lay not in its argument but in the intensity and frequency of its applications. The Dutch heard warnings from every side, in periodicals, in theological treatises, in sermons (those on the creed but also those concerning Christian comfort and divine grace), in occasional addresses, and even in popular novels. One favorite novel, *Erich Ohlson,* had the orthodox-liberal conflict as its central problem, pitting the "godless modernism" contracted at a distant university against the old faith, love of parents, and loyalty to native region in a battle for the hero's soul. Young Ohlson is "saved" by the tender ministrations of his wife, a terrifying brush with death, and an absurd coincidence.[30] The novel *Westhaven* played local variations on this theme. Its hero, Harry Jones, had attended a "liberal" church in "the East" in his youth, there receiving only the dry husks of sociological and literary lectures. But in a small west Michigan city, where he is exiled to conquer his pampered shiftlessness, Harry is brought to Christ by the charms of a Christian young lady and the sermons of an orthodox minister. Harry's father, unfortunately, is last seen floundering in his prosperity and in the "treacherous seas of Modernism."[31]

The assault had as many targets as sources. To H. J. Kuiper, liberalism seemed to have the omnipresence usually reserved for God. Like a plague it bred wherever the religious waters had gone stagnant: in the pulpits, journals, radio programs, and Sunday School papers of mainstream denominations; in public school textbooks and the ceremonies of state; above all in state universities, sophisticated seminaries, and (most grievously) the camp of "moderate" Protestants. In words that might well have been inscribed on the *Calvin Forum*'s masthead, Clarence Bouma declared,

> The greatest menace to genuine Christianity in our day is not found in the attack of the atheist, the naturalist, and the outspoken unbeliever, but in the compromising stand of those who claim to be Christians, yet are in reality the champions of principles alien to the Christian faith.[32]

Even opponents of liberalism came under suspicion if they used new weapons or carried the fight to new ground instead of defending the old. For instance, the Reformed relegated much of Neo-Orthodoxy to the modernist camp because of its concept of revelation. Some critics did not hesitate to equate the Niebuhr brothers or even Karl Barth with Harry Emerson Fosdick. Cornelius Van Til actually declared that the primary purpose of Neo-Orthodoxy was to undermine the traditional Reformed faith.[33]

Clearly, one corollary of Antithetical thinking was potent as ever—the fear of principial infection. As in the Janssen case (which some of them had prosecuted), current CRC leaders kept close watch over "tendencies," "undue emphases," "possible implications," and "which way the wind blew." Their weathervane was extraordinarily sensitive, registering the slightest breeze, and their method of forecasting interpreted each gust as the harbinger of a hurricane. Thus Reformed treatments of American church history, no matter what their specific topic, all became commentaries on declension.[34] John Kuizenga in the early 1920s turned out to be the last advocate of progressive orthodoxy,[35] for both the *Banner* and the *Calvin Forum* urged "Withstand beginnings" as the group's motto.

The "erring cousins" on the Right posed a different problem. The salient features of the Dutch subculture—devout piety, strict orthodoxy, conservative politics, and sober if not Puritanical mores—had so many correspondences within Fundamentalism that the guardians of "distinctiveness" had good cause for alarm. In 1929 both the Reformed and Christian Reformed Churches lost entire congregations to the undenominational movement,[36] and over the next two anxious decades of depression and war, revival meetings, "tabernacle-ism," and Fundamentalist radio programs had considerable appeal in Dutch circles.

Moreover, for everyone who actually joined a sect, a dozen who remained wondered if the N.R.A. Blue Eagle might indeed be "the mark of the beast" and whether Mussolini, Stalin, or Hitler might be the Antichrist.[37] Thus H. J. Kuiper launched periodic campaigns against Fundamentalism in the *Banner* and sundry authors took to dissecting its theology. All found it "sound in the essentials" but wrong on points of critical importance. Said Kuiper, in characteristic rhetoric,

> The Arminian odors which permeate the religious atmosphere around us will surely penetrate into all . . . our religious organizations and gatherings unless we put forth every effort to fill them with the aroma of a vigorous and consistent Calvinism. . . . What will happen if Arminianism is allowed to leaven our church life? We shall lose precisely those things which are the stability and strength of our religious life and . . . the fruits of our Calvinistic conception.[38]

In resistance, the Reformed returned to the grounds of the Bultema case, dispensational premillennialism. In fact, eschatology was second only to liberalism in the attention it received during these years, creating a sizable commentary on the books of Daniel and Revelation, on dragons, saints, and the whore of Babylon. Some of dispensationalism's "errors" had been rehearsed before—its literalistic and futuristic understanding of prophecy, its double resurrections of the dead and returns of Christ, its special role for the Jews.[39] But now Reformed authorities particularly decried its sensationalism, the global fortune-telling by which the Soviet Union was found to be the biblical "kingdom of the North," Hitler's and Mussolini's names were adroitly translated into the fateful 666, and the beginning of the end was calculated to have occurred with the stock market crash, the coming of the New Deal, or the attack on Pearl Harbor.

The "constructive" phase of the commentary softened this critique, however, for the Reformed fixed on the same "signs of the times" as did catastrophic premillennialists—and reached much the same conclusion. Economic distress, global war, "apostasy" within Christendom, sexual immorality, and the centralization of society and growth of government all foretold the imminent rise of Antichrist and terrible calamities on earth.[40] The Reformed differed from dispensationalists in refusing to "rapture" the faithful out of this suffering, but their doleful readings, combined with the controlling image of Jesus as avenging judge, betokened the same profound disaffection with the course of contemporary civilization.

The Reformed-Fundamentalist congruence was most signally demonstrated in the mid 1940s when Calvin Seminary Professor D. H. Kromminga espoused a type of premillennialism possibly at odds with the Confessions. This doctrinal deviation to the "right" was treated far more mildly than the slightest alleged glimmering of Modernism.[41] Also in the '40s, H. J. Kuiper helped found the Reformed Bible Institute, an answer—and a parallel—to the famous Fundamentalist institute in Chicago named after Dwight Moody. During World War II, the CRC joined the National Association of Evangelicals, the Fundamentalist counterpart to the Federal Council of Churches (with which the CRC had affiliated in the previous war), a step Kuiper approved, for all his insistence on "Reformed distinctiveness," despite the NAE's non-Reformed creed and constituency. On the RCA side, the revivalistic style, vocal premillennialism, and treacly hymnody typical of conservative evangelicalism continued in evidence, and the community's publishers achieved their long-awaited impact outside the ethnic circle by issuing a large body of literature of the same sort.[42]

All this is evidence for seeing in Dutch America in this era an ethnic parallel to Fundamentalism. The modernist enemy, the sense of pervasive declension, the response of separation and militancy resulting in a fortress mentality, which in turn engendered a complete "underground" community—these and more the two shared.[43] Why then the sharp Reformed discomfort in the Fundamentalist presence? Certainly ethnicity was involved, but not simply in terms of a drive to maintain community; rather they sought to preserve a cultural heritage that, as immigrant leaders had seen, infused Reformed religion with qualities and conceptions at variance with those of American evangelicalism.

The most obvious difference lay in spiritual styles. With the Fundamentalist "Sunday morning" of "black gown and immense dignity" the Dutch had no quarrel, but its "vaudeville with xylophone and frenzied indignity on Sunday evening" was something else.[44] The whole revivalist focus of religion into intense personal feeling was seen as misguided. It was functionally Arminian, trimming God to human cloth. Surely the Lord of the cosmos had purposes beyond the "saved" individual and the present moment. Surely he held a distance and unfathomability that the faithful had to respect.[45]

The Reformed counterorientation was toward covenant, not revival; history, not the millennium. The covenant grounded individuals in the present *body* of the faithful and in the rich heritage of Christianity in its centuries of development. Both anchored believers against the trials of life and faddish "winds of doctrine." So also they impelled them into the present work of the kingdom of God—that is, to make a witness in all areas of life, not to retreat into futuristic fancies or sacred/secular dichotomies.[46] Thus the Reformed tradition offered a deep, systematic, nuanced philosophy of life equal to the challenges of modern culture—challenges that Fundamentalism, with its short and narrow compass, its emotional and individualistic approach, could not meet. "They [the Fundamentalists] are not only digging the very foundation for a sound and lasting church and spiritual life from under their own preaching," wrote Clarence Bouma, "but are also instrumental in preparing the next generation for an easy transition to the infidelity of liberalism."[47]

Thus, part of this era's tremendous stress upon creedal consciousness served to reproach the Right. As John Kuizenga said concerning "Bible-only" evangelicalism,

> To turn one's back on the historic creeds is therefore to turn one's back on what God has given us through the struggle of centuries, and to run the risk of trying to build up once more what has already been tried and found wanting. . . . To preach a creed is one of the very best methods possible of understanding the book [the Bible], of avoiding tangents and vagaries, of securing a balanced and full-orbed presentation of the Bible as a whole. . . .[48]

But for the most part theology was to bear unceasing witness against Modernism. Sermons and systematic treatises alike casually rejected the objections raised against orthodoxy over the previous hundred years and took pains to reaffirm the doctrines most offensive to the theological "Left": a limited, substitutionary, and "blood" atonement; the seven-day creation; the virgin birth; the physical resurrection, ascension, and return of Christ; and the total depravity of man. Above all they stressed the tenet that, via old Princeton orthodoxy, linked the Reformed to Fundamentalists—the authority and infallibility of Scripture. Louis Berkhof gave more space and intricate argumentation to this point in his *Reformed Dogmatics* than to any other; indeed, he made it the cornerstone of the entire three-volume edifice. Not reason, personal experience, or ecclesiastical tradition but Scripture constituted the sole source for and reliable authority over religious knowledge. "We know absolutely nothing of God's revelations . . . in Christ, except from Scripture. If this is set aside, we abandon the whole of God's special revelation."[49] Small wonder the Christian Reformed were sometimes said to worship the Bible more than God.

More significant than specific doctrines was the psychology that doctrinalism fostered. Faith became knowledge, and that not an intuitive grasping but a rational assent to specific propositions. Religious feeling became secondary in the sequence of salvation, and so also in value and importance. The regenerated mind held it in check, wary of the emotional vagaries that could lead to error and damnation. Intellectualism did not make the path to salvation any easier, however; to the contrary, it served to double its hazards, because it demanded that the genuine experience of salvation, which remained mandatory, conform strictly to the pattern cut by doctrine.[50]

The CRC's emphasis upon doctrine in these years was, in fact, unprecedented. The RCA's orthodoxy had never been so obsessive; the Netherlandic ancestors, whether Seceder or Neo-Calvinist, had never made doctrine the whole of religion as their descendants were now close to doing. Likewise, the prewar Confessionalists had given experiential piety equal place with orthodoxy and had campaigned for one among several refinements of the Reformed tradition, not—as the present generation—for the whole of Christianity against an antithetical faith. This made Berkhof's *Reformed Dogmatics* more than a mere product of the age; it made it the monument of the age. As Professor of Systematic Theology at Calvin Seminary for two decades and president of that institution for fourteen years, Berkhof already had unsurpassed influence over the training of the CRC's future leaders. His *summa* was meant to follow them into their parish studies, and its one-volume distillation, *Manual of Reformed Doctrine,* extended his influence on the rank and file; it would be used to catechize the young for thirty-five years.[51] In either format, Berkhof's intent was clear. Here was a final, comprehensive statement of the true faith and a touchstone with which to test all other opinion. As he said in the preface to his *Manual,*

> The work seemed particularly important to me in view of the widespread doctrinal indifference of the present day, of the resulting superficiality and confusion in the minds of many professing Christians, of the insidious errors that are zealously propagated even from the pulpits, and of the alarming increase of all kinds of sects that are springing up like mushrooms on every side. If there ever was a time when the church ought to guard her precious heritage, the deposit of the truth that was entrusted to her care, that time is now.[52]

But in building this fortress the Christian Reformed trapped themselves in a paradox. For all the contempt they poured upon liberal Rationalism, their own structure was exceedingly rationalized. Berkhof's work, the model of faith, was well-ordered, logically argued, and thoroughly systematic; it was filled with prooftexts, rebuttals, and appeals to authorities ancient and Reformed, and utterly devoid of imagination and feeling. With the ascendance of doctrinalism, the instinctual dimension Kuyper and Bavinck had so valued in the faith almost vanished. This generation had no place for a vibrant "folk consciousness" breaking down the confinements of the intellect; rather, those confinements seemed the ultimate protection. The new structure had advantages, undoubtedly. The Reformed now could readily detect and repel external assault, internal digression, and all the threats that variety posed. But all the while they were opening themselves to the very problems they perceived in liberalism: the insufficiency of reason alone before the needs of the soul, and contradictions from daily life.

The RCA did not follow this path quite so far, but it did add appeals to denominational loyalty per se. Its involvement from the very outset in American history lent itself readily to such purposes; so did promotion of the denomination's multiple activities. The *Intelligencer-Leader* and *Church Herald* were often little more than booster sheets for the denomination's fund-raising projects ("Greater Things," "United Advance"), colleges, missions, youth societies, and social-improvement agencies. In contrast to its ethnic sister, the RCA did not cast these programs in some epochal cause (e.g., promotion of the True Faith or Christendom's battle for survival) but rather as ends in themselves or as ways to maintain institutional prestige against the religious and secular competition. Ironically, loyalty waxed strongest where the heritage was shortest—in the church's western sector. Not only did the West supply most of the funds for the RCA's ventures and agencies, but twice (at the start of this era, 1929, and at the end, 1947) it vetoed eastern proposals for union with Presbyterian denominations. Its reasons were simply ethnic-communal. Considerations of Presbyterian orthodoxy, biblical mandate, or related issues mattered little; the prospect of being "swallowed up" mattered a great deal.[53]

All this left piety without much impulse for originality. Never before had so many sermons—by such Confessionalists as H. J. Kuiper and Louis Berkhof but also by such Neo-Calvinists as Henry Beets and J. K. Van Baalen—dealt entirely with the explication of doctrine or digressed from their topic to promote orthodoxy.[54] Certain uniquely Dutch-Calvinistic characteristics remained in evidence, such as proscription of emotional flamboyance and stress on divine sovereignty, but others, especially its social, corporate emphasis, were missing. *Leader* editor Evert J. Blekkink's series on "the fatherhood of God" never broached the correlative "brotherhood of man" but limited itself to God's transcendence and the believer's dependence. A series on the kingship of Christ by *Intelligencer-Leader* editor Bernard Mulder restricted itself to the personal realm, failing to examine any of the cultural implications that Abraham Kuyper had pointed out in his magnificent three-volume treatise.[55]

The Reformed pulpit still prescribed abstention, pilgrimage, and the faithful remnant as the normative motifs of life. If these were abused, they were also becoming surprisingly apt; tough-minded obedience before a mysterious Providence fit a darkening age.[56] Variations from this type of piety either recalled other strains in the Reformed tradition or adopted contemporary motifs. In the honorable Dutch genre of the Passion series, Henry Beets depicted the sufferings of Christ with drama enough to move the most jaded heart in his audience. In contrast, Simon Blocker, an RCA cleric, recast the gospel in the terms of the psychology of positive thinking.[57] His Christianity of "triumphant living" echoed that of his denominational colleague in New York, Norman Vincent Peale, and presaged that of Robert Schuller, at this time a Hope College student destined for greater things in southern California. Finally, the most sophisticated church in the Dutch Midwest, the Central Reformed Church of Grand Rapids, dined with the comfortable set of the Protestant mainstream. Trailing sentimental imagery of Nature and Home, sermons such as "Soul Sunshine," "Gospel Shoes," "A Mother's Day Salute," and "Philosophies False and True" espoused the "development of personality," the encouragement of "religion," and the triumph of the "spiritual" over the "material" (the warfare of spirits apparently being passé). By such faith, perhaps, the Dutch-American elite found security in troubled times: as the title of a collection of these sermons proclaimed, the early '40s were "Heavenly Days."[58]

Deflected from the pulpit, pietistic energies poured into the ethical sphere. The object of this attention was traditional, but its popularity in this era was striking: the specter of "worldliness" dominated the community's social horizon. Like orthodoxy, moral strictures provided Dutch denominations with a bond to each other, to their European ancestors, and to other conservative Protestants in America; but also, like orthodoxy, these moral strictures were now taken to a new extreme. Antiworldliness was to be the second ring in the Dutch-American fortress. As such it stood against the second current of declension. As the very Simon Blocker of "triumphant living" cried,

> The lid is off. Things are wide open. The carnal mind holds sway. License, looseness, lewdness, are brazenly rampant and contemptuous of moral imperatives and sanctions. . . . Sensuality is glorified and praised in songs of lust as heavenly and divine. . . . It is distasteful to contemplate to what extent America is becoming cursed with gambling, drinking, card-playing, dancing, smoking, and innumerable other forms of self-indulgence, unbridled behavior, undisciplined lust and lawless self-seeking. . . . The church needs more than anything else to be convicted of sin. . . . The world is full of sin. The church is full of sin. . . . May God show us our sin.[59]

Again, not everything in the world was "worldly" and not all worldly things were equally troubling. Sobriety and gentility had been placed high among Dutch ethical priorities in the prewar era—as witness the hostility toward saloons and other haunts of lower-class urban life—but the tracts of this later age showed reverence and chastity ascendant. This became clear from the simplest register of emphases, sermons on the Ten Commandments.[60]

Befitting their opposition to Modernism, Dutch ministers used every available occasion to condemn "undue" stress upon the "second table" of the Law (the items concerned with human relations) relative to the "first" (those treating man's relationship with God). Explications of the latter manifested elements of a sacral world view supposedly foreign to a modern society. In discussing profanity and the Sabbath, for instance, the Dutch pulpit did not resort to rational demonstration or utilitarian calculation. God's name and day were holy in themselves, and all "needless" work (much less pleasure) on the Sabbath and all swearing were evil per se, regardless of the consciousness or intent of the person involved.[61] This stress on reverence reflected the Reformed passion for divine authority as the bulwark of virtue and order. At the same time reverence was an appropriately personal, "spiritual" trait, yet one allowing public—even ostentatious—demonstrations of sanctity.

In such forays as they did make into second table of the Law, the Dutch accepted the 1928 Synod's reduction of immorality to sexual impurity, and felt they now had only to apply appropriate strictures to a multitude of phenomena around them: (in ascending order of concern) women's dress, popular songs, Freudian psychology, dancing, birth control (and the associated root evil of apartment living), divorce, and the movies. The pulpit did its work in this regard by detailing the prohibition of adultery the most minutely in matters of its tangents, corollaries, and implications. Nor were these just for the common folk. The *Calvin Forum* offered weighty prose decrying the evils of birth control, and a treatise on ethical philosophy by Cecil De Boer, one of the keener critics, gave economic and legal issues complex, even-handed treatment but lapsed into simplistic diatribe on matters of sex. Sex for any other purpose than procreation was gluttony; the very survival of civilization depended on self-control—absolute chastity outside marriage and severe continence within it.[62]

Popular novels played on the matter too, as the title of one, *Desires of the Heart,* attests. This book etched the community's quintessential image of worldliness when it showed the Dutch covenant girl Vera at the local country club, now whirled in her suitor's arms, now assaulted by whiskey, oaths, and praise of Sinclair Lewis in the cloakroom. Properly horrified, Vera refused any further sorties into suave Sam's world, finally winning him over to godliness instead. Alternatively, *Westhaven* taught by positive example alone. Beautiful, virginal Laura Hadley lived contentedly with her mother; Harry Jones had not the first flicker of fleshly desire during their entire courtship; the couple's physical contact before marriage consisted of a heartfelt handclasp on the occasion of Harry's religious conversion. More admirable yet was the recurrent type of the selfless neuter. The maiden daughter devoted to mother, a nurse to her patient, and bachelor minister to the fellow cleric who won the girl but almost lost his soul—all showed that Rome had no monopoly on vows of celibacy or on admiration therefor.[63]

As usual, H. J. Kuiper took the crusade to the limit. But then, having been appointed editor by the same Synod of 1928, he had good reason to think he was putting the *Banner* to its intended use. As the titles of his editorials indicate, he also qualified as the leading theoretician of sinfulness: "Worldliness: The First Stage of Modernism," "Worldlymindedness and Earthlymindedness." Nor did he mince words in pointing to the heart of the problem:

> Our present age is sex-mad, sex-crazy. Our amusements, our art, our music, our literature reek with sex filth. . . . Our age is not only brutally but frankly sensual. . . . There is no domain where sin has wrought more havoc than in that of the sexual instinct.[64]

Kuiper's arguments against his favorite target, "the godless movies," were representative of a larger psychology. First he practiced reductionism, singling out from all the movies' offenses those sexual. Then he generalized from the part to the whole, judging any given film by its worst moments and the entire industry by its worst products. Thus he concluded that commercial movies were an "open sewer," showing "unspeakable indecencies," constituting all in all a "moral bubonic plague."[65] Finally, recalling the stringent principles of 1928, he called on the Reformed to boycott the theater entirely. Discriminate attendance was not permissible, (1) because no one knew in advance whether a film was indeed "good"; (2) because the odds against purity were high, inasmuch as no movies were made from a Christian, much less a Calvinistic, point of view; (3) because occasional attendance bred "the movie habit"; and (4) because support of a single production amounted to support of the entire industry. Here was a domino theory of morals to match the fear of principial infection. To glimpse was to yearn; the slightest exposure induced total corruption. Consequently, Kuiper's antidote had familiar ingredients: abstinence, absolutism, and defensiveness.

The obsession with sexuality reflected one of the Dutch-Americans' primordial values:

> In these critical days for the kingdom of God we deem the defense and strengthening of our Christian homes to be the most urgent of all its needs. The denial of marriage as a divine institution, the breakdown of parental authority, the crumbling of the family altar, the loss of home life through the automobile, the pollution of home life through the radio, the constant, insidious, and almost invisible opposition to its Christian ideals by means of the newspaper, and many other hostile forces besides—all these are jeopardizing the Christian home and threatening to destroy it. Its enemies have never been so outspoken, circumstances have never been so subversive of its welfare as in our modern day.[66]

Their social theory had posited the home as the seed of society; their theology had made the family *the* channel of the covenant.[67] Now it was shown to have a third critical function: it provided a context in which sex itself, the most evil of man's propensities, might be domesticated, reduced to a few innocuous forms.

The RCA's more genteel bearing led them around such distasteful specificity to mourn more general evils: "A life devoid of sympathy and love, a life of selfish pleasure and personal desire—of such is worldliness."[68] They also worried more about external than internal corruption, so, instead of itemizing prohibitions, held up the old hope of regnant Protestantism, that the "leading men" of a locality could halt the march of sin by upright example. Thus they supported ecumenical institutions (such as the YMCA) designed for this purpose.

But the virtues both denominations stressed were the same. Close behind chastity and reverence came the preeminent traits of what might be called the pietistic ethic. First was diligence, which, on the ninetieth anniversary of the Van Raalte settlement, Samuel Zwemer of RCA missionary fame honored as a signal feature of "the kolonie's" motivation and heritage. Similarly, one of the more independent minds on the CRC side followed an expose of the American corporate economy with a call for individual frugality, honesty, and industriousness.[69] Popular novels predictably but pointedly castigated the idle rich. Harry Jones, a pampered college bum, was sent by his father to "Westhaven" to learn the value of hard work; his enterprise brought saving faith and true love in its train. As the Dutch maiden of *Desires of the Heart* had to learn, worldliness lurked among the decadent country club set, while piety came with the humble board of the common folk.

Notably, the driving ambition characteristic of the classic Protestant ethic had no place—officially—in the Dutch canon, perhaps because they knew it produced the very wealth that ruined character. Contentment to the point of resignation was to be the partner of diligence. Misfortune was to be borne the same way as the ridicule of the world, though, happily, God did not customarily postpone economic rewards until eternity. There were once two neighboring farmers in the Midwest, began a Christian Reformed parable: "John Smith," who ceaselessly complained about the weather, government policies, and market forces; and "Harry Baker," father of two "rosy-cheeked boys," owner of a six-year-old car, diligent in his work, "never on the street talking politics" but constant in his praise to God. Smith suffered weeds, hailstones, and one meager harvest after another, but Baker's fields escaped the scourge and brought forth abundantly. The silliness of this homily might have been excusable were it not for its circumstances: it appeared in the *Banner* in the depths of the Depression, and it came from the pen of a son of Johannes Groen.[70] Unlike his father, the child had missed the point of Abraham Kuyper's political-cultural writings; rarely were the consequences of that failure so blatant.

The pietistic mode of social thought was not new to Dutch America in the '30s and '40s; it was unprecedented only in its popularity and manifest inadequacy. Given the community's perceptions and predilections, it served sensible purposes as far as it went, elevating a distinctive religio-cultural norm against a hostile world. But it did not go nearly far enough. Inside the fortress, it left bad habits of thought. Was all religious concern for social problems "modernistic" because Modernists preached a "social gospel"? Outside the fortress it failed before the mounting horrors of the time. To talk only about the family and chastity, the Sabbath and dirty movies in the face of Depression, war, and concentration camps was to forfeit too valuable a part of the Calvinist tradition, not to mention of common humanity. For catastrophes of this magnitude, other visions were needed.

10

Calvinists in a Darkening World

Few periods could better fit the Dutch Calvinist temperament than the 1930s and '40s. War and economic calamity had always seemed the ultimate mournful measure of humanity. Now they unfolded in a drama profound enough for the most zealous world-historical Kuyperian, while evoking on the more common level an ancient trust in that Sovereign who directed destinies from afar. The situation begged for fundamental critique—of American civilization as well—and that was a task both suitable and essential for a community still somewhat alien in a new land.

That critique still envisioned a Christianized culture and cultured Christianity. Finding neither Fundamentalism, Modernism, nor Neo-Orthodoxy able—or even willing to try—to hold both at once, the Dutch reached back to appropriate one sector after another of their Netherlandic sources: theology and confessional-devotional reflection, as we have already seen; Herman Bavinck's educational philosophy rendered into the Calvin College textbook for future teachers; Neo-Calvinist theological and political principles in a 250-page compendium for general circulation; and a running Kuyperian commentary on contemporary social problems.[1]

Even so, it is surprising, given the climate of the times, that the old positive Calvinist spirit survived at all. Nevertheless, a few voices carried it on: J. K. Van Baalen and H. J. Van Andel, who had led its defense in the '20s; William Harry Jellema, by all accounts the greatest teacher Calvin College has ever had;[2] and Bastian Kruithof, who as Calvin graduate, RCA minister, Hope College professor, and *Calvin Forum* contributor was one of few to surmount the prevailing denominational division. If these spoke little of common grace per se, they worked directly from its corollary—that "the cause of God's Kingdom is the cause of religion and culture." Furthermore, they advanced that cause with eloquence, simplicity, and a sense of humor rare among their contemporaries. For instance, in a series of semipopular lectures entitled *The Christ of the Cosmic Road,* Kruithof's skillful mix of natural imagery, literary allusion, and Christian theology showed how sensitivity to art and nature could deepen faith. In the best of the popular novels of the era, he used the setting of pioneer days in Holland, Michigan, to the same end. Some settlers succumbed to materialism, bitterness, or negative Calvinism; others heard in the majesty of the Dutch Psalms and of the Michigan forest intimations of a guiding God.[3] Such use of "general revelation" transcended the one more common at the time. Theirs was genuine appreciation of nature and culture, not just the abstract legitimation needed to make Calvinism a "comprehensive world view" superior to "dualistic" systems.

This camp also reversed the usual direction of critique, away from the world's sin (which they genuinely mourned) and toward the elect. It was all very fine to chastise worldliness and Modernism (which, after all, remained external threats), but legalism and asceticism, fatalism and gloominess were well entrenched within. Dutch Americans, Van Baalen mused, had managed to absorb the worst from both ends: with the Right, neglecting the social dimensions of the gospel; with the Left, languishing in a dessicated piety. As for their millennialist persecution complex, it was a delusion. Christianity's cross in the twentieth century was not oppression by Antichrist but a well-deserved reputation for self-absorption and complicity with injustice.[4]

More generally, however, Kuyperianism in this era was bred to a defensive outlook and antagonistic tone. The *Calvin Forum* was not looking for allies or for broad-based causes that might help prevent some calamity or promote the general welfare. Not that it wished the world to suffer; it simply saw nothing in prevailing forces that promised substantial improvement. Hence it was resigned to maintaining the heritage, demonstrating the inadequacy of rival ideologies, and calculating the proper portions of praise and blame to be assigned the trends of the time.[5] The quest for "consciousness" lived on.

These attitudes followed inevitably from their controlling perception. What Kuyper had attributed to "the Revolution" the *Forum* assigned (in more "American" idiom) to "Modernism"—hegemony across the entire cultural spectrum. This unified the group's otherwise jumbled critical agenda: pragmatism, pacifism, progressive education, nonrepresentational art, opposition to capital punishment, the secularization of public values. The diagnosis fit (or was made to fit) specific instance and general category, the local scene and international affairs. Above all it explained the West's looming apocalypse. As John Kuizenga said at the 1939 Hope College commencement,

> After a hundred years or more in which man has done as he pleased
> with no fear of God before his eyes, [we know] that man can neither
> know himself nor can he behave himself, and the thick gloom of
> defeatism and pessimism and misanthropy settles down upon the
> peoples, while the staggering preparations for suicidal war go on.[6]

The heart of the matter remained, for them as for Kuyper, authority. Without authority, the structure of freedom and justice, order and
security would collapse. The difficulty was, of course, to make authority strong but not oppressive; the solution was to legitimize it in the eyes
of the people but strictly control its actual use—and this could happen
only when the consciousness of divine sovereignty imbued rulers and
ruled alike.[7] In steadily weakening that consciousness, Modernism had
fostered the West's turn to pernicious substitutes—"the people," "the
state," or "the folk"—with consequences ranging from spiritless stagnation (in France) to utter tyranny (in the USSR). It was no coincidence,
the argument concluded, that the most degenerate nation of the twentieth century (Germany) had been the bastion of liberal theology in the
nineteenth.

> The favorite dream of the 19th century was that you could destroy
> all Christian doctrine and preserve all Christian morality. . . . [It is
> now clear that] if you destroy Christian doctrine, you destroy Chris-
> tian morality. The terrible scourges of Fascism, Nazism and Marx-
> ism are the literal fulfillment of this prophecy. If you banish God,
> ultimately you destroy the reasons for a good life, and finally make
> man a worthless creature no better than the wolf or tiger.[8]

The regimes here cited served to recall Kuyper's warnings about
authority degenerating into authoritarianism. Accordingly, the *Forum*
kept most of the solution away from the state. Juridical suasions, such
as capital punishment, were in the province of the latter and should be
enhanced therein, but foundational consciousness belonged to other
institutions, particularly church and school. Thus *Forum* writers, contrary to some in their own community and many more American evangelicals, rejected campaigns to extend religious tokens in national life.
Not that they envisioned great triumphs elsewhere. Given the strength
of Modernism, the struggle would for the time be at best a holding
action. Later, the *Forum* hoped (this too borrowed from Kuyper), as the
failures of secularism became increasingly obvious, the country might
return to the alternative that faithful Christians had been keeping in
good repair.

For the rest, the *Forum* focused on specific cultural realms. Some
places it could perform only a negative function—the fine arts, for
instance, where precious little "Christian" material deserved recommendation. Jacob Vanden Bosch took the pietistic tack, condemning

modernist literature for its immoral (i.e., sexual) content. H. J. Van Andel remained relentlessly Kuyperian. Romanticism's Revolutionary principle, the rejection of aesthetic rules, had come in twentieth-century painting to its *reductio ad absurdum*. How much better (Van Andel was ever the ethnic champion too) were Rembrandt's order and balance.[9]

On the other hand, this group was well suited for positive advocacy in the area of education. Professionally, most of its members taught at Calvin College (itself largely a teacher's college in this era); ideologically, they regarded the school, along with church and home, as the seedbed of popular consciousness. Their proposal had two parts: to counter secularization they looked to separate Christian schools; to bolster authority they advocated the classical as opposed to the "progressive" philosophy of education. Religion might not be forced into public education, but the proper model of learning should be for the welfare of student and society alike. Learning, simply, was not creation of new knowledge but appropriation of established truth. The student's much-discussed "self-discovery" could occur only through immersion in and counterpoint to tradition. If this pedagogy again manifest the *Forum*'s passion for order, it also carried a quieter insistence on intellectual enrichment. Progressive education's undisciplined subjectivism and demeaning practicality undermined both, but the classical model subjected mind and will alike to eternal standards while opening the doors to the West's cultural heritage.[10]

This appreciation saved the *Forum* from pure negativism and distinguished its mentality from that of its neighbors. During World War II, for instance, Calvin President Henry Schultze complained of pressures to sacrifice the liberal arts to the "practical needs" of the current emergency. Actually, he said, such demands were just the latest expression of "the American spirit"—specialized, technical, materialistic, and present-minded. Precisely the "emergency" had made broad cultural education all the more essential, for only there could the nation find the values to direct its practical energies.[11] Closer to home the impulse cut two ways. Obviously it contradicted the pietistic contempt for culture characteristic of many *Banner* readers. On the other hand, it made a sharp contrast to the theory of education prevalent on RCA campuses. For the Christian Reformed, the distinctly Christian element of education entered at the intellectual level. Each subject was to be taught from a "Christian point of view," and the conclusions thence derived were to be compared to those of other world views. The RCA's was more a moralistic approach, emphasizing "Christian atmosphere," the personal piety of professors, the solid "character" and "life of service" thereby encouraged.[12]

The aversion to "practicality" also appeared in the *Forum*'s second field of concentration. As good Neo-Calvinists, its staff was extraordinarily inclined toward philosophy. As holistic critics, they saw American academic criticism as a mirror of popular values: the naturalism of the elite corresponded to the materialism of the masses. The first worshiped science, the second gadgetry, and together they regarded "technical, scientific progress as the great end of human living. . . . When will we learn that all these things touch only the fringe of life? When will we wake up to the fact that improvement of the tools of existence is not the same as perfecting the art of living?"[13] The concluding act of World War II clinched the argument, the *Forum* thought. If Hiroshima did not break the worship of Science and Self, these idols would soon complete the process of devouring their worshipers, just as the ancient poets had prophesied.[14]

Here was an excellent opportunity to connect with like-minded "outsiders" and to analyze all dimensions of American materialism. But introversion and the theoretical again prevailed. The *Forum*'s chief energies went to justifying religion against a perceived imperial science, although they turned out to follow a strange ecumenical path indeed. Like any other kind of thinking, the *Forum* argued, the scientific was not self-contained but proceeded from unprovable assumptions and required extrascientifically established interpretations to render its findings meaningful. Thus, maintained Calvin chemistry professor John De Vries, theories contradicting Christianity depended fully as much upon belief as did their opposites.[15] Calvin philosopher Cecil De Boer took the next step. Science constituted only one of several ways of knowing, addressed only one of several dimensions of reality, and could analyze only one of many types of data. Its achievements hardly invalidated the alternatives, and since one of these, religion, touched upon the issues of greatest significance, everyone (consciously or not) pursued knowledge there first of all. And since understanding in the religious realm required a commitment of belief, passive objectivity, supposedly the scientific pose, was utterly out of place: "these verifying consequences [i.e., religious knowledge] come only in the course of a venture to which a man is committed with his entire being."[16]

These two arguments involved an old tradition and a great paradox. The first recalled Abraham Kuyper's assertion of science's ideological presuppositions. But the second repeated, to all appearances unconsciously but nonetheless exactly, the reasoning of William James in "The Will to Believe." Here was the dread ogre pragmatism in the heart of the Reformed camp. More, the *Forum* did its borrowing in this regard precisely when it followed the strategy of principial competition. Whatever the field of battle—theories of education or natural science, society or academic disciplines, or total world view itself—the superiority of Calvinism was demonstrated by the application of a pragmatic test: the biblical account of creation satisfied human longing better than did evolution; Modernism could not endure the dark nights of the soul or explain the dark state of the world; Neo-Calvinism's ordered society would be a better place to live than the present interest-group democracy; and so on. Apparently the great war of principle against principle came down to James's conclusion: results determined the victor.

Such conundrums were not the immediate problem in political and economic affairs. In fact, the community was slow to realize the immensity of the era's crises. Regarding the Great Depression, for instance, the *Banner* showed little awareness of any economic distress until 1932 and even in that year's elections thought (along with many others) Prohibition to be the major issue.[17] On the other hand, Henry Geerlings provided coverage in the *Leader* from the very start, but always from his Chamber of Commerce office. In 1929 he assured his readers that the stock market crash was merely a temporary check on excessive speculation. For the next three years he announced that the worst was over, the corner turned. When all his predictions failed, Geerlings could only fall back on the bedrock of his faith: "We can say nothing about the cure of the situation beyond the fact that we believe in the uprightness, the humanity, the sense of brotherhood, and the ability of the men who control business."[18]

As such reactions imply, the Depression shocked Reformed Church circles more deeply than Christian Reformed. Hard upon the revolution in morals experienced in the 1920s came another challenge to their basic assumptions. Perhaps the America they so confidently celebrated contained radical flaws they had never imagined. In any case, the Depression induced one of the denomination's recurrent periods of self-examination, of cries against pleasure and softness, and reassertions of orthodoxy.[19] Meanwhile, the energy its leaders had left for economic analysis followed the pattern of moderate pietism. Their worries were traditionally conservative—about governmental interference in the economy, the dole's effects on its recipients, and so on. And their solutions were typically individualistic and "spiritual": personal character (integrity, charity, seriousness) would cure the Depression, and a vague "Christianization" ("following the example of Jesus") would put an end to the inequities it had so forcefully brought to light.[20]

The Christian Reformed nursed a bit longer the grim comfort of theological confirmation. God was punishing America for its materialism, licentiousness, and humanism; now all could see that man reaped what he sowed. Or could they? How exactly did sexual sin, Sabbath desecration, and irreligion bring on *economic* disaster? Had the Depression's worst victims been the worst offenders? H. J. Kuiper, prime exponent of this rationale, felt it necessary to add an otherworldly element by way of explanation: the Depression induced repentance, thereby delaying the final destruction of the world and allowing the church to save a few more souls.[21] When he did address the problem in purely earthly terms, Kuiper turned upon the one sector of capitalism the Dutch had always been willing to criticize, the "speculators" ("gamblers") of "Wall Street," "the unscrupulous money-changers who have undermined the very foundations of our national well-being."[22]

Upon these two points—God's purpose and Wall Street's guilt—everyone agreed. They disagreed over the solution, particularly over the solution then being applied, and most particularly over how that solution stood over against the social theory they had inherited. In other words, their discussions amounted to measuring the New Deal by Neo-Calvinism, arguing about how far the United States might depart from that ideal, how much the model itself needed revision, and in fact what the model actually entailed.

H. J. Kuiper's support of the New Deal crested in January 1934 with his approval of President Franklin Roosevelt's admonitions to Wall Street. Thereafter it declined rapidly—to mistrust by late 1934, antipathy in 1935, and shrill hostility by 1936. The reason for his shift was simple:

> We are now specially concerned with the vicious principle underlying the persistent efforts of our administration to extend the powers of the State into fields which are not its own. . . . Any intrusion of the State into matters which can be taken care of by the people themselves . . . is an evil and to be regarded as a menace to civilization.[23]

That the New Deal constituted such an intrusion Kuiper had no doubt. Thereafter he saw nothing in Roosevelt's program but an insidious extension of state power; soon he could see no other problem in American politics at all. With each succeeding election the trend seemed worse, and his denunciations kept pace.

Actually, such had been Kuiper's fear from the start. His condemnation of Wall Street had concluded, "Socialism or Communism will be our fate unless our present system is purged of its abominations."[24] And Kuiper, like his predecessors, abhorred (and caricatured) few things as much as "socialism." It was completely materialistic and anti-Christian, he maintained. It assumed man's inherent goodness and was therefore unworkable. It crushed personal liberties, sacrificed the individual to society, stifled prosperity, and installed a totalitarian state. On the other hand, while he would be "the last one to defend" capitalism, Kuiper said with less than complete veracity, that system was merely non-Christian and not thoroughly materialistic. It allowed personal liberties, "gave room" to the individual, produced prosperity, and above all correctly dealt with human nature by grounding itself in selfishness. (The warrior against worldliness praised capitulation here.) From these perceptions, principial psychology led to one conclusion. Socialism was the abyss; every extension of state power amounted to socialism; therefore, the New Deal was demonic. Capitalism's "abominations," like the Depression, would disappear if the capitalists were left alone.[25]

Kuiper's obsession with "statism" did not grow from callousness to suffering, though it often made him oblivious to it. Rather, it reflected the tenacity with which he clung to his version of Abraham Kuyper's "free and spontaneous" society. Then too, his disposition allowed him to perceive only the best possibilities in his own system, only the worst in another. This blinded him to questions he could have most profitably pursued. Had the sort of society Neo-Calvinism envisioned ever existed in America? If it had, how could it have produced and how would it have responded to an economic crisis of the magnitude of the Depression? Would a "return to laissez-faire" restore such a society? Did the present domination by corporate business—which even Kuiper recognized—in fact constitute laissez-faire? In the end Kuiper could not even allow that Roosevelt was addressing serious problems or wonder by what other means these could be solved.

The *Calvin Forum* tried to replace such reactionary Kuyperianism with a more moderate brand. It gave the New Deal, on balance, slightly favorable reviews, approving of its Social Security, collective bargaining, and regulatory measures, while rejecting Roosevelt's Supreme Court plan and alleged encouragement of CIO violence.[26] But its major concern was criticizing mindless opposition to these programs. Clarence Bouma in particular championed Roosevelt and condemned Kuiper by name for his distortions and scare tactics. H. J. Van Andel (with Bouma, one of the few professed Democrats in Dutch-American leadership) attacked not the person but an equally august premise: "Republicanism . . . has nothing to do with Calvinism, because it has nothing to do with . . . sound Scriptural principles."[27] So also with the hallowed "laissez-faire" capitalism. The two decried its origins (Adam Smith was an Enlightenment Deist—a Revolutionary, in Kuyper's terms) and its current status: "the old laissez-faire policy is not only inadequate but positively immoral in its actual operation in modern economic society. To plead for freedom in the old unrestricted sense is not to champion freedom but economic slavery." Edward J. Tanis, the *Banner*'s "current events" commentator, took the additional step of addressing corporate realities, not laissez-faire rhetoric. His survey left him less charmed than his editor by the compatibility of capitalism and human sinfulness:

> The system has given the natural man so much opportunity to reveal the worst side of his corrupt nature. . . . How true it is that in the economic life of our day souls are sacrificed for dollars! How true that human life is sacrificed all the time on the altar of selfishness and greed, and to satisfy the lust for wealth and for the social and political power that goes with wealth.[28]

Tanis also documented how the community's own traditions (the principles and policies of Calvin, Kuyper, and the postwar Anti-Revolutionary Party in the Netherlands) sanctioned state intervention and regulation in the economy. Likewise, Henry Meeter's summary of Neo-Calvinism allowed the possibility of a broad, affirmative state and noted the Anti-Revolutionaries' positive action against the depression in the Netherlands.[29] These works did not sound all of Kuyper's democratic dimension, but they communicated more of it than this generation had ever heard. Perhaps they also forestalled such reactionary excesses as the Roosevelt-Jewish-Communist conspiracy theory in the Dutch community.

Nevertheless, instinctive wariness of the state balanced every positive note with a precaution. Meeter's compendium still held out the passive, decentralized state as ideal; Tanis warned against the socialist alternative and Bouma about bureaucratic build-up and labor aggressiveness.[30] These men loved the idea of free, spontaneous society as much as H. J. Kuiper did and suffered some of the same intellectual limitations as a result. They differed from him merely in allowing—not without worry—that modern circumstances necessitated certain modifications of the old ideal.[31] The premise of this position emerged most clearly in Cecil De Boer's treatise on ethical problems. De Boer worked long exposing "laissez-faire" capitalism as vicious and hypocritical, only to declare it preferable to the alternatives of socialism or planned capitalism. The latter two had a utopian tinge, he complained; they did not follow from America's natural course of development and possessed unknown deficiencies of their own. So to earlier emphases on order and authority De Boer added a third article of the conservative credo:

> Any economic system, however just and wholesome theoretically, is necessarily subject to the ubiquity of human weakness and depravity. . . . Only if it can be shown that . . . the present system must necessarily have greater irremediable evils than some other possible system are we justified in proposing a change.[32]

A divergent line came from Henry J. Ryskamp, Professor of Economics and Sociology and dean of Calvin College, who was distinguished no less for his quiet luminosity than for his more liberal slant. Without clanging "Calvinistic" apparatus, he let social action make its own argument for total depravity and original sin. The first guilt for the Depression clearly lay with corporate business, he maintained, but only because its greater power had given it greater opportunity. *Every* social unit was incurably selfish and shortsighted. The cures for the ills of the age—honest self-examination, cooperation, and charity—were precisely the least likely responses of a selfish people. Thus Ryskamp's analysis, whether of specific legislation, the New Deal as a whole, or the international crisis, followed the same scenario to a gloomy conclusion:

> From the long time point of view, [cooperation] would have meant greater prosperity for all, but from the short time point of view that would have meant a change of policy and some sacrifice. That no one cared to do if others did not, and they could not or would not agree to do it together.[33]

This diagnosis also applied at home. How difficult it was even for Calvinists to find the will of God, Ryskamp gibed. How ambiguous was divine revelation, how complex the situation in which it had to be implemented, how inadequate to the task were neat systems of principle. His were the only *Forum* articles ending with troubled questions rather than confident proclamations. In the face of economic stagnation at home, totalitarianism abroad, and global conflagration drawing near, Ryskamp manifested a strong, struggling faith aware of the magnitude of the calamities confronting it and of the full measure of human—and Christian—weakness.[34]

Although the topic of war displaced that of economics by 1940, already in the mid '30s it had posed the foremost ethical question in American Protestantism. The RCA's deeper involvement in that world gave it priority in this dispute, by the same token placing the issue in more "American" terms than any uniquely its own.

Bernard Mulder led the pacifist party from his editorial post. Like so many others, Mulder had enlisted enthusiastically in World War I, suffered the full force of postwar disillusionment, and vowed never to forget the lessons so learned. Thus, as the next war approached in Europe, he warned his readers of conspiratorial makers of munitions, commercial interests, and British imperialism. To his consideration of the broader ethical problem he brought unmatched moral intensity and rather simple logic: since "Christ is love," all war is wrong, and Christian participation is forbidden. Mulder left aside considerations of contingency, paradox, or power in international affairs; rather, as one of his colleagues suggested, earnestness and idealism brought their own solution:

> By our Lord's token, therefore, militarism must go. The decrees of destiny have pronounced its doom. It will be cut down, and cast into

the fire. For there is a will to peace . . . the strong will of nations to understand and respect one another, to serve one another in sacrifice and love. . . . More than we dare to hope . . . the ax of the will to peace is laid at the root of the evil tree. Moral and spiritual forces will supplant militarism.[35]

The antipacifists countered with jingoism, a malicious tone, and an intellectual rigor as undistinguished as that of their opponents. At worst they hinted of subversion or fixed guilt by association: were not political and religious "radicals" prominent in the pacifist movement? In better moments they pressed an argument that was also popular in the CRC, where the friends of pacifism were fewer: first, they cited the hoary examples of Old Testament Israel, the Netherlands' eighty-year struggle against Spain, and the American Revolution to show that war could not be condemned absolutely; then they appealed to the ultimate communal values, authority and order, and mandated obedience to the government. Admittedly, since most wars did turn out to be unjust, such obedience could bring the Christian into sin, but even so he had to obey, because the complexity of the modern world made it impossible for a private citizen to determine the morality of any war while it was being waged. For the duration of the war the Christian had to defer to the government's greater wisdom, said H. J. Kuiper, "assured that the responsibility for the lives he may take will be the government's, not his."[36]

The novelty of this reasoning was a tribute to the depth of certain commitments. In no other case would these spokesmen countenance "moral environmentalism" or allow the individual to escape accountability for his own sin, much less to commit it willfully. Indeed, one wonders how long H. J. Kuiper would have sanctioned obedience if the government mandated dancing or movies instead of killing. The Dutch also endorsed here the very tenet they rejected in economics, that "the complexity of modern life" required intervention of governmental expertise. Equally interesting was the rhetorical shift. The threatening "state" of social and economic affairs gave way to "the government," "our government," or "the servant of God" in military-juridical affairs.[37] And finally there came desperate biblical exegesis. Christ's Sermon on the Mount (the favorite text of Christian pacifists) pertained only to relations among Christians, H. J. Kuiper declared; for conduct toward unbelievers, the mandates of the Old Testament Jehovah applied. An RCA pastor determined that the Decalogue's prohibition of killing did not have literal, inclusive implications like all the other commandments, but a narrow "symbolic" meaning.[38]

The notable exception to all this was Clarence Bouma's thirty theses on "War, Peace, and the Christian," one of the more sophisticated documents of the era. Conscious of the great variability of circumstance, Bouma endorsed both the yearning for peace and the duty of obedience and tried to establish a framework for resolving the resulting dilemma. The statement also displayed his cardinal traits. The traditional Calvinist, Bouma scorned Fundamentalists who welcomed war as a harbinger of Christ's return. The "tough-minded realist," he dismissed confidence in the power of love as sentimental. Above all the ideological purist, he took the occasion to emphasize the fallacies of the largest school of pacifist thought (the "Modernist-Humanist") instead of exploring how Calvinists could cooperate with others against a terrible scourge.[39]

Given the instinct for obedience, events soon rendered the discussion moot. When war first broke out in 1939, spokesmen in both churches voiced skepticism. E. J. Tanis repeated Mulder's warnings about duplicitous industrialists and English propaganda, and H. J. Kuiper recounted the "utopian," "humanistic" assumptions of those who wanted the United States to enter the war to crush tyranny.[40] But with the fall of France, the isolation of England, and especially the German invasion of the Netherlands, sentiment turned. Both Tanis and Mulder caught the first glimpse of an ideological factor in the war, and Kuiper endorsed material aid to the Allies. Still, most shared Tanis's ambivalence:

> The whole situation is a terrible revelation of human wickedness and stupidity. As Christians we are bound to condemn Hitlerism, but we are also bound to condemn the equally godless regime of Stalin in Russia. And as Christians we cannot forget that the many evils in the old capitalistic system of Europe and America are at the bottom of the present world war. In this respect all the nations have been guilty, and all should repent.[41]

The full dramatic force of Pearl Harbor was required to remove this hesitancy. In its wake, Mulder himself declared that "The record is clear. We did not seek this war. It was forced upon us. And thus may we rise to our defense, that our people may live and that freedom and democratic principles may continue." Since compliance did not have to be coerced, the hysteria, vigilantism, and hatred for the enemy characteristic of World War I were far less in evidence.[42] This was particularly true of the RCA. Its repentance for the "excesses" of the last war held, so that it celebrated a rather innocent patriotism and avoided grandiose conceptualizations. In and after this contest between "the will to power" and "the will to service," it was argued, Christians should work on hearts and institutions to eliminate hatred and injustice and thus prevent war's recurrence.[43]

CRC types could not remain that banal and so moved everywhere from the absurd to the ominous. As to the first, H. J. Kuiper located

America's war guilt in the materialism that kept her from sending more missionaries to Japan; as to the second, another minister fondly described the war as God's eagle sent to pluck the carcass of Western civilization.[44] Such theodicies, however, ran into what by now was a familiar problem. If God had sent the war to punish America's political corruption, its irreligion, its worldliness, why did both denominations have to fear most the temptations with which army life surrounded their soldier sons? Why, once again, did the instrument of God's wrath either miss or increase the sin it was sent to strike?[45] These puzzles were soon submerged in a "deeper" legitimation: Fascism was an "antichristian system of thought" for reviving paganism and deifying the state. Notably, Nazism *reinforced* everyone's belief in authority and order, being regarded (as Bouma and Kuizenga had said) as the ultimate consequence of Modernism.

This framework contained significant variation, however. H. J. Kuiper spoke of World War II as an ideological war, but never a holy one. America remained too wicked, and postwar possibilities too meager, for that. But enough of the denomination disagreed with him to make it *this* time the Christian Reformed who wrote the misty-eyed hymns to the flag and dwelt on "the bright side of the war." Of interest for the future, the most aggressive tones came from John Vander Ploeg, an Iowa minister who would succeed Kuiper as *Banner* editor in the mid 1950s.[46] For now, the shift was led by the academic and least conservative sector. The Calvin College faculty replaced its "traitorous" sympathies of World War I with vigorous expressions of patriotism. Clarence Bouma cast the conflict in ideological terms earlier and more completely than anyone else; similarly, he was least troubled by domestic violations of civil liberties.[47] In both cases Neo-Calvinism's world-historical impulse was unmistakable, as was its mix of religious, political, and philosophical elements. Nazism revived Teutonic paganism and racism; it violated religious liberty and persecuted the Jews; it regimented society and followed the ethics of force. Combine this with traditional German aggressiveness, the *Calvin Forum* concluded, and Nazism became a supreme menace to Christianity and civilization, to be resisted at every opportunity with every available means.[48] Thus Bouma interpreted the conflict exactly in the terms popular during World War I: the two sides were ultimate incarnations of antithetical principles—Hitler the incarnation of terror, tyranny, and paganism; and the Allies the incarnation of Christianity and freedom. The triumph of one entailed the annihilation of the other. Others writing in the *Forum* held back from this extreme, reflecting on American culpability and positing more restrained connections between Christianity and American democracy. But no one dared believe that anything less than the highest values of Christian civilization was at stake.[49]

This conception of the war would have important long-range effects. For the short run, it brought disillusionment hard on the heels of peace. Bouma himself greeted war's end with singularly little joy, and within three years Schultze was saying, "it is generally conceded that the nations have hated, impoverished, and killed each other in vain." Conditions had reverted to the *status quo ante*. Greed and hatred ruled international relations; Humanism and Naturalism ruled the American mind; and the populace bowed down to materialism, science, and secular culture.[50] The less excited also felt this futility. Just as he had prophesied, said H. J. Kuiper, this war had done nothing but sow the seeds for the next; the nations were unrepentant, and the United States was more sinful than ever.[51] The new editor of the *Church Herald,* Louis H. Benes, manifested the RCA disquiet by launching new campaigns for orthodoxy and purity.[52]

Disillusion bred uncertainty: "progressive" and reactionary strains emerged together, sometimes from the same pens. On the one hand, there were defenders of internationalism and critics of America's cold war posturing; for E. J. Tanis, the Pentagon's contingency plans against the Soviet Union constituted "reckless," "irresponsible," "barbaric," "unpardonable warmongering."[53] But on the other, the tolerance for suffering workers evident during the 1930s vanished with the postwar resurgence of labor unions. "Today the labor union has become the oppressor," declared H. J. Kuiper. "It is the most dictatorial force . . . the most privileged class in our country." Clarence Bouma repeated this opinion more subtly; Cecil De Boer, his successor as *Forum* editor, propounded it at great length. Similarly, with federal power enlarged by the war, anti-"State" sentiment flourished again.[54] These tendencies merely lacked their crowning element. With the "fall" of China and the Korean War, that need was supplied.

Thus the Dutch community entered the 1950s racing toward what seemed the end point of acculturation, that complex of "pure Americanism" made up of fervent nationalism and anti-Communism, celebration of "free enterprise," and antipathy to labor and the Washington bureaucracy. Such had hardly been the goal of the 1930s and '40s leadership. Even less had the postwar characteristic of uncertainty been its dominant trait. Both changes stemmed from a deeper shift, the replacement of liberal secularism with totalitarianism as the chief enemy, making nations so recently described as "Modernistic" into heirs of "Christian democracy." Such critical confusion cost some of the best insights of a generation that had labored hard to make them. The cost fell particularly on the "progressive" sector, which had most stressed acuity only to lead (as in World War I) the war effort that blunted it. Fitting these reversals, perhaps, was the sight of this new "Americanism" taking shape from a European thought pattern—specifically, the world-historical, principial, and antithetical elements of Kuyperian psychology.

In the wake of the war, the Dutch-American fortress would have to be reconsidered—defended anew, dispensed with, opened up, or redefined. All these options and more were soon proposed. But before engaging these, we should take another look around that fortress through the eyes of some who were in it, and out.

PART V

REBELLION AND REFRACTION

11

Four Renegade Novelists

Not all the Dutch who emigrated to the United States entered the ethnic community, and not all those raised in the community remained there. Of the first group, the cultural-historical record is slight. Except for a few prominent individuals, they have left little account of their motives and sentiments (none of which is assuredly representative).[1] In contrast, those who were born into the subculture but grew up to reject it are more easily traced. They form a diverse group: the farmers who moved to peripheral tracts and broke with the church, sometimes living in sin, meeting for mutual support at rural taverns; the city boys who became labor organizers, sportswriters, ballplayers, or horseplayers; the denominational college graduates who fled to state graduate schools and became distinguished scholars. But the greatest fame belongs to Dutch America's renegade novelists: Arnold Mulder, David Cornel De Jong, Frederick Manfred, and Peter De Vries.

Allowing for the peculiarities of their profession, this chapter will treat these authors as spokesmen for the larger body of rebels.[2] For one thing, they represent the full range of Dutch-American social geography. De Jong, the only Dutch-born of the writers, arrived in industrial, mid-sized Grand Rapids in his adolescence; Mulder grew up in Holland, Michigan, when it was a small country town; Manfred was born and raised on a farm in northwest Iowa; De Vries, in cosmopolitan Chicago. Second, they grew up entirely in the confines of the ethnic community and received a full dose of its religiosity. Their parents seem to have been devout churchgoers and strict disciplinarians who educated their children at denominational institutions. (Mulder graduated from Hope College; the other three, of Christian Reformed background, attended Christian schools from first grade through college.) Finally, their careers were launched out of the community's pivotal moment. Mulder (born 1885) came to maturity in Holland, Michigan, in the first decade of the twentieth century—that is, just after the RCA West had come to terms with the American world. The others grew up twenty years later, graduating from Calvin College within five years of each other (1929–34), on the heels of the CRC's decisive decade of Americanization.[3] No doubt the experience of cultural collision has fed their artistic productivity. They set out torn between inside and outside, memory and desire, but therefore able to bounce native group off adopted society to the keener perception of both.[4]

Their work can serve two interrelated functions here: revealing more of the character of the community they rebelled against, and demonstrating that rebellion's thrust and bounds. These writers expose some of the underside of Dutch America, the sorrier aspects glossed over in official accounts. More inadvertently, they exhibit the community's true fundamentals, for the predominant concerns of all their work remain exactly those of Dutch ethnicity: religion, family, and sexual conduct. Their temper and "message" can be traced back to their origins. So can their weaknesses—the very insistence on spelling out a "message," on preaching like a dominie; tendencies toward reductionism and caricature; and difficulties handling intellectual matters. Thus, if their stories rehearse one after another the theme of youthful rebellion against oppressive society, if they lay out the full range of strategies that the disaffected might pursue, if they detail all the motives and arguments of the process, all its pain and relief, they come out showing no more the new worlds substituted for the old than the old persisting in the new.

ARNOLD MULDER

"He is a modern apostle, preaching a new social gospel. He preaches that gospel with a fervor that can be described only as spiritual fury. . . . He is eager to translate this vision into human action."
—FROM BRAM OF THE FIVE CORNERS[5]

Of these writers, Arnold Mulder was first in time and least in talent. He succumbed to all the flaws of the popular fiction of his time. He also remained the closest to the ethnic community; in fact, he achieved considerable standing within it, and that despite the low opinion of its ways evidenced in his books. After receiving a relatively advanced education (Hope College B.A., University of Michigan M.A., and eventually an honorary doctorate from the University of Chicago), Mulder returned to his hometown and married into one of its leading families (the Kollens, themselves connected with the Van Raaltes). He edited the Holland *Sentinel* for seventeen years, long wrote a nationally syndicated library column, and taught English literature at Kalamazoo College for two decades. His four novels appeared between 1913 and 1921, during the high tide of the Progressive movement. Mulder's work can be taken, therefore, as speaking for the "better sort" of Dutch Americans at a time when their confidence was strong but their community was at its burgeoning, most "embarrassing" stage.

Neither his attitudes nor the ethnic world thereby revealed are very pretty. In general, Mulder worked by extreme condescension and caricature. The Dutch of his west Michigan villages are a rude, narrow, suspicious lot. The best among them are merely subdued and inoffensive; the worst are reactionary bigots. The latter, of course, also hold the political power and are the most traditionally religious, and in this Mulder does catch some of the nuances in the community. In one novel the villain is a harsh pietist; in another, an antithetical Kuyperian. More genially, Mulder notes some gender role contradictions—as when he has women, officially subordinate, instructing their husbands how to vote.[6]

In such unpromising environs springs up one of Mulder's favorite character types, the sensitive lad yearning for love and learning, or, in a later phase, defying the community to win great fame in a noble cause in the outside world. *Bram of the Five Corners* (1915) depicts this figure most thoroughly. Upon discovering that his Dutch fiancee is feebleminded (a significant choice of debility), Bram breaks their engagement—for the children's sake—consequently losing his church membership and his hopes for a ministerial career. But by diligence and compassion he excels as a journalist, finds marital bliss with an "outsider," and takes up the crusade for eugenics—or, as Mulder puts it with classic Progressive charm, to rid society of its "useless lumber" (p. 82).

The decisive role in his stories, however, falls to Mulder's other model character, the older man who "lights the flame of learning" in the youngster's heart. This figure is typically an insider-outsider: ethnic-born, educated at "the state university," inspired by a "great professor," he returns to the ethnic community with the gospel of uplift and enlightenment. A large portion of this program turns out to be saving a promising boy for "higher things," a task that sometimes breaks the man but never before he sees his final triumph. *The Dominie of Harlem* (1913), on the other hand, gives that triumph greater sweep. Its hero, manly and tender, brilliant and charitable, not only inspires the boy but wins the girl and brings the entire village to a sweeter brand of faith.[7]

Obviously, these patterns contain sizable portions of autobiographical projection. It is easy to see Mulder's self-image in the young aspirant rebelling against provincial dogmatism and yearning for the realm of high culture, where great achievement, great fame, and—not least—getting even would be his. If Mulder's ascent took him no higher than Kalamazoo, he could take comfort in conceiving himself to be a beacon guiding a few bright minds out of the ethnic wilderness along the trail he himself had blazed. In any case, Mulder had no doubts about his own choices. His novels portray rebellion with unqualified approval. No mixed motives, no sense of loss mark these pages—only the picture of a perfect idealist rejecting a shabby world.

It is interesting to note, therefore, the role Mulder assigns religion. His rebellion against the Dutch brand did not imply disgust with faith itself. Quite the contrary, Mulder was sure nothing else could so elevate the race. But "the modern world" demanded a "nobler" kind of Christianity, which Mulder found in the Social Gospel. His dominie of Harlem has his heart set "afire with dreams of the social salvation of the world" at the state university and adopts the Dutch village as his "rural slum." There he brings the gospel of regular exercise and proper ventilation, of "uplift and purity" and abstinence from tobacco.[8] Love and common sense, if only fired with high ideals, will suffice in America.

Mulder supplements the "conflict of ideals" with the tensions of romance. At first this only seems to open him to the worst cliches of the genteel tradition—the blushes and swoons, the obligatory seasons of misunderstanding, the final rapture in the sunset. But there also emerge a significant ambivalence and an attempt at transvaluation on the author's part. On the one hand, Mulder finds the Dutch farmer embarrassingly earthy;[9] on the other, he specially stresses his heroes' physicality in protest of the community's spiritualized tone. Mulder's females have perpetually heaving bosoms; his young men are forever flexing their muscles, feeling "the eternal call of the race—the call that brings into being the teeming generations."[10] Yet his lovers go childless (as did he and his wife). Mulder is thus pouring all the significance the Dutch usually assigned to the family into the couple. The romantic pair is the central, sacred institution. Emotionally they always stand in the sharpest contrast to their surroundings—joy and vitality opposed to drudgery and rancor, genteel sentiment providing refuge from monotonous Calvinism. Mulder therefore concludes with a cardinal formula of American popular mythology: romantic success always interlocks with professional achievement and personal integrity; having one, the other two must follow.

For romance, ideology, and ethnicity, Mulder's preferred course is best exemplified by the title character of *Bram of the Five Corners,* who exchanges the ministry for muckraking journalism and the feeble-minded Dutch girl for the beautiful American Cordelia, herself a social missionary to Grand Rapids's benighted Poles. Mulder's strategy thus combined substitution and transcendence, rebelling against the community by rising above it to join the likeminded in the outside world. His novels display the ingredients necessary to this alliance: noblesse oblige, militant idealism, mild Protestantism, and emasculation of ethnic culture. His work's simplicity reflects the Progressive Era's confidence in these virtues; his silence after 1920, when that confidence was shattered, indicates that such a resolution was neither good for art nor likely in life.[11]

DAVID CORNEL DE JONG

This is the city of my anger, the warden of my pain.
—FROM "STATE OF SOUL IN GRAND RAPIDS"[12]

David De Jong was raised a world away from Arnold Mulder, and he showed it. Born in a Netherlands fishing village in 1905, De Jong emigrated with his family in 1918, settling in one of the poorer Dutch neighborhoods in Grand Rapids. For several years he had to work assorted odd jobs to relieve his family's financial plight; somewhat belatedly, he completed his education in 1929 at Calvin College. Having had his fill of "the Grand Rapids Dutch" by this time, he taught school for a year in rural Michigan, took an M.A. at Duke University in 1932, and started a Ph.D. program in English at Brown. At that moment he published his first novel to favorable reviews and so spent the rest of his life in Providence, writing fiction and poetry of his own and translating that of others from the Dutch. His skill and reputation climbed steadily in the '30s and peaked in the mid '40s; thereafter his career slowly declined, partly because of illness. His death in 1967 was little noticed in the literary world.

However long or far De Jong moved away, his Grand Rapids experience apparently continued to dominate his thoughts. As befits a sensitive youth who suffered much and kept it all to himself, his fiction takes an intricately psychological approach. The best part of it is overtly autobiographical, constituting the most detailed, poignant record of the immigrant experience that Dutch America has ever produced. His other novels press the themes and dynamics arising from this experience upon non-ethnic materials, and his poetry strives toward a philosophical statement about the problems his heritage bequeathed to him. In brief, De Jong exemplifies the case of the rebel unable to get over his rebellion. That accounts for the considerable power of his work, as well as its weaknesses.

De Jong's ethnic fiction recapitulates the entire immigration sequence. His first novel, *Belly Fulla Straw* (1934), comes from the point of view of the father; his last, *Two Sofas in the Parlor* (1952), from that of the son. In between, he wrote *With a Dutch Accent* (1944), an autobiographical record of his first fifteen years, and *Old Haven* (1938), a novel of village life in the Netherlands that establishes the European backdrop against which immigration occurred. Significantly, *Old Haven* is the best of the cycle, and indeed of De Jong's entire corpus.[13]

The key to *Old Haven* is its pervasive sense of harmony and wholeness. The novel's deliberate pace captures complete cycles of time—the course of a day, the passing seasons, a full lifespan. Its wealth of detail establishes the village as a microcosm of society at large. Each class— the landfolk and fisher-folk, the "leading families" and ne'er-do-wells—has its own customs, loyalties, and prejudices and fills its own place and purpose. Village traditions arch broad unities across time and space. The three-hundred-year-old family business, the thousand-year-old church tower, and the ancient courting rituals of the town square all bind the present generation to the past; in one of the book's most memorable images, the bells of the surrounding villages call the field workers home at sundown, each bell having its distinct timbre and blending with the others to sound the close of day. Thus within and among the villages there exists a great diversity, which tradition has wrought into subtle harmony. Here is a whole society, an integrated life establishing precise relations and rich meaning.

The same resonance marks the Old World portions of De Jong's other works. These pages are colorful, vibrant, and full of pleasure. In his American settings, by contrast, a grim tone prevails and people simply try to survive the worst. When things go wrong in De Jong's Netherlands (but not in his America), the memory and hope of better times endure; even the young rebel appreciates what the community has given him and part of him longs to remain.[14] While De Jong's poems show he later regained a sense of the cycles of life, he never found a new form of community, never stopped suffering its loss, never ceased searching for a replacement.

Of course, so integrated a community as Old Haven requires strict discipline to survive. Here lay the cause of De Jong's fictional parents' emigration. The father figure marries a "foreign" girl (one from a different Dutch province) who violates a host of unwritten village rules, eventually leading to the couple's being ostracized. De Jong's other stories are less romantic. *Two Sofas in the Parlor* refers to the family's "trouble back in Martensluis, something involving embezzlement, loans, and mortgages, and a breach of honor to an ancient ancestral firm, for which Mother's younger brother was largely to blame" (p. 109). *With a Dutch Accent* and *Belly Fulla Straw* tell of an ill-considered impulse to find "something better": "trials at home suddenly become unbearable in this glint of light which was America, free, lush with chances."[15]

That "glint of light" turns out to be a cruel mirage. The cattle pens of Ellis Island are bad enough, but at least quickly passed; the degradation of the Grand Rapids ghetto is not so easily escaped. In three different works De Jong shows the immigrant family crammed into a shabby bungalow on a crowded alley, factories all around. The place comes equipped with outhouse but no running water, and with a boundless supply of meddlesome neighbors. The family's landlord never misses a chance to gouge them, quoting Bavinck and Kuyper all the while; their peers exploit the children's ignorance of American ways; the father's employers, Dutch and American alike, scorn his European craftsmanship and force him to do shoddy work for poor wages, lecturing him all along on the superiority of American techniques. The most blatant viciousness wears off after a few years—not least because the family learns the defense of a hard shell and swift reciprocation—but the greed and cruelty always remain. Small wonder that De Jong recalls in his autobiography that "steadily, unflaggingly, almost unconsciously, I started to hate these self-righteous Grand Rapids Dutch"; this hatred mellowed later, "but not quite to the point of forgiveness"—nor of an even-handed fictional treatment.[16]

De Jong indicted his neighbors with succinct comprehensiveness:

> They were all neat as pins, and thrifty, and though poor and benighted, full of great moral virtues and strict behaviors, and they all kept their neighbors in rein likewise. Everyone living in them [the alleys] was stubbornly intent on being or becoming an American with Christian principles. . . .[17]

Just as reputed, in other words, religion seems the community's foundation. But the reality, De Jong contends, was quite different. Religion is not root but product—product particularly of the fear and desperation caused by immigrant uprooting. The mother in *Belly Fulla Straw*, religiously indifferent in Europe, becomes Calvinistic with a vengeance in America, partly to conform to community standards, partly as "a substitute for family ties and for the old familiar things, which were becoming only faded memories."[18] Her daughters, the much-awaited "American generation," turn this into full-fledged psychosis. Yet De Jong honored enough other characters who did have religion (including the parents in his autobiography) to make it clear that his target was the perversion of Dutch Calvinism, not its substance. Piety turned vile precisely to the extent that it served rather than mastered the community's passions.

Dutch America's real god was mammon, De Jong declares: "Be-

neath a hard surface shell of religiosity they were undeviatingly materialistic in a thousand petty ways."[19] The disjunction wrought hypocrisy, which accounted for some of the ghetto's sins. The other faults were
more ironic. By their pecuniary scale of values, the Dutch had to regard
themselves as failures—their poverty told them that, and their inno-
cence of American ways made improvement unlikely. Consequently
they adopted delusions of grandeur (conceiving of themselves as the
elect children of God, a light to the American gentiles) and of respectability. Maybe the kitchen pump poured rusty water, but there were *two*
sofas in the parlor. These poses have their comic side and a good deal of
pathos, but De Jong concentrated on their connection with the community's worst flaw, conformity. The official illusions required daily and
unanimous reaffirmation. Besides, everything quietly shaped in the old
country was now consciously prescribed, overtly enforced, and that by
the raucous gossips of the ghetto. For this, naturally, religion provided a
ready sanction. Thus, in De Jong's portrait each vice feeds upon the
other, eventually coming full circle to make a prison, or better, an
asylum. His ghetto is a seething bed of neuroses from which contempt
for self and neighbor issues in endless protestations of love for God.

While De Jong's opinion of Dutch America is clear, his assessment
of America in general is not. On the one hand, as already noted, the
admiration and beauty common to his European settings are absent
from the American. *Belly Fulla Straw* condemns the new land explicitly.
The father is treated as badly by vulgar, conceited America as by the
ghetto. His family lost, the promise of the new land gone to ashes, he
returns to the Netherlands to restore his life as best he can. On the other
hand, De Jong's autobiography describes "the real America" as a refuge from the Dutch version thereof, a conclusion shared by the boy
protagonist of *Two Sofas in the Parlor:* "Looking at all that unkempt,
uncouth, gray, and churned-up landscape" that constituted the American countryside, he thinks: "Why it's right, it is wonderful that it has no
recognizable pattern, that it can turn itself into anything whatsoever,
any which way" (p. 220). By inference the Netherlands is old, patterned
to the point of torpor.[20]

These attitudes correspond to the course of De Jong's own life. The
Netherlands is the ideal land for community, childhood, and nurture;
America is the ideal land for the individual, adolescence, and rebellion.
Perhaps "America" was also, in his eyes, the metaphor for adulthood
and modernity—not nearly so colorful as it had once been, but after all
providing for a more honest, mature form of existence. One notable
deficiency in his work—namely, a reluctance to trace male characters
past adolescence—makes such speculation problematic. At the same
time it suggests that De Jong could neither synthesize nor finally choose
between the two models of experience. For all the bravery of his auto-

biographical assertion, however, the weight of the evidence in his novels tilts the scale to the other side: America did not compensate for the
pain it inflicted.[21]

This conclusion is amplified by the other, non-ethnic half of De
Jong's work. Dashing around all his "American" settings, De Jong
manages to produce books more forlorn by far than those set in the
ghetto.[22] In these novels there can be found none of the vitality and
poignance, none of the subtle currents of affection that redeem his
memories. A reviewer's characterization of one applies to them all: De
Jong "subjects the reader to long, dreary sessions with the insides of
foolish minds," constructs "purely synthetic" characters, "tracks his
game with weighted boots and whacks at them with a bludgeon."[23] In
short, they are morality plays, set in abstraction, pitting cliches of good
and evil against each other in tedious battle, and exhibiting De Jong's
problem in bold relief. Insistently, almost helplessly, he makes over
every setting in the image of Grand Rapids. The same conjunctions of
propriety and pretension obtain, the same sources of desperation and
self-hatred, the same neurotic results and presiding old shrews. Against
them rise two character types straight out of the autobiography: the
wondering or rebellious youth battling for identity and integrity, and
the grande dame (modeled on De Jong's forceful Frisian grandmother)
who lends guidance and protection in the effort. Her virtues supply his
need. Boldly defiant, utterly solid, kind, and competent, she is above all
clearheaded. Thus recurs De Jong's autobiographical moral—the sa-
credness (no less than the necessity) of attaining, always via harsh
struggle, direct and honest perception. Only that can break the unholy
trinity that haunts De Jong's world: the "huge insensitivity, huge or-
derliness, huge respectability" that corrupt and suffocate in their
strength and betray in their inevitable fall.[24]

De Jong was equally bound to the seminal structure of his youth, as
is evident from the fact that he consistently wrote family novels.
Whether he saw family as the only substitute for the ideal community
lost in Europe, as the sole survivor of the fearful reductions of immigration, or simply as a reliable ground of communication with a non-ethnic
audience, De Jong's choice unwittingly corroborated Dutch America's
dearest social doctrine. After witnessing the animosity and yearning
that tear through his families, Dutch and American alike, one cannot
help but recall with new irony B. K. Kuiper's paean to the home as the
school of experience and locus of deepest intimacy.

The focus is implicit in De Jong's very technique. He typically
develops plot and characterization by putting family members in counterpoint. The power and color of *Old Haven* derive largely from the
novel's aura of family tradition; the parents and children of the ethnic
novels spell out among themselves the full range of responses to Amer-

ica. The non-ethnic works provide even less social backdrop, narrow-
ing the world to the confines of a single family (e.g., *Light Sons and
Dark* [1940]). In settings bereft of natural families, De Jong insistently
builds substitutes: school children replacing their fragmented homes
with a blood-brothership and adopting their teacher as mother (in *The
Desperate Children* [1949]); and boardinghouse residents, the most
atomistic members of modern society, finding their lives woven together through sheer circumstance (in *Benefit Street* [1942]).

As to the other fundamental of Dutch America—religion—it sours
De Jong's non-ethnic settings as it does his ghettos, in this case without
any redeeming exceptions. In "America" the hideous person will be the
churchgoer, and the smug establishment will use pious sanctions.[25] Yet
De Jong grants more to the religion he rebelled against than one might
think. The fathers in *Old Haven* and *Two Sofas in the Parlor* in particular have a genial faith and are kind, tolerant of weakness, and mellowed
by skepticism about man's ability to know ultimate things. *Two Sofas
in the Parlor,* De Jong's last novel on his ethnic past, closes with the
father welcoming his wondering, wandering sons back to the family
table and grace. For the faith that soothes an aged grandmother
through death; for the faith, in *Old Haven,* that is dubious of church
but stirred by the Psalms; and for the Great Beppe's shrewd appraisal of
God in *Day of the Trumpet,* De Jong shows profound respect.[26]

De Jong's fictional treatment of religion has much to do with its
psychological and ethical dimensions, and almost nothing with its intellectual dimension. The latter is left for his poetry, and even then it
derives from the former. His mature profession was a rather commonplace philosophical materialism, yet pervaded by a familiar tone.
The best critic of the poetry notes its "religious austerity," its sense of
"the harshness of God and the seasons."[27] The autobiographical child
and the adult poet both sense an awesome spiritual Power abroad in the
world, brooding in judgment, punishing the folly of man. De Jong
accepts the scourge of a pleasant land ("He . . . broke us as grass beneath / an ox," turning "the spicy land to a nunnery gray") as a check
upon illusions of comfort. In one tantalizing poem, he might even be
acknowledging the wages of his own rebellion:

> . . . let remembering be stone after stone to throw
> at the windows of this once lucid head, wherein my
> pride sat winding its skein of self so long.
> . . . Let it be so until
> hell stands at last with its legs apart
> pointing agonies and dreams to an everlasting place.[28]

Obviously, young David had listened well when the village dominie preached on sin and sovereignty. Rarely have these doctrines been better symbolized than in the opening pages of *Old Haven*, in which the town huddles at the foot of the dike, the sea thundering above it every minute, until one night it bursts through as the church bell rings the alarm in the darkness (pp. 3–16).

Even more basically, De Jong's stringent realism rests on a Calvinistic sense of human weakness. His poems speak one after another of limitation, disillusion, and slow decay, while his whole fictional program follows the first Calvinist mandate. This struggle for absolutely honest perception, this piercing of the pretenses and proprieties that mask the human problem but cannot solve it—what do these recall but that famous Puritan conscience probing relentlessly to the utter realization of sin? Even his spare salvation unmistakably evokes the sermons of his Grand Rapids youth. De Jong's stricken selves run a lonely course, ever struggling against duplicity within and without, against sentimentality and despair, a winnowed remnant on pilgrimage.

But De Jong's pilgrimage had no known destination; it led him to circle always backward to his point of departure, with ever diminishing artistic results. One insufficiency becomes apparent in his poems. Contrapuntal without resolution, in a sympathetic reviewer's words, De Jong "seems incapable of a philosophical conclusion."[29] In the context of his generation, his values were hardly original, nor even exceptional, and their potential banality was all too fully realized in his non-ethnic novels. His once-momentous struggle became tiresome when told and told again in other guises. Values authentic in that struggle lost their depth in being simply projected on a broader span. Unable either to forget his rebellion or to transcend it, De Jong bound himself and his art ever tighter to the world from which he longed to be free.

FREDERICK MANFRED

"This land's got a history, a story. It means something. . . . If you'll only stop to understand it, you'll have a good life with it."
—FROM THIS IS THE YEAR[30]

With Frederick Manfred and Peter De Vries, the shift to non-ethnic materials goes much further. But the dynamics and values of the Dutch subculture go along, refracted if not replicated. And these writers' privileged access to legendary "Dutch" characteristics that Dutch America had suppressed—Manfred earthiness, De Vries humor—must account for a substantial part of their artistic power.

Manfred's journey began in 1912 on a farm in northwest Iowa. There he passed the normal round of a Christian Reformed youth—

hard work to help support a large and close family, church twice a Sunday, catechism every week, and Christian school from the primary grades through high school. But at the same time he absorbed other lessons from the field and barn. His years at Calvin College multiplied his religious doubts and ethical chafings (both he and De Vries were marked permanently and negatively by the CRC's fixation on "worldliness" during their teens), so that his graduation in 1934 did not see him become a minister (as his dying mother had wished), but a hobo.[31]

For the next three years he wandered around the country—New York, the Great Plains, the West Coast—doing odd jobs and factory work. Then he settled in Minneapolis, working in turn as a reporter, labor organizer, public opinion poller, and political assistant (for Hubert Humphrey's first mayoral campaign).[32] After two years in a sanitarium with tuberculosis, he finally became a full-time novelist in 1944. This did not mark the end of his trials, however, for along with praise his early work received sharp criticism. Both were deserved. Finally in the mid 1950s Manfred emerged as a mature author—a stage he marked, strikingly, by moving back to the region of his birth. There, in southwest Minnesota, he has created a large body of work that effects a complete philosophical replacement for the religion of his youth—a body of work that, ironically, has been made possible only by the emotional sustenance he has drawn from the nearby Dutch Reformed community. Manfred cannot believe with his fathers, but he must live with them and will be buried with them.[33]

It was not always so. Manfred's early work resolutely tried to do without the fathers; its protagonists are all orphans, literally or figuratively. Manfred's autobiographical trilogy, *Wanderlust,* exemplifies this feature as well as his substitutionary strategy.[34] Its first part, *The Primitive,* shows the hero, Thurs, at Calvin College, oppressed by its regime of narrow dogma and repressive mores. The confrontation aggravates his intellectual difficulties with Christianity and offends his moral sense, which by now has become heavily infused with sexual desire. Thurs leaves for the East, as part two, *The Brother,* records it, to find freedom and to fight for the working man. Here, in the New York artist-intellectual set, he at last finds sex but not love, and enters leftist politics only to find Marxism as dogmatic and venomous as Calvinism. So he returns to the heartland (in part three, *The Giant*), where he gravitates to liberal politics and science only to see the first prove ineffectual and the second (at Hiroshima) ultimately destructive. Forsaking social involvement, Thurs retreats to the countryside to create a final metaphysical-ethical statement through art. Manfred thus describes a classic arc of Dutch Calvinist rebellion: rejecting one strict ideology for another and then rejecting ideology altogether; moving

|54|

GURUS OF REFORMED PHILOSOPHY

William Harry Jellema [54] personified the progressive school but was best known for teaching like Socrates, to the joy of students if not of his clerical watchdogs. H. Evan Runner [55], a convert to the Antithetical cause, attracted as devout a following through a fervent style buttressed by trilingual blackboard references (as this photo attests).

|55|

DUTCH AMERICANS IN AMSTERDAM   *Netherlandic influences continued via graduate education. Among these U.S. students at the Free University, ca. 1950, were (standing, from left) Harry Boer (third), John Vriend (ninth), Calvin Seerveld (tenth), Andrew Bandstra (twelfth), Gordon Spykman (fourteenth), and Lewis Smedes (fifteenth).*

|50| |51|

1950s COMBATANTS

George Stob [50] and Harry Boer [51] (pictured here in his days as a naval chaplain) represented the "progressive" impulse that came out of World War II. Cornelius Van Til [52] and Henry Van Til [53] articulated the Antithetical opposition.

|52| |53|

Arnold Mulder
Takes Position
at Kalamazoo

ORMER HOPEITE, AUTHOR,
EDITOR ASSUMES NEW
ROLE AS PROFESSOR

Arnold Mulder who has been a
wspaper editor in Holland for a
ore of years, has severed his con-
ections with the Holland Evening
entinel, he having been tendered
e chair in English at Kalamazoo
ollege.

The position at Kalamazoo was
ndered Mr. Mulder after the
hool year had begun, a vacancy
aving occurred through the death

|46|

|47|

DUTCH-AMERICAN NOVELISTS

Arnold Mulder [46] is pictured is the 1920s as he shifted from editor to professor. David Cornel De Jong [47] changed from aged undergraduate (inset, 1929) to vigorous author; Frederick Manfred [48] from pensive graduate (inset, 1934) to lionized alumnus; Peter De Vries [49] from elegance achieved (inset, 1931) to elegance satirized. (De Vries photo by Evelyn Floret/ People Weekly © 1980 Time Inc.)

|48|

|49|

|57| |58|

FOUR EDITORS

Louis Benes [57] edited the Church Herald *from 1945 to 1975. Peter Y. De Jong [58] managed the* Torch and Trumpet *in the '60s. John Vander Ploeg [59] took over the* Banner *in 1956 and was succeeded by Lester De Koster [60] in 1970.*

|59| |60|

THE SUBURBANIZATION OF THE CHURCH

After half a century on the Franklin campus, Calvin College and Seminary moved in the 1960s to a new site on the edge of Grand Rapids. The new campus name (Knollcrest) and architecture (cf. the old Hekman building [61] with the new home for the seminary [62]) evinced the suburban style so captivating in postwar America.

|62|

MORE INTELLECTUALS AT PLAY

Mainstays of the Reformed Journal staff pose at a picnic in the mid '70s. Left to right: Roger Verhulst, Richard Mouw, Nicholas Wolterstorff, Lewis Smedes, George Stob, James Daane, Harry Boer, Martin Van Elderen, Henry Stob.

|64| |65|

FOUR AMBASSADORS

In the 1970s, Lewis Smedes [64] and Howard Hageman [65] brought a critical Calvinistic voice to the west coast and the east, respectively, while Robert Schuller [66] and the Amway Corporation (Center for Free Enterprise [67]) reached out with the gospel of success.

|67|

|66|

from religious enclave to political cell to suspicion of all sects; judging orthodoxy by science but leaving science for humane naturalism.

Manfred's other early work selects certain segments of this cycle for closer study. *Boy Almighty* (1945) shows a young writer–labor organizer recuperating in a tuberculosis sanitarium, devoting equal time to romantic and philosophical quests. The latter involves breaking free from a boyhood religion—a vengeful, puritanical variant of Dutch Calvinism—to a new secular faith. The universe, young Eric determines, is not malevolent but merely chaotic. Neither threat nor answer lies beyond man; they reside only within him. In *Morning Red* (1956) Manfred returns to political concerns. A young journalist raised on the Bible graduates to Tom Paine and *The Rights of Man* only to learn that politics does not follow civics-book proprieties and that reformers can be as corrupt as the establishment. This sours the protagonist on political involvement, though not on his democratic convictions.

Already in these works Manfred's merits and defects are in full bloom. His unexcelled descriptive powers render moments and milieus unforgettable: a lowering bank of clouds, an enveloping snowstorm, a 1930s industrial slum, the vagabond's endless highway. Surely no one who attended Calvin College between 1920 and 1970 can read *The Primitive* with a quiet heart, and if one came to love and learning there from a constricted past, the book can be overwhelming. Yet the difficulties of the substitutionary strategy are evident too. The philosophical ruminations by which Manfred moved from Calvinism to naturalism appear distressingly rudimentary; so also his political exchange of Dutch Reformed conservative authoritarianism for celebration of "the common man." Surely by the 1950s, eighteenth-century radicalism and nineteenth-century evolutionary naturalism were utterly conventional, a condition Manfred's presentation does nothing to change. In considering them revolutionary, Manfred persisted in the opinion of his native folk, just as his reductionism and naivete recalled all too clearly their intellectual methods. Indeed, *Wanderlust* indicates that Manfred's dying mother got her wish: her son did become a preacher. As the trilogy follows its hero from Christ to Marx to Science to Nature and Love, interspersing invocations to Evolution throughout, *Wanderlust* shows how deeply Manfred had absorbed his native group's impulse toward metaphysics and holistic system.[35]

The connection even appears where Manfred deems himself farthest removed from his upbringing—on the sexual terrain. Manfred's frequent—and often graphic—renditions of sex reflect its preeminence as standard and symbol in his naturalistic vision. Sex is *the* index of health and integration, as well as of perversion and error. It is here that both intellectual left and religious right go astray, and in the same

way—by interposing dogma between instinct and action. It is sex that
the rebel's cogitations and authority's repressions either mask or express. Sexuality, in short, has the place in Manfred that the family has in
De Jong: it pervades every book, can monopolize the subject matter,
and serves to define character, construct motive, and propel plot.[36]
That such may be simplistic Manfred also proves. Some of his characters develop like cases in a psychology textbook, replete with trans-
parent devices (dreams of snakes, glimpses of mother naked), heavy-
handed symbolism (short stature, thumbsucking), and ready explanations (orgasm as epiphany being a favorite). Too often, in sum, Manfred merely inverts the image presented by his native church. Both give
sex far too much power in explaining behavior and measuring morality.
Manfred merely exchanges the church's negative conclusion for a
positive one, and in doing so demonstrates that reaction to one cliche
might only produce another, thwarting the development of a richer
vision.

By the end of his first decade as a writer (1954), these deficiencies
were evident enough; final proof came when his publisher (Doubleday)
dropped him after his trilogy was severely received. So he undertook a
dramatic new course, beginning with an appropriate symbolic gesture:
he changed his given Frisian surname, Feikema (used in his publications
thus far), to its English equivalent, Manfred. Obviously, Manfred
wanted to dissociate himself from a sullied literary reputation; but he
was also building a new, more "American" identity. At the same time
he adopted a new subject matter, the history of the upper Midwest. Far
more than a geographical expression, "Siouxland," as he labeled it, was
to Manfred a "spiritual" region. In fact, it was something of a savior,
for there he found a claimable heritage and a fictional space made for
his philosophy and style. There he could enact his values instead of
preaching them.[37]

Manfred constructed this world in a five-part "Buckskin Man"
series reviewing the different epochs of the region's past: pre-white
Indian times (*Conquering Horse* [1959]), the mountain-man era (*Lord
Grizzly* [1954]), the Indian-white wars (*Scarlet Plume* [1964]), the
eclipse of the frontier (*King of Spades* [1966]), and the 1890s range
wars (*Riders of Judgment* [1957]). As a functional postscript to the
series, *This Is the Year* (1947) brings Siouxland into its settled, agricultural stage, introducing as well the ethnic culture of Manfred's other
world. To his credit, Manfred made this history as much natural as
human and as much Indian as white. He also aimed at broader significance by using the epic form and incorporating themes and types from
classical literature.[38]

These stories, like the earlier ones, are built around the male of epic
stature, but give him rather a different fortune. If the earlier pro-

tagonists are perpetually involved in search and doubt, the later ones are distinguished for their confidence and achievement. They come sooner to self-knowledge and vocation and have sure convictions and a clear moral code. They combine self-reliance with loyalty, and honesty with charity—conjunctions unfamiliar before. Most strikingly, the Siouxland heroes operate within the social order. Where *Wanderlust*'s quest had to take the form of rebellion, and its vocation had to take the form of the artist thundering in isolation, the title character of *Conquering Horse* receives his vision precisely by following tribal ritual and at story's end becomes chief of the village, both without cost to his integrity. *Lord Grizzly*'s Hugh Glass, who must struggle for survival through weeks of solitude, might seem the archetype of individualism, but he cannot exist without the moral structure and emotional sustenance provided by the mountain men and their code.

These harmonies obtain because Siouxland makes possible Manfred's other fundamental: harmony with the land. Where this principle had been evident in his earlier novels by negation (sexual perversity and intellectual dessication are tied directly to urban environment in *The Brother* and *Morning Red* [1956]), Manfred's Indian novels in particular allow him to present a cosmology quite congruent with his own. His description of a ritual dance in *Conquering Horse* shows man sharing with the animals, the earth, the whole universe the same fabric of being:

> Every time the drummer's stick fell . . . the cottonwoods along the river seemed to thresh their leaves in an agony of joy. Through the beating drum the cottonwoods at last had heartbeat. The drumbeat became the heartbeat of all living things; the rooteds and the wingeds, the twoleggeds and the fourleggeds. The drum beat the tempo of their common origin. (P. 55)

Man could fit the earth's mold (i.e., achieve wholeness) because he had indeed been formed from its dust—not by God but by natural process. This cosmology also reverses the Christian spiritual-physical ordering. The white woman of *Scarlet Plume,* having lived captive in the Indian world, comes to see that

> the white man had things backward. . . . He believed that all things spiritual were heaven-sent. . . . The real truth was that they were earth-born. Stone was not just stone, dust was not just dust . . . but utterances dark and from far out of the deeps of time. . . . The dancing and crying . . . the drumming and the singing, were voices out of the heart of Matter. (P. 141)

In such a framework Manfred's stress upon sexuality also achieves fuller purpose. As the elemental link of the physical and the spiritual, sex becomes a sacrament, the communion of the saints of the earth, the field for realizing coherence within and with all things without.[39]

The glory of Manfred's naturalism lies not in its concepts but in its total aesthetic realization. Through a thousand details—rock formations, pebbles in a stream, acres of wildflowers under the noon sun, signs of cloud, bird, wind, and frost—his novels attain an aura of utter physicality. (*Lord Grizzly,* for one, might be "the most physiological narrative ever written.")[40] Certain episodes capture perfectly what might be considered Manfred's ideal state: resistant symbiosis with nature. Pier Frixen, the central figure in *This Is the Year,* slaughters a cow and crawls into its carcass to wait out a blizzard; Hugh Glass survives in the wilderness by wearing the skin of the grizzly that had mauled him. Above all, the land itself is the eminent presence in all these novels, its contours and constraints indelibly fixed on character and reader alike. The region becomes at Manfred's hands more than an authentic setting: it becomes a living being profound in history and meaning. From Conquering Horse's Badlands to Pier Frixen's farm, Siouxland is an unforgettable place and an artistic achievement of the first order.

That Manfred had to turn to a remote setting to realize his values, however, is a measure of their limitations. Siouxland's charm weakens as modernity sets in.[41] To redeem the more recent past, Manfred has had to return to family memory, restoring something of the ethnic factor and reconsidering his native religion. Among a good bit of dross, two of Manfred's finest works, *This Is the Year* and *Green Earth* (1977), show that recovery to be luminous indeed.

Within Manfred's corpus, these two volumes round off the regional saga and connect it with the autobiographical. A sense of completeness infuses them individually as well, as does a poignant affection missing from his other modern settings. Between the two we have a full picture of Dutch midwestern farm life in the past generation—the landscape, the pace, the customs and mores, every shade and shape of character, and the signal Dutch conjunction of piety and earthiness. The summit of that religion is the mother in *Green Earth,* a thoroughly (and surely American literature's most thoroughly developed and admired) Christian Reformed lady. Manfred honors the person and the faith both, but *it* for *her* (the reverse of her own injunction), so that her early death foretells his eventual lapse of faith. Yet in late career Manfred can recall that religion lovingly: the prayers and reading at every meal, the Christian schools and catechism classes, church and dominies and deacons—all of it as intertwined with the commonplace as any Calvinist could wish, neither caricatured nor sentimentalized, warts next to virtues, standing firm at the end.

Manfred's "father" book, *This Is the Year,* coming much earlier

(1947), treats more typical themes (principally, the issue of harmony within the man-woman-land triad) and so submerges religion entirely within ethnicity. Manfred arranges the shift, a rare if not unique occurrence in Dutch-American letters, by identifying Pier Frixen's family as Frisians—a free, heroic race—in contradiction to the plodding Hollanders who dominate the area. Pier has little use for his heritage beyond such invidious distinctions, however. A second-generation immigrant, he scorns his father's dream of establishing a colony of "free Frisians" in Iowa and boasts about using "new ways" in the "new land." The traditions persist in Pier only unconsciously, in certain personality traits. It is left to his son to absorb the legends of the race at the grandfather's knee. Himself an erstwhile partisan of melting-pot Americanism, Manfred obviously spoke some of Pier's bold declamations. Yet Pier is shown here, as everywhere, pushing a good thing too far. Having severed himself from his roots and fellows, Pier ends the story as a bum on the road, his wife dead, his son alienated, and his farm washed out.[42]

Since *This Is the Year*, Manfred has continually drawn upon his Frisian identity, but with changing purpose. Early on he used it not only to tweak Dutch noses but, given the old Frisian–Anglo-Saxon link, to endow himself with an ancestral claim on American culture.[43] That much was good 1940s political liberalism. More recently, however, in view of the mass culture that assimilation was producing, he has apparently come to find a separate place against the stream more valuable. Such also was the West, the Siouxland carved out from amnesia and "progress." Whether with Yankton Sioux, the tribal mountain men, or the Dutch/Frisian Reformed of northwest Iowa, Manfred's resonances arise only amid peoples set apart.

Perhaps Manfred's achievement in *Green Earth* indicates a reconciliation with his origins, a congruence at last between their formative influences and his artistic purpose. Manfred's rhetoric has always borne the mark of the King James Bible; the three daily readings of it throughout his youth (one at every meal) did shape his spirit, if not entirely as intended.[44] His naturalism has a distinctly Old Testament, Calvinistic cast, characterized as it is by an emphasis on elemental powers, a cosmic scope, an air of judgment, and above all by foreordination. Besides the land without, there is in Manfred always the inherited trait within, fixing destiny; for each character that trait is established early and returned to often. Consequently, Manfred's plots are usually picaresque. His characters, like his younger self, do not develop so much as pass through one situation after another on the way to their appointed home. But if the old catechism lesson on predestination struck deep, so did the one on grace: the gift of being reconciled to, and even joyful in, one's destiny. For both lessons Manfred's work itself would seem to be the best evidence, for its qualities—earthy detail, metaphysical sweep, both set to biblical cadence—are precisely those of his native faith.

PETER DE VRIES

"We have to try to be understanding. It's the least we can do, especially when we don't understand."
—FROM REUBEN, REUBEN[45]

Peter De Vries has a point of contact with each of his fellows: dreams of glory with Mulder, the psychological focus of De Jong, and a signal style (though its diametric opposite) like Manfred's. Yet De Vries has pursued a unique strategy, has in one way maintained his inheritance most while moving farthest away from it. And he has achieved the widest fame.

De Vries was born in the heart of Chicago in 1910 to immigrant parents who ran a used-furniture business. The cosmopolitan setting threatened and so reinforced the ethnic world. For the De Vries family, an additional tension came from the counterpoint of scrappy manual labor and high-flown Calvinism. In one fictional reminiscence, De Vries describes his narrator's father backing his garbage truck too close to the edge of the pit and leaping out of the machine as it begins to sink, only to disappear himself beneath the muck, finally emerging crowned with a cantaloupe rind and singing the doxology.[46] De Vries's years at Calvin College merely put these strains up a notch. He distinguished himself there as an extraordinary public speaker with what were in that context radical political tendencies. At the same time, by restructuring the college paper he showed the editorial talent that would one day serve him well. At the time it served him ill, however, especially after he labeled the Calvin Board of Trustees "the 1930 vest-pocket edition of the Sanhedrin," whose deliberations amounted to "stern circumnavigations around the perimeter of doughnuts."[47]

After graduation, De Vries executed a turn worthy of his best characters: he broke with his origins by moving back home to Chicago, and he set out on a writing career by undertaking the most mundane jobs possible (selling taffy apples and servicing vending machines). He first won attention with stories and verse published in little magazines and *Esquire* and eventually became coeditor of the esteemed Chicago-based quarterly *Poetry*. A written tribute therein to James Thurber plus an insightful speech at a *Poetry* fund-raising dinner in Thurber's honor prompted the latter to "adopt" De Vries, ensconcing him at the *New*

Yorker in 1944.[48] There at last De Vries found his element and honed his style, preparatory to the novels that made his name.

New York and the *New Yorker* are indeed, as one commentator has said, "a long way from three little rooms full of religious agony and theological comedy and ethnic tragi-farce behind [a] moving-company office on South Halstead Street."[49] But throughout his career the two worlds have dwelt side by side in De Vries's mind, never synthesized but juxtaposed, supplying the creative tension that has generated no end of humor. De Vries does not give the two worlds equal barbs, however. Before an audience of literati, he felt no need to reenact the rituals of liberation. Rather his rituals have been those of half-reparation, keeping him a permanent alien in his adopted milieu. The importance of his criticism is commensurate with that of its target, for the "suburbia" that De Vries is famous for satirizing is special—the commuter exurbia of New York City, laid out along the Manhattan-Westport axis, wherein dwells America's cultural ruling class. Indeed, much of the recent "new class" critique was anticipated by De Vries two decades ago.[50]

Several recurrent character types convey De Vries's assessments of his two worlds. High in the ranks of his artistic successes stand old-fashioned common folk, representing his childhood elders with religious and ethnic nubs removed. These "characters" have little formal education and no professional credentials but show far more intelligence that those so endowed. Their marvelous verbal style might be one measure of De Vries's affection for them. Certainly their ready charity, independence of mind, and self-criticism constitute De Vries's moral compendium.

Such is the title character of *Mrs. Wallop* (1970), the mother—natural and surrogate—of several budding writers who pay the dues of cultural fashion by insulting her values and then follow their bright minds into a maze of difficulties from which only she can rescue them. Such also is Frank Spofford of *Reuben, Reuben* (1964), a Connecticut chicken farmer whom commuter sprawl has made a displaced person in his own hometown. Spofford drives a model-T Ford with license plates reading "SCAT" and keeps the yards of the chic in trim (the pioneers of suburbia prove helpless in their vaunted "country life") in order to spy on them for the coming war of revenge.[51] Yet these characters themselves move a little toward the world of glitter, De Vries perhaps imagining his parents by the waters of Babylon, dabbling a toe or two.

They come under judgment only when they fall into the sins of the chic. Stan Waltz, furniture mover extraordinaire in *Let Me Count the Ways* (1965), is the funniest case. He spouts Ingersollian atheism as the latest word in religion and attempts an affair with a woman who gleans her revolutionary ideas from *Cosmopolitan*. Stan loses his pretensions with remarkable inelegance: he is caught window-peeping on his own wife, stricken with hiccoughs after reciting the books of the Bible in beer-fueled belches, and shamed into a decade-long hangover by unwittingly entering an Elizabeth Barrett Browning poem as his own in a local poetry contest (whence the book's title). Still, he retains his particular charm to the end.

A second character type is more directly autobiographical, divided perfectly between disparate worlds. Al Banghart of *Into Your Tent I'll Creep* (1971) rises from his lower-middle-class Chicago origins, but ambivalently. He counters business success with sorties to skid row, appreciates his wife's intelligence but not her academic posturing, and rescues her after the liberal cleric with whom she elopes "gets religion" ("that's a bad thing in a minister" [p. 178]). To considerations of social class De Vries adds those of ethnicity and religion in one of his best creations, Tom Waltz of *Let Me Count the Ways*. Tom is a complete repository of De Vries's own contradictions. For parents he has a raging agnostic father (Stan) and a raving fundamentalist mother; Mrs. Waltz, in Stan's words, is not one of your "intellectual converts to Catholicism or cetera [sic] . . . [but] plain lowdown, cornball, meat-and-potatoes Jesus *Saves* saved" (pp. 4–5), and bears witness to her Lord by giving her husband tracts on the street and a hand-tooled Bible belt for his birthday. Tom further brings a midwestern (Slow Rapids, Indiana), ethnic (Polish) background to a culturally elite job (college professor). He tries to bridge his divided soul by visiting revival halls and saloons in the same evening, by teaching Shakespeare on campus and sobbing to sentimental ballads in his room. But when his composure snaps in the face of "The Three Little Prigs," faculty colleagues of Harvard pedigree against whom he wages a guerrilla campaign for bad taste, Tom is given a (mental) health leave which he uses to go on pilgrimage to Lourdes. There he falls *ill,* triggering a convoluted religious conversion, a split decision for the provincial side of De Vries's past.

Other autobiographical figures come to a different conclusion. Jim Tickler of *The Glory of the Hummingbird* (1974) is brought up in an intensely religious Dutch midwestern home, "Hogarthian in its wealth of steamy detail" (p. 17). Naturally, all this disgusts one whose dream is, in T. S. Eliot's words, "to glitter with the glory of the hummingbird." Jim escapes to the Chicago Gold Coast by marriage, oblivious to his in-laws' delight, rather than embarrassment, with his family. His comeuppance is left for the later occasion—stemming from his involvement in a fixed TV show—when he discovers the rise to fame to be simultaneously a spiral to disaster.[52]

A bolder representation of this course occurs in *The Blood of the Lamb* (1962). Here De Vries reduces disguise to a minimum, giving a first-person narrative of Don Wanderhope's journey from a Dutch Calvinist Chicago boyhood to advertising-writer adulthood in Westchester County. Even more pronouncedly than Jim Tickler, Don keys his rebellion to the community's mores. "Worldliness to a reared Calvinist is not a vague entity but a specifiable sin of a higher order," a height Don is determined to attain. When, sneaking in from a date with an "outsider," he is confronted by his father standing in long underwear, "scrubbing his teeth with the dishrag, as was his wont," and thundering, "Any girl you go out with you take here, *verstaan*, because I want to see what Jesus would say," Don can take flight into his fantasy of the future—

> of high life, of standards and of suavity, certainly dedication to the arts. . . . I laughed softly as I hurried to my bedroom, a chuckle of affection for origins from which I would soon be gone, had already in spirit flown. I had a vision of polished doors opening, and myself in faultless tweeds in a party moving toward dinner across a parquet floor, under a chandelier like chiseled ice. (Pp. 33–36)[53]

But corroborating the pulpit of his youth, De Vries brings this moral process to a climax on the plane of intellect, and that—again, as the dominies had said—in the hour of death. As Don slowly loses his daughter to leukemia (as had De Vries shortly before writing this book), he reenacts in the suburbs of New York the theological disputations his elders had conducted on Sunday afternoons in Chicago parlors redolent of coffee, cigar smoke, and the cologne-scented handkerchiefs "of Old World women . . . listening respectfully while their menfolk gave each other chapter and verse" (p. 157). In the moment of crisis, Don touches the faith of his childhood, reciting the benediction over his daughter's body and, by means of De Vriesian convolutions, casting his cares on Christ and falling prostrate at the foot of the cross.[54] A few months later, however, after he presumably has returned to his senses, Don reaffirms the secular stoicism proclaimed decades before by his brother on *his* deathbed, deciding to live "without the consolations we call religious" (pp. 240–42).

Between the two of them, Don Wanderhope and Tom Waltz strike the close balance in which De Vries holds his past. Even if Don's renunciation outweighs Tom's conversion—and there is no agreement that it does[55]—the rest of De Vries's work quite amply demonstrates him to be a secular Jeremiah, a renegade CRC missionary to the smart set. In book after book he pricks every balloon the sophisticates launch: fads of dress, architecture, child rearing; the rituals of cocktail party and business lunch; liberal theology and liberal politics; and above all, "psychological analysis, that major industry of today. Not by their fruits shall ye know them, but by their roots. Criminals are understood, do-gooders unmasked. All that."[56] De Vries's thoroughness is that of the reverse pilgrim who has discovered Vanity Fair to be exactly what its name indicates, at once arrogant and empty.

De Vries's worldlings show themselves to be innovative but hardly original sinners. Their first fault is hubris. One after another, his suave males contrive schemes whereby lost luster can be restored, freedom regained, or a mate, mistress, or fancier job captured. But they each discover that events are not susceptible to management, much less people, and least of all oneself; as the postmortems of all their "plans" would conclude, "complications set in." "The inexplicable crashing through our pat explanations" produces the brilliant incongruities and sense of the grotesque that lie at the heart of De Vries's talent.[57] Appropriately, of all the weapons in the comic arsenal—wit, slapstick, parody, and puns—his best are wonderful paradoxes: "We must love one another, yes, yes, that's all true enough, but nothing says we have to like each other"; "Self-esteem is what others think of you, no use in denying that"; "I don't want any pleasures interfering with my happiness."

His sophisticates are equally liable to the classic Puritan charge: a false confidence of grace, rooted in self-deception. They deem themselves free of the pressures that make so much of their inferiors' lives commonplace. Of course they are not free; they merely pursue pettiness on a higher plane. Here "psychology" is invaluable—simplifying the complex, complicating the simple, and installing blithering ignorance in the guise of "understanding." As *Forever Panting*'s Stew Smackenfelt (still another exurbanite of Dutch, Chicago background) comes to learn, " 'Id' isn't just another big word, either. Far from it."[58] And finally there is conformity. These are the "Babbitts of Bohemia," "trapped in a snare of cliches."[59] Their naivete touches the most precious aspects of their self-image, for they pride themselves on their independence precisely as they run the cultural establishment, and on their modernity just as they perform rituals of insurgency that are a century old. Exposing rebellion as the preeminent convention, De Vries embalms the very myth he and his compatriot novelists had followed out of their native world.

Typically, these sins bring their victims to pratfalls; the would-be boulevardier is exposed as an altogether average man. But De Vries's work also has a darker strain that was fully realized in a series of novels written in mid career.[60] Here the generative problem is more than individual pretension. Dislocations originating in a religious crisis render Joe Sandwich of *The Vale of Laughter* (1967) unfit for this world: a broker, he gets seasick watching stock quotations glide across the board; his wife, "Naughty," is frigid. Only a universe out of joint could kill the children in *Blood of the Lamb* and *The Cat's Pajamas & Witch's Milk*. The trend crests in the latter volume, a pair of interlocking novellas. If De Vries's Professor Tattersall begins his slide because of the familiar concern for reputation (as the title of his novella suggests, he wants to be thought of as the cat's pajamas by one and all), a metaphysical force makes sure he ends in the abyss. Tattersall, "left with [a] mongoloid boy and [a] mongrel dog, and a free hand to affirm negation as he could" (p. 160), proves a master at doing just that: he cooks his meals in a bedpan and freezes to death trying to get back into his house through the dog's trapdoor.

Themes of human inability and a hostile universe evoke De Vries's religious past, of course. The institutional setting of his stories does so even more. With good reason De Vries has been called the most domestic of American writers. He uses the home fully as much as did David De Jong, only shifting from the sibling and parent-child relationship to the marital. This leads to the source of the Dutch family concern, sexuality, to which De Vries returns as compulsively as Manfred.[61] In most of his books the action springs from romantic scheming, the centerpiece of the male drive for glory. But sexuality is also the great complicator, the element of self least under control, as Stew Smackenfelt best exemplifies by his turning from wife to mother-in-law and back to wife again. More routine, conventional sexuality is no better, however, marriage being in the De Vriesian dictionary the "arena for the display of private contradictions."[62] The snug conventions of hearth and home mask a ceaseless battle for "moral credit," complete with strategies, truces, and reparations. De Vries typically concludes both intra- and extra-marital escapades with apologies for matrimony, but the very repetitiveness of such assertions, appended to the unconquerable allure of adultery, render them suspect. The effects of De Vries's fixation are showing, too: his work is becoming increasingly monochromatic and formulaic; the sexes are suffering battle fatigue.[63]

About the other bulwark of Dutch-American culture—religion— De Vries speaks less but more. He resists making any final statement of belief, perhaps for the same reason that a character in *Blood of the Lamb* stands mute when confronted by an angry Don Wanderhope:

> "Dr. Simpson, do you believe in a God?" He just perceptibly raised his eyes, as if in entreaty to Heaven to spare him at least this. It took me some years to attain his mood and understand my blunder. He resented such questions as people do who have thought a great deal about them. The superficial and slipshod have ready answers, but those looking this complex life straight in the eye acquire a wealth of perception so composed of delicately balanced contradictions that they dread . . . the call to couch any part of it in a bland generalization. (P. 111)

Instead, he sometimes offers wit ("The universe does reflect some divine intelligence. Mirror my God to thee"), sometimes only cuteness.[64]

De Vries's fictional-autobiographical work would seem to leave him in the agnostic camp, if only on its fringe. Yet as Don Wanderhope recognizes at the end of his theological peregrinations, the questions asked have as much to do with one's faith as the answers found.[65] Certainly De Vries sees in the religion of his birth more profound apprehensions (in both senses) than he does in the tenets of Modernity. Accordingly, he suspects proposed replacements. "Laodiceanism?" Tom Waltz snorts in reply to the suggestion of "a middle course." "That I particularly abhor. To the angel of the church of Laodicea write, 'because thou art lukewarm, and neither hot nor cold, I will spew thee out of my mouth.' No, don't come to me with your tepid accommodators."[66] Above all, De Vries wishes to avoid the substitutionary strategy of his colleagues. In *The Mackerel Plaza,* the Reverend Andrew Mackerel epitomizes the substitutionary approach. Pastor of People's Liberal Church (where the "worship area" constitutes the smallest part of the building and the pulpit is made of four different types of wood to signify the disagreement of the Gospels) and purveyor of tired Marxian-Jungian-humanist bromides (he is "working on" a book, *Maturity Comes of Age*), Mackerel is running from a boyhood Calvinism to aggressive Modernism, taking all the flaws of the original faith along. "Your anti-Calvinism is the most Calvinistic thing I've ever seen," an intimate declares. "This all-or-nothing idea. Whole hog. It's got to be one thing or another, splitting hairs right down to the finish. All right, not hairs, essentials" (p. 259).

Still, De Vries is no more immune to the memory of the pulpit than is Manfred. Little sermonettes appear like a constant refrain throughout his work—brief perorations by Frank Spofford, Stan Waltz, Joe Sandwich, Stew Smackenfelt. The cheerleading routine Emma Wallop's husband liked to practice shows their method and their message: "PER . . . SPEC . . . TIVE!"[67] Scarred by the catechisms of both Calvinism and Modernity, De Vries finally offers the philosophy of simple compassion. Beneath and between the ideological blocs flow the universals of human existence: joy, pain, limitation, forgiveness. These demand nothing more—or less—than patience, tolerance, and charity. Their most eloquent expression is left to him who has suffered most. Don Wanderhope concludes his "book of the dead" by saying,

> for we are indeed saved by grace in the end—but to give, not to take. . . . [We feel] again the throb of compassion rather than the breath of consolation: the recognition of how long, how long is the mourners' bench upon which we sit, arms linked in undeluded friendship, all of us, brief links, ourselves, in the eternal pity.[68]

Thus at the last, De Vries sounds the fundamental note of the Dutch-American experience, for this is common grace indeed.

De Vries's work does not always maintain this level of power. Delicate ambivalence carries the price of contrived conclusions, questions forever begged.[69] Yet there are certainly worse ways to meet contradictions than by knitting them together in humor, and De Vries has brought that approach to its summit. In so doing, he has spoken not only for his fellow renegades from Dutch America but for a whole civilization at odds with itself for a hundred years.

> So I am like all of us, reluctant thinkers, emotionally resisting truths toward which we are intellectually borne, still dreaming of islands though the mainland has been lost, swept remorselessly out to sea while we spread our arms to the beautiful shore.[70]

PART VI

AT HOME AND UNEASY, 1948–1970s

12

Americanization Again, 1948–1963

If Calvinists are born to suffering and strife, for them good times must be bad. To the evidence supporting so De Vriesian an aphorism, the Dutch-American 1950s can be added. The unparalleled calamities of the '30s and '40s had somehow sadly fit expectations; the '50s, on the other hand, brought prosperity on all fronts, a tougher challenge by far. In this decade the whole community, especially the long-lagging Christian Reformed, joined America's mythic middle class. Materially, that meant partaking of the move to suburbia and the plunge into consumer utopia for which the '50s are legendary. Mentally, it showed in unwonted displays of the tender side of their faith and in a new sense of settling down into the nation that so recently, it appeared, had joined right with might to save the world—and, coincidentally, become its master in the process.

That is half the story. The other half entails severe theological disputes, or more precisely, an eerie return to the battles of the 1920s. While the RCA again reevaluated its American settlement, the CRC again took up common grace. The old mentalities reemerged in stark polarity, new journals were founded to carry on the causes, and Calvin Seminary went through another purge. Only the outcome was different.

In all, the 1950s constituted Dutch America's latest watershed decade. The questions of Americanization dominated attention, once more in the wake of war. Those questions were answered by new voices; like the '20s, this was a decade of marked generational shift. That the old issues carried across this shift nonetheless, testifies to the continuities in Dutch-American history and to the power of the patterns we have been using to explain it.

Events in 1948 can be seen as initiating these developments. On the side of conflict, the CRC Synod that year made the second of two appointments that would shortly bring Calvin Seminary to complete discord. Harry Boer (chair of Missions), like the previous year's appointee, George Stob (Church History), was a veteran of the war chaplaincy, a young Turk par excellence, and a protégé of Clarence Bouma. "That you were not the choice of a number of the Seminary faculty you may know by this time," Bouma wrote Boer, "but that you were my first and outstanding choice I trust you will understand. . . . [Still,] it was not necessary for some of us to fight for a candidate as had proved quite essential the previous Synod in the case of the Church History chair."[1] The opposition alluded to had been set five years before when the Synod had replaced two lions of the faculty, Louis Berkhof and Henry Schultze, with two thoroughgoing traditionalists, William Rutgers and William Hendriksen. These lacked their predecessors' repute, however, so that to those so inclined the Seminary's Confessionalist hegemony seemed quite open to challenge.

On the side of success, 1948 saw a memorable triumph for Dutch Reformed politics. A reform movement called the "Home Front" (trading on wartime patriotism) had arisen in west Michigan in the early '40s to fight the Kent County Republican machine of Frank McKay. Though the group had corporate-professional WASP leadership, Hollanders supplied its rank-and-file, its moral outrage, and its launching pad— the local CRC Morals Committee's expose of machine "corruption." Calvinist politics Grand Rapids style at last came into its own. Unencumbered by old principial baggage—or insight—the Home Front erected a platform of "clean government," merit appointment, and suppression of public vice; they decorated it with all-American rhetoric and broke the machine in consecutive elections (1948 and 1950). But the ultimate measure of its meaning came in the career of Gerald Ford. First elected to Congress in 1948 on the reform ticket, Ford defeated Bartel Jonkman not so much on the morality issue—Jonkman was after all an elder in the Sherman St. CRC—as on "internationalism." Ford was eager to have the United States seize its "responsibilities" as a "world power"; Jonkman demurred. Ethno-religious loyalty paled beside such solemnities, and the Dutch Reformed supported Ford all the way to the White House.[2]

Among other things, the Home Front campaign signaled the full arrival of American civil religion in Dutch circles.[3] Its coming in such a rush, however, swelling from calm to crest in little more than a decade, indicated that various of its elements had already been in place. The RCA had been speaking its language since before World War I, and the CRC's academic-progressive sector had used some of it in World War II. Certainly anti-Communism and free enterprise advocacy were no strangers to the *Banner*. Yet only the 1950s supplied the linkages and passion that forged these into a coherent, potent ideology. Previously, "church/world" or "modernism/orthodoxy" had constituted *the* cruxes of the tension of history for the Reformed, and in those the United States had by no means stood comfortably on the right side. The categories changed with the Korean War.[4] Now "America" and "Russia" divided the world between them: "Free World" and "Communism," right and wrong, truth and falsehood, all set in dichotomous array. Thus, even though every writer who broached the topic reproached America for its sins, its faithlessness, its neglect and defiance of God, its sloth, greed, carelessness, fornication, and Sabbath-breaking, the very structure of the argument said something different. Certainly God could not be on the side of Communism. Just as certainly he was not outside the fray. Therefore, America must somehow be the object of his special concern, and so the center of history. Simple logic—at least the principle of guilt or virtue by association—led to various practical evaluations. If Communism despised religion, free enterprise, democracy, the bourgeois ethic, American might, wealth, and expansion, then these must automatically be the Christian's preference, even his passion, to be guarded against slippage or criticism. Surely they adorned the credit side of God's ledgers.

Many people knew better than this and some of them said so, but no one could avoid the logic entirely. "Communism" simply set the boundaries and agenda of discussion. Thus, though E. J. Tanis denounced American militarism in 1948, by 1953 he had so entirely entered the Cold War frame of mind as to defend the "investigations" of Senator Joseph McCarthy; Louis Benes had done the same for the RCA four years before.[5] On economics, W. Harry Jellema and H. J. Ryskamp, no enthusiasts of American business, were issuing apologies for free enterprise in the early '50s and naming government "interference" rather than corporate power as the problem of the day. Clarence Bouma expressed the new alignments perfectly: "The battle that is going on in every civilized country today is the battle between Christianity, democracy, and free enterprise on the one hand, and Marxian atheism, dictatorship, and a collectivized economy on the other."[6] With that being the tenor of statements issuing from the "left," we need not recount the tirades, lamentations, calls to arms, and even hysteria that emanated from all points to the right.

Yet the civil religion turned out to allow as much variety as the Reformed; and when the two spectra fused, they intensified each other's claims and conflicts. The signal collision occurred in 1950 between H. J. Kuiper and Lester De Koster (the latter a young "progressive" addition to the Calvin College faculty) over John T. Flynn's *The Road Ahead*, a right-wing prospectus for American civilization. Kuiper found the book magisterial—for its alarms about Big Labor and Big Government, and even more for its domino psychology, which assumed that the slightest step in a "collectivist" direction would herald the full onslaught. At this De Koster vented his considerable scorn (in him Kuiper had met more than his match for clever, unforgiving argumentation) and proposed the cold war Democratic alternative: federal planning in a mixed economy would co-opt the socialist appeal by correcting capitalism's worst abuses. It was a sign of the times that despite De Koster's subsequent thirty-year career of anti-Communist polemics Kuiper could deem him a radical subversive, as he did. Indeed, the whole college came under suspicion, not just for "collectivist thinking" but for theological and ethical laxity (read "worldliness") too. The faculty responded first with protests and then with abject apologies for any misleading appearances, and the trustees were satisfied. Kuiper had won a half victory but only a half, sign enough of a turning in the road.[7]

Concurrent hostilities at Calvin Seminary proved less tractable. The "progressive"/"traditionalist" quarrel was now breaking out on every occasion. For instance, the conservatives proposed that the seminary offer its own doctorate so that CRC students might have a "safe" education through the terminal degree. The progressives saw neither reason nor—in light of the opposition's meager scholarly qualifications, which they took pains to point out—means for the plan. Then too, there were rumors of "Barthian" deviations in certain students' ideas of Scripture. But the real problem involved personalities, as a reading of the brutal documentary record of the case reveals. Passions reached such a level in 1951 that faculty meetings degenerated into shouting matches, and Clarence Bouma suffered a nervous breakdown that left him in a psychiatric hospital for the ten remaining years of his life.[8]

The 1952 CRC Synod resolved the situation for the short run by removing almost the whole faculty. Bouma's protégés, Stob and Boer, were "terminated"; the two more recently appointed traditionalists, Rutgers and Hendriksen, were "not reappointed"; a third was retired; a fourth was "severely admonished." Their replacements over the years were quiet and better balanced individually, collectively, and ideologically. But that just served to shift the battle to other grounds. Although the Synod dismissed all accusations of heresy in the case—even H. J. Kuiper announced himself satisfied on this score[9]—the charges would not so easily down. Besides, behind all the personality clashes and petty disputes lay ideological differences of a fundamental and familiar sort. The "progressives" were positive Calvinists in slightly different dress; the "traditionalists" were Confessionalists in the old; and the "Seminary situation" led on to a new round over common grace.

The question was reopened by Cornelius Van Til. The last of the CRC's sons to follow Geerhardus Vos to Princeton Seminary, Van Til had then been taken by his other mentor, J. Gresham Machen, to the faculty of the new "orthodox Presbyterian" Westminster Seminary. There he carried on a relentless campaign against all forms of theological liberalism, including, to his mind, neo-orthodoxy (his critique titled it *The New Modernism*).[10] With "Barthian" vapors in the air, therefore, CRC stalwarts welcomed him to Calvin Seminary during its year of turmoil. Van Til declined their invitation to stay on permanently, but he did remain long enough to shatter the delicate settlement of 1924. Common grace, he declared, was no continuing and renewing work of God but a fund given to mankind in general before the Fall that had been diminishing ever since. "Civic righteousness" was but a weak memory of ancestral blessings. Humanity was dividing ever more sharply into two religious camps as the mist of common grace lifted from human consciousness, revealing to the reprobate their true enmity with God and thus triggering ever more thorough, forceful enmity toward his elect.[11]

Van Til made his most controversial applications in the realm of philosophy. In the Idealist framework he had learned, nicely, from W. Harry Jellema at Calvin College, he made God the Absolute Universal; every fact had meaning *only* in relationship with him. Therefore, Van Til declared, metaphysically the elect and reprobate had everything in common; epistemologically, nothing. Every part of thinking was different for them, even in the natural sciences; they were poles apart not just in their conclusions but in initial perceptions and at each step and in each process along the way. There were no such things as simple "brute facts" the same for both sides. In their very argumentation, however, unbelievers testified to their suppressed knowledge of God, to their awareness that Christianity (and that of the Reformed type) constituted the only rational, self-consistent system of truth. Accordingly, Van Til concluded, believers should at once take nothing from the opposition, but press a rational offensive to break the "ethical alienation" that kept unbelievers from faith—and, actually, from any real knowledge.[12]

Others drew the more spiritual implications. Various Confessionalist ministers, though acknowledging the existence of the 1924 concord, argued the antithesis to be the supreme need of the day.[13] Van Til's namesake and protégé, Henry R. Van Til, supplied 250 pages of religio-cultural analysis and bold rhetoric. The antithesis was no abstract concept hidden in the mind of God but a deepening reality in the lives of men. Since "the real value of culture does not pertain to the things produced, as pieces of art and modern inventions, but in preparing . . . the arena for Christ and the antichrist," it was held to be the Christian's cultural calling to exacerbate the differences, to catalyze the conflict. Those who "softpedal the antithesis" should remember such to be "one of the most subtle tactics in the arsenal of Satan." As to common grace, it should never be discussed "without its correlate, common curse," and is always "in the service of special grace, which is tantamount to saying it is in the service of the antithesis."[14]

The passion of the response this drew showed theology to be once again carrying more than its own weight. The progressives not only felt contradicted; they were mortified. Having passed through a noble war—some in Europe, some in the Pacific, some in the Home Front— and the nation's stellar graduate schools, they were veterans at once of common truth and righteousness. Now as they turned to lead their people out of parochialism, they faced first off the old embarrassment, the philosophy of "separation" and self-righteousness.

Some established voices did join the protest. Another old student of Machen, William Masselink, took on Cornelius Van Til in public debate, defending common grace with "evangelistic fervor."[15] Cecil De Boer, who had succeeded Bouma as editor of the *Calvin Forum*, de- voted that journal ever more to refuting Van Til's position;[16] indeed, the *Forum* rode the issue to death, as De Boer's passing in 1956 found no one able or willing to take his place. Despite the fact that such critiques as De Boer's had bite ("a bad argument for the truth does more damage than a good argument against it"), his was not the group to carry on the cause. Above all, he held no illusions about postwar prospects:

> The younger generation is too well adjusted ["progressive" educa- tion was one of De Boer's favorite targets] and, therefore, too apa- thetic to care. . . . It has simply reverted to the life of a satisfied animal. . . . Never since the Reformation has a younger generation had less to fall back upon. . . . But . . . considering the kind of world they are about to inherit, perhaps one should pray for them rather than complain.[17]

It was left to the younger generation to confute De Boer on this point and the Van Tils on all others. To do so they created an indepen- dent voice, the *Reformed Journal.* The *Journal* first appeared during the heat of the seminary crisis (March 1951) with Stob and Boer as two of its five editors, and it immediately called forth the opposition's voice; *Torch and Trumpet* (later the *Outlook*) had its debut one month later. The coincidence of the emergence of both publications at this time underscores the significance of the seminary struggle for this era and also for the longer run, although their persistence to the present indi- cates that each had a larger program of concerns. The *Journal*'s agenda sprang from an eagerness to see and seize opportunities for "Reformed advance" in the postwar world. That in turn evinced a double-barreled conviction: that the American scene was better than rumored and the Dutch-American worse. Compared to the positive Calvinists of forty years before, the *Journal*ists stressed the first less and the second considerably more. Our churches, they said apropos of a dozen different issues, are caught in the cake of custom, in reflexive defensiveness and insularity. They needed to subject all things again to the light of Scripture. Such would not only prove obedience, however, but open up the way to progress. The rhetoric of James Daane, the group's major theologian, caught the spirit well. The past thirty years had been "sterile," "commonplace," "repetitious," he said; the new times demanded "a Reformed theology bristling with vitality and restless with creative power."[18]

Daane immediately lived up to his challenge by beginning what was in essence a thirty-year series on the nature of divine grace. (His other inaugural-year concern was eschatology, the second issue of '20s controversy.) Linking Cornelius Van Til to Herman Hoeksema, Daane faulted them both for being speculative, abstract, and nonbiblical. They began and ended with God's secret counsel in eternity, but the Bible with his relations with living people, Daane argued. Theirs was a system of "timeless logic" and "unconditional theology"; the Bible's is a theology of history and response to changing people. They gave "equal ultimacy" to election and reprobation, which had to lead to a priority on the latter and so to fascination with damnation, wrath, and hell; the Bible characterizes God above all as gracious and loving, repenting and causing repentance. While Daane's categories revealed his quasi-neo-orthodox training (under Josef Hromadka at Princeton Seminary), he also addressed the key Dutch Reformed terms. Common grace did not diminish over time but expressed God's most earnest desire. The antithesis remained hidden in the mind of God, was overcome at the Cross, and would be realized only at the very end of time; meanwhile, the Christian "task is not . . . to fan the antithesis into brighter burning but to proclaim the well-meant divine disposition."[19]

While certain of Daane's traits were personal, others exemplified the *Journal*'s whole enterprise. The very repetitiveness of his critique over the years evinced negative symbiosis with adversaries. If Herman Hoeksema was, as another critic said, "a theologian in reaction," then Daane was long in reaction to a reaction, and his constructions suffered as a result (particularly on points of balance, nuance, and fairness).[20] Oddly, with all his enthusiasm for the field, theology at his hands lost some of the wide range and resonance it had had among his forebears. The occasional socio-political comments he did make lacked organic connection with his doctrinal system, which seemed reserved for matters ecclesiastical and soteriological. The Christocentrism on which he so insisted approached the theological truncation for which Kuyperians had faulted it within pietism. Daane's work finally served to announce the domestication of Dutch-American theology. Grace dominated his system to the point of being exclusive, minimizing considerations of evil. The Lion of Judah never roared in these pages.

The *Journal*'s other two editors were more explicitly Kuyperian but no less cordial. Both Henry Zylstra, Professor of English at Calvin College, and Henry Stob, Professor of Philosophy there until the seminary upheaval brought him aboard *its* faculty, used the full presuppositionalist approach ("fideism," Stob preferred to call it): searching out the "world-and-life views" behind a figure or civilization, dissecting the descent and defects of cultural modernism, and forming a Christian perspective in every field.[21] They did not conclude with "principial antithesis," however. Rather, Zylstra urged a severely classicist model of literature and education by which the best of the Western heritage could be appropriated for the contemporary struggle against specialization, technicism, and cheapness.[22] Stob was not convinced that a Christian approach to some fields would render distinct and definitive results. Indeed, his "Note to a College Freshman" sounded very much like late Victorian Idealism: "You must leave behind the subjectivity of your narrow self and reach out for the broader mind of Man."[23] Study the great teachers of the race, then subsume them under (more like "frost them with," the critics said) the teachings of Christ. Stob's prescription for his denomination was equally genial—and imperial. In the most striking demonstration of the *Journal*'s lineage, Stob replicated the strategy first proposed by the *Christian Journal* in the afterglow of World War I. Of the three parties in the Church, Stob said, two were marked by "fear," "eccentricity," and "imbalance" and only one by love and wholeness. The "mind of safety" (Confessionalist-pietist) sought to protect the church from the world; the "militant mind" (Antitheticals) sought to attack the world; but the "positive mind" would appropriate the good elements in each for its own larger, balanced system, working to effect "progressive and saving penetration of the world in love."[24]

The one thing needed for this was freedom, Stob said: "freedom from the weight of custom . . . freedom from fear and reprisals . . . freedom from enervating suspicion."[25] And it was precisely that that the opposition was determined to withhold. Over against the *Journal*'s excruciating refinement, its opponents modeled themselves on Gideon and fell, torches blazing, trumpets blaring, on the camp of the Midianites. Tact, tolerance, and broadmindedness became suspect as the first steps of deviation, and on the high road at that. So let us not be afraid to hunt heresy, Henry Van Til exhorted, for truth is the absolute foundation of the church. To those who would put "love" or "conduct" in that place, R. B. Kuiper had the time-honored reply: "To belittle truth in the interest of love is folly. . . . And, never to be forgotten, he who disparages doctrine undermines not only truth, but good-ness also, for one's beliefs determine one's conduct."[26]

This was the Confessionalist motto supreme, and the rest of *Torch and Trumpet*'s work followed that party's program. First and last, to repeat—as its writers did ceaselessly—doctrinal orthodoxy had to be maintained in absolute purity. Second, the whole way of life that ex-pressed and upheld that orthodoxy was similarly to be preserved. The Confessionalists *celebrated* the cake of custom, the mores of Sabbath observance, the rigorous intellectualism of the pulpit; they distrusted the "dilution" that aggressive evangelism might bring into the church; and they attacked any proposed "loosening" of strictures against worldliness and divorce.[27] Beyond that they had little to say; indeed, they took pride in the absence of innovation that allowed, for example, Louis Berkhof to publish unchanged, in 1951, his Stone Lectures of 1922. There was no need to change, as Truth was finite, final, and in hand; nor was there any gain to be found in change, for they already constituted the establishment. Thus they could only oscillate between preservation— "Withstand beginnings," R. B. Kuiper's last testament concluded—and lamentation, the forte of H. J. Kuiper.[28]

As in the strife of the '20s, however, the Confessionalists took on—or were put upon by—Antithetical Kuyperian allies. Cornelius Van Til had exhibited the connection on the philosophical level as had Henry on the cultural-practical level. But the latter represented the Confes-sionalists' restricted interest in the matter: separation served to protect doctrinal and behavioral purity. A more expansive approach came from the newest bloc of Dutch North Americans, the postwar immi-grants to Canada. In this immigration staunch Calvinists held as dispro-portionate a share as earlier: ten percent of the home population, they composed thirty percent of the immigrants and the core of those most likely to maintain ethno-ideological identity. Quickly they put the CRC in their debt; by 1965 their addition of fifty thousand accounted for some twenty percent of the denomination's membership.[29] Equally important was the matter of cultural memory. Theirs showed some signs of internal strain but nothing like the degree of difference between their experience and that of the CRC in the States. The new immigrants had grown up in the full system of separate institutions, very often under Calvinist-run governments, and amid sophisticated post-Kuyperian developments in Neo-Calvinist theory. On the other hand, they had suffered five years of Nazi occupation, they resented the post-war reimposition of a proprietary regime in the Netherlands, and they had passed through all the travail of emigration. Whatever mood they were in, it was not that of success or of narrow defensiveness.

The man who mobilized them compounded the dissonance with

rich irony. It was H. Evan Runner who pushed the Canadians to rebuild the Dutch system—a Christian labor union, political caucus, and educational network—in the new country. It was Runner who proselytized for the same in the States, who appeared in full Antithetical regalia in *Torch and Trumpet* next to wary traditionalists. But if his head was full of Holland, his veins were utterly devoid of it. Runner was an American of the Americans, a Philadelphia Old School Presbyterian raised with revivals, dispensationalism, and Keswick holiness on the side, and a Wheaton College education to round them off. He met Dutch Calvinism in the person of Cornelius Van Til at Westminster Seminary and, impressed with the way it addressed various American evangelical weaknesses, pursued it at Kampen Seminary and the Free University in the Netherlands. From thence he returned, brimming, in 1951 to join the Calvin College Philosophy Department.[30] So thoroughly did he contradict his new colleagues' aspirations—by *adopting* Dutch ethnicity and with a vengeance, forsaking a Harvard for an Amsterdam Ph.D., rebuffing common grace for antithesis—that their amazement shortly turned to outrage.

Runner not only taught antithesis but sought to revive its practice. His classroom lectures (as much preaching as teaching, one protégé has recalled)[31] rehearsed the breathtaking reductions of Antitheticalism. The history of Christianity, he maintained, amounted to a string of fatal syntheses with Hellenism, the Renaissance, the Enlightenment; to break them, Christians were called to ideological and institutional separation. Publicly, Runner scorned the most precious of Grand Rapids achievements. If one saw superficial discussions and anti-beano campaigns as the summit of Christian politics, he allowed, then one could happily join Citizens' Action (the successor to the Home Front); but if Christians wished to make full, consistent, radical witness, they would have to tyrannize or quit such an organization—that is, be unfair or ineffectual. The solution: a separate Christian party that would throw off America's reigning liberal-conservative ideology. When most Americans, to put it kindly, did not accede to his suggestion, Runner turned to the Canadians—and the Canadians turned to him. His Groen (van Prinsterer) Club at Calvin College became their refuge amid American smugness for twenty-five years. If nothing else, the whole process served as an ironic turn for the American Christian Reformed whose forebears had undergone the same cycle at the hands of the RCA three generations before.[32]

Perhaps it was fitting, then, that the most startling turn occurred in the RCA itself. The denomination's Western leadership, proudly "American" and "practical" for fifty years, now exhumed their own Netherlandic past with the result, eventually, of a theological renaissance. The latter we shall review in the next chapter; its signal now was the overdue emergence in this quarter of a scholarly forum, the *Western Seminary Bulletin* (after 1955, the *Reformed Review*). The journal first distinguished itself by its openness to neo-orthodoxy: it shared the '50s fascination with Reinhold Niebuhr, gave Barth and Emil Brunner plaudits rarely heard in the CRC, and recast the church's mission to the world in existential, eschatological, and paradoxical terms.[33] But these in turn mirrored developments in the Hervormde Kerk in the Netherlands (NHK), the National Church which the RCA had long reflected. Its emulation became explicit and excited in the 1950s, however, because of the mother church's postwar rejuvenation (involving a revision of doctrine and polity by which the NHK sloughed off a century of state-dependent lethargy). A "broad" yet "confessing" church, addressing "the whole nation" with vibrant faith that was expressed above all in "action," the NHK fit perfectly the RCA's ideal of what it should be in America—and of no less import, in Dutch America. The model's key concepts were so regularly juxtaposed to their opposites— "narrow," "separated," faith as "intellectualism" or doctrinal watchdog—that one can only infer a relief on the part of many at finally being able to pay back the CRC in Netherlandic coin.[34]

Their real opposition, though, lay closer to home. The 1950s saw almost as strong (and certainly as public) a Confessionalist campaign in the RCA West as in the CRC. Its partisans were parish clergy and "concerned laymen" who, feeling alternately neglected or denigrated by the denominational leadership, seized critical junctures to rise in protest.

> Where is a denomination going which cooperates with all of the liberal organizations of Protestantism [e.g., the Federal Council of Churches] and none of the conservative organizations, that has at least one seminary [New Brunswick] and one college [Hope] in a very serious condition in regard to the faith, and whose Boards are controlled by one area of the church [the East] in which there is not enough spiritual life to make a reasonable contribution to the benevolent work of that church?[35]

These sentiments appeared in the late '40s as the RCA once again debated ecumenical actions. Western disaffection proved strong enough to block one of these (merger with the United Presbyterians) but not another (membership in the FCC), and manifested itself thereafter in a variety of pamphlets on doctrinal and behavioral matters: "The Authority of the Bible," "The Ordination Vows of Ministers and Elders," and "Marriage-Divorce-Remarriage," and one book, *The Doctrine of Eternal Punishment*. This party too had self-conscious Netherlandic sources, but in the Seceder, not the National

Church tradition, and it urged upon the church at large its own model: heartfelt conversion, devout homes, unbudging orthodoxy, and personal faithfulness rather than social concerns in a declining world.[36]

The only problem was that the world was not declining, at least not ecclesiastically. The RCA had in the 1950s a decade of growth unparalleled in a hundred years, the result of an aggressive church extension program. Its strategy—evangelism outside the ethnic orbit—satisfied both wings in the church. One of its consequences, however, would one day please neither: southern California became the greatest growth area, and Robert Schuller's the model program.[37] Schuller's ascent from drive-in theater to Crystal Cathedral empire, which began in the mid '50s, improved denominational statistics but rode a gospel of success that comported ill with Seceder and neo-orthodox strains alike. In any case, these developments seemed to augur a major break with the past and in the Dutch-American community. While the CRC reached out to Calvinist immigrants, the RCA brought American suburbanites into "community churches."

There remains the other side of our project—determining the socio-cultural correlations of the various mentalities, their field of consensus, and the ways they advanced or complicated acculturation. The consensus can be easily stated. America and Communism stood ready to battle for the world. Would the United States prove strong and vital and moral enough? Not likely, since the Communists were disciplined and utterly committed to their creed, awful as it was, while Americans were slipping into the swamps of carnal ease. Only Christianity had the creed and calling equal to the day. Thus it was the Christian's—and especially the Reformed Christian's—urgent duty to call the nation back to the gospel, with all its social and political implications.[38] This formula allowed of several applications, however, which manifest, now as fifty years before, different perceptions of Christianity and America.

The dominant RCA voice, being most closely tuned to the Protestant mainstream, provides a good standard for comparison. No one in Dutch America repeated their formula with more passion or frequency than *Church Herald* editor Louis Benes. The secular objects of his attack were nineteenth-century traditional—sexual license, political corruption, gambling, liquor. The religious targets were twentieth-century innovative—Christianity "demythologized" or turned into social reform, formal ritual, or mere "peace of mind." And his proffered solution entailed simple evangelical orthodoxy—sin, repentance, and regeneration—vigorously proclaimed.[39] But Benes distinguished his from the other mentalities on two points. First, he gave scant attention to means and models by which the proclamation of the gospel might be turned into social transformation. "Somehow" and "indirectly," he argued, Christianity's "basic principles" and "moral dynamic" would span out from the individual (at whom they must be aimed) to society; but the church was resolutely to avoid specifying programs or any one type of social order.[40] This left Benes for the most part with little more to do than make ardent repetitions (his readers got virtually a weekly dose); he appears to have believed that much speaking in his paper and then in all the pulpits would be enough to ensure that the old Protestant ethos might again cover the land. But Benes *did* get specific on certain issues, which provide the second point of contrast: he stood fast on the RCA's Prohibition heritage, and he was persistently anti-Catholic. Both emphases demonstrated an American Protestant identification. By contrast, the CRC operated either under Seceder shibboleths (the negative triad of dancing, gambling, and theater) or by Kuyperian precedents, which had *entertained* both of Benes's demons.[41]

The Confessionalists, Reformed and Christian Reformed alike, differentiated themselves from any such liberal attitudes by their stricter standards and dolorous tone. In their estimation, the best Christians could do would be to rise in one voice to tell the nation where it was going, but even that would not likely change its course. So in actuality, Christians were called to survive, a faithful remnant in a degenerate land, which in turn demanded that faith and mores be kept in absolute purity.[42] The attitude was not bereft of insight. H. J. Kuiper caught the 1950s' famous religious revival well: no wonder "More Religion" was begetting "Less Morality," he said, since Christ was being reduced to "community" and the Bible to bromides. John Vander Ploeg, Kuiper's successor at the *Banner,* turned the last point to denominational ends. What did it say about the RCA that one of its ministers, Norman Vincent Peale, led the "peace of mind" movement?

> If Dr. Peale has nothing better to offer young Americans as an interpretation of Christianity . . . then his popularity is a serious indictment for him and for his denomination as well as a menace for the millions who turn to him for help and guidance.[43]

But this approach did not forestall other duplicities. Hearing that the world was going to hell, Dutch Americans kept moving to the suburbs. Their children by 1970 might regard the two as synonymous, but it is doubtful the parents did. So pulpit proclamation began to separate from pew experience and could be reclaimed only by partitioned or self-serving minds. But even the doomsayers did not berate all things equally. They condemned "materialism" only as it was evidenced in the ranks of a clamoring labor force. They condemned "worldliness," but not advertising and not much the consumer ethic— and that in the decade of their florescence. They condemned bureaucratization in government but not in corporations. The full measure of inconsistency came clear in an ecumenical venture. The CRC had joined the National Association of Evangelicals (NAE) in 1943 (again, as a wartime measure), but was having second thoughts a few years later. Some wanted to continue membership, since the NAE was "Reformed as far as it goes." Their opponents sounded the venerable cry of "Reformed distinctiveness":

> The heart of our calling to the American world is to bring to it the power of a full and undiluted Reformed witness. We can scarcely in good conscience unite for that purpose with those who do not share our Reformed convictions.

Amazingly, the second voice was heard in the pages of the *Reformed Journal*, whereas the first was none other than H. J. Kuiper.[44] Kuiper thus earned for his camp the epithet of "Reformed Fundamentalism," veering close—and uncritically—to the American movement in all things political and theological, the five points of Dort excepted.[45]

The two Kuyperian camps addressed the issues with more finesse, yet the Antitheticals ever invoking "principle" and the *Reformed Journal* ever invoking "practice" managed to miss each other more often than meet. The Antitheticals' theoretical, holistic, and Canadian immigrant outlook resurrected discomfiting reminders—of the wholesale co-option of American labor unions by corporate materialist values and of the permeation of American politics by Enlightenment ideas.[46] But their "solutions" exhibited old infirmities as well. Their calls for separate organization bore world-flight rhetoric belying their intention; and for all the "action" such organizations were to undertake, their likely status as discussion clubs, as Christian-theory constructors, seemed evident enough.[47] Some progressives noticed a reactionary strain besides: "*Upon what principle* is labor singled out?" Lester De Koster demanded; why not separate organization also in business, medicine, and law? And finally, the sublime proved father to the prosaic. The "Work Program" of the Calvinistic Culture Association, which was founded with an H. Evan Runner oration extraordinaire, spoke to art and science with vague pledges and to international affairs with vague warnings, but to hearth and bed with startling directness—namely, glorification of marriage as a sacred ordinance and proscription of all birth control.[48] For Antitheticals too, it was family first.

The "progressives," being more hopeful, allowed more variety. On the one hand, they struck most consistently at American materialism, from consumer frenzy to the idolatry of technique. On the other hand, they gave the most esteem of any CRC party to public religiosity. James Daane, from his *Christianity Today* desk in Washington, D.C., celebrated America for having a churchgoer in space (John Glenn), presidents at prayer breakfasts, and evangelists in public print (Billy Graham in the *Saturday Evening Post*). Two Calvin College professors saw America as so open to cooperative witness that such could be extended—to the Democratic Party as well as the Republican.[49] But this side too fell into the mundane. In the face of the "terrifying" moral and religious collapse of the West, Harry Boer invoked as a hopeful example the old campaign against dirty politics in Grand Rapids. The Calvinistic Action Committee's symposium on "God-Centered Living" finally got specific on the points of "worldliness" and "government interference" in business.[50] And George Stob's answer to proposals for a Christian labor union not only ignored the ideological presence in institutions (thereby also admitting corporate and consumer materialism through the back door), but substantially shrank the dimensions of cultural witness. "The ends for which the Christian is supposed to work in his social task are specific and concrete, and relate to the immediate and present needs of our common society," Stob announced; thus, he is called "to preserve, not to recreate or transform, what is already decaying."[51] With that, Stob stepped over into pietism, though of the outgoing sort, in token of which his presentation duplicated exactly (though unconsciously, it seems) the RCA's arguments against Christian schools and the truncations James Daane had brought to theology.

Others were more eager still to erase the Kuyperian line, no one more than Leonard Verduin, long the pastor of the CRC outpost at the University of Michigan. For Verduin, "Constantinism" (i.e., a religiously "monolithic" society) accounted for all the evil in Christian history, and Anabaptism for most of the good. Kuyper, and in fact Dutch Calvinism as a whole, epitomized the first; the United States epitomized the second. A decade hence it would seem most odd to remember the "progressives" wrapping themselves in the flag, but such was the logic of their '50s development. Verduin's series on Dutch church history ended with a paean to the U.S. Constitution and a deep draught of civil religion all the more striking for its sneers at European versions thereof:

> We in America will have to take the lead in pioneering for a new and better way. And we shall ask our brethren in the faith in Europe to come clear, if indeed that is possible for them, of the errors of the past and to embrace a philosophy of culture more in keeping with the Word.[52]

Lester De Koster was not quite so dismissive; he would cite Dutch precedents for New Deal measures. But he wished to get back to Geneva itself, unmediated by Amsterdam. His Calvin turned out to look quite American, however, and his Calvinism served his epic anti-Communist struggle. This was positive Calvinism, to be sure: the Christian's first duty in crisis was to examine his own faults, and then to work to cure the sources of social distress. But these by no means precluded militant worldwide American action. The U.S. needed the Pentagon, De Koster insisted, because "there may be other cities [besides those bombed in World War II] to be cleansed." For the home front he nominated two models: John F. Kennedy, who was proof positive (also, presumably, in his personal life) that "Christian politics" could happen in America; and J. Edgar Hoover, "whose administration of the police power of the modern state cannot be sufficiently lauded. Start your anti-Communism from this [Hoover's *Masters of Deceit*] and be thankful for the F.B.I."[53]

If the sorrier revelations about Kennedy awaited a later day, and those already available about Hoover could be subordinated to anti-Communist imperatives, other elements of the '50s accommodation seemed noxious already. It was a younger generation still—one coming of age after rather than before World War II—that raised these questions, and not timidly: *Youth Speaks on Calvinism,* they intoned; *Youth Speaks on Christianity and Civilization.* Their reception was typical. For all the catastrophes they described, the turnings of the ages, the crisis of the West, H. J. Kuiper met them on the ground of moviegoing. In that context, their turn to Netherlandic Neo-Calvinism became all the more significant. They rediscovered the radical side of Abraham Kuyper, linked him with contemporary American social critics, and arraigned "every sphere" as well as the presiding spirit of the new American age. As for Dutch America, their satire bore the mixed tones of hope and anger:

> It is . . . difficult to see how a Calvinistic community whose discussions of Christian action are confined, with a few exceptions, to questions of whether Halloween parties are allowed, or whether movies shown over TV can be safely watched . . . can produce Christian action [commensurate with that of its Dutch past]. Or how a rising generation of high school graduates fed a diet of Spanish, social adjustment, shop, and basketball can produce the leaders equipped [for such] Christian action.[54]

In thus moving different directions at once, Kuyper's reputation fit the overriding pattern of the time. Dutch America opened outward in the postwar era, but almost inattentively; most of its commentary was introspective, churchy in tone and concern. Second, "Americanization" proceeded under the conscious appropriation of Dutch links and models. Each group had a Netherlandic patron it invoked, perhaps for psychological stability as much as direct usefulness.[55] Third, external accession occurred simultaneously with internal pluralization. Partly this involved geography. Like the California-suburban additions to the RCA, the Canadian newcomers in the CRC had their own mind, and soon their own para-ecclesial institutions. When the Christian Reformed built colleges in Iowa and Chicago besides, they discovered the mixed blessings of regionalism that the RCA had been living with all along. More striking was the new state of ideological pluralism, signaled by the persistence rather than the purging of parties and their periodicals, and by the dedication of the new Calvin Seminary faculty above all to moderation, coexistence, and peace. This spelled the end of Confessionalist hegemony.[56]

The remainder of the 1960s, and the years beyond, would be thick with efforts to restore that regime; but early in the decade a kind of peace prevailed. This owed not as much to internal resolution (since the most portentous issues were only sprouting) as to external mood, especially as set by the image of John F. Kennedy. Here was the final irony, for Dutch America had reached new depths of passion—the sectarian factor redoubling the partisan—in opposing his candidacy in 1960. Kennedy's circumspection on religious matters, however, together with the events of Vatican II, tempered even the most virulent; and his Cuban missile crisis in 1962 gave everyone hope that the Communist tide might have been turned. But above all there was his death, uniting the parties for the moment with each other and with the nation as a whole, all reconciled by the blood of the young messiah.[57]

13

Evangelical and Ethnic, 1964–1970s

Among the more charming features of history is the way it allows speaking to the present without speaking about it. This chapter, undertaking the latter, jeopardizes the former. To try to save perspective, we will discuss most recent developments in conjunction with some summary conclusions about the entire span of our study. That at least spares us the most tiresome fatuity, "engaging the future."

The event with which this period began signaled its two overriding features. The Kennedy assassination wrenched Dutch Americans' attention to external politics, and the whole series of issues that followed—civil rights, Vietnam, urban disorders, campus ferment, ecology vs. technology, Watergate—kept it there. The result was some turning away from the sort of ecclesiastical, introspective discussions that prevailed during the '50s and a resurgence of socio-cultural critique of the sort that was prominent in the prewar era. At the same time, determining how representative the published discourse of this period in fact was is problematical, given the impact of the national media evident in the assassination coverage. The denominations never had exclusive access to their parishioners' minds, especially since the advent of radio, but television constituted an intrusion that was at once wholesale and more intimate. More than ever before, Dutch Reformed identity faced becoming just one option in a big market, one compartment in a many-chambered mind; to that prospect leaders and laity alike responded with several stratagems. Analyzing these, however, first requires a turn to internal developments, where the period began on two perennial notes—a theological argument among the Christian Reformed, and the question of church union in the RCA.

The Reformed had entered merger negotiations in 1962, this time with the Southern Presbyterians (the Presbyterian Church in the United

States [PCUS]). The doggedness with which they pursued union (this was the third attempt in little more than thirty years) showed its supporters' commitment not only to the American scene, as they emphasized, but also to a "mainstream" strategy. Ecumenism had been a rising cause in the Protestant establishment during the whole middle third of the twentieth century, and it crested in the '60s with the Consultation on Church Union (COCU) formed among nine major denominations. The same RCA elements—the entire Eastern bloc and the Western elite—supported this merger, and both with arguments the brevity of which indicated that the cause involved fundamental faith more than labored analysis. Christ had prayed that all his followers be one; unity required erasing denominational lines; Christians must obey regardless of the consequences, although, indeed, these would prove to be beneficial.

Beneficial especially in the East, the supporters added, where demographics were vitiating Reformed Church identity and zeal. Precisely the problem, the opponents replied. Why should the healthy sector of the church, the one that supplied most of the ministers, missionaries, and money, weaken itself by appeasement? Besides, Christ wanted his followers united *in truth*. Southern Presbyterians might not threaten orthodoxy, but the inevitable *next* merger would. Further, merger would do nothing to enhance the spiritual quality of the church, which depended on sound preaching and discipline in holiness. Finally, administrative centralization had little to do with unity in faith; a more tightly defined identity, history indicated, would breed greater dedication.[1]

As usual, the two sides argued past each other so that the matter came down to a question of power. By small majorities, both the COCU (in 1967) and the Southern Presbyterians (in 1969) were rebuffed, though for the merger, which required a two-thirds approval, this amounted to a substantial defeat. The voting pattern was more striking than the result, showing complete regional polarization. All twenty-two of the Eastern classes favored the merger; twenty-two of the twenty-three Western classes rejected it.[2] Predictable bad feelings and name-calling ensued, accompanied by some ironic twists. The East now generated proposals that the RCA be split in two with local churches retaining their own property. Western conservatives, who had been discussing the same idea before the vote, nevertheless returned all the East's earlier invocations of unity and central control. The whole episode ended on one of the sorriest notes in RCA history when the 1969 General Synod appointed a committee to consider "the orderly dissolution" of the denomination at a time when it was itself being blasted and having its offices occupied by James Forman's "Black Manifesto" group.[3]

The revelatory significance of the affair lies in its being a middle term between deeper sources in one direction and broader implications in the other. Both sides had true conviction no less than self-interest at heart, but even after a century together they turned out to be moving from divergent experiences. Ethnicity still mattered substantially in the West, where the Particular Synods averaged a sixty-seven percent "Dutch or part-Dutch" membership, compared to a twenty-one percent average in the East.[4] The descendants of the nineteenth-century immigration retained a natural community that merger hardly figured to enhance. They also retained Seceder traditions in doctrine and polity—hence the prominence of cries of "dilution" and "centralization" in the anti-merger litany. Indeed, *intra*-Seceder differences persisted, as a Western conservative stalwart showed in rejecting subsequent proposals for an RCA-CRC union. The latter denomination was hierarchical and clergy-run, Gordon Girod replied; the RCA's localist polity allowed "Gospel preaching," "Bible believing" congregations a safe autonomy.[5] This amounted to a recapitulation of the ancient dispute between the "Northern" (CRC) and the "Geldersche" (Van Raalte) factions some 125 years later.

In sum, the Western presence worked now as before to "de-Americanize" the RCA somewhat, a phenomenon more common than noted in other churches as well. The RCA was blocked from a purely "mainstream" approach, affiliation, and character. But the Easterners could argue that such represented not *less* but a *different* Americanism, that the antimerger agenda was not so much Dutch as American evangelical drawing on certain Dutch compatibilities. Their clearest evidence came from the presence (signaled by the Forman incident) of socio-political purposes in the merger fight. The localists opposed not only union but recent Synodical "activism," such as support for the civil rights movement and declarations of distress about U.S. involvement in Vietnam. Their operative concern turned out not to be "politicalization" itself, however, but the "left wing" nature of the politics. Thus, they called for the church's restriction to "spiritual" concerns, but they also passed resolutions about alcohol, tobacco, and prayer in public schools.[6]

Perhaps it was fitting, then, that the solution to the crisis arrived in evangelical dress. Two extraordinary assemblies (appropriately labeled "festivals") given to evangelistic activism put the denomination on a new track. They offered something for all: missions and "witnessing" emphases for the conservatives and a full array of countercultural worship styles (e.g., rock hymns, communion out of a dixie cup) for the disaffected.[7] With evangelicalism rising in the nation anyway and repenting of some of its offenses in the process, the option was sufficient to cover everyone.

The Christian Reformed dispute, which also began in 1962,

marked something of a departure in that it involved not "common" but "special" grace. Actually, it was a return to the core of Dutch Calvinist formulations, the Synod of Dort's article on limited atonement. Various progressives, headed by Harold Dekker, Professor of Missions at Calvin Seminary, worried that the tenet had undermined their church's outreach, and so they worked to recast it in very positive terms, or, more accurately, to put it low and late in the train of doctrine. God loved all people with one and the same love, they said; he hated no sinner, only the sin, which he punished to the end of salvation. The atonement was universal in sufficiency, availability, and divine desire, and limited only in efficacy. Certainly there was a paradox here—"that God loves all men while not all men are saved"—but that should remain "where it belongs—in the infinite mystery of the heart of Him who is Himself love." Instead of stressing God's wrath or the number who would perish, in other words, the Christian Reformed should "carry out our mission to all men according to the plain Biblical givens."[8]

The Confessionalists' response proceeded along two lines: defending the CRC past against these aspersions and emphasizing the graver side of the question. Louis Berkhof (the traditional authority) *had* taught this sort of atonement, they replied, though with closer attention than Dekker to the balance—not to say the correct exegesis—of particularistic and universalistic texts in Scripture. Moreover, to respect the solemnity of salvation, it was better rhetorically and theologically to distinguish between two kinds of divine love than between different relationships under the same love. Such might seem a distinction without a difference, but the Confessionalists sensed portentous developments at hand. Obviously the formulations echoed different church-world conceptions; to that extent the dispute had the traditional base. More ominously, R. B. Kuiper saw the progressives imposing on Scripture a logic (he enjoyed returning James Daane's charge for once) that stemmed from incipient liberalism.[9] This proved the more popular tack and so increased the stakes in the case that the Confessionalists, on the verge of its final disposition (at the 1967 Synod), pronounced the church to be at *the* fork in the road. The Synod took the extraordinary step of convening a second session to decide the issue, only to see its mountain of labor, in the words of one delegate, bring forth a mouse of a decision: "admonish[ing] Professor Dekker for the ambiguous and abstract way in which he has expressed himself," and consigning the matter to the churches for study.[10]

The dispute clarified certain matters nonetheless. The Confessionalists' dominance was now broken on the official level. One need only compare the present scene to that of their latest (and last, it turned out) unqualified triumph, a 1959 case involving biblical infallibility. At that time suspicion still reigned—the case arose from articles in a seminarians' in-house periodical—and disposition was quick: the Synod spoke first (and within a year of the first publication) and discussed later.[11] Symbolically, between that case and the 1967 controversy, three Confessionalist stalwarts had died—Henry Van Til (1961), H. J. Kuiper (1962), and R. B. Kuiper (1966)—and in the latter year the church broke with its long-standing behavioral symbolics by declaring movie attendance (in the proper Christian critical frame of mind) quite permissible.[12] Nor was the scent of protoliberalism entirely imaginary in the Dekker case. The progressives' insistence that "faith" be separated from "theology," that the intelligentsia be allowed more latitude for discussion, that cases be settled slowly and in good order, that traditional terminology cover new meanings, that the creeds be regarded in their historical conditioning as testimonies to as well as statements of the truth, all had ample precedent in the early stages of liberalism some ninety years before.[13] Finally, the case provoked troubling questions about the role of theology in the community as a whole. The progressives seemed to be abstracting it into a professional preserve, the Confessionalists into a static test of communal membership, but both away from vital contact with heartfelt concerns.[14]

Part of the reason lay in the growing concern with politics. The crisis of the '60s bore hard upon the Dutch on all counts, from their most recently acquired civil religion to their ancestral conservatism. For this era, accordingly, it was politics that served to disclose internal differences and the twisting uses of tradition.

The Confessionalists had always played weakest here, and they stood fast in that heritage now. At the hands of John Vander Ploeg (H. J. Kuiper's successor at two periodicals but—since Kuiper at least addressed the significant issues—more the heir of Foppe Ten Hoor), Vietnam, Watergate, and the civil rights movement passed with marginal comments amid months of silence. Events that demanded a response could evoke zany pietistic irrelevancies. The Kennedy assassination, for instance, became a parable of the fleeting nature of glory, of the divine-human disparity (Kennedy left his agenda undone, but Jesus could say, "it is finished"), of the need for deliverance from fear and sin. Comments more to the point showed closure with right-wing values now to be as complete as it was unexamined. Condemning Lyndon Johnson's "Great Society" for its horrible materialism, the Confessionalists kept content with their share of the curse. Acknowledging racial injustice, they could find no acceptable means of amelioration but did point up every facet of the "sin" of civil disobedience. If their grandfathers, strictly by their immigrant status, had kept free from such entanglements, the present generation plumbed the depths of Americanization. John Vander Ploeg, invited to a White House briefing on Vietnam, could barely contain his awe at having shaken hands with the President.

In retrospect he felt a little bad that the King of Kings did not receive all the glory, but added his voice nonetheless to the chorus eager, in this time of trouble, to say what was *right* about America.[15]

The outgoing piety in the RCA showed a better heart, a bit more rigor, and one additional major concern—the Supreme Court's limit on prayer in public schools. For the CRC the last was predictable, even just; for the RCA it cut to the core of the civil religious settlement.[16] As to the rest of the agenda, the Reformed had less trouble than the Christian Reformed with civil rights, though more with Black Power (ethnicity again); on the war, while both allowed dissenting voices, the *Church Herald* came sooner to skepticism than did the *Banner*.[17] The two were united—in scorn—for the New Left and hippie counterculture, waxed equally indignant on Watergate, and came up with the same diagnostic formula. Lawlessness Left and Right was the reflection in ethics of "death-of-God" notions in theology; both breathed the era's love of the jumbled and garbled, the dissonant and upside-down.[18] The RCA's distinction lay again in the type of "American" solution it envisioned. In this era Louis Benes found his exemplar in John Wesley—no American to be sure, but British anyway, and the source of so much of the nineteenth-century Protestant complex that Benes idealized. For current troubles, Wesley gave a shining example of combining personal conversion and social reform; for denominational precedents, he provided the right mix of established-church and pietist strains. That Wesley represented the purest Arminianism as well would have given Benes pause perhaps, had he not been so confident of the sufficiency of the simple essentials of biblical faith.[19]

The Antitheticals made a living exposing such simplicities and they continued to do so now, only under strangely new auspices. By 1970 they seemed the farthest *left* of all the factions. In part this reflected affinities with New Left approaches, in part the youth of the group's new leaders, and for the rest a consistency of basic perceptions: they had stood firm, and the world came round to meet them.[20] Marx's dialectics met Kuyper's: the West stood at the crisis, in fact the greatest crisis in two thousand years. Liberalism was the culprit; Christianity's syntheses therewith (which among "conservatives" took the form of bourgeois pieties) the problem; and institutional introversion was the church's pathetic response. All this they presented in urgency always, in rage often. The Christian Reformed too, read the longest reverberating pronouncement of the Antitheticals, had experienced "the wet dream of self-gratification" and gone "awhoring after that great American Bitch: the Democratic Way of Life."[21] The extremity of the rhetoric almost hid the familiarity of the analysis. The hundred griefs of the day led back to one common root—human self-arrogation—so the solution lay in "the radical message of the Gospel," "that God still gives life to the man who will lose his life [i.e., surrender autonomy] for the Word Incarnate [divine sovereignty]." What did that entail? That the church break in general with the competitive-materialist system of values that pervaded America, and, in its own house, with bureaucratization, mere soul-saving, mere do-gooding, and mere preservation of orthodoxy in order to find and proclaim and implement "the full counsel of God." What was that? The kingship of Christ over *all* areas of life. And the strategy? First of all, creating a piercing Christian critique (read "distinctive Christian mind").[22]

Safe to say, this upset everyone. The Confessionalists, who had been making overtures to the group up to the very appearance of its manifesto, were hurt by its denigrations ("mere") of evangelism and orthodoxy. The progressives, in turn, were puzzled—outflanked on the left, outdone in daring and chic, and deprived even of the "separate organization" bogey, which the new Antitheticals had removed from discussion.[23] This let the real issues come to light, exposing emergent fissures in the progressive camp. Those still convinced of a Christian America supported both of Lyndon Johnson's Great Society ventures, the one in the U.S. and the one in Vietnam. Having done signal duty in raising consciousness on race, they were frustrated as events left their sort of progress behind. Leonard Verduin was put in the position of disowning Anabaptists (their young left) for the sake of American centrism, while Lester De Koster alternated between crusading against the Far Right (which at least had a comfortable familiarity) and for the Vietnam War. The latter he supported, even after the fall of Saigon, as *the* locus of the world-historical antithesis, *the* test of American will, and, more happily, a theater for American distinctiveness: "Our construction of refugee camps, our good habit of playing . . . foster parent to orphans, *that* is our style!" Accordingly, the war would be justified only when the U.S. established the principles of the Declaration of Independence ("surely the noblest political document yet struck by the hand of man") in Vietnamese political culture.[24]

That such could not be done without creating an unconscionable number of orphans to "foster-parent" most of the *Reformed Journal* circle came to realize. That recognition, growing with the awareness of the profundity of the nation's domestic flaws, worked some sharp reversals.[25] America changed from ideal to negative referent; Dutch America changed from shabby province to a place insufficiently apart. "Progressive" went out as a self-description, connoting as it now did a smug view of history and a naive if not noxious political agenda. "Calvinist," even "Kuyperian," came back in, with resources made for the day: a sense of comprehensive Christian engagement, informed by structural-institutional analysis; a presuppositional epistemology exposing the ideologies at work in scholarship and society alike; and a critique of the reigning ideology—corporate, materialist, liberal—that, far from producing reactionary conclusions, would allow a radical Christian alternative instead.[26] Of the two Kuyperian directions, the times brought out the antithetical even here, though not the full trailing apparatus, and the positive impulse took a new track. Witness was possible not because the world was so good, but because it was so ill. On the political level that was evident enough; on the cultural, it required Kuyper to be put on his head twice over in order to land him on his feet. It was precisely modernist art, the *Journal*'s literary critics reminded, that had restored "myth and mystery and miracle" to Western culture. If twentieth-century poetry was one of disillusionment, the illusions broken were those of secular optimism, and "the growing sense of the absurdity of life pushes [man] perilously near to the absurdity of the Cross." From this—and from positive Calvinism's oldest animus (namely, that against American materialism)—followed sympathy for countercultural discontent with dehumanized, technological society.[27]

Yet, how much of Kuyper was—and was not—involved here? What did "Kuyperian" mean, anyway, after a hundred years of use and neglect? At many points in its critique during this period the *Journal* cited some other authority than the Dutch master: Jacques Ellul on technocracy, Dostoevsky on the utopian hubris of the New Left. Against death-of-God theology it repeated much of Kuyper's "fata morgana" argument against Modernism, but unconsciously; Peter Berger served instead.[28] Of course, this was much as Kuyper would have preferred—not repristination but conversation with contemporaries. Then, too, the agenda had changed. Kuyper had spoken well to class struggle, but little to technology, and badly on race and empire. The verdict about lines of influence, therefore, must be mixed. That the *Journal*ists, compared to other Dutch Americans and vast reaches of American evangelicals, spoke so fully to these crises, by such approaches, and with such conclusions, manifests a strong, continuing Kuyperian impulse. Perhaps other traditions enabled such an address, but for this community Kuyper's was still the one that obtained. On the other hand, Kuyper himself had intended much more than the general "social action" and "cultural critique" that his name was now taken to imply. These elements were part of a larger constellation that had been reduced over time. American constrictions on separate organization and overt ideological discussion were the most familiar development. But the more important involved Kuyper's insistence that critique and action be *distinctively* Christian, and not just Christian but Calvinist. Both were predicated on principial psychology, which had fallen into disfavor over the years, along with the German Idealism whence it had sprung. By 1970 "heart commitment" still mattered but was scarcely understood to explain or assess everything. This left "distinctiveness" in trouble; indeed, the *Journal* showed as reflex (if less naive) an inclination toward a moderate Left agenda as the Confessionalists had toward the Right. As for confident Calvinism, the Vietnam era was not for imperial spirits. The *Journal*ists insisted they used the name to start conversations, not to end them, and made good on their profession by engaging in all manner of "dialogue" hereafter.[29]

Above all, Kuyper had depended on a nineteenth-century historical sense that allowed the driving forces of development to be isolated, assessed, and traced over time. The key trait of Kuyperian Calvinism was its comprehensiveness, drawing history, ideology, social structures, university theology, commoner piety, and all the proverbial "spheres" into an organic union with a biblical hermeneutic to match. Everything from the hearth to the heavens was one integrated whole. All that had suffered—more from the twentieth century than from America, but with troubling possibilities either way. Without a measure of history or a sense of system, his followers could be as "Kuyperian" as they pleased but still fall into the serial good works, the ad hoc critique, the theology-by-the-week that Kuyper had so memorably exposed as the essence—and bane—of pietism.

That such has not entirely eventuated indicates the interposition of more recent models, models that have also served to give the complexities of acculturation one more twist and make the current profile of "positive Calvinism" difficult to draw. From the American side, the brothers Niebuhr have had the greatest effect: H. Richard, in whose "Christ and culture" spectrum the *Journal* could find its perennial ideal, the "transformationalist" option; and Reinhold, for his tough-minded analysis of all human pretension and programs, those of Christians included. Indeed, Lewis Smedes's critique of "radical"/"secular" theology culminated with words that Niebuhr himself (but also Bavinck and various Dutch Americans) might have written. To say that stress on transcendence vitiates Christian social action, he suggested, is "simply wrong . . . historically and logically." To say that "the kingdom of God is identical with useful efforts to improve the quality of human life" is to trivialize the gospel. To specify "which efforts embody God's kingdom" is to court the gravest temptations. At best certain proposals may seem

> consistent enough with kingdom norms to deserve our involvement . . . [always accepting] the reservation that we may be wrong. And even when we might be right, is there not always enough human obfuscation and human duplicity in all our efforts that they deny even as they signal the promise of God's kingdom?[30]

But equally prominent have been Netherlandic figures, such as

Gerrit C. Berkouwer, from the '30s to the '70s occupant of Kuyper and Bavinck's chair at Amsterdam, author of the tradition's latest encyclopedic dogmatics, and exemplar, by his friendly criticism of Barth and Vatican II, of the constructive engagement the *Journal* desired. And, more apt still (because younger), there is Harry M. Kuitert of the same faculty, whose approach to the most contemporary theological problems quickly resonated in the *Journal*'s pages. "The way between orthodoxy and existentialism," he has said (using the phrase as a subtitle to his book *The Reality of Faith*), lies in appropriating the historical development of the faith, appreciating the historical conditioning of Scripture, and subordinating oneself to the corporate claims of both.[31] Together the two represented the approach of mediation and relativity (in both senses of the term). That the *Journal* could use them compatibly with native influences might have been due to the "Americanization" of the Netherlands that had been proceeding since World War II, with special force in the mid '60s. Developments in both countries— "horizontalism" in theology, erosion of confessional boundaries (Dutch Protestant and Catholic political parties merged in the '70s), and popular infatuation with the symbols and substance of media culture—seemed to be one.[32]

But again, affinities were selective according to underlying disposition. The young radicals of Canada turned not to Berkouwer but to his contemporary Herman Dooyeweerd for inspiration. Professor of Law (a "secular" field) at the Free University, Dooyeweerd nonetheless was much given to traditional antithetical themes and systematic theoretical approaches. He and his colleagues proposed nothing less than realizing the "purely biblical" philosophy Neo-Calvinism had always dreamt of. If his North American followers became so identified with that project as to be labeled "Dooyeweerdians," they used other Kuyperian elements as well, undiluted and without apology. The cure to the crisis posed by secular theology lay in the institute-organic church conception; problems of biblical authority and ecclesiastical deadness alike were soluble through appreciation of the "Law-Word"—the third mode of revelation supplementing the Incarnate and Inscripturated Words and amounting to "creation ordinances" or "norms" for "every sphere" of life.[33]

In the RCA, meanwhile, the return to Continental sources now came to a harvest unprecedented in the church's modern history, a harvest sufficient to make it at last the equal—and in some areas the superior—of the CRC in theological productivity. Calvin himself was the chief object of attention, but, as always, a particular Calvin was apprehended—in this case, the moderate churchman of liturgical, sacramental, and ecumenical concerns. The decrees and any extremities of thought or practice were absent. This perspective was supplied partly by the general renaissance in Calvin studies, and partly by Dutch spirits such as Bavinck, Berkouwer, and A. A. van Ruler. The first two appealed to the Reformed irenic side, the third to problems that came with taking a mainstream trajectory. For one thing, van Ruler had been instrumental in the revitalization of the Dutch National Church after World War II; in addition, he saw himself as an appreciative critic of Abraham Kuyper, adapting his better ideas to twentieth-century usefulness. Thus van Ruler spoke with a voice of Protestant establishment (he was not only antisectarian but a theocrat), yet with the sense of dynamic, "full-orbed" Christianity that had made Kuyper compelling. His principal transformation lay in substituting existential and eschatological terms for Kuyper's Idealist and tradition-historical terms; or, *vis-à-vis* Dooyeweerd, an all-embracing "Holy Spirit" for "creation ordinances." Christian engagement thus went forward under the sign of "hope" rather than "principle," by intuition more than program. If that comported well with the American pragmatic style, and even better with the requirements of negotiating National Council of Churches mazeways, it produced in the RCA itself a proposed addition to the Reformed confessional standards—*Our Song of Hope* by van Ruler student Eugene Heideman—and another note for the chords of optimism the RCA preferred.[34]

Other parts of the revitalization extended these themes. M. Eugene Osterhaven began his study of the Reformed tradition on the topic of church rather than Scripture, and underscored the comprehensive Christian mandate but hesitated over specific means and programs, especially those of "separatism." Others explored the liturgical, confessional, and even architectural dimensions of church life; for the four hundredth anniversary of the Heidelberg Catechism (1963) it was the RCA that produced the more noteworthy observance.[35] Some discontent appeared over all this "avoidance" of the "real" issue—namely, "soul salvation"—and perhaps these measures did represent an attempt to overcome the pietist and activist burden of the denomination's past, but an unlikely source made clear that they also rebuked prevailing American religious patterns. Howard Hageman, born "outside" Dutch circles, long a pastor in New Jersey, and eventually president of New Brunswick Seminary, should have been, in light of his "easternness," a sure advocate of "Americanization." But it was he who led both confessional and liturgical causes, not only in scholarship but in his weekly column in the *Church Herald*. More, these channels bore a witness to "Calvinism" startlingly compatible with some CRC traditions. Its sources were different, certainly (e.g., a German Reformed ancestry and Perry Miller's lectures in Harvard College), but its scope and substance were familiar: catechism, not revivalism; corporate cultural witness, not individual "soul saving"; the Genevan Psalter, not "the latest picnic music," which "in the name of sound Calvinism" had become "the badge of orthodoxy" in the RCA. From the middle of the American metropolis, Hageman knew the limitations of ethnic provincialism, but he also knew, better than most, the limitations of the opposite: "the overwhelming theological temper of this country has been and remains an Arminian Pietism," he proclaimed, and its seduction of all sorts of Calvinists provided a sad historical lesson. Far from accommodating, the Reformed should reassert their distinctive calling—"to make the justice and righteousness of God visible in the structures of human community and human society"—beginning from their classic base: the "foundation of the whole Christian enterprise is neither the regenerate man nor his decision [but] the saving and electing act of God."[36]

But if the most "American" sector had turned toward the Netherlands, it was only fitting that the most "traditional" should turn away. In fact, the "old country" *had* become distressingly "new" for the Confessionalists, a font of bad influences from political radicalism (as witness the Free University's awarding an honorary degree to Martin Luther King, Jr.) to confessional latitude to "weakening" of biblical authority. The last became the overriding concern. This group's most persistent argument throughout the '60s had been with certain Dutch scholars' reinterpretation ("rejection") of the first chapters of Genesis in accord with evolutionary theory; that, in turn, helped generate a wholesale reconsideration of Scripture and hermeneutics by the CRC Synod in the early '70s.[37] Given their denominational loyalty, it is not surprising that the traditionalists put a friendly construction upon the final result, but the facts militated against them. The Bible's authority, the Synod declared, lay not simply in divine inspiration but in its redemptive message. Its meaning and truthfulness emerged accordingly, inhering not so much in propositional statements concerning empirical "facts" in all sorts of domains (geological, biological, historical) as in its purpose of salvation and focus in Christ. The emphases of the Confessionalists diminished at every point, as ensuing years made clear. The group's cases against assorted professors failed one after another, while proposed changes in gender roles within the church, they believed, took rise from "the new hermeneutic." Capping the defeat once again was yet another behavioral issue—this time (1977) Synodical permission of dancing. "Never in all the years I have attended Christian Reformed Synods," reflected John Vander Ploeg after that decision, "have I felt so heartsick regarding the future of the church."[38]

With the Dutch church gone and the Dutch-American going, the Confessionalists could only look to the American in the name of maintaining their heritage. They kept close watch on denominations going through similar struggles (contradicting to that extent their opponents' accusations of insularity): the Missouri Synod Lutherans, among whom the conservatives won; the Southern Presbyterians, from whom some conservatives left; and the Orthodox Presbyterians, among whom the biblical hermeneutic (propositional, empiricist) was held to be still correct. From these reconnoiters, they gleaned a strategy for the home front: polarization, not secession—yet. Said Vander Ploeg,

> I do not envision polarization as a *permanent* solution to the conservative's problem in the CRC but rather as a *prelude* or *precursor* to what ought to follow. For liberals and conservatives to remain in tension under the same denominational roof . . . will eventually become intolerable.

Such had to be endured for the time being only to gather the solid core of support needed against the day when the cause would become clearly and finally hopeless.[39]

In some ways the Confessionalists might be seen as cutting the path of the future—forsaking a divided ethnic house for compatible American evangelicals. Indeed, the evangelical resurgence in the 1970s stirred every group in Dutch America, though not bringing their long-hoped-for unity, since each was stirred in its own way. The Confessionalists not only connected with traditionalists elsewhere but applauded an "outsider's" indictment (that of Harold Lindsell in *The Battle for the Bible*) of their own denomination. The *Church Herald* had been running material from evangelicals old and new already in the '60s, while the *Reformed Review* acknowledged the upsurge of the born-again and waited for them to gain maturity.[40] Even the Antitheticals recognized the need to adjust their appeal if not their ideas. The largest effort, however, belonged to the *Reformed Journal*. Positive Calvinism had always dreamt of having an impact on America; now, with suitable allies at hand and growing more powerful by the month, the moment seemed to have arrived.

But how could "fundamentalists," even of the "reconstructed" sort (according to Lewis Smedes's label), appear suitable to the group that customarily had the least use for them? Part of the answer appeared from Smedes's own career: he left Calvin College for Fuller Seminary in 1970, just as the *Reformed Journal* was opening to wider evangelical circles. More importantly, those circles (some of them, anyway) had dropped their Fundamentalist offenses—the millenarian fixations, the revivalistic mode, the right-wing reflexes, and the spiritual/secular dualism. Concepts of the Kingdom of God, of comprehensive divine sovereignty, of covenantal hermeneutics (for Scripture and history) seemed attractive, and the *Journal* was eager to supply the need. But most of the work was done in socio-political contexts. That reflected the hot climate of the early '70s, when the connection was forged, but even more (in the *Journal*'s mind) evangelicals' greatest need. "Without address to the core," said Smedes of one social congress, "the evangelical 'new sound' . . . will be muted to clichés and bromides, phrased into a thousand isolated opinions from as many corners." *Journal*ists contributed quite disproportionately to that "core address," participating in such signal gatherings as the Chicago Declaration of Evangelical Social Concern (1973) and the Hartford Appeal for Theological Affirmation (1975). But the periodical was also given more and more—in some issues, almost exclusively—to ethnic "outsiders," as if in pursuit of the other side of the positive Calvinist dream, that American contacts might rub away Dutch defects.[41]

But ethnicity, especially in its religious manifestation, is more than so many "positions" in or on society, theology, and life style; it is also a matter of the sensibility in which all these are lodged, the pervading spirituality that makes inner differences beneath smooth surfaces. Here we skirt upon an area where all sorts of silliness have been committed, not least in American historiography—notwithstanding which (and without trying to define *an* "American spirit") we must proceed, for the differences have been felt and are real. But inklings of convergence and ambivalence have also arisen of late. For example, the title of Richard Mouw's volume on Christian social duty, *Called To Holy Worldliness*, expresses something of what other observers have noted as a "fundamental American perspective," drawing off Puritan, Wesleyan, and Pentecostal sources.[42] That Dutch-American leaders around 1900 had found just these sources extremely problematic gives one measure of relative acculturation. But the fact that contemporary leaders are still troubled by other elements of this complex is an index of resistance. The "charismatic" movement of the early '70s met a swift and effective retort in Dutch America, and from every point on its spectrum. Here Confessionalist and Calvinist, innovator and preserver could meet—as could past and present. The argumentation of the '70s repeated exactly the charges brought three generations before against "Methodism": individualism and privatization (read "subjectivism"); feeling at the expense of intellect; frenetic "practicality" that follows first the "soul saving," then the bureaucratic imperative (now in the form of evangelists' personal empires); and through it all an Arminian "bootstrap theology" ("human potential") that displaces divine grace for human faith (read "anthropocentrism").[43]

But the deepest soundings of all have come from poets, as if theology, supposedly culture-free, cannot deal adequately with the latest conformities and so must yield to the old form of rebellion. The protest comes from the far side of experience. Having hailed ecumenicity—not, to be sure, the lust for "semantic clarification and ecclesiastical merger" that the word connotes among theologians, but the common spirit "at pre-creedal, pre-denominational levels, especially in literature and in the other arts"—Calvin College English professor Stanley Wiersma felt free to recall the Dutch portion of that spirit in the persona of "folk poet."[44] The approach, the naivete projected over critical sophistication, allows all the finesse necessary to capture Calvinist farmers plowing in bib overalls and neckties, committing their professed theology sometimes despite themselves. The poems pour out the signal disparities of the group. In pace and rhythm they evoke the contrast of noble Psalms with daily conversation. In theology they highlight the relationship between awesome Jehovah and petty man, as in life, some of those petty men, "saved," assume (even as they speak better) some of the divinity, thereby producing the final contrast of highest ideals and most catch-penny realities. Wiersma resolves this contrast neither in sentimental nor in denunciatory pieties but in the humor of a most mundane grace. Faithfulness is funny here, earthy and arduous; God is mercury, close but not to touch.[45]

A starker view comes from an insider gone out—Roderick Jellema, a member of Dutch America's preeminent intellectual clan now living in the American capital, but needing the first community, the home, to survive the second. As one of his poems puts it, birds sail free but "when they sing grip their hands down hard / into bark that is rooted and cuts the wind." Accordingly, "the gift is tension, drag"—the cultural lesson, but also the final religious lesson. From the very first poem of his first volume, recalling a classmate's "one gold period/When, crimson phrase against a darkly sky, / His jet purred into a green Korean hill," Jellema cuts to what for Calvinists must be the heart of the matter: believing in the face of death.[46]

Jellema's are poems of all "the lost faces": the three daughters stillborn; the severance from hometown; the loss of childhood patriotism, of white liberal dreams; the death of uncle, of father, and above all of adolescent son, killed in a car accident. Why do not all these add up to the death of God? How is God spoken of between secular apathy and evangelical bumperstickers? By indirection and silence, and so not spoken of at all, but listened to and heard, and that especially, for Jellema, through creation and covenant. As to the first: life is time, forms, and fleshly things, not

> that ancient Greek ghost
> the Immortal which is only
> the pressed light leaking the loss
> of what ticks tight and incarnate in apples.

As to the second: life's meanings even more than its substance are passed down through generations, through rituals and memories, lessons cleft in nuance. Sailing at night,

I am not quite lost in these reflection of stars.
Pakke's [Frisian for "grandfather"] old cells call through my bones
to say "you are losing your son,"
but a neighbor's light on the dune points home. . . .

Some night as he sails here alone
my son will pick up and bring back
senses the mind can never know about wind,
his past, work, losses, his hands.

When the son's death breaks the line, the father climbing the dune ascends into St. Peter's temptation at the Transfiguration, yearning for the unbearable perfect light. Yet he knows to return instead to "all the empty corners . . . back to these tangled things they [the dead boys] knew . . . back down to love and the faces in the street." His father's death, in turn, evokes two Exoduses—the one of Moses falsely, the one of immigration truly, with the still, small voice of Elijah in between:

His [father's] eyes pleaded with red cancer to hurry
as though it were a skyriding pillar of fire,
but it was cancer flowering down in the flesh,
and down in grey cells under skull-bone,
in an old synapse, is where God the Father
was speaking Dutch to a child
when my father said *tot ziens* and died.

Tot ziens, old carer: "until we see."
Never mind *wiedersehen*, seeing again,
that German illusion. God and the Dutch tongue know
we have never seen much.

Face by false ascent by phrase
by face by riot I learn, learn that words matter
like bodies, learn not to look up
for some pure-spirit godkin
Christ but down the lost faces
the Word became
before we made it mere word again.[47]

These expressions, like much in the '70s ethnic revival, are not naive but reclaimed, testifying by their very resistance to both the power and pall of acculturating pressures. The tension may resolve itself toward one pole or the other, but for the near future will likely persist. A few concluding observations, therefore, are in order. The question of "Americanization," this study has shown, breaks down into another: "which America?" The whole force of Dutch-American experience on both sides of the Atlantic led them to their present answer: "evangelical America." But which evangelicals? The groups within the ethnic community have picked out different elements exactly in line with their inherited mentalities. Furthermore, whatever convergence obtains has developed bilaterally, *after* the evangelicals selected and pruned away certain repellent features. It is a fair question indeed whether the Dutch have "Americanized" more than certain Americans have "Dutchified"—that is, have come to models of theology, society, and hermeneutics that were pioneered by Dutch Calvinists a hundred years ago and that they predicted would mark the path America itself would have to take as the problems of modernity struck home.[48]

The slowness of accommodation also deserves note. Having all the marks of the WASP profile, the Dutch did not melt into American society on schedule; in fact, they vociferously resisted the same. Socioeconomic dysfunction cannot explain the anomaly, for in these areas the Dutch have adjusted well enough. The reason must lie in considerable part in the realm of "outlook," religion, and "mind."

The Dutch, like many evangelicals in America, responded negatively to crucial features of modern development. This bred "ethnicity" (of an ideological-communal sort) already in the Netherlands, which easily redoubled in the process of emigration. When the surface marks of ethnicity disappeared (as in the language crisis around World War I), the older mode reemerged. This accounts for some of the similarities in structure and agenda (though often not of substance) between the Christian Reformed and Fundamentalists in the interwar era: both were "underground" and insular, fortressed against the modernist tide. And both faced the same problem when, after World War II, Modernism collapsed as a credible threat. What now would be the negative referent, the source of cohesion? There was none, and so Reformed and Fundamentalists alike surfaced willy nilly, with a set of answers—if not a complete grasp of the questions—that the larger society has found interesting, and an agenda that now faces the dubious honor of being tried.[49]

A final irony should also be mentioned: it has been the group most critical of America recently, the positive Calvinists, that has done most to legitimize opening up to the American world. Certainly the motive was to liberate others from civil-religious bondage, even to reform the nation itself, but just as certainly the process will not end with that. For one thing, the positive Calvinists have always aspired to both critique and acceptance, and their performance after both World Wars shows that in the pinch the latter will win. Whether that also proves to be the legacy of the Vietnam War cannot yet be determined. But certain trends must be less than thrilling from their point of view. "Opening up" to America can take any number of directions, not just toward the "right kind" of evangelicals.

With the religious media expansion of the '70s, the Dutch laity have unprecedented access to—and from—evangelists, institutes, methodologies, and theologies of every sort. That these for the most part offer less than the sort of rigorous, Reformed, critical spirit that the *Reformed Journal* esteems is the mildest statement of the case. That alienation of the rank and file from the elite in Dutch circles will accordingly increase is likely, auguring still another break between intellectuals and their natural constituency that will leave the latter to the mercies of pop wisdom while the former talk among themselves. One need not look far to see such happening. If the empire of Robert Schuller in the RCA is not enough, it is now matched on the CRC side by the Amway Corporation—a business, to be sure, but a gospel as well, combining militant capitalism, nationalism, materialism, and the success ethic with gestures toward that Big Fella Upstairs who loves those most who love themselves. Radical "outreach" may thus have eased precisely at the point at which it criticized new inroads of the "American Way."[50]

The Reformed, as part of a faith with universal claims, cannot rest easy with ethnicity, but neither, in their Dutch-American phase, can they rest easy without it. Or perhaps without it they would rest all too easy. Whatever critique they have been able to make of American ways has risen from a distinctive consciousness shaped by a particular culture and history, just as the remarkable loyalty and longevity that consciousness has attained are due to the intense community that has given it nurture. The parallel increases of late in pluralization of consciousness and affiliation perhaps give the negative demonstration of the case.[51] Whether that process—from community to network to holding company of assorted interests—will, should, or can do anything else but advance is a question for other observers. Only the destination is clear: this way lies the full measure of freedom and banality that is the promise of American life.

APPENDIX
DENOMINATIONAL STATISTICS

TABLE I
CRC AND RCA MEMBERSHIP STATISTICS, 1875–1980

	Churches				Families			
	CRC	RCA WEST[1]	TOTAL RCA	RCA % WEST	CRC	RCA WEST	TOTAL RCA	RCA % WEST
1875	26	78	490	16	NA[2]	5,997	42,277	14
1880	39	86	510	17	2,014	6,440	43,289	15
1885	65	92	543	17	4,645	6,843	45,654	15
1890	79	127	551	23	6,833	8,617	49,135	18
1895	121	166	618	27	9,774	11,264	55,934	20
1900	144	179	643	28	10,614	12,552	60,716	21
1905	165	191	649	29	12,186	13,272	62,623	21
1910	177	211	684	31	14,031	14,497	64,950	22
1915	223	240	718	33	16,412	17,298	70,859	24
1920	245	257	731	35	18,861	19,142	75,198	25
1925	251	256	730	35	21,430	21,996	81,537	27
1930	263	268	738	36	22,886	24,630	87,602	28
1935	279	266	726	37	23,845	26,724	87,771	30
1940	298	271	723	37	26,008	29,607	91,104	32
1945	311	290	742	39	29,315	33,415	97,499	34
1950	341	316	763	41	35,597	39,046	105,990	37
1955	466	374	831	45	44,992	46,845	119,981	39
1960	541	444	897	49	52,689	53,211	126,748	42
1965	610	480	927	52	58,699	59,975	130,736	46
1970	658	519	928	56	62,421	66,409	134,802	49
1975	688	497	919	54	65,004	74,034	134,465	55
1980	828	515	930	55	68,729	80,845	136,796	59

| | Communicant Members | | | | Total Members[3] | | | |
	CRC	RCA WEST[1]	TOTAL RCA	RCA % WEST	CRC	RCA WEST	TOTAL RCA	RCA % WEST
1875	NA[2]	8,682	70,628	12	8,065	NA[2]	92,804	—
1880	3,698	10,503	80,208	13	12,001	19,903	112,003	18
1885	6,942	10,372	83,702	12	21,156	21,555	112,119	19
1890	10,291	13,960	90,878	15	33,964	35,900	129,350	28
1895	15,598	18,885	103,348	18	47,349	46,888	144,797	32
1900	15,581	21,214	109,899	19	53,794	51,730	154,154	34
1905	21,767	24,142	116,668	21	62,572	54,021	156,320	35
1910	27,306	27,437	116,815	23	78,427	60,132	161,359	37
1915	34,648	32,726	126,847	26	86,799	69,310	175,162	40
1920	41,795	37,582	135,885	28	94,843	73,616	183,452	40
1925	47,873	44,351	145,373	31	103,668	84,068	195,491	43
1930	52,905	51,299	159,325	32	108,864	92,255	213,240	43
1935	58,554	57,629	160,065	36	116,414	99,781	216,009	46
1940	64,263	62,884	163,233	39	121,755	104,982	220,299	48
1945	73,143	70,171	173,975	40	129,979	114,455	233,112	49
1950	84,358	78,097	183,178	43	148,881	125,423	248,640	50
1955	105,947	91,456	207,732	44	196,822	147,419	289,311	51
1960	124,268	103,755	225,927	46	236,145	168,525	324,413	52
1965	140,179	115,459	232,414	50	268,165	200,007	385,754	52
1970	152,670	123,258	226,830	54	284,737	211,874	379,506	56
1975	160,660	131,486	215,827	61	286,371	210,515	360,227	58
1980	172,786	139,769	214,500	65	292,379	218,931	352,773	62

[1]"RCA West" = 1875–1915, Particular Synod of Chicago
1920–1950, Particular Synods of Chicago and Iowa
1955–1960, Particular Synods of Chicago, Iowa, and Michigan
1965–1980, Particular Synods of Chicago, Michigan, and the West

[2]NA = Not Available

[3]Baptized and Communicant Members (RCA figures 1965–1980 include the category "Inactive Communicant Members").

TABLE II
CALIFORNIA IN THE RCA

	Classis California		Cl. Calif. % of RCA West		Cl. Calif. % of Total RCA	
	COMMUNICANT MEMBERS	TOTAL MEMBERS	COMM.	TOTAL	COMM.	TOTAL
1955	3,167	5,607	3	4	1.5	2
1960	5,574	9,810	5	6	2.5	3
1965	8,275	14,856	7	7	3.5	4
1970	11,787	21,102	10	10	5	5.5
1975	15,965	25,573	12	12	7.4	7
1980	18,117	29,100	13	13	8.5	8.2

TABLE III
CANADIAN MEMBERSHIP IN THE CRC

	COMMUNICANT MEMBERS	TOTAL MEMBERS	% of CRC	
			COMM.	TOTAL
1945	1,116	2,274	1.5	1.8
1950	3,528	8,216	4.2	5.5
1955	18,031	37,865	17	19
1960	24,060	53,202	19	23
1965	28,392	64,736	20	24
1970	32,049	71,971	21	25
1975	34,681	74,893	22	26

SOURCES FOR TABLES I–III
Acts and Proceedings of the General Synod of the Reformed Church in America (New
    York: Board of Publications, RCA), years stated, 1875–1950; years subsequent,
    1955–1980.
Jaarboek/Yearbook, Christian Reformed Church (Grand Rapids: Board of Publications,
    CRC), year stated.

Notes

PREFACE

1. Michael Novak's *The Rise of the Unmeltable Ethnics* (New York, 1972), which describes the first-mentioned groups' mentalities and their confrontation with American culture, helped instigate this study.

2. An exemplary essay is Samuel P. Hays's "Modernizing Values in the History of the United States," in *American Political History as Social Analysis* (Knoxville, 1979), especially pp. 264–76.

3. The traditional histories are Jacob van Hinte's *Nederlanders in Amerika* (Groningen, 1928), and Henry S. Lucas's *Netherlanders in America* (Ann Arbor, 1955). For the newer approach, see Robert P. Swierenga's "Local-Cosmopolitan Theory and Immigrant Religion: The Social Bases of the Antebellum Dutch Reformed Schism," *Journal of Social History* 14(Fall 1980): 113–35; Robert P. Swierenga and Harry S. Stout's "Dutch Immigration in the Nineteenth Century, 1820–1877: A Quantitative Overview," *Indiana Social Studies Quarterly* 28(Autumn 1975): 7–34; and the first half of *They Came to Stay: Essays on Dutch Immigration and Settlement in America*, ed. Robert P. Swierenga (New Brunswick, N.J.: Rutgers University Press, 1984).

CHAPTER ONE

1. See Lambertus Mulder, *Revolte der Fijnen: De Afscheiding van 1834 als Sociaal Conflict en Sociale Beweging* (Meppel, 1973), pp. 126–37; H. Algra, *Het Wonder van de 19e Eeuw: van vrije kerken en kleine luyden* (Franeker, 1966), pp. 95–105; F. Ernest Stoeffler, *The Rise of Evangelical Pietism* (Leiden, 1965), pp. 109–17; and Ph. de Vries, "De Nederlandse cultuur in de eerste helfte van de 18e Eeuw," in *Algemeene Geschiedenis der Nederlanden*, ed. J. A. van Houtte, et al. (Utrecht, 1964), 7: 256–60.

2. The Dutch, indeed, produced or harbored some of the leading lights of all European pietism: William á Brakel, Friedrich Lampe, William Teellinck, William Ames, Jadocus van Lodensteyn. For descriptions of pietism in general and the Dutch brand in particular, I have relied primarily on Stoeffler's *Evangelical Pietism*, pp. 6–22, 109–79. See also Algra, *Wonder*, pp. 39–51.

3. See Mulder, *Revolte der Fijnen*, pp. 126–37; de Vries, "Nederlandse cultuur," pp. 256–60; and Stoeffler, *Evangelical Pietism*, pp. 127–79.

4. William á Brakel, for example, stressed contemplation and precisianism; his father, holy emotion; Lampe, asceticism; and Bernardus Smytegeld, human impotence (to the extent of writing 145 sermons on a text in Jeremiah likening man to a broken reed). See Stoeffler, *Evangelical Pietism*, pp. 151, 156, 157; and L. Knappert, *Geschiedenis der Nederlandsche Hervormde Kerk: Gedurende de 18e Eeuw* (Amsterdam, 1912), 2: 23–27.

5. Algra, *Wonder*, pp. 23–36.

6. De Vries, "Nederlandse cultuur," pp. 256–60.

7. Stoeffler outlines this alliance in *Evangelical Pietism* (pp. 116–17) and describes its operation among prominent authors of the period (pp. 127–48).

8. On Voetius, see Otto de Jong in *Geschiedenis van de Kerk in Nederland*, A. G. Weiler, et al. (Utrecht, 1963), pp. 138–40; on Brakel, see Stoeffler, *Evangelical Pietism*, pp. 156–57. As late as 1900, Dutch parishioners in America were reading these "fathers" in the pulpit and in private, and using their authority to clinch an argument; see Henry Beets, *De Christelijke Gereformeerde Kerk in Noord Amerika* (Grand Rapids, 1918), pp. 22–27.

9. See Stoeffler, *Evangelical Pietism*, pp. 178–79.

10. See Mulder, *Revolte der Fijnen*, pp. 84–85, 94–97; J. S. van Weerden, *Spanningen en Konflicten: Verkenningen rondom de Afscheiding van 1834* (Groningen, 1967), pp. 3–10; and Algra, *Wonder*, pp. 62–81. With the reorganization of 1816, the church's name was changed from "Gereformeerde" to "Hervormde." The former name was later claimed by the Seceders for their own denomination. Although the Hervormde was not technically an Established or State Church, it was officially preferred by the government and defended by its sanctions. In these and other ways it served the function of a National Church; therefore I will use "Hervormde Kerk" and "National Church" interchangeably.

11. Regarding the nation as a whole, see Mulder, *Revolte der Fijnen*, pp. 62–67, 84–88, 154–55; Jacob van Hinte, *Nederlanders in Amerika* (Groningen, 1928), 1: 83–91, 128–38; and Henry S. Lucas, *Netherlanders in America* (Ann Arbor, 1955), pp. 53–58. Regarding the province of Groningen alone, see van Weerden, *Spanningen en Konflicten*, pp. 81–84, 91–92, 220–30, 267, 281, 299–304.

12. So called because it was centered in the university of that city.

13. See C. W. Mönnich, in *Geschiedenis van de Kerk*, Weiler, et al., pp. 237–41; Mulder, *Revolte der Fijnen*, pp. 94–97, 142–43; Weerden, *Spanningen en Konflicten*, pp. 8–10; and Pieter R. D. Stokvis, *De Nederlandse Trek Naar Amerika, 1846–1847* (Leiden, 1977), pp. 38–39.

14. See Algra, *Wonder*, pp. 107–22; Mulder, *Revolte der Fijnen*, pp. 150–75; and Weerden, *Spanningen en Konflicten*, pp. 16–23.

15. See Mönnich, *Geschiedenis van de Kerk*, pp. 240, 253–58; and M. Elizabeth Kluit, *Het Protestantse Reveil in Nederland en Daarbuiten, 1815–1865* (Amsterdam, 1970), p. 256. As the Seceders saw it, the new hymns, one of which *had* to be sung at every service, were permeated with "the rationalistic-moralistic trio of God, virtue, and immortality," not "the classic-Christian trio of sin, salvation, and gratitude" (Stokvis, *Nederlandse Trek*, p. 39).

16. On the nation as a whole, see Algra, *Wonder*, pp. 245–50; Mönnich, *Geschiedenis van de Kerk*, pp. 240, 250, 253–58; Mulder, *Revolte der Fijnen*, pp. 154–57; and Stokvis, *Nederlandse Trek*, pp. 41–42. On particular provinces, see Mulder, pp. 237–44, 275–80, 283; and van Weerden, *Spanningen en Konflicten*, pp. 81–84, 91–92, 360–61. These studies agree that locally and nationally the Secession had sizable over-representations of the "lower-middle" and "upper-lower" classes (the former being defined as those who were self-employed but had no employees, or who had a little capital in tools, skills, or land; and the latter, as those at hire by the day or year, who had no capital, yet were not paupers [Stokvis, pp. 28–30]). The Hervormde Kerk, in comparison, had larger representation from the upper, upper-middle, and lower-lower (i.e., pauper) classes.

17. See Algra, *Wonder*, pp. 119, 241; and Mulder, *Revolte der Fijnen*, pp. 205–21.

18. See Algra, *Wonder*, pp. 126–32; Mulder, *Revolte der Fijnen*, pp. 159–75, 205–25; and Lucas, *Netherlanders in America*, pp. 50–53.

19. See Algra, *Wonder*, pp. 99–100; and Mulder, *Revolte der Fijnen*, pp. 250–57. The Secession was one of a great many instances of ecclesiastical "separation" in nineteenth-century Europe and is best categorized under the theory originally generated

in response to those cases, that of sect formation. As one recent summary presents it, the typical nineteenth-century sect drew its constituency from the lower-middle class, that sector which, in the face of commercializing and/or industrializing trends, was rendered most "marginal"—plagued by failures of experience to match expectations and by uncertainty concerning place, function, and future following the demise of established rules and roles, and thus made to suffer "relative" or "social deprivation" and often considerable *economic* stress as well (see Roland Robertson, *The Sociological Interpretation of Religion* [New York, 1970], pp. 136–37, 158–63).

As to the actual course of formation, John Wilson's depiction of American sectarianism (see *Religion in American Society: The Effective Presence* [Englewood Cliffs, N.J., 1978], pp. 51–78) applies equally well to this case. A "presectarian" body (in this case the conventicles) exists within the established church but rejects its double standard of religiosity and fosters a "leaven in the lump" self-image. It moves toward separation only when the established church presses its opposition keenly. "Schism usually involves fundamental conflicts of value . . . and result[s] from intensification of long-standing, perhaps inherent contradictions in a denomination's teachings" (p. 74). The new sectarians become highly self-conscious and articulate, maximizing doctrinal differentiation, insisting on the necessity of separation, and depicting the parent church as so far lost in worldliness or error that truth can no longer dwell in its house (p. 73). Their cause is aided by the established church's state of advanced centralization, lack of charismatic leadership (or effective symbols of unity), and erratic response to protest (now repressive, now tolerant—the course of the Dutch government in this case as well).

We would only note, in light of recent emphases upon sects' future-oriented and innovative character, that traditionalist elements were prominent in the Secession. The Seceders wished to "return to the Fathers," to restore "the true Church," which had atrophied under the establishment's heretical innovations; this task, they thought, could be best accomplished by revivifying the old Confessions. That the Secession proved a fit mode of "adapting to modernity" gives the obvious reminder that adaptation can proceed as well under the spell of "history" as of "the future."

20. See Algra, *Wonder*, pp. 144–56; Mulder, *Revolte der Fijnen*, pp. 192–201; Weerden, *Spanningen en Konflicten*, pp. 388–89; J. Bosch, *Figuren en Aspecten uit de Eeuw der Afscheiding* (Goes, 1952), pp. 84–88; and Stokvis, *Nederlandse Trek*, pp. 47–53.

21. A good overview is provided by William Petersen, *Planned Migration: The Social Determinants of the Dutch-Canadian Movement* (Berkeley and Los Angeles, 1955), pp. 29–31, 45–56; see especially pp. 49–51. Quoted material appears on pp. 30–31. See also Lucas, *Netherlanders in America*, pp. 53–58; van Hinte, *Nederlanders in Amerika*, 1: 83–91, 128–38; 2: 128–34, 144–69; and Stokvis, *Nederlandse Trek*, pp. 8–17.

22. See Robert P. Swierenga and Harry S. Stout, "Dutch Immigration in the Nineteenth Century, 1820–1877: A Quantitative Overview," *Indiana Social Studies Quarterly* 28(Autumn 1975): 22–23.

23. Ibid., p. 17.

24. Ibid., pp. 16–22, 25. See also Stokvis, *Nederlandse Trek*, pp. 6, 18, 28–30.

25. See Petersen, *Planned Migration*, pp. 47, 48, 186, 200, 229.

26. See Swierenga and Stout, "Dutch Immigration," p. 21. My estimate of the Seceders' portion of the total Dutch population is based upon Mulder's figure for Friesland (see *Revolte der Fijnen*, p. 254). The Seceders' seven percent there was higher than their nationwide share since the movement was stronger in Friesland than elsewhere.

27. See Mulder, *Revolte der Fijnen*, p. 254; and Swierenga and Stout, p. 21.

28. What percentage of Seceders emigrated has been a matter of contention and of

wildly contradictory estimates. Lucas (*Netherlanders in America*, pp. 471–78) places it at well over half; Stokvis (*Nederlandse Trek*, pp. 36–37) finds this far too high. I have arrived at my figure by taking the 2,151 Seceder "heads of households and individuals" ("h.h. & i.") who emigrated from 1844 to 1857 (according to Swierenga, "The Impact of Reformed Dutch Immigrants on the American Reformed Churches in the Nineteenth Century" [Paper presented to the American Society of Church History, Toronto, 18 April 1975], p. 37) and multiplying by 2.92—a figure derived from comparing his "h.h. & i." and "total" (adding women and children) figures for 1831–77 ("Dutch Immigration," p. 18); this yields a total of 6,281 Seceder emigrants for 1844–57. Stokvis gives the Seceder population in the Netherlands as 40,000 in 1849 and as 65,721 in 1859 (pp. 36, 37). Assuming an even rate of growth, the figure for 1857 would be 60,580. Without emigration it would have been 66,861, of which 6,281 is 9.4 percent.

29. See Swierenga, "Impact of Reformed Dutch Immigrants," p. 33; and Stokvis, *Nederlandse Trek*, p. 36. (Protestants composed eighty percent of all emigrants; .64 × .80 = .51.) The starkest comparison comes from the years 1846–47, when Netherlanders in general emigrated at a rate of 1.7 per thousand, and Seceders at a rate of 44 per thousand. That this was a *religious* skewing holds up even after adjusting for economic status (see Stokvis, p. 17).

30. See Petersen, *Planned Migration*, pp. 43–48; and Swierenga and Stout, "Dutch Immigration," pp. 15–16.

31. See Stokvis, *Nederlandse Trek*, pp. 53–60, 121–29.

32. A quantitative study is available for the post–World War II Dutch emigration to Canada that again finds the orthodox Calvinist sector disproportionately large. See Petersen, *Planned Migration*, pp. 167, 189, 200, 209.

33. For further elaboration on this theme, see G. J. ten Zijthoff, "Het Reveil en de Christelijke Gereformeerde Amerikaanse Nederlanders: Mythe en Realiteit," *Nederlands Theologisch Tijdschrift* 21(1966): 21–23, 31–35.

34. See Stokvis, *Nederlandse Trek*, pp. 49–56. In the "exodus years" of 1846–47, the general rate of Dutch emigration (per thousand of population) was 1.7; the Seceder rate was 44; their rates from the three provinces where Scholte dominated were 136, 97, and 78; their rates from the two provinces under Van Raalte's influence were 78 and 71; and in the "Northern" provinces their rates were 36 and 35—and 8 in de Cock's Groningen (p. 54). Notably, in the provinces with higher emigration rates, the Seceders formed smaller than average (1.3 percent) minorities of the population (≤1 percent), while in the north they were above average (in Groningen and Drenthe 5.7 and 6.2 percent, respectively). Moreover, the former areas were more "cosmopolitan"—more vulnerable to international economic competition and open to "outside" religious influences (p. 56). Robert Swierenga has elaborated upon this point (in "Local-Cosmopolitan Theory and Immigrant Religion: The Social Bases of the Antebellum Dutch Reformed Schism," *Journal of Social History* 14[Fall 1980]: 113–35), applying it as well to developments in Dutch America (see below, pp. 38–40).

Timothy L. Smith (in "Religion and Ethnicity in America," *American Historical Review* 83[1978]: 1155–85) has suggested that what might be called the "innovative-sectarian" type was *the* typical immigrant from most European lands. We would note here that while these did indeed form the immigrant vanguard among the Dutch, the composition of immigrants changed markedly over the next decades so that "traditionalist sectarians" of various sorts came to dominate in Dutch America, modifying the "mild" innovators (e.g., Van Raalte) and extinguishing the "radicals" (e.g., Scholte).

35. Albertus C. van Raalte and Antonie Brummelkamp, "Appeal to the Faithful in the United States in North America, May 25, 1846," in *Dutch Immigrant Memoirs and Related Writings*, ed. Henry S. Lucas (Assen, 1955), pp. 14–20. The authors were "appealing" here to the descendants of the earlier Dutch emigration to the United States. Cf. Stokvis, *Nederlandse Trek*, pp. 18–25, 61–72.

Two centuries earlier English Calvinists had cited identical complaints—economic hardship, an undesirable program of education, fears for the morals of their children, all rooted in religious corruption—in justifying their move across the Atlantic. See Edmund S. Morgan, *The Puritan Dilemma: The Story of John Winthrop* (Boston, 1958), pp. 29–30, 38–40.

36. I have relied chiefly upon the most comprehensive study of this movement, Kluit's *Protestantse Reveil.*

37. Regarding these personalities, see Kluit, *Protestanse Reveil,* pp. 62–73, 132–41; concerning their conventicle-like arrangements, see pp. 160–61, 167–68, 177–78, 394–95, 414–16.

38. See Kluit, *Protestantse Reveil,* pp. 67–70, 189–92, 400–402, 455–58.

39. See Kluit, *Protestantse Reveil,* pp. 248–49. One of da Costa's poems is entitled, "Aan Mijn Vriend, Den Theol. Stud. H. P. Scholte." See *Da Costa's Kompleete Dichtwerken,* ed. J. P. Hasbroek (Leiden, 1870), 2: 195–96.

40. See Kluit, *Protestantse Reveil,* pp. 403–10, 423–26; and Algra, *Wonder,* pp. 125–26, 132–40.

41. Isaac da Costa, *Bezwaren tegen den Geest der Eeuw* (Leiden, 1823), pp. 10–11, 81.

42. Kluit describes the political and cultural dimensions of the movement and paraphrases some of its critique in *Protestantse Reveil,* pp. 67–70, 143–52, 159–61, 189–92, 409–15, 426–44. J. C. van der Does's *Bijdrage tot de Geschiedenis der Wording van de Anti-Revolutionaire . . . Staatspartij* (Amsterdam, 1925) is a more detailed and analytical study. Typical Reveil works are da Costa, *Bezwaren,* and Abraham Capadose, *Le Despotisme Considere Comme le Developpement Natural du Systeme Liberal . . .* (Amsterdam, 1830). The best critique was made by G. Groen van Prinsterer in *Ongeloof en Revolutie,* ed. P. A. Diepenhorst (1848; Kampen, 1922); and "The Anti-Revolutionary Principle," in *La Partie Anti-Revolutionaire et Confessionale dans l'Eglise Reformee des Pays Bas,* 1860 (E. T. by J. Faber, Grand Rapids, 1956, Mimeographed).

43. See Groen van Prinsterer, *Ongeloof en Revolutie,* pp. 7–14, 58, 127–39, 182–48; and "Anti-Revolutionary Principle," pp. 1–2; Capadose, *Despotisme,* p. iv; da Costa, *Bezwaren,* pp. 3–5, 9, 12–17, 37–40, 81–89; and van der Does, *Bijdrage,* pp. 91–92.

44. See Groen van Prinsterer, *Ongeloof en Revolutie,* pp. 2–3, 7, 14, 87, 125–28, 190–97, 204; and "Anti-Revolutionary Principle," pp. 1–2; Capadose, *Despotisme,* p. iv; da Costa, *Bezwaren,* pp. 46–57.

45. See Groen van Prinsterer, *Ongeloof en Revolutie,* pp. 90–99, 132–55, 198–222, 240–44; and van der Does, *Bijdrage,* pp. 44–51, 108–12. Groen's ties to conservative thinkers are quite evident in *Ongeloof en Revolutie* (e.g., pp. 31–38). One critic divides his thought into two phases—before and after 1848, the year of both the Revolution and the publication of *Ongeloof en Revolutie.* Before 1848, Groen followed von Haller in regarding the state as all-encompassing and authoritarian, the bulwark against upheavals from below. Afterward, under the influence of Stahl, he began to see the encroaching state as the chief danger, and the protection of smaller social units as the optimal (and conserving) end. See James W. Skillen, "The Development of Calvinistic Political Theory in the Netherlands" (Ph.D. diss., Duke University, 1974), pp. 218–23.

46. See Groen van Prinsterer, *Ongeloof en Revolutie,* pp. 6, 44–47, 141–45; and "Anti-Revolutionary Principle," pp. 1–2, 6, 25–27, 35–36, 45; Capadose, *Despotisme,* pp. 48–58; da Costa, *Bezwaren,* pp. 47–48, 63–64; and van der Does, *Bijdrage,* pp. 72, 93–95, 108–12.

47. See Groen van Prinsterer, *Ongeloof en Revolutie,* pp. 48–54, 108–15, 140; and "Anti-Revolutionary Principle," pp. 1–7; da Costa, *Bezwaren,* pp. 9, 46–48, 94–

97; and van der Does, *Bijdrage,* pp. 24–27, 65–67, 91–95, 118, 123. Abraham Capadose was the most obsessed with this theme and the most extreme in expressing it (see
his *Despotisme,* pp. 46–68). For instance, he found his colleagues' comparison of the
monarch-subject relationship to the parent-child relationship insufficient; he preferred
the husband-wife model, because therein the dominated partner could never grow out of
her subjugation.

CHAPTER TWO

1. There are some disparities in the available statistics. Henry Lucas (in *Netherlan-
ders in America,* p. 641), using official U.S. records, gives 45,183 as the 1840–1880
count, and 172,439 for the 1881–1920 period. Robert Swierenga (in his essay "Dutch
Immigration Patterns in the Nineteenth and Twentieth Centuries," in *They Came to
Stay: Essays on Dutch Immigration and Settlement in America,* ed. Robert A. Swierenga
[New Brunswick, N.J.: Rutgers University Press, 1984]), working more from
Netherlandic records, gives 55,676 as the total for 1840–1880, and 125,049 for 1881–
1920. In any case, the numerical preponderance of the later over the earlier period is the
historiographical corrective I wish to make here.
2. The standard biography is P. Kasteel, *Abraham Kuyper* (Kampen, 1938). The
best short interpretation in Dutch is Jan Romein, "Abraham Kuyper: De Klokkenist der
Kleine Luyden," in Jan and Annie Romein, *Erflaters van Onze Beschaving* (Amsterdam,
1971), pp. 747–70. The best short interpretation in English is Dirk Jellema, "Abraham
Kuyper's Attack on Liberalism," *Review of Politics* 19(October 1957): 472–85. More
information and analysis are available in Th. L. Haitjema, "Abraham Kuyper und die
Theologie des Höllandischen Neucalvinismus," *Zwischen den Zeiten* 9(1931): 331–54;
Simon J. Ridderbos, *De Theologische Cultuurbeschouwing van Abraham Kuyper*
(Kampen, 1947); and Justus Vander Kroef, "Abraham Kuyper and the Rise of Neo-
Calvinism in the Netherlands," *Church History* 17(1948): 316–34. Jellema aptly characterizes Kuyper's writings as "not so much reports on a changing set of ideas
as . . . constant reiteration of already formed ideas; reiteration, development, expansion, reiteration—a constant hammering away at his readers" (p. 479). I have abstracted major themes from several of his works, rather than reviewing the latter
seriatim.
3. Kuyper's multiple roles, broad scope, and holistic vision put him in a class with
such other often overlooked nineteenth-century "revitalizers" as Hans Nielsen Hauge of
Norway (1771–1824), N. F. S. Grundtvig of Denmark (1783–1872), and England's
John Henry Newman. These figures all moved first and last from a religious base but
envisioned religious transformations working wholesale social and cultural (or "national," in the era's sense of the term) transformation as well—from political structure
to personal ethic, from high literature to (often their great love) folk culture. We shall
discuss Kuyper as a "revitalizer" in a technical sense later (see note 22 to this chapter).
Politically, Kuyper's achievement, combined with his philosophical-ideological
concern, offers interesting possibilities for comparison with his contemporaries
Gladstone and Bismarck, with both of whom, however disparate, he identified on many
different points.
4. See Kasteel, *Abraham Kuyper,* pp. 10–21; Haitjema, "Abraham Kuyper," pp.
333–35; and Jellema, "Kuyper's Attack," pp. 472–79. The novel he read while ill was
The Heir of Redclyffe, by English author Charlotte Yonge.
5. See Abraham Kuyper, *Lectures on Calvinism* (1898; Grand Rapids, 1961), pp.
73–77; *Pro Rege, of Het Koningschap van Christus* (Kampen, 1911), 1: 267–69; and
Antirevolutionaire Staatkunde: Met Nadere Toelichting op Ons Program (Kampen,
1916), 2: 288–94, 433–46.

6. Many of the meditations he wrote for his religious weekly, *De Heraut*, were later published in book form. I have consulted two of these collections in English translation: *To Be Near unto God* (Grand Rapids, 1924) and *The Practice of Godliness* (Grand Rapids, 1948). Some regard these as his best work; in any case, he excelled by the standards of the genre.

7. See Kuyper, *Lectures on Calvinism*, pp. 14–19, and the entire lecture "Calvinism and Religion," pp. 41–77.

8. Ibid., p. 171.

9. *Lectures on Calvinism* constitutes one (but by no means his only) great elaboration and repetition of this message. It is stated briefly on pp. 32–41; developed in its particulars in the lectures "Calvinism and Politics," "Calvinism and Science," and "Calvinism and Art"; and capped on pp. 187–99.

10. Quotation from Romein, "Abraham Kuyper," p. 754. On the more general point, see Romein, pp. 751–56; and Haitjema, "Abraham Kuyper," p. 345.

11. Kuyper edited the Netherlands' first mass-circulation newspapers (made viable only in the late 1860s), organized its first mass political party, and profited from franchise extension in political and ecclesiastical realms. See Kasteel, *Abraham Kuyper*, p. 24; and Johan Westra, "Confessional Parties in the Netherlands, 1813–1946" (Ph.D. diss., University of Michigan, 1972), pp. 150–54.

12. Kuyper, *Lectures on Calvinism*, p. 162. The motif is so prominent in Kuyper's writings that it is hardly possible to cite all its appearances. Some concise statements appear in *Lectures on Calvinism*, pp. 30–31, 43, 53, 54, 66, 119ff.; in *De Gemeene Gratie* (Amsterdam, 1902–1904), 1: 7, and 2: 659–60; and most famously in *Souvereiniteit in Eigen Kring* (Amsterdam, 1880), p. 35: "there is not a single inch on the whole terrain of our human existence over which Christ . . . does not exclaim, 'Mine'!" The most comprehensive treatment appears in the three volumes and 1,700 pages of *Pro Rege*, the purpose of which was to propound this idea in all its ramifications; for summary statements see 1: v–vii, 560–70, and 2: 589–90. For a secondary treatment see Ridderbos, *Theologische Cultuurbeschouwing*, pp. 88–93, 96–97, 106–18, 131–38, 265.

13. Kuyper, *Lectures on Calvinism*, p. 171.

14. Kuyper did not elaborate this model as much as operate by it. On one occasion he expressed it concisely in the following manner: "As truly as every plant has a root, so truly does a principle hide under every manifestation of life. These principles are interconnected, and have their common root in a fundamental principle; and from the latter is developed logically and systematically the whole complex of ruling ideas and conceptions that go to make up our life- and world-view" (*Lectures on Calvinism*, p. 189; see also p. 11). He was also more concerned with its application on the collective than on the individual level. A good indication of this emphasis can be found in "Calvinism a Life-System" (*Lectures on Calvinism*, pp. 9–40), especially in his analysis of the progression of world civilizations (pp. 32–40). Also illustrative is his discussion of the role of assumptions in natural science (pp. 130–38).

15. Kuyper developed this theme most forcefully in *Ijzer en Leem* (Amsterdam, 1885) and *Tweeërlei Vaderland* (Amsterdam, 1887), and used it as the ideological foundation for *Souvereiniteit in Eigen Kring* and *De Verflauwing der Grenzen* (Amsterdam, 1892). For specific statements of it see *Lectures on Calvinism*, pp. 11–12, 34, 189–91, 198, 199; and *Verflauwing der Grenzen*, pp. 8, 45. Ridderbos describes it in *Theologische Cultuurbeschouwing*, pp. 233–57.

16. Kuyper, *Lectures on Calvinism*, p. 199; *Verflauwing der Grenzen*, p. 45.

17. *Ijzer en Leem* appeared in 1885, the year before Kuyper's split with the Hervormde Kerk; *Tweeërlei Vaderland* appeared in 1887, the year after. *Souvereiniteit* was the principal address at the founding ceremonies of the Free University, and *Verflauw-*

ing der Grenzen came out on the heels of a severe electoral setback for the Anti-Revolutionary Party.

18. Quite notably in contrast to his more cursory, episodic treatment of the antithesis, Kuyper developed the doctrine of common grace in a separate treatise of monumental size—*De Gemeene Gratie*, three volumes and over 1,625 pages. Therein he provided a full biblical and historical exegesis and a lengthy description of the theory's practical implications. A brief English summary of the doctrine appears in *Lectures on Calvinism*, pp. 121–26. Ridderbos explicates it in detail in *Theologische Cultuurbeschouwing*, pp. 30–131, and S. U. Zuidema adds important insights in "Common Grace and Christian Action in Abraham Kuyper," *Communication and Confrontation* (Assen/Kampen: Van Gorcum/Kok, 1972), pp. 52–105.

19. Kuyper, *Gemeene Gratie*, 1: 7, and 2: 4–7; and Ridderbos, *Theologische Cultuurbeschouwing*, pp. 100–110.

20. Romein's is the best statement of this point. Common grace was "the valve through which Kuyper pumped fresh air into his people. . . . Through the doctrine of common grace, and through that alone, the basis of his system became broad enough to build Calvinism up from a one-sided church dogma to a many sided life- and world-view. . . . Through common grace he not only made his own group acceptable to the 'thinking part of the nation' . . . but at the same time opened the world of science and art for his fellow-believers" ("Abraham Kuyper," p. 754). S. U. Zuidema's commentary ("Common Grace and Christian Action") refines this point and in particular draws the connection between the doctrine and Kuyper's critique of pietism (p. 67). See also Ridderbos, *Theologische Cultuurbeschouwing*, pp. 98, 117–51.

21. Such as advancement of science and technology, increase in education or wealth, and European colonialism. See Ridderbos, *Theologische Cultuurbeschouwing*, pp. 192–213.

22. Kuyper's strategy conforms best not to the model used to analyze sect dynamics (as for the earlier Secession) but rather to the model of "revitalization" propounded by Anthony F. C. Wallace in *Religion: An Anthropological View* (New York, 1966), pp. 30–39, 140–65, and refined by that author in "Paradigmatic Processes in Cultural Change," an appendix to his book *Rockdale* (New York, 1978), pp. 477–85.

According to Wallace, revitalization is a group's attempt to counter its experience of stress—with the outside world (issuing particularly in feelings of anomie) and within itself (factionalism)—by changing both its own conceptual scheme (or "world view") *and* outside reality in a deliberate, persistent, and substantial way. That is a perfect depiction of Kuyper's own quest. Equally fitting is the model's prediction of leadership by a visionary, charismatic "prophet" (Kuyper was called "Father Abraham" by thousands). As forecast, the leader's new vision generated "disciples," communication networks, and eventually full organizations.

The sequence described by this model (see *Religion*, pp. 159–62) applies to Dutch Neo-Calvinism roughly as follows:

(1) Experience of *"increased stress* by many *individuals"*—1860s. Kuyper, for example, has his own conversion and delivers his first great speech ("Uniformity the Curse of Modern Life," 1869, replete with sentiments of protest and anomie) in this period.

(2) *"Cultural disorientation"*—1870s. Disaffected individuals come into contact under Kuyper's lead. The catalyzing issue is the *"school-strijd,"* an eruption of protest against state-mandated secularization of elementary education. The ensuing petition campaign mobilizes the constituency and creates the communication network upon which all succeeding Neo-Calvinistic institutions are built. The drive for a separate school system is (in terms of "Paradigmatic Process") the crucial "innovation," the "major breakthrough" that solves an immediate, concrete problem but in so doing ushers in "a whole new line of development," pointing the way to a comprehensive "solution"—in this case, the confessionally pluralistic model of society.

(3) In the 1880s, *revitalization* proper proceeds. Neo-Calvinism generates its own institutions—signally, a university (1880) and a church (1886)—and elaborates the core insight into a full ideology ("antithesis," "sphere sovereignty," etc.). (In "Paradigmatic Process," Wallace calls this "paradigmatic core development.")

(4) There follows (beginning in the 1890s) *"adaptation"* of both ideology and assessments of the outside world to account for changed conditions wrought by the "revitalizeds'" forceful actions. "Common grace" (1894) and cooperation begin to come to the fore, Kuyper looks to "the social question" for new momentum (1891), and the movement experiences new unities and schisms (1892, 1894—see below, pp. 29–31). At this stage the "transfer model"—the "temporary" structure (pluralism) under which society was to move toward the ultimate goal (a re-Christianized nation)—edges toward permanence.

(5) *Routinization* occurs after Kuyper's death in 1920. The pluralistic "transfer culture" is accepted as a permanent *modus vivendi* with larger society. The movement shifts from aggression and innovation to maintenance (precisely the tone of the Anti-Revolutionary Party during its rule in the inter-war decades under Kuyper's successor, Hendrik Colijn; the political tone colored the entire movement).

Overall, Neo-Calvinism was a mix of the "revivalistic" (aiming to restore a lost golden age) and "utopian" (aiming to achieve a golden age in the future) types, with quite the stronger stress on the former.

One part of Wallace's "Paradigmatic Process" model (of which revitalization movements form a subset) *not* applicable to Neo-Calvinism is the *"exploitation"* stage, where the larger society "captures" the emerging paradigm for its own purposes. In the present case, the paradigm was "seized" by the very group it mobilized. Ongoing tension (an option Wallace fully recognizes) rather than assimilation would be the lasting relation.

23. In *Christian Democracy in Western Europe: 1820–1953* (Notre Dame, Ind., 1957), Michael P. Fogarty describes a pattern of reworkings similar to Kuyper's occurring all over Western Europe at the same time. Before 1880, the organized Christian voice in politics, economics, and social philosophy alike had generally been traditionalist in a negative, reactionary way. After 1880 it transformed this heritage to make its critique from within the new order, accepting democracy, fluidity, disestablishment, and other central features of "modern" society (see pp. 102–10, 151, 196).

24. *De Verflauwing der Grenzen*, pp. 5–30, provides a classic expression of this historical survey. See also *Het Modernisme een Fata Morgana op Christelijk Gebied* (Amsterdam, 1871), pp. 16–28; and *Lectures on Calvinism*, pp. 18–23, 173–83. On Modernism in particular, see *Verflauwing der Grenzen*, pp. 18–20; and *Modernisme*, pp. 25–28.

25. See Kuyper, *Modernisme*, pp. 12–16, 33–34, 42–45; *Souvereiniteit*, pp. 22–25, 29; and *Ons Instinctieve Leven* (Amsterdam, 1908), pp. 17, 30.

26. Kuyper, *Verflauwing der Grenzen*, p. 19. This theme is most fully treated in *Evolutie* (Amsterdam, 1899), and recurs in *Modernisme*, pp. 53–54; *Souvereiniteit*, pp. 13–14, 29–35; and *Lectures on Calvinism*, pp. 130–38. A detailed and contextual treatment including Kuyper is provided by Ilse Bulhof, "The Netherlands," in *The Comparative Reception of Darwinism*, ed. T. F. Glick (Austin, 1972), pp. 269–306.

27. See Kuyper, *Verflauwing der Grenzen*, p. 35. More general statements are contained in *Modernisme*, pp. 28–48; *Verflauwing der Grenzen*, pp. 21–26, 37–39; *Lectures on Calvinism*, pp. 172–80; and *Souvereiniteit*, pp. 14–17.

28. See Kuyper, *Souvereiniteit*, pp. 14, 31, 33–36; *Verflauwing der Grenzen*, pp. 45–50; and *Lectures on Calvinism*, pp. 139–41.

29. A poignant expression of this appears in the conclusion of *Souvereiniteit* (pp. 34–37), where Kuyper considers the Free University's prospects for success.

30. By now anyone acquainted with the work of Peter Berger will have noted his

pertinence to many points raised here. (I have in mind particularly his analyses in *The Sacred Canopy: Elements of a Sociological Theory of Religion* [Garden City, N.Y., 1967], and *A Rumor of Angels: Modern Society and the Rediscovery of the Supernatural* [Garden City, N.Y., 1969]).

In Berger's view, "secularization" and the other mixed boons and banes of "modernity" accelerated to critical tension under industrialization—precisely the experience of the Netherlands and the context in which Neo-Calvinism emerged. The "pluralization of world views" therein entailed was graphically (and, in his own country, perhaps first) seen by Kuyper, whose response tallied nicely with Berger's theory. He undertook a "social [re]construction of reality" (the title of Berger's first book on the subject). Kuyper's efforts here, however, were *self-conscious* (as opposed to the workings of premodern societies, which were, presumably, subliminal, though no less potent). He wrote out the psychology, the principles, and the implications by which "Calvinistic reality" (both empirical and "meaning" structures) was defined, and worked constantly with his associates to fit events to that framework. But no world view, Berger insists, can long exist without "plausibility structures" (i.e., social networks of the like-minded) around to educate and uphold their membership in its "reality definitions." This Kuyper labored at with startling comprehensiveness, creating a distinct "Calvinistic world" of institutions and associations in which his group could live from the cradle to the grave. (Recall his injunction that "they who still have faith must begin by drawing a boundary around themselves, that within this circle they might develop a *life of their own*" [*Verflauwing der Grenzen*, p. 45].)

Kuyper anticipated Berger on other points as well. We shall note later their mutual resort in social philosophy to "mediating institutions" (see note 47 to this chapter). Theologically, they saw the same problem but gave radically divergent answers. Berger proposes "a return to some of the fundamental concerns," and also the spirit, of Protestant liberalism (see *Rumor of Angels*, pp. 60, 105]; he elaborates on the proposal in *The Heretical Imperative: Contemporary Possibilities of Religious Affirmation* [Garden City, N.Y., 1979]). That movement's classic form (that which is assumed in the nineteenth century) and figure (Schleiermacher), whom Berger repeatedly invokes, drew, of course, Kuyper's greatest animus. He chose an option—namely, reaffirming confessional traditions—that Berger regards as impossible; but Berger, Kuyper would retort, cannot have the religious option he prefers without the correlative ills of modernity he fears.

31. On the "historicism" of European Christian Democracy in general, see Fogarty, *Christian Democracy*, pp. 16–26. Precisely these emphases would keep Dutch Neo-Calvinism at odds with the next generation's "neo-orthodoxy," led by Karl Barth, which rejected such "earthly" mediations of absolute transcendence.

32. *Christianity and the Class Struggle*, pp. 33–34. See also *Niet de Vrijheidsboom maar het Kruis* (Amsterdam, 1889), p. 14; *Ons Instinctieve Leven*, p. 30; *Lectures on Calvinism*, pp. 87–88; and "Calvinism: The Origin and Safeguard of our Constitutional Liberties," *Bibliotheca Sacra* 52(1895): 389–90.

33. See *Christianity and Class Struggle*, pp. 35–40; *Lectures on Calvinism*, pp. 88–89, 179; and *De Christus en de Sociale Nooden en Demokratische Klippen* (Amsterdam, 1895), p. 81. See also Jellema, "Kuyper's Attack," pp. 480–81, 484; "Abraham Kuyper: Forgotten Radical?" *Calvin Forum* 15(May 1950): 211–13. Kuyper reviews the oscillation of secular politics between excessive individualistic freedom and collective authoritarianism in *Vrijheidsboom*, pp. 5–7.

34. See Kuyper, *Sociale Nooden en Demokratische Klippen*, pp. 77–85; *Vrijheidsboom*, pp. 5–7; *Lectures on Calvinism*, pp. 173, 176–80; and *Christianity and Class Struggle*, pp. 20–21, 34–36. See also Kasteel, *Abraham Kuyper*, p. 207. The diagnosis, denunciation, and (Christian) solution show remarkable parallels to those of

Leo XIII's great encyclical *Rerum Novarum*. That declaration and Kuyper's *Christianity and the Class Struggle* appeared in the same year, 1891.

35. See Kuyper, *Sociale Nooden en Demokratische Klippen*, p. 74; *Vrijheidsboom*, pp. 5–7, 10–12; and *Ons Instinctieve Leven*, p. 30.

36. See Kuyper, *Christianity and Class Struggle*, pp. 33–46. See also Jellema, "Kuyper's Attack," pp. 480–81, 484; and "Kuyper: Forgotten Radical?" pp. 211–13.

37. See Kuyper, *Sociale Nooden en Demokratische Klippen*, pp. 68–74; and *Vrijheidsboom*, pp. 10–12.

38. Nieuwenhuis, quoted in Kasteel, *Abraham Kuyper*, p. 144. The same impression emerged among the religious parties. H. A. M. Schaepman, leader of the Dutch Catholic party, wrote to A. F. Savornin-Lohman, leader of the conservative Calvinists, that "He [Kuyper] has one great onesidedness: his hatred for the conservatives" (quoted in Kasteel, *Abraham Kuyper*, p. 130).

39. *De Kleyne Luyden* (Kampen, 1917), one of Kuyper's last major speeches, expresses his particular democratic sentiments well. See also *Ons Instinctieve Leven*, pp. 29–35; *Sociale Nooden en Demokratische Klippen*, pp. 55, 61, 65, 68–70, 84–87; and *Lectures on Calvinism*, pp. 27–28. And see Kasteel, *Abraham Kuyper*, pp. 190–93; Jellema, "Kuyper: Forgotten Radical?" p. 211; and "Kuyper's Attack," p. 485; and Romein, "Abraham Kuyper," pp. 756–58.

40. See Kuyper, *Christianity and Class Struggle*, pp. 25–32, 34–36; and *Sociale Nooden en Demokratische Klippen*, pp. 77–80. Romein cites a business magazine's calling Kuyper a "greater danger than Nieuwenhuis," the Socialist leader (p. 766).

41. Quoted material from Kuyper, *Christianity and Class Struggle*, pp. 43, 50; and *Sociale Nooden en Demokratische Klippen*, pp. 77, 33. Kuyper presents this argument most thoroughly in the latter on pp. 5–56, and in the former on pp. 25–32, 44ff. See also Kasteel, *Abraham Kuyper*, pp. 205–09. To remove all doubt about his meaning, Kuyper declared that an antithesis existed between Christianity and capitalism (*Sociale Nooden en Demokratische Klippen*, p. 47), and that the *most* "special grace" (recalling Christ's reference to the camel through the eye of a needle) was required for a rich man's salvation.

42. See Kuyper, *Ons Instinctieve Leven*, p. 30; *Sociale Nooden en Demokratische Klippen*, p. 73; and *Vrijheidsboom*, pp. 10–12, 17.

43. See Kuyper, *Antirevolutionaire Staatkunde*, 1: 261–65; *Sociale Nooden en Demokratische Klippen*, pp. 72–75; *Vrijheidsboom*, pp. 7–12, 17; *Lectures on Calvinism*, pp. 83, 89–90, 98; and "Calvinism: Origin and Safeguard," pp. 662–63, 675—all especially on political authority. For the broader social dimension, see *Christianity and Class Struggle*, pp. 44ff.

44. It first appeared in systematic form in *Ons Program* (1879); *Antirevolutionaire Staatkunde* (1916) provided an updated version. Fragments and motifs of this theory recur throughout Kuyper's writings. The organizational pattern of his massive treatises *Gemeene Gratie* and *Pro Rege* reflects it also, since their volumes devoted to practical application draw the implications of the works' central themes for (in turn) the family, society, the state, and various "spheres" of society—art, education, science, and the church.

45. See Kuyper, *Antirevolutionaire Staatkunde*, pp. 201–07; and *Lectures on Calvinism*, pp. 91, 96.

46. Again, this is one of the most frequently recurring themes in Kuyper's work. It is especially evident in *Eenvormigheid, de Vloek van het Moderne Leven* (Amsterdam, 1869); but it also appears in *Christianity and Class Struggle*, pp. 40–43; *Souvereiniteit*, pp. 11–12, 24–26; *Lectures on Calvinism*, pp. 91, 94–96; *Vrijheidsboom*, pp. 18, 21; and *Sociale Nooden en Demokratische Klippen*, p. 71. A convenient catalogue of the terms of approbation (and their antonymns) in Kuyper's social thought appears in an

otherwise wrongheaded book by Jacob van Weringh, *Het Maatschappijbeeld van Abraham Kuyper* (Assen, 1967), pp. 55–56.

47. Again, these and other elements of his social philosophy and program fit the general European Christian Democratic pattern (see Fogarty, *Christian Democracy*, pp. 41–91). In the mid 1970s, Peter Berger (whose comparability to Kuyper on other points we have already noted) responded to the same problems—namely, "modernity's" bureaucratized state and depersonalized society—with praise for "mediating structures" (see *To Empower People: The Role of Mediating Structures in Public Policy* [Washington, 1977]; and "In Praise of Particularity: The Concept of Mediating Structures," in *Facing Up to Modernity: Excursions in Society, Politics, and Religion* [New York, 1977]—a Kuyperian subtitle indeed!). Kuyper's anticipation (better—Berger's following?) here was by nearly a century.

48. See Kuyper, *Lectures on Calvinism*, pp. 79–82, 92–94, 97; *Vrijheidsboom*, p. 20; and *Antirevolutionaire Staatkunde*, pp. 96–99, 122. Kuyper's concern for the poor and powerless *reinforced* (however wisely) rather than contradicted his fear of more state power and activities. "The fixed rule prevails that the stronger devours the weaker; and the stronger . . . have always known how to bend usage and magisterial ordinance so that the profit was theirs" (*Christianity and Class Struggle*, p. 22).

49. See Kuyper, *Lectures on Calvinism*, pp. 85, 88–90; and *Sociale Nooden en Demokratische Klippen*, p. 81; and Kasteel, *Abraham Kuyper*, pp. 47–57.

50. Of his many expressions of praise for and hope in "the small people," see especially *De Kleyne Luyden; Vrijheidsboom*, pp. 6–7, 20; and *Ons Instinctieve Leven*, pp. 29–35. From this and other evidence Jellema concludes that "Kuyper's social thought thus tends more toward syndicalism or Guild Socialism than it does toward a hierarchically organized corporative state" ("Abraham Kuyper's Attack," p. 483).

Kuyper's ultimate impatience with programmatic detail was perhaps reflected in and drawn from the frustrations in his term as prime minister (1901–1905). His intentions were preempted by demands of foreign policy (the Boer and Russo-Japanese Wars) and by the reverberations of an attempted general strike spearheaded by railroad workers. By the time of the next Anti-Revolutionary cabinet (1909), Kuyper was too old (72) and the younger generation too restless to allow him the first position. Thus much of his program, especially the parts concerning education and social welfare, was passed under his successors' supervision (see Westra, "Confessional Parties," pp. 202–09).

51. This is the burden of most of *Souvereiniteit in Eigen Kring* ("Sovereignty in Our Own Circle"), and of all of *De Verflauwing der Grenzen* ("The Obliteration of the Boundaries"), *Eenvormigheid, de Vloek van het Moderne Leven* ("Uniformity the Curse of Modern Life"), and *Ons Instinctieve Leven* ("Our Instinctual Life"). For concise statements of the point, see *Ons Instinctieve Leven*, pp. 15–17, 29–30, 32–35.

52. The Doleantie involved some 200 churches and 100,000 members. I have relied for my information on this matter on R. H. Bremmer, *Herman Bavinck als Dogmaticus* (Kampen, 1961), pp. 46–54; and *Herman Bavinck en zijn Tijdgenooten* (Kampen, 1966), pp. 53–90, 110–75. Though these tensions persisted for a long time, a *modus vivendi* was achieved with the decision in 1902 to allow Kampen Seminary (Secessionist) to remain independent of the Free University and with the doctrinal compromises of the Synod of Utrecht of 1905. (This matter will be discussed more completely in Chapter 3 herein.)

53. See Kasteel, *Abraham Kuyper*, pp. 99–104.

54. See Kasteel, *Abraham Kuyper*, pp. 43–76. The dispute had been building ever since 1870, when Kuyper had left his second pastorate (at Utrecht, in a church of this character) with a stinging farewell address, "Conservatisme en Orthodoxie: Valsche en Ware Behoudzucht" (Amsterdam, 1870). See Haitjema, "Abraham Kuyper," p. 335.

55. See Kasteel, *Abraham Kuyper*, pp. 173–90, 195–202; Bremmer, *Bavinck en zijn Tijdgenooten*, pp. 91–107; and Romein, "Abraham Kuyper," pp. 766–67. In both

battles Kuyper's chief opponent was Alexander F. Savornin-Lohman, a prominent figure in Neo-Calvinist circles, the Anti-Revolutionary Party's parliamentary floor leader (Kuyper controlled the party newspaper and central committee), and professor of law at the Free University (where Kuyper was on the theological faculty).

56. I have relied on Bremmer, *Herman Bavinck als Dogmaticus* and *Herman Bavinck en zijn Tijdgenooten,* for much information about Bavinck's life, writings, and involvement in Neo-Calvinism. Two of Bavinck's rectoral addresses nicely capture the basic motifs of his thought: *De Algemeene Genade* (Kampen, 1894) and *Christelijke Wereldbeschouwing* (Kampen, 1904). Two of his major works are available in English—an abridged version of *Gereformeerde Dogmatiek* (Kampen, 1895–1901) entitled *Our Reasonable Faith* (Grand Rapids, 1956), and *The Philosophy of Revelation* (New York, 1909).

57. Sample statements of his critique are available in *Philosophy of Revelation*, pp. 7–17, 33–42, 94; *Algemeene Genade*, pp. 34–36; *Christelijke Wereldbeschouwing*, pp. 30–38; and "Christendom en Natuurwetenschap," in *Kennis en Leven: opstellen en artikelen uit vroegere jaren* (Kampen, 1922), p. 200. In these places Bavinck almost duplicates Kuyper's survey of nineteenth-century European intellectual history. See also Bremmer, *Bavinck als Dogmaticus*, pp. 142–47; and *Bavinck en Tijdgenooten*, p. 249. For Bavinck's "solution," see *Christelijke Wereldbeschouwing*, pp. 11–18, 38–43, 60–88; *Algemeene Genade*, pp. 34–36; *Philosophy of Revelation*, pp. 17, 27, 35, 85, 104, 254, 309; and "Christendom en Natuurwetenschap," pp. 200–202, among other sources.

58. See Bremmer, *Bavinck als Dogmaticus*, pp. 376–81; and *Bavinck en zijn Tijdgenooten*, pp. 14–36, 127, 138, 250, 262–64.

59. In *Algemeene Genade,* 1894.

60. *De Algemeene Genade,* pp. 33–34. Bavinck put the doctrine to the same use as did Kuyper (see pp. 44–53; see also "De Navolging van Christus en het Moderne Leven," in *Kennis en Leven,* p. 135).

61. See Bavinck, *Algemeene Genade,* p. 10.

62. See Bavinck, *Philosophy of Revelation,* pp. 18, 243, 250–51, 269; and "Navolging," pp. 138–39; and Bremmer, *Bavinck en Tijdgenooten,* p. 226.

63. William Shetter's *The Pillars of Society* (The Hague, 1971) provides a fine interpretation of this social system and its effects. The Dutch word for the phenomenon is *verzuilen,* also meaning "pillars." See again the comments concerning Peter Berger's theories in relation to this matter in note 30 to this chapter.

CHAPTER THREE

1. For numerical totals, see Chapter 2, note 1 herein. Henry Lucas's table (*Netherlanders in America,* p. 641) shows the clear correlation between economic and immigration cycles. The first wave of Dutch immigration arose out of a severe agricultural depression in the Netherlands in the mid 1840s. It was curtailed by the panic of 1857 and the Civil War in the United States. There was a brief reprise between the end of the Civil War and the depression of the mid 1870s. The second phase, 1880–1920, saw a much larger scale of movement among the Dutch, as among Europeans in general. Nearly four times the 1840–1880 number (according to Lucas; 2.25 times according to Robert Swierenga) immigrated in response to a prolonged agricultural depression in the Netherlands. This wave fell off only in the worst of the hard times of the American 1890s and ended with World War I. For a description of economic conditions in the Netherlands, see Jacob van Hinte, *Nederlanders in Amerika* (Groningen, 1928), 1: 83–91, 128–38; 2: 128–34, 144–69.

2. See William Shetter, *Pillars of Society* (The Hague, 1971).

3. In Lucas's account, the church stands prominently in almost every Dutch settlement. One instance of a devout minority taking over a larger enclave occurred in Chicago; see *Netherlanders in America*, pp. 231–32. For the often sad story of settlements founded on economic schemes, see pp. 240–47, 265–67, 306–21, 391–97, 399–417, 428–40.

4. See Herbert J. Brinks, "Ostfrisians in Two Worlds," in *Perspectives on the Christian Reformed Church*, ed. Peter De Klerk and Richard De Ridder (Grand Rapids, 1983), pp. 21–34.

5. Even the non-Reformed Dutch communities that endured in some form had a religious orientation—either Catholic or Mennonite or (in an intriguing sub-tale) Mormon (see Lucas, *Netherlanders in America*, pp. 203–25, 247–49, 397–99, 444–59).

6. The original settlements were (1) Holland, Michigan, and the surrounding constellation of towns also named after the settlers' places of origin (Zeeland, Drenthe, Overisel, Vriesland, Groningen, Graafschap, Noordeloos); (2) Pella ("a place of refuge"), Iowa; (3) South Holland and Roseland, Illinois (both on the outskirts of Chicago); and (4) Alto and Sheboygan, Wisconsin. Of the Seceder ministers involved, Albertus Van Raalte (who founded Holland) and Hendrik Scholte (Pella) were the most eminent. Cornelius Vander Meulen, Koene Vanden Bosch, Maarten Ypma, and Seine Bolks worked in communities around Holland; the latter two later ministered in the Illinois and Iowa settlements as well. Pieter Zonne was a Secessionist lay leader of the Wisconsin settlements. (See Lucas, *Netherlanders in America*, pp. 87–210, 225–31.)

Over time, the settlements around Holland, Michigan, expanded contiguously and, as farmland became scarce, poured thousands into nearby cities. Thus the area bounded by Muskegon, Grand Rapids, and Kalamazoo contains the largest concentration of Dutch in the United States. The Holland settlement also fostered "daughter colonies" some two and three hundred miles northward in Michigan. The latter was a strategy also followed by the Pella, Iowa, group. The only land within their sons' means was in northwest Iowa, and the communities founded there in turn mothered settlements in the Dakotas and Minnesota, and later in California and Washington state. With their proximity to a major metropolis, the Chicago-area groups could easily absorb their own growth. A few other Dutch enclaves did develop on their own, scattered along the route between East Coast ports of entry and the midwestern settlements (e.g., Rochester, New York); on some overlooked farmland in Kansas, Idaho, and Montana; and in healthful climes such as Denver and Arizona. The later that immigrants arrived, of course, the poorer their chances were of finding farms. Thus, more and more of the latecomers settled immediately in the cities, where they joined growing numbers of Dutch Americans born in but crowded out of the countryside. These cities were those close to original settlements (especially Grand Rapids and Chicago) but also the last major area of Dutch concentration, Paterson, New Jersey, located close to the port of the Holland-American line and connected with the communities remaining from Dutch immigration in the colonial period.

7. Here and throughout I use "ideology" more broadly than in its strict political-social sense. I mean by it essentially what Abraham Kuyper called "world- and life-view" (which I avoid because of its status as cliche in Dutch Calvinist circles); that is, I refer to an integrated set of assumptions, ideas, and values encompassing the philosophical, cultural, and religious as well as the social.

8. At this time, the denomination was called the Reformed Protestant Dutch Church in America; it changed its name to Reformed Church in America in 1867. From its inception this group had been marked by strong orthodoxy. It was infused with pietism during the first Great Awakening under the influence of Theodore J. Frelinghuysen, and emerged from its Americanization crisis in the Revolutionary era

with a combination of these two traits that it has retained ever since. See John P. Luidens, "The Americanization of the Dutch Reformed Church" (Ph.D. diss., University of Oklahoma, 1969); and Johannes J. Mol, *The Breaking of Traditions: Theological Convictions in Colonial America* (Berkeley, 1968).

9. Van Raalte belonged to the "Scholte club" in Leiden and was related by marriage to Seceder pastors Antonie Brummelkamp and Simon van Velzen.

10. Besides being the Kolonie's cleric, Van Raalte also functioned as its banker, land agent, treasurer, secretary, and mayor. Concerning provincial origins, Henry Beets determined the dissidents' leadership to be "Northern" and the Van Raalte party to be "Geldersche" (see *De Christelijke Gereformeerde Kerk in Noord Amerika* [Grand Rapids, 1918], pp. 79–87). Robert Swierenga disagrees with this characterization of the membership of the two factions, although he does agree that over the next decades "Northerners" became predominant in the new group (see "Impact of Dutch Reformed Immigrants," p. 17).

11. See Swierenga, "Local-Cosmopolitan Theory and Immigrant Religion: The Social Bases of the Antebellum Dutch Reformed Schism," *Journal of Social History* 14(Fall 1980): 123.

12. This has been the most controversial issue in Dutch-American history, generating a large body of literature concerning the events and the dissident church's "right of existence." The final word from the Reformed side was William Van Eyck, *Landmarks of the Reformed Fathers* (Grand Rapids, 1922); from the dissenters' side it was Henry Beets, *Christelijke Gereformeerde Kerk,* pp. 66–120. For a review of this literature, see Herbert J. Brinks, "The CRC and RCA: A Study of Comparative Cultural Adaptation in America" (paper delivered at the Great Lakes History Conference, Grand Rapids, May 1979), notes, pp. 14–19.

13. Contrariety of cultural outlooks, so central to our understanding of "Americanization," already figured here. The eastern RCA and its midwestern loyalists saw Masonry as the prestigious social institution it had become in the U.S.; both the perception and the reality reflected the Anglo-Saxon tradition in Masonry. Midwestern opponents had Continental perceptions of the lodge as *the* Revolutionary network and of its rituals and ideology as a complete religion of an anti-Christian sort. The 1870s and '80s, of course, were Neo-Calvinism's years of mobilization via "antithesis" to "the Revolution."

14. From 1873 to 1899 the CRC grew 831 percent, while the RCA grew 111 percent. The CRC grew faster than the RCA in every three-year period within this era but never so starkly as during the years of the Masonic controversy (1881–84), when the CRC grew 66 percent and the RCA grew only 3 percent (see Swierenga, "Local-Cosmopolitan Theory," p. 121). In a sense, the events of the early '80s continued an established trend. By 1881, 37 RCA congregations had joined the CRC (which in 1880 had a total of 39 churches). But this was a continuation with a difference: in 1882 alone, 8 churches switched, helping bring the CRC total for 1885 to 65.

The CRC surpassed the western (immigrant-derived) section of the RCA in total membership in 1895 with 47,349 to their 46,888 (including baptized children). In communicant membership ("professing" or "confirmed" adults), by 1915 the CRC had 34,648 to the RCA's 32,726. By 1970 the latter count stood at 152,670 to 123,258 and the former at 284,737 to 211,874, according to the *RCA Yearbooks* and *CRC Jaarboeken/Yearbooks.* The RCA as a whole (the eastern section included) is, of course, larger than the CRC. (For more complete denominational statistical data, see Appendix.)

15. For this reason, as well as because of its having captured the largest number of the immigrants and their descendants, the CRC receives more attention in this study. This is not to suggest that the place the RCA has had in Dutch America is in any way unimportant, however. Moreover, the fact that this study is oriented toward the Dutch

in Michigan does not imply that other Dutch Americans are less significant; I have adopted this emphasis simply because about half of all Dutch Americans, the ethnic press, and the headquarters of both the CRC and the RCA "West" are located there. The RCA's Western Theological Seminary and Hope College are both in Holland, Michigan; the CRC's Calvin College and Seminary is in Grand Rapids. Parenthetically, from this point on "Dutch" means Dutch Americans, not the Dutch in the Netherlands, unless otherwise indicated.

16. See Lucas, *Netherlanders in America,* pp. 499–500. Whether such tendencies are indeed "typically American" is, of course, open to question; perhaps "famously American" is a more accurate term. Nonetheless, Timothy L. Smith makes this constellation of features normative for immigrant religious acculturation (in "Religion and Ethnicity in America," *American Historical Review* 83[1978]: 1175–83), a thesis the Dutch case contradicts.

17. According to Swierenga, "Local-Cosmopolitan Theory," pp. 123, 130.

18. According to Swierenga, "Local-Cosmopolitan Theory," p. 130. "Northerners" numbered about one-third of the CRC in 1857, and one-half of its joiners between 1857 and 1880. See also Brinks, "CRC and RCA Comparative Adaptation," notes, p. 12.

19. Brinks gives the figure as 84 percent ("CRC and RCA Comparative Adaptation," notes, p. 12); Swierenga says 77 percent ("Local-Cosmopolitan Theory," p. 130). All the developments around 1880—the new sources of Dutch immigration and their effects on CRC character, the Masonic schism and the sanction the CRC gained from it, the rise of Neo-Calvinism in the Netherlands—make that year, as much as 1857, a definitive point in Dutch-American Reformed history.

The demographics of immigration would have one additional, perhaps ironic, interaction with theology. If indeed the first members of the CRC did originate, as Swierenga argues (in "Local-Cosmopolitan Theory"), in more isolated and parochial places in the Netherlands and the RCA loyalists came from a more urban background, then this pattern was reversed in America. The majority of post-1880 immigrants entered the CRC, as we have seen, and they also increasingly began to settle in urban areas (see note 6 to this chapter). Thus the CRC slowly became more urban than the RCA West. By the mid 1920s, 34 percent of the CRC membership was in Michigan cities (Grand Rapids, Muskegon, and Kalamazoo), compared to 27 percent of the RCA West. The percentages for Chicago are virtually equal—7 and 6, respectively. But in the almost totally rural classes of Iowa, Minnesota, and the Dakotas, the opposite held; these groups constituted 19 percent of the CRC and 27 percent of the RCA West (according to *Census of Religious Bodies, 1926* [Washington, 1930], 1: 1223, 1241, and Tables 31 and 32; and 2: 1219, 1239).

Urban dwelling does not necessitate urbane attitudes, of course (on this, see Samuel P. Hays, "Political Parties and the Community-Society Continuum," in *American Political History as Social Analysis* [Knoxville, 1980], p. 297). But along with other factors it does make a simple localist-cosmopolitan comparison of the two denominations difficult to uphold. The CRC had national scope already early in the twentieth century, and it retained (more than the RCA) strong international connections (with the Netherlands); neither of these factors comports well with an ascription of "localism." It *did* recognize other churches and (again, perhaps more than the RCA) non-Christian movements in the American world. It was in strategies of response, as the following pages will argue, that the differences lay. The RCA envisioned a normative national Protestantism that befit alike its rural bastion in Iowa, its Western headquarters in small-town, homogenous Holland, Michigan, and its Eastern center in New York. The CRC, headquartered in the mid-sized (and by no means ethnically or religiously uniform) city of Grand Rapids, opted for a near sect-like denominational loyalty in a fully recognized diverse field. All of which argues that Confessional emphasis and Neo-

Calvinist strategies can stand in a pluralistic society and be just as "modern" as ostensibly "ecumenical" attitudes.

20. The discussion was catalyzed additionally by the accession in the 1890s of a few English-speaking churches in New Jersey to the CRC. These were descendants of a group that had seceded from the RCA in 1822 over allegations of Arminianizing trends in that body, the seceders having taken the conservative side. Most of these churches (seven out of the original ten) broke with the CRC early in the twentieth century, leaving it with only a small net numerical gain but an important regional entree. Still, the standard textbooks (e.g., Sydney Ahlstrom's *Religious History of the American People* [New Haven, 1972], and Winthrop Hudson's *Religion in America,* 3d ed. [New York, 1981]) tend to exaggerate the importance of this accession.

21. The first full articulation of this position was in 1886 by the Reverends J. H. Vos and L. J. Hulst in response to the formation of the first English-speaking Christian Reformed congregation in Grand Rapids (see Beets, *Christelijke Gereformeerde Kerk,* pp. 242–45).

22. B. K. Kuiper, *Ons Opmaken en Bouwen* (Grand Rapids, 1918), p. 128. This book was a collection of the articles Kuiper had written on "Americanization" in the *Banner* between January 1911 and June 1914. In quality, its only peer can be found in two series by Foppe M. Ten Hoor in *De Gereformeerde Amerikaan:* the first, "De Amerikanisatie onzer Kerk," appearing in 1898; and the second—including "Wat is het hoofddoel van *'De Gereformeerde Amerikaan'*?"; "Amerikanisatie"; and "Hoe moet onze Amerikanisatie Beginnen?"—appearing in 1909.

23. See B. K. Kuiper, *Opmaken en Bouwen,* pp. 5, 92; and *The Proposed Calvinistic College at Grand Rapids* (Grand Rapids, 1903), p. 40.

24. See the following articles by F. M. Ten Hoor in *De Gereformeerde Amerikaan:* "Verscheidenheid en Eenheid in de Gereformeerde Kerk en Theologie," 1(February 1897): 6–13; "De Amerikanisatie onzer Kerk," 2(August 1898): 289–96; and "Hoe moet onze Amerikanisatie Beginnen?" 13(March 1909): 153–61.

25. Henry Beets, "Not Ashamed of the Basis of 1857," *Banner,* 11 April 1907, pp. 184–85.

26. F. M. Ten Hoor, "Verscheidenheid en Eenheid," p. 13. Perhaps every immigrant group passed through a thought process like this, but the German Catholics, organized through their Central Verein, offer one of the clearest parallels. For them, as for Dutch Calvinists, the reformulation of ethnic identity (from the level of language and Old World–specific loyalties) and the institutional redirection that went along with it were conscious, deliberate, and quite sophisticated. Their change also exhibited the following two characteristics: (1) it evolved under a strong sense of a European heritage that, notably, had emerged out of sharp political-philosophical conflicts there (i.e., the *Kulturkampf* had distanced German Catholics from simple "fatherland" loyalties as the Secession and Neo-Calvinism had the Dutch), and (2) it produced a remarkable critique of American society and culture and of the proposed "Progressive reforms" thereof in the early twentieth century. For more on this, see Philip Gleason, *The Conservative Reformers: German-American Catholics and the Social Order* (Notre Dame, Ind., 1968), especially pp. 208–11.

27. According to B. K. Kuiper's reckoning in 1911, Christian Reformed authors in America had written six books concerning infant baptism, four on other theological issues, eight on the denomination's controversy with the RCA, five congregational histories, four treatments of the Reformed Confessions, four concerning missions, twenty catechism manuals, and thirty collections of sermons (see the *Banner* of 12 June 1911, pp. 394–95; of 29 June 1911, p. 410; and of 13 July 1911, pp. 426–27). I have used the following collections on the CRC side: Hendericus Beuker, *Leerredenen* (Holland, Mich., 1901), *Uit Eigen Kring* (Grand Rapids, 1903), *Van de Onzen* (Grand Rapids, 1910), and *Tot de Volmaking der Heiligen* (Holland, Mich., 1911); and two on

the Reformed side: *Leerredenen der Predikanten der Gereformeerde Kerk in Amerika* (Holland, Mich., 1911), and *Messages from the Word* (Holland, Mich., 1912).

28. J. Post, "Het Karakter en het Geluk van den Wandelaar naar het Zion Gods," in *Van de Onzen,* p. 73. Exemplary on this point are Hendericus Beuker, "Ze waren gewaar dat zij naakt waren" and "Des Christens innerlijke Strijd," in *Leerredenen,* pp. 18–26, 88–95; E. Breen, "Gods groote Barmhartigheid jegens zijn ontrouw Verbondsvolk," and S. B. Sevensma, "De Toevluchtneming der Ellendigen tot den nooit beschamenden God," in *Van de Onzen,* pp. 74–88, 166–83; P. Ekster, "Eene opwekking tot ernstig zelfonderzoek," in *Uit Eigen Kring,* pp. 315–30; John Karsten, "Biddag voor het Gewas," James DePree, "De Hemel Geopend," and Peter Bouma, "Het Ware Evangelie," in *Leerredenen, Gereformeerde Kerk,* pp. 29–38, 53–68, 254–63; and John Kuizenga, "The Unchanging Christ," and Nicholas Boer, "The Mercy and Goodness of God," in *Messages from the Word,* pp. 53–66, 78–86.

29. F. Hulst, "Het Leven door het Geloof," in *Uit Eigen Kring,* pp. 100–118, is perhaps the best portrait of the Reformed ideal in the sermonic literature. Other representative samples can be found in L. Hulst, "De Overwinning der Wereld," also in *Uit Eigen Kring,* pp. 55–70; J. Keizer, "De Liefde van Christus," and L. Veltkamp, "Maaien Wat We Zaaien," in *Van de Onzen,* pp. 7–20, 31–44; H. Beuker, "Het Zout der Aarde," in *Leerredenen,* pp. 230–39; John Lumkes, "De Rechtvaardige Nauwelijks Zalig," in *Leerredenen Gereformeerde Kerk,* pp. 127–37; and Benjamin Hoffman, "Lost Power," in *Messages from the Word,* pp. 185–96. The motif of heavenly rest is especially clear in H. Beuker, "Ingaan in de Rust," in *Leerredenen* (see the quotation on p. 269); and John Vander Meulen, "De Rust," in *Leerredenen Gereformeerde Kerk,* pp. 217–26.

30. The pilgrimage motif was most clearly expressed in J. Post, "Het Karakter en het Geluk," in *Van de Onzen,* pp. 60–73; Hendericus Beuker, "De Vreemdlingen en het Vaderland," in *Leerredenen,* pp. 96–104; F. Doezema, "In vreeze wandelen," in *Uit Eigen Kring,* pp. 475–84; and John Lumkes, "De Rechtvaardige Nauwelijks Zalig," in *Leerredenen Gereformeerde Kerk,* p. 131. Timothy Smith notes the pilgrimage motif among various immigrant groups but integrates it into the perfectionist, millennial, zestful complex of Progressive Era America (see "Religion and Ethnicity in America," pp. 1174–80); Dutch Americans, however, constitute at least one group that did not make this sort of synthesis.

31. Neo-Calvinist examples are G. A. DeJong, "De ware godsdienst"; K. Kuiper, "Alles is uwe"; and J. Groen, "De Uitverkiezing," in *Uit Eigen Kring,* pp. 428–41, 442–56, 525–42.

32. As I will suggest in the rest of this chapter, the acculturation of later Dutch immigrants did not simply follow the pattern J. J. Mol posits for the colonial era Dutch in his book *The Breaking of Traditions.* Briefly, Mol sees an American-context pietism overcoming a Netherlandic-derived orthodoxy. The pietist/orthodox comparison does to some degree describe RCA/CRC differences in the twentieth century, but to a larger extent it does not. Different types of pietism were present in both denominations, and in addition to Confessional orthodoxy the Neo-Calvinist movement had great impact in the Dutch-American community. Acculturation therefore involved conflict among *all* these elements and various (and shifting) combinations thereof. Moreover, Mol's sense that pietism is more "American" and bound to surpass orthodoxy in the new world does not hold for the later Dutch immigrants, who were more attracted to the confessionally emphatic CRC, and it ignores the perennial resurgence of confessional movements in American Protestant history. Finally, even for his own case Mol underestimates the Netherlandic roots of pietism and the tendency for some pietist leaders to revert toward orthodoxy in discomfort over the effects evangelical pietism can engender. For more on this, see James Tanis, *Dutch Calvinist Pietism in the Middle Colonies* (The Hague, 1968), a study of Theodore J. Frelinghuysen; see also Herman Harmelink, "Another Look at Frelinghuysen and His 'Awakening'," *Church History* 55 (1968): 423–38.

33. Blekkink was born in Oostburg, Wisconsin, in 1858, attended Hope College and New Brunswick Seminary, and was pastor of Third Church in Holland from 1905 to 1912 and Professor of Systematic Theology at Western Seminary from 1913 to 1928. Dubbink was born in Overisel, Michigan, in 1866 and attended Hope and Western, where he was professor from 1904 until his untimely death in 1910. Kolyn was born in Franklin, Wisconsin, in 1856, attended Hope and New Brunswick, pastored Second Church in Grand Rapids from 1901 to 1910, and taught at Western from 1910 to 1918. Moerdyke was born in the Netherlands and came among the first immigrants; he attended Hope and Western and pastored churches all over "the West."

34. Of the twenty faculty at the RCA's Western Academy (Hope College) and Seminary in the nineteenth century, thirteen had been trained at the New Brunswick Seminary, two in the Netherlands, and five elsewhere in the U.S. (See Brinks, "CRC-RCA Comparative Adaptation, " p. 19; for more detail, see Elton Bruins, "The Contribution of the Theological Seminary in New Brunswick to the Church in the West, 1850–1884," *Reformed Review* 13[December 1959]: 42–47.)

35. See John Higham, "Hanging Together: Divergent Unities in American History," *Journal of American History* 61(June 1974): 13. Higham's article (pp. 13–18) treats this theme succinctly, contrasting it to earlier and later "hegemonic ideologies." Fuller explications are offered in Robert Handy, *The Protestant Quest for a Christian America, 1830–1930* (Philadelphia, 1967), and Martin Marty, *Righteous Empire: The Protestant Experience in America* (New York, 1970).

Politically, evangelical Protestantism had become embodied in the Republican party from the late 1850s on, and in fact had played a fundamental role in the formation and definition of that party as it had in the Whig party before. (For this major theme of the ethno-cultural interpretation of nineteenth-century American politics, see Paul J. Kleppner, *The Cross of Culture: A Social Analysis of Midwestern Politics, 1850–1900* [New York, 1970]; Ronald P. Formisano, *The Birth of Mass Political Parties: Michigan, 1827–1861* [Princeton, 1971]; and Richard Jensen, *The Winning of the Midwest* [Chicago, 1971]). Appropriately, the RCA seemed to vote more Republican than did the CRC in the nineteenth century, although the data are fragmentary. Kleppner gives the RCA a 70/30 Republican/Democratic "intensity" rating, the CRC a 55/45. According to Formisano (pp. 185–88), the Dutch as pious Protestants had seemed "natural" Whigs from the start but had been repelled by that party's aggressive, meddling evangelical character. (Van Raalte called them "cold" and "egotistical.") The RCA began the movement toward the Republicans just before the Civil War; the CRC seems to have completed it around the 1896 election—notably, just when the Republicans moved from a "moralistic" toward a "purely economic" basis (see Formisano, p. 308; Kleppner, pp. 360, 361, 369; Jensen, p. 298).

36. As an indication, the RCA West's periodical and leadership were opposed to Abraham Kuyper's Doleantie. (See Nicholas Steffens's letters to Kuyper, 4 January, 27 October, and 1 December 1888, Steffens papers, Calvin College and Seminary Archives, Grand Rapids, Michigan.)

37. *Leader*, 29 April 1908, pp. 417–18.

38. Gerrit Dubbink, "Christianity and Man's Personality," *Leader*, 6 March 1907, pp. 296–97. Cf. John Beardslee, Jr., "God's Ideal Man," *Messages from the Word*, pp. 131–39. Such statements recall the "Groningen Theology" against which the Secession of 1834 had formed.

39. Evert Blekkink, "True Democracy," *Leader*, 19 July 1911, p. 610.

40. Henry Geerlings, *Leader*, 4 September 1912, p. 729.

41. Evert Blekkink, "The Religious Press," *Leader*, 13 September 1906, p. 1; and "True Democracy," *Leader*, 19 July 1911, p. 610.

42. The exemplar of this zeal, and long the RCA's proudest emblem, was Samuel Zwemer, born (in 1867) in the Michigan "kolonie," a legendary missionary to Arabia and Egypt. Zwemer's many books on Islam and missions gave him a national reputation in mainstream Protestantism, as his professorship of Christian Missions at Princeton

Seminary (1929–36) signifies. Missions could facilitate elite acculturation in other ways too. John Van Ess, an RCA immigrant's son, married Dorothy Firman on the Arabian field, thus joining a family that traced its ancestry on both sides to the *Mayflower* and *Arbella*. Firman's father was a Marshall Field executive, her mother an associate of Jane Addams. She herself had attended Mount Holyoke and taught at Carleton College. In Arabia the two mingled with British military and diplomatic officialdom in a galaxy far removed from the muck-farm parishes Van Ess's father had served. (See Dorothy Van Ess, *Pioneers in the Arab World* [Grand Rapids, 1974]).

43. Evert Blekkink, "Behind the Times," *Leader,* 13 February 1907, p. 242; cf. "The Theology for the Twentieth Century," *Leader,* 24 May 1911, pp. 482–83. Vigorous sermonic defenses of orthodoxy from the Reformed Church are presented by Matthew Kolyn in "The Inspired Word of God" and Siebe Nettinga in "The Persecution of Jesus," in *Messages from the Word,* pp. 89–103, 177–79.

44. Nicholas Steffens, *The Christian View with Regard to the Sins and Disorders of the World* (Holland, Mich., 1910), p. 12; and "Calvinism and the Theological Crisis," *Presbyterian and Reformed Review* 12(April 1901): 213.

45. Steffens, in a letter to Abraham Kuyper, 12 February 1890, Steffens papers, Calvin College and Seminary Archives. Thus frustrated, Steffens, who had taught at Western Seminary since 1884, left in 1895 for the German Reformed Seminary at Dubuque, Iowa. He returned to Western in 1903 and taught there until his death in 1912.

46. His infralapsarian opponents' passion on the matter was one of the factors inducing the CRC's brightest theological star, Geerhardus Vos, to leave the Grand Rapids school for Princeton Seminary in 1893. Vos's Neo-Calvinist inclinations were clear. Kuyper himself had offered him the Old Testament chair at the Free University, an invitation Vos regretfully declined. His rectoral address in Grand Rapids and inaugural address at Princeton ("The Doctrine of the Covenant in Reformed Theology" [1891] and "The Idea of Biblical Theology as a Science and as a Theological Discipline" [1894], respectively) speak in typically Neo-Calvinist accents: "Theology as a science," "the present universe as an organic whole . . . restored to its ideal state," "deepest root idea," "distinctly Reformed principle," and so on. (See *Redemptive History and Biblical Interpretation: The Shorter Writings of Geerhardus Vos,* ed. Richard B. Gaffin, Jr. [Phillipsburg, N.J., 1980], pp. 8, 235, 241. Vos's Supra position is evident in pieces on pp. 247 and 263ff., and his Neo-Calvinist stress on theocentricity in theology is pronounced throughout, notably on pp. 231ff. and 242–47.) Nicholas Steffens mentioned the Infra attacks on Vos in a letter to Abraham Kuyper of 25 January 1891, Steffens papers, Calvin College and Seminary Archives.

47. On this matter, the Synod followed the lead of its mother church in the Netherlands (the Synod of Utrecht, 1905).

48. Van Hoogen was born in Groningen in 1836, graduated from Kampen in 1865, and served churches in the Netherlands until 1893, when he came to the United States. He occupied pulpits in three central posts: Roseland (Chicago); Holland, Michigan; and Prospect Park (Paterson), New Jersey. Beuker began his ministry in 1862 and edited the Seceder and often anti-Kuyperian journal, *De Vrije Kerk.* He emigrated to America in 1893 and in 1895 became Professor of Systematic and Practical Theology at Calvin Seminary. Beuker died in 1900, Van Hoogen in 1907.

49. See Jacob Vanden Bosch, "Lammert J. Hulst," *Reformed Journal* 7(December 1957): 17–26.

50. That being the Oakdale Park Christian Reformed Church.

51. Hulst presented his views intermittently in *De Gereformeerde Amerikaan* (1912 through 1916) and more compactly as coauthor, with Gerrit K. Hemkes, of *Oud-en Nieuw-Calvinisme: Tweeledige Inlichting voor ons Hollandsche Volk* (Grand Rapids, 1913). Ten Hoor conducted two major offensives against the Supras, one in

1905 (see *Gereformeerde Amerikaan* 9[February–September]), the other in 1916 (see *Gereformeerde Amerikaan* 20[February and May–October]). These coincided with the two terms (1902–06 and 1914–22) on the seminary faculty of Ralph Janssen, a graduate of the Free University of Amsterdam and devotee of Kuyperian theology; in the interim Janssen studied in Europe and taught at Knox College in Illinois. His second term saw ascending controversy with Ten Hoor and others, culminating (for Dutch America) in an epochal battle that cost Janssen his job and sent him into permanent exile (see pp. 105–10 herein).

52. See Hulst, *Oud- en Nieuw-Calvinisme*, pp. 19, 24.

53. Gerrit K. Hemkes, *Oud- en Nieuw-Calvinisme*, p. 114.

54. Ten Hoor returned to this topic almost annually. See especially "Principieele Bezwaren," *Gereformeerde Amerikaan* 9(August 1905): 295–302; and "De Naam Calvinisme," *Gereformeerde Amerikaan* 20(September 1916): 403–16.

55. Hulst, *Oud- en Nieuw-Calvinisme*, pp. 26–27; see also 46–51.

56. F. M. Ten Hoor, "Principieele Bezwaren," *Gereformeerde Amerikaan* 9(May 1905): 21.

57. See Ten Hoor, "Het Waardelooze der Wereld door God Uitverkoren" ("The Worthless of the World Elect by God"), in *Volmaking*, pp. 280–302. Notably, this was the only sermon Ten Hoor chose to publish. A similar sermon from the Reformed Church is Jacob Vander Meulen, "Honey Out of the Rock," in *Messages from the Word*, pp. 151–61.

58. See Ten Hoor, "Principieele Bezwaren," *Gereformeerde Amerikaan* 9(August 1905): 361.

59. In this I follow Henry Zwaanstra, *Reformed Thought and Experience: A Study of the Christian Reformed Church and Its American Environment, 1890–1918* (Kampen, 1973), p. 69.

60. See F. M. Ten Hoor, "Slotwoord," *Gereformeerde Amerikaan* 20(December 1916): 497–500.

61. In his article "Abraham Kuyper—A Modern Calvinist" (*Princeton Theological Review* 19[January 1921]: 131–47), Van Lonkhuyzen presents an apt indication of this party's priorities: it devotes one sentence to common grace and two paragraphs to the antithesis.

62. Klaas Schoolland, "De Antithese," *Calvinist,* 27 February 1915. This series started sometime early in 1913 (the available *Calvinist* run is incomplete) and finished 6 March 1915. It shows how Schoolland borrowed Kuyper's journalistic structure completely. As had Kuyper in *Pro Rege* and *Gemeene Gratie*, Schoolland began with the presentation of principles in the abstract (articles 1–10) and went on to consider their implications for the church and home (11–15), for society (16–24), for various facets of politics (25–64), for voluntary association (65–73), and for art and science (74–85). (See his resume of the series in *De Calvinist*, 6 March 1915.) Schoolland's basic principles are also evident in the initial articles of his other series, especially "Onze Beginselen," *Gids*, 28 December 1907, and "Onze Taak," *Calvinist*, 20 May, 27 May, and 3 June 1911.

63. Schoolland, "Onze Taak," *Calvinist*, 19 August 1911. For example, Schoolland saw this as the chief purpose of his municipal political organization (see "Calvinisme en Nationaliteit," *Calvinist*, 4 November 1911). So strong was his group's insistence upon separate organization that Henry Zwaanstra labeled its members "Separatist Calvinists" (see *Reformed Thought and Experience*, p. 69). My label highlights the generative principle rather than the tactic deduced therefrom.

64. Schoolland, "Onze Taak," *Calvinist*, 9 September 1911. These were the concluding words of a four-month series of articles.

65. Schoolland, "Ons Hollandsch," *Gids,* 14–28 April 1906; and "Het Hoog Belang der Nederlandsche Taal voor de Calvinistische Beginselen in dit Land," *Cal-*

vinist, 3 June 1911. Henry Zwaanstra records other members of this group on this issue in *Reformed Thought and Experience,* pp. 64–65.

66. See his *Koop de Waarheid en Verkoop Ze Niet* (Den Haag, 1909). See also Ten Hoor, "Tweeërlei Uitgangspunt," *Gereformeerde Amerikaan* 5(January and March 1901); and "Beginsel en Nuttigheid," *Gereformeerde Amerikaan* 14(July–October 1910). Though accepting principialism as a method, Ten Hoor still insisted on clear Confessional authority, and his "antithesis" turned out to be the persecution by the mighty of a holy remnant, not the clash of sophisticated systems.

67. Van Lonkhuyzen, *Banner,* 20 November 1913, p. 739.

68. Groen was pastor of the Eastern Avenue Christian Reformed Church in Grand Rapids from 1900 to 1919. Beets served as the denomination's stated clerk (secretary) and director of missions for many years, and edited its English-language periodical, the *Banner,* for twenty-four years. Kuiper also wrote the first comprehensive defense of Calvin College, *The Proposed Calvinistic College at Grand Rapids,* where he taught from 1900 to 1902 and from 1907 to 1918. He also edited the denomination's Dutch-language periodical, *De Wachter,* for four years; the *Christian Journal* (successor to *De Calvinist*) for two years; and served as chief editor at the principal Dutch-American publishing house, Eerdmans-Sevensma, for four years.

69. Groen, "Onze Roeping en Idealen voor de Toekomst," in *Gedenkboek van het Vijftigjarig Jubileum der Christelijke Gereformeerde Kerk* (Grand Rapids, 1907), p. 228.

70. Henry Beets, "Prospectus," *Banner,* 1 January 1904, p. 3. Beets followed up this declaration with a nine-part series on aspects of Calvinism, often paraphrasing Kuyper's Stone Lectures (see the *Banner* of 26 February, 25 March, 22 April, 20 May, 17 June, 29 July, 9 September, and 4 November 1904, and of 17 March 1905). Groen became a Kuyperian through prolonged, intensive, and self-initiated study of Kuyper's works. B. K. Kuiper's records of his reading in the 1910s frequently list Kuyper titles (see B. K. Kuiper papers, Calvin College and Seminary Archives).

71. We should caution here *against* assuming such correlations to have been universal. Not all American-born Christian Reformed became positive Calvinists, nor were all Confessionalists or Antitheticals born and trained in the Netherlands.

72. Groen was born at Vriesland, Michigan, in 1865, the son of Secessionist parents and Van Raalte immigrants. He graduated from the Christian Reformed Church's Theological School in 1891, but only after enduring an examination by pastors who distrusted his Supralapsarian mentor, Geerhardus Vos, so ruthless that the latter intervened with indignant protests. This was the first of many trials for Groen, but the last for Vos, who left for Princeton soon after. Kuiper came to the United States in 1891 at the age of 14, graduated from the University of Chicago in 1899, and studied at the Free University from 1903 to 1907. Beets came to America in 1886 for educational purposes, occupied (Dutch-speaking) pulpits in Sioux Center, Iowa, from 1895 to 1899 and at the La Grave and Burton Heights churches in Grand Rapids (both English-speaking) from 1899 to 1920, besides editing the *Banner* from 1904 to 1928. The Beets quotation is taken from his Liberty Loan Speech (1918), Beets Papers, Calvin College and Seminary Archives.

73. See R. B. Kuiper, *Christian Liberty* (Grand Rapids, 1914).

74. Johannes Groen, "De Oude Paden," *Gids,* 29 February and 25 April 1908. See his "De Lijdende Messias," in *Uit Eigen Kring,* pp. 143–48, and Henry Beets's "Christus in Gethsemane," also in *Uit Eigen Kring,* pp. 190–204, for examples of the pietism that also marked this group. Technically "confessionalists" because of their Reformed orthodoxy, they were not obsessed with the Confessions as was the party of that name.

75. On principialism, see *Christendom en Leven* (Grand Rapids, 1916), pp. 10–13, 29–31. On the French Revolution and its consequences, see *Christendom en Leven,* pp.

86–87; *The Church and Social Problems* (Grand Rapids, 1913), p. 5; and *The Christian Laborer in the Industrial Struggle* (Grand Rapids, 1916), pp. 6–7. On separatism, see *Christian Laborer*, pp. 29–31. A prime example of his ability to assert and balance contrary tendencies can be found in *Church and Social Problems*, p. 16. Of pietist appeal are the concluding half of *Church and Social Problems* and the essay "Christendom en Beschaving," in *Christendom en Leven* (pp. 105–27). Concerning Americanization, see "Ware Beschaving," *Gereformeerde Amerikaan* 12(January 1908): 2–12.

CHAPTER FOUR

1. Tanis, "Christianity and Politics," *Calvinist*, 8 May 1915. Kuyper published reflections on his 1898 American tour (in connection with the Stone Lectures at Princeton) in *Varia Americana* (Amsterdam, 1899). Cf. his *Antirevolutionaire Staatkunde: Met Nadere Toelichting op Ons Program* (Kampen, 1916), 1: 349–53, 445–81, 705–14. Kuyper's conception of America as a Christian country (see *Varia*, p. 22) anticipated a great deal of the discussion and difficulties that we will proceed to consider: an excessive regard for the symbols of public religiosity and underestimation of the scope and depth of Enlightenment, secular, and civil religious influences throughout American life. The only surprise is that a man of Kuyper's critical acuity fell into the same mistakes.

2. Beets, *Het Leven van William McKinley* (Holland, Mich., 1901), p. 3. Beets wrote this book at the height of the public bathos over McKinley's death; *Abraham Lincoln: zijn tijd en leven* (Grand Rapids, 1909) appeared at Lincoln's centennial.

3. Marc Hanna has a small role in Beets's *McKinley* and business corporations none at all.

4. See Beets, *Abraham Lincoln*, p. 35.

5. Vennema, "The Process of Americanization," a speech delivered at the Semi-Centennial Celebration in Passaic, New Jersey, 3 August 1897, p. 7; archives, Netherlands Museum, Holland, Michigan. The second quotation is taken from M. J. Bosma's essay "Our American Churches," in *Gedenkboek van het Vijftigjarig Jubileum der Christelijke Gereformeerde Kerk* (Grand Rapids, 1907), p. 79.

6. Kuiper, *Ons Opmaken en Bouwen* (Grand Rapids, 1918), p. 7. The preceding quotation of F. M. Ten Hoor is taken from his article "Bij het Einde van den Vierde Jaargang," *Gereformeerde Amerikaan* 5(January 1901): 5. The Antithetical contribution to the chorus came from Klaas Schoolland in the *Calvinist* of 5 June 1911: "Calvinism [is] in this our new fatherland in great danger of degenerating, yes, even of perishing. The spiritual atmosphere [here is laden] with heretical doctrine and human practices in the ecclesiastical area, and with revolutionary ideas and purely humanistic hobbies on the broad terrain of Family, Society, and State."

7. Johannes Groen took this position in trying to placate those troubled by changes in language and customs (see his article "Onze Roeping en Idealen voor de Toekomst," in *Gedenkboek van het Vijftigjarig Jubileum der Christelijke Gereformeerde Kerk*, p. 219).

8. Particularly in "De Amerikanisatie onzer Kerk," *Gereformeerde Amerikaan* 2(May and June 1898): 180–87, 206–15; and in "Wat is het hoofddoel van 'De Gereformeerde Amerikaan'?" "Amerikanisatie," and "Hoe moet onze Amerikanisatie Beginnen?" (a series in three parts), *Gereformeerde Amerikaan* 13(January–March, May, and September 1909).

9. See Ten Hoor, "De Amerikanisatie onzer Kerk," *Gereformeerde Amerikaan* 2(May and June 1898): 182; with regard to what follows, see also pp. 180–87, 206–15.

10. Ten Hoor, "Wat is het hoofddoel van 'De Gereformeerde Amerikaan'?"

Gereformeerde Amerikaan 13(January 1909): 2. For his attack upon English civilization written in the context of the Boer War, see "Het Engelsch Christendom," *Gereformeerde Amerikaan* 5(October 1901): 457–63.

11. He did so especially in the following articles in *De Gereformeerde Amerikaan:*
"Het Engelsch Christendom," 5(October 1901): 457–63; "Een Woord ter inleiding van
den derden Jaargang," 3(February 1899): 1–10; "Bij het Begin van het Nieuwe Jaargang," 8(January 1904): 1–4; and "Is het Christendom in Strijd met de Rede?"
18(March 1914): 106–20.

12. Quoted matter from Ten Hoor, "Bij het Begin van der Nieuwe Jaargang,"
Gereformeerde Amerikaan 5(January 1901): 2–3.

13. Quoted matter from P. Jonker, "De Emmanuel Beweging," *Gereformeerde
Amerikaan* 13(November 1909): 569. In an interesting use of American idiom, Ten
Hoor once said that "it pays to be Reformed, that it pays better for the internal and
external life than any other system of truth" ("Hoe moet onze Amerikanisatie Beginnen?" *Gereformeerde Amerikaan* 13[March 1909]: 160).

14. Significantly, *De Gereformeerde Amerikaan*'s board of editors warned against
"Methodism" in its inaugural statement, "Een Woord Vooraf," 1(February 1897): 1–
5. For the views of spokesmen I do not treat below, see Zwaanstra, *Reformed Thought
and Experience: A Study of the Christian Reformed Church and Its American Environment, 1890–1918* (Kampen, 1973), pp. 43–49. The sermonic literature does not use the
term explicitly but in nearly every instance commends a type of spirituality at odds with
the perceived "Methodist" type: cyclical rather than linear-progressive; objective and
cognitive (with heart and mind) over against subjective and emotional; introverted;
oriented toward endurance and obedience instead of triumphalistic; and cognizant of
the large reaches of the unfathomable in God, life, and self. A prime example, which
sums these all up as solid "faith" vs. fleeting "feeling," is provided by F. Hulst, "Het
Leven door het Geloof," in *Uit Eigen Kring* (Grand Rapids, 1903), pp. 105–12.

The Dutch were not alone in this usage. For instance, people from both state and
dissenting churches in Scandinavia spoke of the "American Methodist type" in reference to evangelical proselytizing (see Frederick Hale, *Trans-Atlantic Conservative Protestantism* [New York, 1979], pp. 170–71), and a German-American Lutheran pastor
associated YMCA activities during World War I with "the Methodists" (see H. C.
Peterson and Gilbert Fite, *Opponents of War, 1917–1918* [Madison, 1957], p. 84).
More recently, historians of religion have called the nineteenth century "'The Methodist Age' in American Church History" (see C. C. Goen, *Religion in Life* 34[1965]:
562–72; see also Winthrop Hudson, *Religion in America*, 3d ed. [New York, 1981], pp.
179–81; and Catherine Albanese, *America: Religions and Religion* [Belmont, Cal.,
1981], pp. 98–101). They too refer not so much to Methodist Churches per se as to "a
generic name for the religious style" that came to dominance in this era and so "helped
to create a national ethos" (Albanese, p. 99; Goen, p. 569). The definitive elements in
that style are much the same for them as for Dutch-American observers: Arminian
theology, a subjective-experiential approach, activistic moralism, and a pronounced
concern with organization. The defects perceived are also similar: revivalistic "technique . . . pushed steadily toward reductionism and individualism"; "the emotion
which came to characterize conversion [and] tended more and more to empty religion of
normative content and to exalt a subjective experience as the essence of Christianity";
and "the influence of popular evangelicalism [which] has left a deceptive veneer of
Christian terminology . . . over a deeply rooted secularism" (Goen, pp. 565, 564, 570).

15. See K. Van Goor, "De Christelijke Gereformeerde Kansel in Amerika," in
Gedenkboek van het Vijftigjarig Jubileum der Christelijke Gereformeerde Kerk, p. 182.

16. F. M. Ten Hoor, "Is het Christendom in Strijd met de Rede?" *Gereformeerde
Amerikaan* 18(March 1914): 111. For the Neo-Calvinist position, see John Van Lonkhuyzen as cited by Zwaanstra in *Reformed Thought and Experience*, pp. 45–46.

17. F. M. Ten Hoor, "De Moderne Positieve Theologie," *Gereformeerde Amerikaan* 13(January 1909): 10. This was the final article in a four-part series on "Modernism" begun in October 1908. Concerning "mysticism," see "Wat is het Verschil tusschen de Gereformeerde Opvatting en die van het Mysticism over de Goddelijkheid der H. Schrift" (2 parts), and "Mystische Neigingen" (4 parts), *Gereformeerde Amerikaan* (March–August 1897).

18. B. K. Kuiper, "Orthodoxy and Christianity," Calvin College *Chimes,* June 1910, p. 16.

19. Steffens letters to Kuyper, 7 May 1886 and 25 January 1891. Steffens papers, Calvin College and Seminary Archives, Grand Rapids, Michigan.

20. Steffens, in a letter to Kuyper, 25 January 1891.

21. Louis Berkhof, "Onze Kerk en de Geest van ons Land," *Gereformeerde Amerikaan* 11(July 1907): 296. Similarly, the farewell address of the old Infra/Confessionalist spokesman Hendrik Van Hoogen, "Onze Gevaren," *Gedenkboek van het Vijftigjarig Jubileum der Christelijke Gereformeerde Kerk,* p. 209. Ten Hoor made this the essence of "safe" Americanization; see the following articles in *De Gereformeerde Amerikaan:* "Verscheidenheid en Eenheid in de Gereformeerde Kerk en Theologie," 1(February 1897): 6–13; "De Amerikanisatie onzer Kerk," 2(August 1898): 289–96; and "Hoe moet onze Amerikanisatie Beginnen?" 13(March 1909): 153–61.

22. Henry Beets, "Hope College Semi-Centennial," *Banner,* 22 June 1916, pp. 396–97.

23. B. K. Kuiper, "Orthodoxy and Christianity," Calvin College *Chimes,* June 1910, p. 13.

24. Klaas Schoolland, "Wel Verstaan," *Gids,* 5 October 1907.

25. See John Van Lonkhuyzen, *Billy Sunday: Een Beeld uit het Tegenwoordige Amerikaansche Godsdienstige Leven* (Grand Rapids, 1916), pp. 150–51, 153.

26. Beets defended Sunday in "Billy Sunday—a Near-by View," *Banner,* 28 September 1916, pp. 608–10. He voiced his earlier objections in the *Banner,* 28 March 1907, p. 158; and in "Revival Methods Becoming Unpopular," *Banner,* 4 May 1911, pp. 280–81. *De Gereformeerde Amerikaan*'s spokesman on current events agreed with Van Lonkhuyzen and the earlier Beets (see P. Ekster, "Op's Werelds Tooneel," 18[March 1914]: 126–28).

27. Henry Geerlings, "A Religious Phenomenon," *Leader,* 28 January 1914, p. 238. See also his "'Saturday' Meetings," *Leader,* 20 January and 17 March 1915, pp. 225, 376.

28. Evert Zagers, "Account," in *Dutch Immigrant Memoirs and Related Writings,* ed. Henry S. Lucas (Assen, 1955), p. 89. The same collection records similar complaints from 1882 (Rieks Bouws, "How I Spent My Earliest Years," p. 110) and 1911 (Sietze Bos, "Our First Settlement," p. 241).

29. The quotations are both taken from *Dutch Immigrant Memoirs*—James De Pree, "Reverend Seine Bolks," p. 383, and G. W. Renskers, "History of Settlements in Campbell County," p. 349, respectively.

30. S. Eldersveld, "Materialisme," *Gereformeerde Amerikaan* 19(May 1915): 229. Cf. Georg Americus [pseud.], "Brief uit Michigan," *Gids,* 5 January 1907: "The dollars flow without principle." Foppe Ten Hoor deplored the greed and commercialization of American life in "Hoe Moet onze Amerikanisatie Beginnen?" *Gereformeerde Amerikaan* 13(September 1909): 479–84.

31. See B. K. Kuiper, *Ons Opmaken en Bouwen,* pp. 126–27; and Jacob G. Vanden Bosch, "A Plea for Higher Education," *Banner,* 29 July 1904, pp. 283–84.

32. See Evert Blekkink, "Theology," *Leader,* 18 May 1910, pp. 465–66.

33. S. Eldersveld, "Materialisme," *Gereformeerde Amerikaan* 19(May 1915): 232.

34. Quotations from John W. Brink, "Making Light of Sins," *Banner,* 28 September 1911, p. 605; and P. Ekster, "Op's Werelds Tooneel," *Gereformeerde Amerikaan*

16(July 1912): 297. "Worldliness" of this sort was at least mentioned in nearly all the sermons of the time and it often constituted the prime object of their "practical application." Good examples include F. Hulst, "Het Leven door het Geloof"; G. D. De Jong, "De Ware Godsdienst"; and J. Manni, "De Vijanden des Heeren Overwonnen," in *Uit Eigen Kring;* and H. Beuker, "Het Zout der Aarde," in *Leerredenen* (Holland, Mich., 1901). On the RCA side there are D. De Bey, "De Invloed van het Geloof"; John Lumkes, "De Rechtvaardige Nauwelijks Zalig"; and A. W. De Jonge, "De Goedertierenheid Gods," in *Leerredenen Predikanten der Gereformeerde Kerk in Amerika* (Holland, Mich., 1912). But materialism as well as licentiousness was part of "worldliness," and some sermons referred pointedly to American examples thereof (see for example K. Kuiper, "Alles is uwe"; and J. Manni, "Het Verlaten der eerste Liefde," in *Uit Eigen Kring).*

35. See Henry Beets, "Dancing a Sinful Pastime," *Banner,* 25 February 1909, p. 124; and P. Ekster, "Op's Werelds Tooneel," *Gereformeerde Amerikaan* 16(April 1912): 166. Besides condemning the theatrical performances (see *Banner,* 12 November 1908, p. 724), Beets also pointed to the low moral character of the actors. These arguments dominated P. Jonker's criticism of the theater, too (see "The Moving Picture Shows," *Gereformeerde Amerikaan* 20[August–October 1916]), and the Reformed Church was equally aroused (see, for example, Matthew Kolyn, "Ad Nauseam," *Leader,* 17 December 1913, p. 130—a horrified denunciation of "sexually explicit" literature, concluding with a call "for a return to the old fashioned Christian home where motherhood and childhood were counted holy").

36. Columns appearing around the time of the municipal elections of 1906 and 1908 constitute a good case in point. The official platform of the local Calvinist political club gave a prominent place to the same concern ("Municipal Program of the Christian Political Society 'Fas et Jus,'" *Banner,* 26 February 1914, p. 148). Similarly, a *Banner* advertisement during the 1906 campaign recommended Alderman Ate Dijkstra to Dutch voters because he "stands for the enforcement of the Sunday closing law, . . . for the licensing and general restriction of clubs where liquor is sold, and also for the saloon districting ordinance" (16 February 1906, p. 60). A Reformed Church pastor applied the lament of lawlessness to all strata of American society: "many a citizen in our good land shows little obedience for the lawful government, many a servant little obedience for his employer, and some children little love and honor for their parents" (Gerhard De Jonge, "Address at the Old Settlers' Meeting," 3 August 1904, p. 1).

37. See Z. Z. Lydens, *The Story of Grand Rapids* (Grand Rapids, 1966), pp. 57–65.

38. See "Municipal Program of the Christian Political Society 'Fas et Jus,'" *Banner,* 26 February 1914, p. 148.

39. John W. Brink, "Op's Werelds Tooneel," *Gereformeerde Amerikaan* 11(January 1907): 16–17.

40. Henry Beets, "Independence Day Oration," 5 July 1899 (Beets Papers, Calvin College and Seminary Archives). The speech also warned about Mormons, Catholics, and secret societies, "the Devil of strong drink," the mob spirit exemplified by the Ku Klux Klan, and "that spirit of Expansion" evident in American operations in the Philippines. By 1911 this list had changed to "Plutocracy," "The Autocracy of Labor," "The Hierarchical Power of Rome," and "Jewish! Power." (Cf. Henry Beets, "Independence Day Oration," 4 July 1899 and 4 July 1911, Beets Papers, Calvin College and Seminary Archives.) If these seem, by later standards, somewhat quirky combinations, they were par for the American Protestant course at the time. (Cf. also Beets, "A Social Creed," *Banner,* 14 October 1915, p. 637.)

41. See Schoolland, "Onze Beginselen," *Gids,* 20 June 1908; and "Voor President," *Gids,* 19 September 1908. Schoolland's coeditor, Dorr Kuizema, repeated this complaint in "Monopolie en Groote Rijkdommen," *Calvinist,* 19 August 1911, the last of a series of

articles which also criticized Frederick W. Taylor's "efficiency" system and American greed in general (see *Calvinist*, 29 July and 12 August 1911).

42. Dorr Kuizema, *Calvinist*, 23 December 1911; and "Het Nieuwste in Stads-Gouvernement," *Calvinist*, 15 April 1911. For an analysis of the 1912 Grand Rapids charter vote, see Bill Westerhof, "The Defeat of the Grand Rapids Charter, 1912," unpublished paper, Calvin College and Seminary Archives. The Grand Rapids case and Kuizema's assessment thereof fit the reinterpretation of Progressive municipal reform catalyzed by Samuel P. Hays in his article "The Politics of Reform in Municipal Government" (originally published 1964; reprinted in *American Political History as Social Analysis* [Knoxville, 1980], pp. 205–32): "The movement for reform in local government, therefore, constituted an attempt by upper-class, advanced professional, and larger-business groups to take formal political power from the previously dominant lower- and middle-class elements. . . ." Thus, reform "involves a paradox: the ideology of the extension of political control and the practice of its concentration" (pp. 215, 228).

Hays's article was also a harbinger of a fundamental reinterpretation of the "Progressive Movement" as a whole, one result of which has been the demonstration of the variety—and contrariety—of elements covered by that label. Since the Dutch response became caught on the same contradictions, we should distinguish three major components of the movement:

(1) Its *"humanitarian reform,"* articulated in "democratic" and egalitarian accents ("the people" vs. "the interests"); indignant at political "corruption," corporate business hegemony, and social suffering; urging governmental intervention to regulate business and improve social welfare (hence its sometimes radical image); and yet envisioning a small state open to direct popular pressure (via initiative, referendum, and recall).

(2) Its *"managerial reform,"* concerned with "efficiency," order, control, and technique; aiming to systematize, rationalize, and centralize the economy and with it society and government; working toward a business-government collusion and direction of the entire society.

(3) The *Protestant-nationalistic tone* in which these and other ventures were proposed: exuberence over the certainty of American progress, the actuality of American greatness, and God's special interest in both, which in turn shed near-religious ultimacy upon the American Protestant bourgeois constellation of "decency," drive, education, moral fervor, and energetic uplift. For more on this, see Robert Wiebe, *The Search for Order, 1877–1920* (New York, 1967); and "The Progressive Years, 1900–1917," in *The Reinterpretation of American History and Culture*, ed. William H. Cartwright and Richard L. Watson, Jr. (Washington, 1973); William L. O'Neill, *The Progressive Years: America Comes of Age* (New York, 1975); and Samuel P. Hays, "The Organizational Society," in *American Political History as Social Analysis*.

43. See Kuizema, *Calvinist*, 10 June, 17 June, and 18 November 1911; see also B. K. Kuiper, *De Hope*, 20 May 1913.

CHAPTER FIVE

1. The *Leader* was especially fond of the "Protestant-nationalist tone" emphasis in the Progressive movement (see note 42 in Chap. 4). It also liked the "humanitarian reform" and "managerial reform" components of the movement, and was little troubled by the contradictions between and within them.

2. See Matthew Kolyn, "That Glory May Dwell in Our Land," *Leader*, 19 July 1913, p. 594.

3. One biographical (autobiographical?) sketch of Geerlings reads, "Henry Geerlings' career is interesting as it shows how the son of an immigrant ascended the social

ladder through his ability and perseverance. His life's story is an epic of steady, uninter-rupted progress, the story of the native son who achieved the most important post in his community. Here we see the highest form of Americanization already in the second generation" (*Hollanders Who Helped Build America,* ed. Bernard Vlekke and Henry Beets [New York, 1942], p. 127).

4. Henry Geerlings, "The Indomitable Spirit," *Leader,* 23 December 1914, p. 190. The extremity of Geerlings's Americanism, perhaps, is evident in his assessment of one particular tragedy: "The [American] Indian has been a true sport. He has not only accepted defeat, but turned it into a triumph. . . . The live Indian has become a good Indian and a help to civilization. He has played civilization's own game and won" ("Assimilating the Indian," *Leader,* 21 July 1915, p. 670). His postmortem appraisal of McKinley reveals, respectively, his sentimentality, his cultural ideals, and the measure of his political sagacity: he suggests that McKinley's life showed that "there may be darkness and clouds but the light and sunshine will dispel them. There may be cost and sacrifice but liberty and education come by them. He [McKinley] championed the cause of the struggling and the weak" ("In Honor to McKinley," *Leader,* 3 February 1909, p. 233).

5. Evert Blekkink, "Criminal Silence," *Leader,* 9 January 1907, p. 162.

6. See Blekkink, "Freedom's Day," *Leader,* 26 June 1907, p. 552; and "The Nation before God," *Leader,* 24 November 1909, pp. 65–66.

7. Blekkink, "The Fourth of March," *Leader,* 8 March 1909, pp. 289–90.

8. The best study is C. Warren Vander Hill's *Gerrit J. Diekema* (Grand Rapids, 1970). William Schrier, *Gerrit J. Diekema, Orator* (Grand Rapids, 1950), devotes some space to his ideas and gives excerpts from many of his speeches. For Diekema's legislative record, see Vander Hill, pp. 16–27; for his defense of temperance, p. 19; for his defense of the tariff, p. 50. Characteristic speeches are "Patriotism and Republicanism, Now and Forever, One and Inseparable" (27 February 1901); "Remarks . . . upon the Occasion of the McKinley Memorial Exercises" (17 November 1901); "The American Busi-nessman"; "The Man of the Hour [Theodore Roosevelt]" (26 November 1906); and "Address . . . on the Occasion of the Sixtieth Anniversary of the Holland Settlements in Michigan" (23 August 1907), archives, Netherlands Museum, Holland, Michigan.

9. Gerrit J. Diekema, "Remarks . . . upon the Occasion of the McKinley Memorial Exercises," and as quoted in Vander Hill, *Gerrit J. Diekema,* p. 26.

10. Vander Hill, *Gerrit J. Diekema,* p. 91. Klaas Schoolland was one who objected, in this case to Diekema's and the community's undying allegiance to the Republican party. During the campaign of 1908, Schoolland noted, the community had been much agitated by propaganda against Bryan and yet had ignored the economic interests and ideology that controlled Taft. More interesting is the fact that in this campaign the Dutch had forgotten their usual concern for the candidates' religious beliefs. Such a lapse would not have occurred, Schoolland averred, had Taft been the "stalwart Presbyterian" and Bryan the "Christ-denying Unitarian" (see "Voor President," *Gids,* 19 September 1908).

11. Schoolland elaborated his theory most completely in a commentary on the Fas et Jus statement of principles entitled "Onze Beginselen," *Gids,* 14 December 1907–12 September 1908. In "Politiek" (*Gids,* 8 June–17 August 1907) he examines the duties and the role of Christians in political affairs. In "Onze Taak" (*Calvinist,* 13 May–9 September 1911) and "Calvinisme en Nationaliteit" (*Calvinist,* 16 September–4 November 1911) he unfortunately did not keep to his announced topics but repeated the substance of the earlier series. The other systematic presentation of Reformed political thought was Dietrich H. Kromminga's "Divine Ordinances for Political Life" (*Banner,* 9 April–4 June 1914), which agreed with Schoolland on most major points.

German Catholic social theory in America ("solidarism") was more advanced than this but shared striking similarities in its critique, response, and weaknesses. It too deplored liberal individualism as a breeder of anomie and, thence, artificial collectivism. It too gave much stress to the organic, to mutuality, and to mediating institutions, advocating vocational economic organization and political representation. Deeply concerned with "the social question" of the time, it supported unions (so long as they had distinct Catholic ideological cells within them); and it rejected the purely materialistic, technocratic, and pragmatic solutions of the Progressive Era as inadequate to the fully humane (i.e., including spiritual cultivation) life central to Catholic theory. But like Dutch Calvinists, its articulators had difficulty with practical application and specific recommendations, returning again and again to elaboration of theory and description of a near-utopian ideal. (See Philip Gleason, *Conservative Reformers: German-American Catholics and the Social Order* [Notre Dame, Ind., 1968], pp. 125–41, 214–16.)

12. Schoolland, "Onze Beginselen," *Gids,* 4 January 1908. Schoolland repeated this point later in this series (7 and 21 March and 23 May 1908) as well as in "Politiek" (*Gids,* 15 June 1907), in "Onze Taak" (*Calvinist,* 20 and 27 May 1911), and in "Calvinisme en Nationaliteit" (*Calvinist,* 17 October 1911).

13. Klaas Schoolland, "Onze Beginselen," *Gids,* 1 February 1908; he expanded upon the family in the 25 January and 18 and 25 April 1908 articles of the same series. Henry Beets, *Het Leven van William McKinley* (Holland, Mich., 1901), pp. 13–18, 37–41; and *Abraham Lincoln: zijn tijd en leven* (Grand Rapids, 1909), pp. 25, 26. Louis Berkhof, "De Emancipatie der Vrouw en het Huisgezin," in *Christendom en Leven* (Grand Rapids, 1916), pp. 67–80. B. K. Kuiper, *Ons Opmaken en Bouwen* (Grand Rapids, 1918), p. 149 (note the exact Kuyperian terminology). P. Jonker added *De Gereformeerde Amerikaan*'s voice to the matter in a series entitled "Het Huisgezin," 11(January, March, and April 1907): 5–9, 119–22, 145–50.

14. See Schoolland, "Onze Beginselen," *Gids,* 15 February and 16 May 1908.

15. See Schoolland, "Onze Beginselen," *Gids,* 25 January, 1 February, and 11 and 18 July 1908; and "Onze Taak," *Calvinist,* 5 and 12 August 1911. D. H. Kromminga gave his strongest emphasis to warnings against encroachments by the state (see "Divine Ordinances for Political Life," *Banner,* 14 and 21 May 1914, pp. 326, 342).

16. See Schoolland, "Politiek," *Gids,* 3–17 August 1907; and "Onze Taak," *Calvinist,* 19 August–9 September 1911.

17. Phrase quoted from John Van Lonkhuyzen, *De Fundamenten Omgestooten* (Grand Rapids, 1913), a sermon that is typical in the way it trumpets the momentousness of concrete social developments (in this case, recent labor strife and exposes of sexual immorality in Grand Rapids) and then offers a strictly theoretical solution.

18. See Ten Hoor, "Slotwoord," *Gereformeerde Amerikaan* 20(December 1916): 497–500; the quoted matter appears on pp. 498–99. Ten Hoor's farewell also illustrated the static nature of the Confessionalist mind. He repeated almost verbatim his opening statement in 1897 and his series on Americanization in 1898 and 1909. In fact, he gave no indication that "his people" had progressed or regressed in the twenty years since his first statement, or that he and his colleagues had reached any settled conclusions about the nature of American society or the process of Dutch adjustment to it.

19. P. Ekster, "Op's Werelds Tooneel," *Gereformeerde Amerikaan* 17(April 1913): 164. The quality of Confessionalist social commentary is exemplified by Ekster's criticism of endurance feats, which he condemned not because they exploited or degraded the participants, but because they forced them to miss regular meals, sleep, and Scripture reading. Similarly, the sinking of the *Lusitania* did not prompt *De Gereformeerde Amerikaan* to discuss international law, political alliances, the world's military situation, or the just means of war; rather, it provoked an allegory concerning "the Christian life." The Christian was likened to the unfortunate vessel—alone and ever threatened by enemies; he therefore should live cautiously and prayerfully; death often strikes without warning and within sight of safety, so the Christian ought to make sure of his salvation now; the redeemed will always constitute a minority, just as most of the passengers went down with the ship to eternal damnation. (See Ekster, "Op's Werelds Tooneel," *Gereformeerde Amerikaan* 16[May 1912]: 205; and 19[June 1915]: 258–61.)

20. See Berkhof, *Church and Social Problems* (Grand Rapids, 1913), pp. 18–20.
21. See Beets, "The Study of Social Problems," *Banner*, 14 May 1914, p. 325; and "Prayer for Our New President," *Banner*, 6 March 1913, p. 148.
22. See Matthew Kolyn, "Have Not Fellowship," *Leader*, 11 October 1916, p. 818; Klaas Schoolland, *Gids*, 19 July 1909; John W. Brink, "Op's Werelds Tooneel," *Gereformeerde Amerikaan* 12(February 1908): 118; and Henry Beets, "A Deplorable Stand against Local Option," *Banner*, 16 December 1909, p. 817. For other attacks on the saloon, see P. Jonker, "Gemeenschapleven," *Gereformeerde Amerikaan* 14(June–December 1910); Edward J. Tanis, "Prohibition," *Banner*, 20 September–2 November 1916; and almost every one of Ate Dijkstra's columns on Grand Rapids politics in *De Gids* between 1907 and 1909, especially "De Drankhandel," 18 April–22 May 1909. Henry Zwaanstra reviews the arguments on this issue in great detail in *Reformed Thought and Experience: A Study of the Christian Reformed Church and Its American Environment, 1890–1918* (Kampen, 1973), pp. 219–39.
This cross-factional agreement should caution against casual use of temperance as an index of Americanization (which standard would indicate all the Dutch to be thoroughly and equally Americanized). True, drinking was common practice in the Netherlands—after all, the Dutch had pioneered in the art of distilling—and even the most orthodox parishioner enjoyed his *slokje* before dinner. But temperance, too, was popular in the Netherlands at this time; no less a figure than Abraham Kuyper, for instance, praised America for its "dry" public ceremonies (see *Varia Americana* [Amsterdam, 1899], pp. 4–6). Besides, the Dutch in the Netherlands had always distinguished between *private* drinking (in the home, among intimates) and *public* drinking (with "strangers" in dubious surroundings); hence the unanimity against saloons. The differences among Dutch Americans arose—and here the issue *can* help measure acculturation—because some joined the "Americans" in proscribing drinking per se while others adhered to the traditional distinction, advocating *voluntary restraint* rather than legal prohibition or total abstinence.
23. See Evert Blekkink, "The King and Duty," *Leader*, 31 March 1909, p. 354; and Gerrit Dubbink, "The Anti-Saloon Movement," *Leader*, 29 March 1911, p. 354. The Dutch case harmonizes with trends throughout the state and nation; higher social status and lower ethnic consciousness (RCA) correlated with greater support of Prohibition (see Larry Engelmann, "Dry Renaissance: The Local Option Years, 1889–1917," *Michigan History* 59[1975]: 69–90). It also comports well with the ethno-cultural political model (see Chap. 3, note 35) that finds the temperance/Prohibition issue of particular importance in explaining local political divisions. Churches of the British-derived evangelical type were strongly for temperance; those of the Catholic, liturgical, or Confessional type were opposed. In the Dutch case, the RCA was well on the evangelical side of the spectrum, while the CRC was nearer the middle (as indicated by its division on the issue).
24. Edward J. Tanis, "Prohibition," *Banner*, 28 September 1916, p. 615.
25. For the war in *De Gids*, see Ate Dijkstra's "De Drankhandel," 18 April–22 May 1909; and Klaas Schoolland, "De Saloon-Kwestie," 3 July–7 August and 16 October 1909 (the quoted material appeared in issues of 10, 17, and 31 July 1909). Schoolland recorded his protest in 1916 in "Prohibitie?" *Calvinist*, 26 August, 10 October, and 4 November.
26. See Beets, "A Deplorable Stand against Local Option," *Banner*, 16 December 1909, pp. 816–17; and "Professor Schoolland on Prohibition," *Banner*, 21 September 1916, pp. 592–93.
27. John W. Brink, "Op's Werelds Tooneel," *Gereformeerde Amerikaan* 15(December 1911): 580. Other typical statements in *De Gereformeerde Amerikaan* include J. Manni, "Eenige Gedachten aangaande het Anarchisme," 4(August, September, and October 1900); Idzaard Van Dellen, "Staatsarmenzorg," 10(March 1906): 97–103; and J. De Haan, "The Struggle of the Working-man in Social Life," 18(September 1914):

397–98. See also Louis Berkhof, *The Christian Laborer in the Industrial Struggle* (Grand Rapids, 1916), pp. 13–23; and John Van Lonkhuyzen, *Het Recht van Werkstaking* (Grand Rapids, 1913).

28. Schoolland, "Onder 't Zoeklicht," *Calvinist*, 12 August 1911; Jacob Manni, "Het Socialisme en Communisme," *Gereformeerde Amerikaan* 6(March 1902): 136–37; and Berkhof, *Christian Laborer*, pp. 6–9; and *The Church and Social Problems* (Grand Rapids, 1913), pp. 4–7.

29. Jacob Manni, "Het Socialisme en Communisme," *Gereformeerde Amerikaan* 6(March 1902): 138; Klaas Schoolland, "Onder 't Zoeklicht," *Calvinist*, 12 August 1911.

30. Schoolland opposed the strikers in his column "Onder 't Zoeklicht," *Calvinist*, 12 August, 2 and 9 September, 11 November, and 30 December 1911; quoted matter taken from the September 9 article. Having no Kuyper among them to correct this thinking, the Dutch were instructed by John Van Lonkhuyzen, who urged Dutch laborers to resist socialists and obey management (see "Het Recht van Werkstaking," p. 6), and by Louis Berkhof, who forgot his list of capitalistic depredations when analyzing the current situation and condemned every labor union in America but not one corporation (see *Christian Laborer*, pp. 21–29). More than a third of Berkhof's treatise is devoted to arguments against socialism.

31. See Berkhof, *Christian Laborer*, pp. 29–31; Van Lonkhuyzen, "Het Recht van Werkstaking," pp. 5, 10–11; and Schoolland, "Onder 't Zoeklicht," *Calvinist*, 30 December 1911.

32. M. J. Bosma, "Socialism," *Banner*, 12 November–24 December 1908; quoted matter taken from the 17 December issue, p. 814. Dorr Kuizema, "Politiek," *Calvinist*, 20 May 1911; Kuizema defended the strikers in this article and others under the same title in the 15 July and 26 August 1911 issues.

33. Groen summarized his views in "Labor Unions and the Church," *Banner*, 30 September 1915, pp. 604–05; he presented them in greater detail in a series of articles in *De Wachter* during 1915, which have been paraphrased by Henry Zwaanstra in *Reformed Thought and Experience,* pp. 264–76.

34. Adding fuel to this fire was the course of events in Grand Rapids. The founding of the Christian Labor Alliance in 1910, the furniture workers' strike in 1911, and the constant increase in the numbers of Dutch workers in the city (coming from rural Michigan or the Netherlands) brought the issue of Christian membership in secular unions to a head. The Christian Reformed Synod received two recommendations in 1914, one from Groen and the other from Confessionalists and antithetical Calvinists. Synod postponed its decision until 1916, setting the stage for a war of words: Groen's report and apologia in *De Wachter* of 1915, countered in 1915 by Van Lonkhuyzen in the same journal, and in 1916 by Van Lonkhuyzen in *De Calvinist*, by Berkhof in *Christian Laborer*, and by Henry Danhof in *De Wachter*. At the height of the controversy, Synod met and adopted a position closer to Groen's than to that of his opponents. For an exhaustive survey of this conflict and its antecedents, see Zwaanstra, *Reformed Thought and Experience*, pp. 239–94.

35. Samples of this thinking can be found in Klaas Schoolland, "Het Feminisme," *Gids*, 3 July–7 August 1909, and "Onze Beginselen," *Gids*, 25 April 1908; Louis Berkhof, "De Emancipatie der Vrouw en het Huisgezin," *Christendom en Leven*, pp. 67–80; John W. Brink, "Op's Werelds Tooneel," *Gereformeerde Amerikaan* 12(July 1908): 404–05; and Jacob G. Vanden Bosch, "A Burning Question," *Banner*, 31 October 1912, p. 684.

Such sentiment reflected that of many other ethnics at this time. Women's suffrage was strongly associated by ethnics and suffragists alike with the issue of temperance/Prohibition and, more variably, with nativist attitudes and "progressive reformism" in general. For the Michigan case, see Lawrence E. Ziewacz, "The Progress of Woman

Suffrage in Nineteenth-Century Michigan," *Journal of the Great Lakes History Conference* 2(1979): 29–39.

36. Groen's speech was summarized and quoted in "Says Bible Favors Ballots for Women," Grand Rapids *Evening Press,* 2 April 1913. Groen's position went beyond Abraham Kuyper's own rather late and hesitant change on the topic. Kuyper advocated the "household franchise," which gave the vote to female-headed families and single women but still kept the polity from being based on "pure individualism," ever his bête noire. Significantly, Groen's departure from his mentor on the latter point came at the cost of his acceding to a fundamental article of American civil religion.

37. See "Groen Scored for Stand on Suffrage," Grand Rapids *Evening Press,* 10 April 1913.

38. As an added misfortune, Schoolland's high Latin title for the organization could easily be modified to "faucet juice."

39. The coincidence was noted by Henry Zwaanstra (see *Reformed Thought and Experience,* p. 292). I have quoted from the published version of this speech of Herman Hoeksema, "Social Christianity and Calvinism," in *Religion and Culture* 1(August 1919): 30.

CHAPTER SIX

1. Van Lonkhuyzen, "Playing with Fire," *Wachter,* 16 June 1915, p. 2. The petition was reprinted in *De Wachter,* 30 June 1915, p. 2.

2. Grand Rapids *News,* 2 July 1915; see also *Calvinist,* 3 July 1915.

3. See Evert J. Blekkink, "The Peace of the World," *Leader,* 29 November 1911, p. 82. Matthew Kolyn, "War," *Leader,* 12 August 1914, p. 674.

4. Geerlings, "A United Nation," *Leader,* 16 July 1916, p. 590.

5. Geerlings, "An Inevitable Conflict," *Leader,* 9 May 1917, p. 469.

6. Jacob Vander Meulen, "Some Responsibilities of the Church in the Present Crisis," *Leader,* 17 July 1918, pp. 3, 11. See also Evert Blekkink, "The Love of Country," *Leader,* 27 June 1917, p. 578. Typical of the *Leader* rhetoric was its description of Germany as "the heartless Hun" and "a leper," "beyond the pale" for its "deliberate crimes against humanity, [its] outrages before which all the outrages of the past are but a drop in the bucket." Antithetically opposed to absolute evil was, of course, the absolute good of Great Britain and the United States (Russia and France apparently not being suitable for inclusion): George V was a true democrat trying to make the world "safe for free and enlightened nations," while American businessmen showed their devotion to high ideals and the public welfare by (so it was said) refusing to take extra profits in wartime (see *Leader,* 10 July 1918, p. 9; and 24 July 1918, p. 4).

Ray H. Abrams, in his *Preachers Present Arms* (New York, 1933), gives dozens of similar (and more extreme) examples from the Protestant mainstream, creating the impression of unequivocal and often hysterical ecclesiastical support for the war. Later works have modified that picture somewhat, but the central thesis remains (see Sydney E. Ahlstrom, *Religious History of the American People* [New Haven, 1972], p. 884) and would seem to describe the RCA case accurately enough.

7. See Henry Beets, "Wars and Rumors of Wars," *Banner,* 6 August 1914, p. 504; and "Editorials," 24 September 1914, pp. 621–22. See also P. Ekster, "Op's Oorlog," *Calvinist,* 7 November–5 December 1914.

8. See Beets, "The War in Europe," *Banner,* 13 August 1914, pp. 524–25. This reflects something of the Netherlands' own attitude. Located between Germany and England, the Hollanders' opinion of the two great powers at any given time depended on which had offended them last. Thus in 1914, with the Boer War being the weight most recently added to the scales, the Dutch in Europe gravitated (though hardly unanimously)

toward Germany. In the next world war, this attitude would be reversed with a vengeance.

9. See Klaas Schoolland, "De Lusitania," *Calvinist*, 15 May 1915: "For ourselves, we are of the opinion that this war above all else was sought and fashioned by England's imperialistic world-politics, to keep down rising Germany." For *De Wachter*'s opinion, see the weekly columns on the war written by A. Keizer and G. De Jong; the latter's "Zelfrespect" (11 October 1916, p. 2) is a good example.

10. See John Van Lonkhuyzen, "De Dreigende Oorlog," *Wachter*, 14 February 1917, p. 3. In *De Calvinist*, see Klaas Schoolland, "Hyphenated Americanism," 13 January 1917; "Stagnatie," 24 February and 10 March 1917; and "De Oorlog," 7 April 1917. In *De Wachter*, see G. D. De Jong's biting column of 7 March 1917, pp. 1–2; and A. Keizer, 28 February 1917, p. 4.

11. See A. Keizer, *Wachter*, 11 April 1917, p. 4. See also Henry Beets, "What to Think about War?" *Banner*, 19 April 1917, pp. 248–49.

12. Such were the demands of the Pella *Weekblad* (in southeastern Iowa) in December 1917 and of a "foreign"-born (i.e., Dutch) and -raised RCA minister in February 1918: "In times when feelings run high we cannot picture true loyalty based on duty without firmly laying hold of one's feelings. . . . That is true American loyalty, not loyalty based exclusively on the idea of duty" (Peter P. Cheff, "Flag in the Church? Sure! Why Not?" Holland [Michigan] *Daily Sentinel*, 15 February 1918).

13. See Jacob Poppen, "The Church Hyphen," *Leader*, 6 and 13 December 1916, pp. 125, 130–31.

14. On Christian schools, see John Van der Beek, *Leader*, 2 and 16 January 1918, p. 9 each issue. On Kuyper, see the Hope College (RCA) *Anchor* (undated clipping in Beets Papers, 1917). Examples of Protestant patriotic propaganda are replete in Abrams, *Preachers Present Arms*. A description of the national propaganda machine is contained in David M. Kennedy's *Over Here: The First World War and American Society* (New York, 1980), pp. 54–62. In the whole nation as among the Dutch, the targets for this propaganda were often ethnics; the most fervent dispensers were "the cultivated classes" (see Kennedy, pp. 63–75; quoted material is taken from p. 73).

15. The quoted material appeared in articles in the Grand Rapids *News* and a speech by the Reverend Dr. A. Wishart (pastor of the city's Fountain Street Baptist Church), which were summarized and quoted by Henry Beets in "What We Dutch Calvinists Really Stand for, and Why," a rebuttal delivered at the Fountain Street Church and printed in the *Banner*, 22 March 1917, p. 184.

That it was the liberal Protestant flagship in Grand Rapids that led this attack is clear and noteworthy. Not *only* liberals gave ardent support to the war of course (see Ahlstrom's examples from all parts of the theological spectrum in *Religious History*, pp. 883–87), and as William R. Hutchison demonstrates not *all* liberals did so (see *The Modernist Impulse in American Protestantism* [Cambridge, 1976], pp. 236–43), but an undefined number were "crusaders." How many there were and what their thinking was exactly is hard to tell; Hutchison spends only half a paragraph discussing them, whereas his treatment of the more moderate camp runs five pages. Among these crusaders were some of liberalism's most eminent figures: Lyman Abbott, Harry Emerson Fosdick, and Shailer Mathews. Mathews is particularly significant for our purposes since he was the midwestern voice of Modernism (and hence the one whom Dutch Americans were most likely to hear), and he used the "conservative-backward-unpatriotic" chain of argument in leading a harsh liberal attack on dispensational premillennialism (see Timothy Weber, *Living in the Shadow of the Second Coming* [New York, 1979], pp. 117–22; and George M. Marsden, *Fundamentalism and American Culture* [New York, 1980], pp. 145–48). Dispensationalists were, arguably, the most alienated segment of the emerging Fundamentalist coalition, as the Antitheticals were among the Dutch. Wartime hostility would cement that position and give these two groups, quite different in their theologies, a similar trajectory in the postwar period.

The Grand Rapids case also illustrates the stake the Progressive movement had in the war. Progressivism's "Protestant-nationalist" and "managerial" streams could take to the conflict quite readily, but so (after some cogitation) could the "humanitarian reformers." Thus the war became a *crusade* for *control* and *democracy*, justified by enormous promises—a wager, in effect, of the prestige and program of the entire Progressive cause (see Kennedy, *Over Here*, pp. 33–51; Wiebe, *The Search for Order, 1877–1920* [New York, 1967], pp. 260–79; and O'Neill, *The Progressive Years: America Comes of Age* [New York, 1975], pp. 140–53).

16. E. A. Stowe, *Michigan Tradesman*, 6 March 1918, and a letter from Stowe to Henry Beets of 15 February 1918. Similar attacks came from within the denomination. One L. Rietdyk of Muskegon, Michigan, complained in three letters to Beets that Professors Samuel Volbeda, Foppe Ten Hoor, Ralph Janssen, and Jacob Vanden Bosch were "strongly pro-German" and that they had misled "our people" and ruined the church's reputation (letters of 10 and 18 September and 1 October 1917, Beets Papers, Calvin College and Seminary Archives). Thus, suspicion did not fall on the Antitheticals alone: the first two named were Confessionalist stalwarts; the latter two, positive Calvinists.

17. Cheff and Diekema's opinions are recorded in the Holland *Daily Sentinel*, 15 February 1918, under the general heading "Flag in Church, Controversy," and "Mr. Diekema's Address at Hope Church Service Flag Dedication." The "best element" statement is Cheff's. For an example of the extremes to which the "good Americans" among the Dutch went in decorating their churches with flags, see the picture of the sanctuary of the Third Reformed Church of Holland, Michigan, photo 30 herein.

18. Hoeksema replied in the *Sentinel*'s 16, 18, and 19 February 1918 issues. Gertrude Hoeksema describes the controversy in greater detail in *Therefore Have I Spoken: A Biography of Herman Hoeksema* (Grand Rapids, 1969), pp. 81–90.

19. See E. A. Stowe, *Michigan Tradesman*, 6 March 1918, pp. 8, 21; and Gertrude Hoeksema, *Therefore Have I Spoken*, p. 89.

20. For materials on the teacher, Cornelia Hulst Steketee (she had popularized the WASP-conspiracy theory in national magazines), and J. B. Hulst, see the Beets Papers, Calvin College and Seminary Archives.

21. The Christian school in Sully, Iowa, was also burned (see John Kromminga, *The Christian Reformed Church: A Study in Orthodoxy* [Grand Rapids: 1949], p. 100). The Dutch were not the only group that showed some hostility to the war and received the same in return; the Irish and Swedes were also "suspicious," and the hostility they encountered pales beside that suffered by "radicals" of various stripes and by German Americans generally (see Frederick Luebke, *Bonds of Loyalty: German-Americans and World War I* [DeKalb, Ill., 1974], especially pp. 218–80). On that different plane, though, the German case shows some similarities to the Dutch. For many "church Germans," identity had centered not so much on Germany the nation as on a religious loyalty historically and culturally rooted there. But that made it harder for them (compared to simply "ethnic" Germans) to drop all things "German" during the war: ethnicity was entwined with things of deepest significance (see Luebke, pp. 310–12). Hence the instances of German pastors refusing to allow flags in the sanctuary, to sell war bonds from the pulpit, or to follow the government's "suggestions" as to appropriate sermon topics (see Luebke, pp. 233, 234, 238). Hence also the resemblances between Dutch and German denominational developments in the 1920s, as we shall see later.

22. Henry Beets, "Our Loyalty Proclaimed," *Banner*, 14 March 1918, pp. 181–82; and "Why We Should Support the United States Government in Its Present Great Crisis" (1918 Liberty Loan Speech), Beets Papers, Calvin College and Seminary Archives; see also Beets, "Reasons for our Loyalty," *Banner*, 21 March 1918, pp. 200–202; and Edward J. Tanis, "The Church, the Christian, and the War," a sermon delivered in Grand Rapids in 1917. Beets's articles of March 14 and 21 also defended Calvinism against liberal

calumnies—in characteristic fashion: far from being autocratic and reactionary, Calvinism was historically early in cultivating civil liberties and patriotism.

23. Schoolland, "Het Naakte Feit," *Calvinist,* 1 June 1918.

24. See Klaas Schoolland, *Calvinist,* 20 September–27 October 1917; Hoeksema's complaints appeared in the flag-in-the-church controversy.

25. Exemplary of this response were the sermons Ymen P. De Jong (former associate editor of *De Gereformeerde Amerikaan*) preached on national days of commemoration in 1918 and 1919: "Een Zwaard des Heeren," for the national day of prayer, May 1918; "Die de Oorlogen doet Ophouden," for Armistice Sunday, 1918; and "Goddelijke Bewaring," for a memorial service, October 1919. The three were published together as *Daden des Heeren: Drie Leerredenen Gehouden in verband met den Wereld Oorlong, 1914–1919* (Grand Rapids, 1919).

26. Clarence Bouma, "Be an American!" Beets Papers, Calvin College and Seminary Archives. In his maturity, Bouma came to be one of the principal figures in the community. Idzaard Van Dellen, "Slotwoord" (Article 78), *Acta Synodi der Christelijke Gereformeerde Kerk, 1918,* pp. 93–94. Henry Beets showed unusual heat in condemning "shortsighted" and "selfish" opponents of language change in "Americanization Unwisely Retarded" and "Americanization Our Bounden Duty," *Banner,* 7 March 1918, pp. 164–66. Other advocates of faster acculturation were G. W. Hylkema (in the *Banner*) and E. J. Tanis (in *De Calvinist*). The year 1918 also saw the publication in book form (under the title *Ons Opmaken en Bouwen*) of B. K. Kuiper's series of articles on Americanization in the *Banner* from 1911 to 1914.

27. Matthew Kolyn, "War and Sin," *Leader,* 12 January 1916, p. 194. See also Henry Beets, "What We Dutch Calvinists Really Stand for, and Why," *Banner,* 22 and 29 March 1917, pp. 184–86, 200–201. R. B. Kuiper also integrated orthodoxy and patriotism in "Patriotism," *Banner,* 6 June–4 July 1918, pp. 418, 433, 452, 474.

28. A. Keizer, "Kijkes," *Wachter,* 9 October 1918, pp. 6–7; Henry Beets, "Thanksgiving Reasons," *Banner,* 28 November 1918, pp. 860–61.

29. Kuiper, *De Groote Oorlog* (Grand Rapids, 1919), p. 20.

30. E. J. Tanis, "Church, Christian, and War," pp. 9–10. Other examples can be found in Henry Beets, "The War in Europe," *Banner,* 13 August 1914, pp. 524–25; R. L. Haan's columns in *Calvinist* throughout the fall in 1914; A. Keizer, "Kijkes," *Wachter,* 6 November 1918, p. 7; and Y. P. De Jong, "Een Zwaard des Heeren," *Daden des Heeren,* pp. 1–16.

31. I differ here with Henry Zwaanstra's interpretation, which sees the war years as "the end of an era," the disputes among the mentalities being resolved in a triumph for the "progressive," "American" (positive) Calvinists (see his *Reformed Thought and Experience: A Study of the Christian Reformed Church and Its American Environment, 1890–1918* [Kampen, 1973], pp. 295, 316–22). Rather, the war was the beginning of a *new* era in which group conflict reached an unprecedented severity, culminating in defeat for the "progressives" and "Americanization" of quite a different sort.

CHAPTER SEVEN

1. Henry Geerlings, "The World's Challenge to the Church," *Leader,* 10 September 1919, p. 8. Herman Hoeksema, "Social Christianity and Calvinism," *Religion and Culture* 1(August 1919): 2–3.

2. See Ymen P. De Jong, *Daden des Heeren: Drie Leerredenen Gehouden in verband met den Wereld Oorlog, 1914–1919* (Grand Rapids, 1919). On Armistice Sunday, see his

"Die de Oorlogen doet Ophouden"; for an October 1919 retrospective, see his "Goddelijke Bewaring"; on the influenza epidemic, see p. 18 of the latter.

3. See Kuiper, *De Vier Paarden uit Openbaring* (Grand Rapids, 1918).

4. See Kuiper, *While the Bridegroom Tarries: Ten After-the-War Sermons on the Signs of the Times* (Grand Rapids, 1919).

5. Kuiper, *While the Bridegroom Tarries,* p. 92.

6. "Modernism" was the only enemy Kuiper attacked in every sermon. For a sample, see "The Church's Departure from the Faith," in *While the Bridegroom Tarries,* pp. 66–88; see also pp. 228, 242.

7 Kuiper, *While the Bridegroom Tarries,* p. 266.

8. E.T., *Maranatha! A Study of Unfulfilled Prophecy* (Grand Rapids, 1917). Bultema was pastor of the First Christian Reformed Church of Muskegon, Michigan, having previously (from 1912 to 1916) served the Peoria, Iowa, church that was burned during the war. In "The Controversy over Fundamentalism in the CRC, 1915–66" (Th.D. diss., Concordia Theological Seminary, 1974), Joseph H. Hall documents the extensive involvement of Dutch-American publishers with premillennial titles at this time and subsequently (see pp. 142–55).

9. Harry Bultema, *Maranatha!* pp. 4, 73, 98. For an extended description of the evils of the day, see pp. 61–75. He had special animus against accolades of culture and progress: "A cultured unbeliever is ten times as unconverted as an uncultured. . . . There has never been in the history of mankind so much natural and spiritual misery on this earth as in our lamentable times" (pp. 246–47).

10. See Bultema, *Maranatha!* pp. 70–75.

11. *Maranatha!* p. 89.

12. See *Maranatha!* pp. 17–30, 199, 241.

13. See *Maranatha!* pp. 199–240.

14. *Maranatha!* pp. 195, 93. Regarding the role of the church in the final days, see pp. 151, 156–61, 185–90, 263–73; regarding the "spiritual" nature of the church, see pp. 191–200 and, for an extended historical millenarian treatment, pp. 305–47. The latter, reminiscent of L. J. Hulst's history of the church, praises the oppressed and powerless and condemns Origen, Augustine, the Catholic Church, and liberal Protestantism for prescribing temporal power and prosperity for the redeemed.

15. Ernest R. Sandeen traces this relationship in great detail in *The Roots of Fundamentalism: British and American Millenarianism, 1800–1930* (Chicago, 1970). Sandeen has been criticized for reductionism on this point, but even when Fundamentalism is portrayed more fully, the central and often generative role of the dispensational element is clear (see, for example, Marsden, *Fundamentalism and American Culture* [New York, 1980], pp. 43–71, 143–61, 184–95).

16. John Van Lonkhuyzen, "Chiliastische Droomerijen," *Wachter,* 19 September and 10 October 1917, pp. 1–2 each issue.

17. Louis Berkhof, *Premillennialisme* (Grand Rapids, 1918), pp. 19–23; Ymen P. De Jong, *De Komende Christus* (Grand Rapids, 1920), pp. 37–61; and Henry Danhof, "Een Woord van Critiek," *Wachter,* 11 July and 19 September 1917 all focus on interpretive method and the doctrinal tradition of the church. For an exposition of errors, see Berkhof, pp. 24–48, and De Jong, pp. 62–230 passim.

18. See De Jong, *Komende Christus,* pp. 231–326; see also Louis Berkhof, *Premillennialisme,* and Henry Danhof, "Een Woord van Critiek," *Wachter,* 18 July and 26 September 1917, pp. 2–3 each issue.

19. See *Acta Synodi, 1918,* pp. 76–80. Commentary on this issue is found in H. Danhof, "Een Woord van Critiek," *Wachter,* 26 September 1917, pp. 2–3; John Van Lonkhuyzen, "Chiliastische Droomerijen," *Wachter,* 3 October 1917, p. 2; and Y. P. De Jong, *Komende Christus,* pp. 103–67.

20. See Idzaard Van Dellen, *Acta Synodi, 1918*, p. 95; R. B. Kuiper, *While the Bridegroom Tarries*, p. 182; and Louis Berkhof, *Premillennialisme*, pp. 7, 18.

21. Edward J. Tuuk, "There's a Silver Lining," *Religion and Culture* 2(August 1920): 163. See also Tuuk's "After the War—A New Vision," *Banner*, 20 March 1919, pp. 184–85; and "The New Internationalism," *Religion and Culture* 2(May 1920): 23–35. Regarding "reconstruction" rhetoric and postwar Progressive hopes, see Kennedy, *Over Here: The First World War and American Society* (New York, 1980), pp. 245–47; and Wiebe, *The Search for Order, 1877–1920* (New York, 1967), pp. 272–79.

22. For instance, Henry Geerlings: "Do we feel as millions of Christians in America are beginning to feel that this is the Day of Days, the glorious opportunity for which through the ages every sincere Christian has hoped and prayed?" ("The World's Challenge to the Church," *Leader*, 10 September 1919, p. 8).

23. See "Editorial Preface," *Religion and Culture* 1(May 1919): 1–3.

24. Ibid. See Kuiper, "Principles," *Christian Journal*, 24 August 1918. For Kuiper 1918 was a significant year. He resigned his teaching post at Calvin College, complaining of an inadequate salary, and became managing editor of the Eerdmans-Sevensma Publishing Company, which at this time had visions of doing "big things" in the world of books. In addition to becoming head editor of the *Journal*, he was also made editor of *De Wachter* by the 1918 Synod, saw two of his books appear (*Ons Opmaken en Bouwen* and *De Vier Paarden*), and was writing a third (*De Groote Oorlog*).

25. Van Andel had been headmaster of a school in the Netherlands, obtained his M.A. from the University of Chicago, and joined the Calvin faculty as an instructor in 1915. His review of recent common grace theology, "Wij en de Wereld," appeared as an intermittent series in the *Christian Journal* during 1919.

26. Quoted matter taken from H. J. Van Andel, "De Crisis," *Christian Journal*, 19 October 1918, and "Ons Program," *Christian Journal*, 6 September 1919. Regarding "harmonization," see "Reconstructie," 14 September 1918; "Wij en de Wereld," 19 October 1918; and "Ons Program," 14 September 1919. See also B. K. Kuiper's prospectus for the *Journal*, 31 August 1918; and John Kuizenga, "Bases of Cooperation," 28 December 1918.

27. Kuizenga was born in Muskegon, Michigan, in 1876 and educated at Hope College, Western Seminary, and the University of Michigan. He taught at Hope and Western from 1906 to 1930, was president of Western from 1924 to 1930, editor of the *Leader* from 1919 to 1930, and professor at Princeton Theological Seminary from 1930 to 1947.

28. Kuiper, "Wat Moeten Wij?" 23 November 1918. See also his articles under the same title of 9 and 30 November 1918 and "Separation," 10 May 1919, as well as H. J. Van Andel, "Wij en de Wereld," 23 November and 28 December 1918 and 4 January 1919; and John Kuizenga, "Bases of Cooperation," 21 and 28 December 1918—all in the *Christian Journal*. Henry Beets attacked the same tendency in " 'Pre' as Harmless as Represented?" *Banner*, 27 March 1919, pp. 196–98.

29. Van Andel, "Eigen Organisatie Een Lapmiddel," *Christian Journal*, 28 February 1920, and "Het Christendom Separatisch," *Christian Journal*, 14 August 1920.

30. Kuiper, "Ons Streven," *Christian Journal*, 21 September 1918; repeated in "Wat Kunnen Wij?" *Christian Journal*, 25 January 1919.

31. H. J. Van Andel, "Reconstructie," *Christian Journal*, 5 October 1918. See also the 28 September and 12 October 1918 articles of the same title as well as "Wij en de Wereld," 21 December 1918, all in the *Christian Journal*.

32. John Kuizenga, "Principieel and Principieelitis," *Christian Journal*, 1 March–5 April 1919; quoted matter taken from the March 8 article, the epithets from March 22.

33. Quoted matter taken from John Kuizenga, "Bases of Cooperation," *Christian Journal*, 28 December 1918; and H. J. Van Andel, "Waar het om Gaat," *Christian Journal*, 9 November 1918. For expressions of these various points, see Van Andel's

"Reconstructie," 28 September and 12 October 1918, and "Wij en de Wereld," 28 June, 12 July, and 1 and 29 November 1919; Kuizenga's "Bases of Cooperation," 14–28 December 1918; Kuiper's "Wat Moeten Wij?" 23 and 30 November 1918; and J. J. Hiemenga's "Reconstructie," 8 March 1919. Neatly summing up their ideals, Van Andel declared: "The full man, the rich life, the harmony and the reconciliation of all antitheses, that is the secret of perfection and the power of the permanent life. . . . Therefore we advocate the all-sided development of spiritual powers and balance between the theoretical and practical" ("Reconstructie," 28 September 1918).

34. See Kuiper, "Wat Moeten Wij?" *Christian Journal*, 2 November 1918; and John Kuizenga, "Bases of Cooperation," *Christian Journal*, 28 December 1918. See also H. J. Van Andel, "Reconstructie," *Christian Journal*, 5 October 1918.

35. See H. J. Van Andel, "Wij en de Wereld," *Christian Journal*, 4 January 1919, 14 June–12 July 1919, and especially 29 November 1919; "Bavinck as a Philosopher," *Religion and Culture* 3(October 1921): 70–72; "Kuyper and Bavinck," *Religion and Culture* 5(November 1923): 86–88. Other instances can be found in E. J. Tuuk, "The Two Bavincks," *Religion and Culture* 3(February 1922): 129–31; and Quirinus Breen, "Bavinck as an Ideal," *Religion and Culture* 3(December 1921): 102–06.

36. Kuiper, "Separatism," 21 and 28 June 1919.

37. Kuiper, *Christian Journal*, 5 July 1919. Henry Beets denounced the League in "The League of Nations Desirable?" *Banner*, 11 September 1919, pp. 564–66.

38. See Geerlings, "Put Heel on Serpent," *Leader*, 11 June 1919, p. 4. Geerlings supported suppression of strikes, widespread deportations, the banning of Victor Berger from his seat in Congress, and outlawing "socialist" unions (e.g., the I.W.W.). He also wanted a strong, mandatory "Americanization" program for the likely victims of "sedition," namely, working-class ethnics. For Christian Reformed declamations against the "Reds," see Henry Beets, "Bolshevism a Peril," *Banner*, 1 January 1920, pp. 5–6; E. J. Tanis, *Banner*, 5 July 1920, p. 490; and J. M. Vande Kieft, "Het Boljewisme en de Antichrist," *Religion and Culture* 2(August 1920): 168–74.

39. See E. J. Tanis, "Tumult of the Peoples," *Banner*, 7 August 1919, p. 488. Cf. Henry Beets, "Problems—After the War," *Banner*, 9 January 1919, pp. 4–6.

40. Kromminga, "How Late Is It?" *Christian Journal*, 28 December 1918; "Hopes That Make Ashamed," *Banner*, 27 March 1919, pp. 198–99; and "Lead Us Not Into Temptation," *Banner*, 3 April 1919, pp. 214–15. B. K. Kuiper replied to Kromminga in the *Christian Journal* of 4 January 1919. Kromminga's "cleaning" imagery was not accidental since one of the "big things" Kuizenga saw God attending to in the postwar world, and so one place for the church's ardent "cooperation," was the matter of public sanitation (see "Bases of Cooperation," *Christian Journal*, 28 December 1918). The American "sanitary" ideal later drew, for instance, Reinhold Niebuhr's disparagement as one example of the social gospel's banalization into "pious utilitarianism" (see *Moral Man and Immoral Society* [New York, 1932], p. 99). Kromminga's indignation evinced a similar insight.

The larger protest shows the continuation of the parallel between the Antitheticals and American dispensationalists noted in Chapter 6. As the two drew off a similar wartime experience, in the postwar cultural crisis they both underwent resurgence and sharp radicalization (see Marsden, *Fundamentalism and American Culture*, pp. 153–63). German Catholics formed a parallel in another quarter. Assaulted on ethnic and ideological grounds during the war, they at the turn into the '20s were also seized by a sense of crisis, pessimism, and unprecedented alienation (see Gleason, *The Conservative Reformers: German-American Catholics and the Social Order* [Notre Dame, Ind., 1968], pp. 159–203).

41. Hoeksema, "Pseudo-Calvinism," *Banner*, 23 January 1919, p. 7. Like Kromminga, Hoeksema thought that the hour of world history was very late, but William B. Eerdmans answered his heavily Neo-Calvinistic analysis by suggesting he go back to the Free University of Amsterdam to get his clock fixed (see *Christian Journal*, 18 January 1919).

42. Hoeksema's series on "The Fallen King and His Kingdom" and "The New King and His Kingdom" went on in the *Banner* for more than a hundred installments (over two years). On this score he undoubtedly wore Schoolland's mantle well. An especially clear picture of the antithesis appeared in installment 28, 10 April 1919, pp. 229–30.

43. See Hoeksema, "The Fallen King and His Kingdom," *Banner*, 10 April–22 May 1919; quoted matter taken from 10 April 1919, p. 230, and 1 May 1919, p. 278. Nicely enough, this declaration was made at the very time that positive Calvinist confidence was reaching its peak, in the spring of 1919.

44. See Danhof, *De Idee van het Genadeverbond* (Grand Rapids, 1920). Concerning the "organic," see pp. 22, 23, and 31; concerning the Antithesis, see pp. 26–28, 32, and 40; concerning the imminence of the "last days," see pp. 30, 31, 37, and 38.

45. See Hoeksema, "Pseudo-Calvinism," *Banner*, 23 January 1919, p. 7. Danhof had been one of Bultema's chief critics in 1917; see notes 17–19 to this chapter.

CHAPTER EIGHT

1. See Chapter 3, pp. 48–49, and especially note 51.

2. *Nadere Toelichting omtrent de Zaak Janssen* (Holland, Mich., 1920). The authors were Ten Hoor, Louis Berkhof, William Heyns, and Samuel Volbeda. Details of these events can be found in *Acta Synodi, CRC, 1920*, pp. 79–81, 95–96; *Nadere Toelichting*, pp. 6–33; and (pro-Janssen) Harry R. Boer, "Ralph Janssen after Fifty Years . . . ," *Reformed Journal* 22(December 1972): 17–22.

3. F. M. Ten Hoor, et al., *Nadere Toelichting*, p. 33. Concerning miracles, see pp. 37–50; concerning Israel's history, see pp. 58–60; concerning the documentary hypothesis, see pp. 34–37; concerning inspiration, see pp. 63–74; concerning distinctiveness and unity of Scripture, see pp. 50–57, 61–63; concerning theology as a science, see pp. 63–74. Examples of judging by "tendencies" are found on pp. 44, 45, 61–64, 80, and 81.

4. See *Nadere Toelichting*, pp. 74–83.

5. For Princeton's view of Scripture and its critical role in Fundamentalism, see Sandeen, *The Roots of Fundamentalism: British and American Millenarianism, 1800–1930* (Chicago, 1970), pp. 103–31; and Marsden, *Fundamentalism and American Culture* (New York, 1980), pp. 109–18. Lefferts A. Loetscher gives a detailed account of the controversy with liberalism in *The Broadening Church: A Study of Theological Issues in the Presbyterian Church since 1869* (Philadelphia, 1957), pp. 48–74, 104–47. Vos had been hired in connection with Charles Briggs's 1891 ouster for heresy (see *Redemptive History and Biblical Interpretation: The Shorter Writings of Geerhardus Vos*, ed. Richard B. Gaffin [Phillipsburg, N.J., 1980], p. xi). The early 1920s climax of the battle at Princeton and for Fundamentalism in general is well presented in Marsden, pp. 141–75, 180–84, 192.

6. See Hoeksema, "Objective Revelation or Subjective Development?" *Banner*, 23 September–7 October 1920, pp. 584–85, 599–600, 615–16; "The Covenant with Noah" (reply to Janssen), 11 November 1920, p. 684; and "Not Satisfied" (a title epitomizing Hoeksema's entire personality and career), 27 January 1921, pp. 55–56, from which the quoted matter is taken.

7. Janssen, *Voorzetting van de Strijd* (Grand Rapids, June 1922), p. 3. Janssen's February 1922 pamphlet was *De Crisis in de Christelijke Gereformeerde Kerk: Een Strijdschrift* (Grand Rapids). He answered his critics concerning science and theology in *De Crisis*, pp. 15–23, and *Voorzetting*, pp. 46–48; concerning miracles in *Voorzetting*, pp. 24–35; and concerning the documentary hypothesis in *Voorzetting*, pp. 44–48.

8. Janssen, *Voorzetting*, pp. 29–30. Janssen attacked Hoeksema in the pages of the *Banner* in "Reply to Rev. H. Hoeksema," 4–25 November 1920, pp. 667, 683, 700–701,

716, and 13 January 1921, p. 24; and in "The Erroneous and Unwarranted Criticisms of Rev. H. Hoeksema," 24 February 1921, pp. 117–18. He attacked the others in *De Crisis*, pp. 5–9, 23, 30, 33–35; and in *Voorzetting*, pp. 3–30 (effectively summarized on p. 102).

9. See Janssen, *De Crisis*, pp. 1–5.

10. The tract was "Waar Het in de Zaak Janssen Om Gaat" (n.p., March 1922). For Janssen on this issue, see *Voorzetting*, pp. 63–80; for the prosecution, see J. Manni, et al., "Report of the Majority Section of the Janssen Investigating Committee," *Reports and Decisions in the Case of Dr. R. Janssen* (n.p., 1922), pp. 57–64, 112–20, 145–51.

11. Quoted matter taken from the pages of *Religion and Culture:* Edward J. Tuuk, "Sense of Humor," 3(May 1921): 3; "The Situation," 3(November 1921): 83–85; and "Orthodox and Progressive," 3(March 1922): 147–48. Anonymous contributions include "A Well-Meaning Curatorium," 3(August 1921), which calls Janssen's forced "vacation" a pitiful surrender to public opinion; and "A Layman Cogitates in Zion," 3(July 1921): 19–21. Kuiper defended Janssen in *De Janssen Kwestie en Nog Iets* (Grand Rapids, June 1922); Van Lonkhuyzen in *Onze Toekomst* ("Our Future"), a Chicago periodical that he edited and opened to this, Groen's last contribution to his denomination's wars.

12. Ten Hoor and Heyns did not participate, apparently being too old for such battles. The *Witness* was bilingual, with some important articles published in both languages simultaneously.

13. Quoted matter taken from the *Witness* 1(December 1921): 3–4. Danhof's article "Faith in the Spade" appears on pp. 10–11 of that issue. See also Hoeksema, "Het Christelijk Offensief," *Witness* 1(February 1922): 37–38; and Louis Berkhof, " 'The Witness,' " *Witness* 1(December 1921): 2. Berkhof repeated his fear of losing "our distinctive tenets" in adapting to "the world of thought around us" in the English inaugural editorial, "Conservative or Progressive," pp. 3–4.

14. Berkhof and H. J. Kuiper were severe enough, but Hoeksema showed himself at his worst, rejoicing in combat for its own sake; nearly slandering B. K. Kuiper, Van Lonkhuyzen, and Groen; and concluding that the Synod might be "packed," but that the packing was of God. See "Met Twee Maten" ("With Two Measures"), *Witness* 2(June 1922): 100–105.

15. Among the most egregious of the procedural errors are the following: some investigating committees had refused Janssen a personal hearing; they had based their conclusions entirely upon students' notes, not his own acknowledged statements; certain of his opponents were on these committees and at Synod, thus serving at once as prosecutor, judge, and jury; delegates to Synod had been chosen in an atmosphere of hysteria; some of these ("the four preachers") were utterly lacking in Christian charity; some (Hoeksema and Danhof) had even publicly contradicted the Confessions.

That all these charges (and more) were true shows further how poisoned the atmosphere was during these years. In addition, Hoeksema, at the time of his *Banner* articles on Janssen, was Janssen's own pastor and attacked him without warning. Janssen showed something of the same spirit, which, along with his refusal to speak at Synod (even though he was in the chamber), did not endear him to others. B. K. Kuiper complained of his abrasive personality in *De Janssen Kwestie* (pp. 5–6), and Janssen showed it in calling Hoeksema "an untrue witness . . . full of falsifications" and praying, "May God open the eyes of our people to the profoundly sinful morality . . . of men like Rev. H. J. Kuiper and his compatriots" (see the *Banner*, 24 March 1921, p. 183; and *Het Synodal Vonnis* [Grand Rapids, November 1922], p. 29).

16. For more detail on Synod's meeting, see Harry R. Boer, "Ralph Janssen: The 1922 Loaded Court," *Reformed Journal* 23(January 1973): 22–28. Janssen protested the decision in two pamphlets, *Het Synodal Vonnis* (1922) and *De Synodale Conclusies* (Grand Rapids, 1923), and, with several others, appealed to the Synod of 1924. Turned

down there, he left academia for a brokerage job in Chicago (see Harry R. Boer, "The Janssen Case: Aftermath," *Reformed Journal* 23[November 1973]: 21–24).

17. "A Layman Cogitates in Zion," *Religion and Culture* 3(July 1921): 19. John Kuizenga, "Special Grace and Common Culture," *Leader*, 31 May 1921, pp. 8–9.

18. Van Andel, "The Foe Within the Gates," *Religion and Culture* 4(July 1922): 27. Kuizenga, "Special Grace and Common Culture," *Leader*, 31 May 1921, p. 9.

19. Besides a series on "the light of nature" during 1922–23, *Religion and Culture* featured G. Hoeksema, "Specific Calvinism," 5(June 1923): 2; H. J. Van Andel, "Luther and Calvin," 5(October 1923): 71–74; "Kuyper and Bavinck," 5(November 1923): 86–88; "Common Grace and Total Depravity," 6(October 1924): 68–69; "Common Grace the Creative Idea," 6(December 1924): 100–101; and R. B. Kuiper, "The Importance of Common Grace," 6(September 1924): 50–52. Henry Beets added his voice (in "The Common Grace Issue among Us," *Banner*, 30 November and 7 December 1923, pp. 732, 748, and 4–18 January 1924, pp. 4, 20, 36), concluding that Hoeksema and Danhof had violated Scripture and the Confessions (14 January 1924, p. 37). Kuizenga's series were "Special Grace and Common Culture," *Leader*, 10 May–13 September 1922; and "If We Deny Common Grace," *Leader*, 5 December 1923–23 January 1924. J. K. Van Baalen wrote *De Loochening der Gemeene Gratie: Gereformeerd of Doopersch?* ["The Denial of Common Grace: Reformed or Anabaptist?"] (Grand Rapids, September 1922); and *Nieuwigheid en Dwaling . . .* ["Innovation and Error"] (Grand Rapids, 1923).

Hoeksema left the *Banner* in August 1922; as if to punish both branches of Neo-Calvinism for making such a fuss, the 1922 Synod had also replaced B. K. Kuiper as editor of *De Wachter*, putting Confessionalists in both positions. Hoeksema and Danhof disappeared from the masthead of the *Witness* in the December 1922 issue. They published *Niet Doopersch Maar Gereformeerd* ("Not Anabaptist but Reformed") in late 1922, and *Van Zonde en Genade* ("Of Sin and Grace") in July 1923. Because Hoeksema took the lead in the entire struggle, I have used "Hoeksema" and "Hoeksema and Danhof" interchangeably below.

20. See H. J. Van Andel, "Common Grace the Creative Idea," *Religion and Culture* 6(December 1924): 101; and J. K. Van Baalen, *Loochening*, p. 84. For additional material on this point, see Hoeksema, *Niet Doopersch*, pp. 9–22, 34–51; and *Van Zonde*, pp. 85–168; and Van Baalen, *Loochening*, pp. 50–74; and *Nieuwigheid*, pp. 9–41, 133–49.

21. See Hoeksema, *Van Zonde*, pp. 85–176, especially 169–76 and 202–04. See also J. K. Van Baalen, *Nieuwigheid*, pp. 58–66 (quoted matter taken from p. 64).

22. Hoeksema, *Van Zonde*, pp. 229, 205. Concerning "inconceivability," see Hoeksema, "The Fallen King and His Kingdom," *Banner*, 17 April and 1 May 1919, pp. 248, 277; concerning natural gifts as curses, see *Banner*, 1 May 1919, p. 277, and *Van Zonde*, pp. 152, 156, 165–68; concerning civic righteousness, see *Van Zonde*, pp. 224–26, 229; concerning privileges of the elect, see "New King and His Kingdom," *Banner*, 15 January 1920, p. 38. Hoeksema expanded upon these points in *The Protestant Reformed Churches in America* (Grand Rapids, 1936), pp. 309–402.

23. Quoted matter from J. K. Van Baalen, *Loochening*, pp. 46–47; reference is being made to a remark Danhof made in the question-and-answer session at the classical meeting after delivering "De Idee van het Genadeverbond." This statement, with its indelicacy, offended the positive Calvinists' sensibilities more than anything else the two said. For the questions asked of Hoeksema and Danhof, see *Loochening*, pp. 5–9, 85–92; and Van Andel, "The Foe within the Gates," *Religion and Culture* 4(July 1922): 27. Regarding natural gifts, natural good, and restraint of sin, see *Nieuwigheid*, pp. 133–60.

24. On Anabaptism, see J. K. Van Baalen, *Loochening*, pp. 75–84; and *Nieuwigheid*, pp. 67–74. On Rationalism, see *Loochening*, pp. 32–49; and *Nieuwigheid*, pp. 99–103, 193–200.

25. See Herman Hoeksema, *Van Zonde*, p. 84. See also D. Zwier, "Een Interessant

Debat," *Witness* 2(January 1923): 19–20; and rev. of *Van Zonde, Witness* 2(October 1923): 171–75; Samuel Volbeda, "Teekenen aan Onzen Kerkelijken Hemel," *Witness* 2(February 1923): 38–39; and H. J. Kuiper, "We Willen Weer Gereformeerd Zijn!" *Witness* 3(December 1923): 11–12. And see Gerrit Hoeksema, "Specific Calvinism," *Religion and Culture* 5(June 1923): 2.

26. See D. Zwier, rev. of *Van Zonde, Witness* 2(October 1923): 171–75; J. K. Van Baalen, *Loochening,* p. 83; and *Nieuwigheid,* p. 79; and Herman Hoeksema, *Van Zonde,* pp. 104, 141, 165–67, 237; and *Niet Doopersch,* pp. 34–44. For the positive Calvinists' use of Bavinck, see *Loochening,* pp. 5–9; Van Andel, "Bavinck as a Philosopher," *Religion and Culture* 3(October 1921): 70–72; Quirinus Breen, "Bavinck as an Ideal," *Religion and Culture* 3(December 1921): 102–06; and E. J. Tuuk, "The Two Bavincks," *Religion and Culture* 3(February 1922): 129–31. Kuizenga put Bavinck against and above Kuyper (see "Special Grace and Common Culture," *Leader,* 28 June and 5 July 1922, p. 9).

27. See Hoeksema, *Protestant Reformed Churches,* p. 15; and Danhof, *De Idee der Genadeverbond,* p. 5; and *Van Zonde,* p. 81. In *Protestant Reformed Churches* (pp. 14–25), Hoeksema presents a thorough, detailed, and—granting his assumptions—accurate review of developments from 1915 on. He has especially good insight into the instincts and vacillations of the Confessionalist party.

28. Samuel Volbeda, "De Antithese en de Gemeene Gratie," *Witness* 3(January 1924): 22–24; J. K. Van Baalen, *Loochening,* pp. 9–10.

29. See *Acta Synodi, 1924,* pp. 145–47; for the entire deliberations, see pp. 114–50.

30. For Federal Council of Churches decision, see *Acta Synodi, 1924,* p. 112. Appeals of the Janssen deposition are described in Harry R. Boer, "The Janssen Case: Aftermath," *Reformed Journal* 23(November 1973): 21–24. It was R. B. Kuiper who called Breen "one of the church's most promising young ministers," in *As to Being Reformed* (Grand Rapids, 1926), p. 49. Breen left his Grand Rapids church for academia, becoming a historian specializing in John Calvin and dedicating his major work (*John Calvin: A Study in French Humanism* [Grand Rapids, 1931]) to Ralph Janssen. Ironically, Breen's father had earlier been Hoeksema's pastor in Chicago and had encouraged his bright young parishioner to go into the ministry.

31. *Acta Synodi, 1924,* p. 147.

32. Ibid.

33. Illustrations of the former tendency can be found in H. J. Van Andel, "Common Grace and Total Depravity," *Religion and Culture* 6(October 1924): 68–69; "Common Grace the Creative Idea," *Religion and Culture* 6(December 1924): 100–101; Fred Bronkema, "The Doctrine of Common Grace in Reformed Theology" (Th.D. diss., Harvard University, 1928), pp. 3–9, 186–89; and Herman Kuiper, *Calvin on Common Grace* (Goes, the Netherlands, 1928), pp. 229–31. Illustrations of the latter tendency can be found in Louis Berkhof, *De Drie Punten in Alle Deelen Gereformeerd* (Grand Rapids, 1925); and Henry J. Kuiper, *The Three Points of Common Grace* (Grand Rapids, 1925).

34. Three of Janssen's prosecutors (Louis Berkhof, H. J. Kuiper, and Samuel Volbeda) as well as his successor at Calvin Seminary (Martin Wyngaarden) were on the board of the *Reformed Herald* and effectively had editorial control. Only secondary figures from *Religion and Culture* wrote for the *Herald* and then not often. The *Herald* ran for only one year (June 1925 through May 1926), the passing of theological controversy apparently making a forum for cultural commentary unnecessary.

35. *Acta Synodi, 1924,* pp. 147–49. Significantly, this was quite close to the treatment Harry Bultema gave common grace: the doctrine was biblical but dangerously open to "worldliness," which opening Kuyper had helped create (see *Wat Zegt de Schrift van de Algemeene Gratie?* [Muskegon, Mich., 1925], pp. 11–12).

36. Clarence Bouma, who wrote the official brief against Hoeksema, led the CRC attack; see his "Dogma and Metaphysics," *Religion and Culture* 1(May 1919): 26–51;

and "Christianity's Finality and New Testament Teaching," *Princeton Theological Review* 29(July 1928): 337–54. For the RCA attack, see John Kuizenga, "Our Double Conflict Today," *Leader*, 11 and 18 October 1922; "What the Liberals Are Driving At," 28 January–18 March 1925; "What We Can Learn From the Liberals," 6 May–10 June 1925, p. 9 each issue. See also H. J. Van Andel's series in the *Christian Journal*, 1 February–5 April 1919; Van Andel, "The Foe without the Gates," *Religion and Culture* 4(September 1922): 56–60; Gerrit H. Hospers, *The Reformed Principle of Authority* (Grand Rapids, 1924); and R. B. Kuiper, *As to Being Reformed*, pp. 55–62.

37. Henry Geerlings, "A Futile Fight," *Leader*, 11 April 1928, p. 2; see also his articles "The Blunder of Liberalism," 26 May 1926, p. 4; and "The Prohibition Battle," 15 September 1926, p. 2. The articles against Al Smith ran 4 and 11 July 1928 and found his constituency to comprise "the menacing alien colonies, . . . every vicious criminal, anti-American, and every destructive force in America" (4 July, p. 3). See also C. Dolfin, "The Roman Catholic Church and Al Smith," *Leader*, 11 April 1928, pp. 2–3. The *Leader* increasingly vacillated between identifications of Christianity with American civilization and an unprecedented note of desperation. For examples of the former, see Ame Vennema, "Religion and Business," 27 August 1919, p. 3 (wherein it is stated that the Bible is a "wonderful book of business maxims"); and Henry Geerlings, "God With Us," 2 July 1924, p. 2; and "The Rotary Creed," 28 February 1923, p. 4 (wherein it is stated that the motto "Service above Self" characterizes Rotary businessmen and Christianity alike). For examples of the latter, see Henry Geerlings, "The Youth Problem," 17 August 1927, p. 2; Albertus Pieters, "Present Day Lawlessness," 29 June 1927, pp. 2–3. Hope College President Edward Dimnent went farthest by voicing doubts during the 1928 campaign about the virtues of mass democracy and intimating his preference for a turn to (Protestant) moral aristocracy instead (see his "Veto by the People," "Saved yet So as by Fire," and "Hold Fast," 30 May, 4 July, and 11 July 1928, respectively). A theological sign of this mood was the outspoken advocacy of premillennialism by Gerrit H. Hospers, an Iowa-born RCA pastor long situated in upstate New York, who wrote *The Calvinistic Character of Premillennialism* in 1915 and reiterated its themes in the *Leader* during the early '20s. Hospers also had strong Kuyperian leanings (see his *Reformed Principle of Authority* [1924]). From both sources he argued against liberalism, identification of Christianity and modern culture, and his denomination's implicit postmillennialism.

38. Positive Calvinist voices included E. J. Tuuk (*As to Being Worldly* [Grand Rapids, 1927]) and R. B. Kuiper (*"Not of the World": Discourses on the Christian's Relation to the World* [Grand Rapids, 1929]). H. J. Kuiper, on the Confessionalist side, led the issue through official channels and wrote on it extensively in the *Witness* and *Reformed Herald*. The two Kuipers and Tuuk formed the Synodical advisory committee on the issue; their recommendation was taken whole. The only dissent in the entire process came from E. J. Tanis, who had no love for sensuality but questioned the itemized prohibition of selected sins by an official church body (see "The Overture to Synod . . . ," *Banner*, 26 March 1926, p. 182).

39. I have relied for details here on Joseph H. Hall, "The Controversy over Fundamentalism in the CRC, 1915–66" (Th.D. diss., Concordia Theological Seminary, 1974), pp. 188–207 (on "legalistic ethics," see p. 188). Hall documents E. J. Tuuk's plagiarism of William Biederwolf (a Chicago-area Fundamentalist leader much published by Eerdmans in Grand Rapids) on pp. 192–95, and discusses the 1928 Synod's more discreet reliance on such sources on p. 199.

40. See "Report of the Committee on Worldly Amusements," *Agenda: Synod of the Christian Reformed Church, 1928*, pp. 4–31; quoted matter taken from pp. 11–12.

41. Edward J. Tuuk, *As to Being Worldly*, pp. 98–99; see pp. 87–101 for his entire rationale. H. J. Kuiper showed in this context, as in many others, how close to the absurd the campaign for holiness could be: "Our parents did not realize that there is a gradual

but no essential difference between flinch and pedro. Today we are reaping the fruits! . . . It is not easy to convince them that every game of chance is a practical denial of divine providence" ("From 1915 to 1925," *Reformed Herald* 1[February 1926]: 143).

42. Henry Beets, "The Menace of the Movies and 'The King of Kings,'" *Banner*, 19 November 1928, p. 840. See E. J. Tuuk, *As to Being Worldly*, pp. 71–83, 103–16, for the full argument against the theater. For the broader scope of attack, see H. J. Kuiper, "From 1915 to 1925," *Reformed Herald* 1(February 1926): 141–43; Beets, "Soul Destroying Doctrines about the Soul," *Banner*, 4 February 1927, pp. 76–77; and three articles by Jacob Vanden Bosch in *Religion and Culture:* "Walt Whitman," August 1919, pp. 98–100; "The Movies," May 1923, pp. 177–78; and "The Philosophy of the Phallic Frenzy" (on Freud), August 1922, pp. 42–45.

43. See "Report on Worldly Amusements," *CRC Agenda, 1928*, pp. 35–36; on dancing, see pp. 40–41; on the theater, see pp. 31–38. The community feared illicit sexuality in other places too (e.g., books), but the two practices condemned involved *public* behavior and admitted of easier supervision.

44. See *CRC Agenda, 1928*, pp. 47–56. Kuiper had been appointed to this post (after apologizing for his statements in the Janssen case) in 1926. After his demotion, in the words of one who knew him, "the remainder of this talented man's life was mournful. . . . With all his talents he ended as a withered branch. While I was studying at Northwestern University, I often . . . came home from there around midnight. I saw him frequently between eleven and twelve walking the almost deserted streets, or just standing on a corner chewing a dead cigar. It must have been 3 a.m. in his soul. I was reminded of the sad words of Edwin Arlington Robinson: 'Familiar as an old mistake / and futile as regret'" (John J. Timmerman, *Promises to Keep* [Grand Rapids, 1975], pp. 37–38). The Kuiper papers (Calvin College and Seminary Archives), largely correspondence after 1930, contain the doleful, at times excruciating, details.

45. The generational change both denominations underwent in the late '20s (the RCA would present new voices in the '30s as well) provides still another resemblance to German Catholic developments. There too these years saw the passing of a group of leaders who had risen with the question of Americanization around 1900 and had often worked out that question brilliantly. Suffering similar setbacks after 1915, they, like the Antitheticals, became increasingly bitter, negative, and aligned by default with reactionary impulses; theirs ended as a "critique by alienated utopians" (see Gleason, *The Conservative Reformers: German-American Catholics and the Social Order* [Notre Dame, Ind., 1968], pp. 199–203). Much the same, of course, applies to Protestant Fundamentalism in this period.

As to the CRC's language change, its pace is reflected in a few statistics. Where in 1915 only 17 of the 223 churches were totally English in usage, by 1926 the English-language *Banner* surpassed the Dutch *Wachter* in circulation, and the 1932 Synod heard the last reports given in Dutch (see Kromminga, *The Christian Reformed Church: A Study in Orthodoxy* [Grand Rapids, 1949], p. 203). The largest German-American Protestant denomination, the Missouri Synod Lutherans, experienced just as rapid a change in these years and also adopted the same ideological course as the CRC: resolute confessionalism and protective-defensive ethics (see Luebke, *Bonds of Loyalty: German-Americans and World War I* [DeKalb, Ill., 1974], pp. 316–17).

46. During all these developments, Kuiper had been pastor of the second oldest English-speaking church in the denomination (aside from the New Jersey acquisitions), the Broadway church on Grand Rapids' west side. A final note on what triumph in such wars as these demanded: R. B. Kuiper left the denomination temporarily because of its actions against his brother-in-law, Ralph Janssen; H. J. Kuiper, on his road to supremacy, agreed to the censure of *his* brother-in-law, Harry Bultema.

CHAPTER NINE

1. There was a resurgence of Dutch immigration after World War I—34,376 from 1919 to 1931—but with the Depression of the 1930s, immigration nearly stopped entirely, with only 2,500 Dutch immigrants between 1932 and 1938 (see Henry S. Lucas, *Netherlanders in America* [Ann Arbor, 1955], p. 641). For denominational statistics of this era, see Appendix.

2. Louis Berkhof, *Aspects of Liberalism* (Grand Rapids, 1951), p. 36.

3. Henry J. Kuiper, "Our Church in the Last Forty Years," *Banner*, 12 January 1940, pp. 28–29.

4. The oldest was William B. Eerdmans Publishing Company, founded before World War I. Zondervan Publishing House was founded in 1932, and Baker Book House in 1939. All three were located in Grand Rapids. For more information, see Joseph H. Hall, "The Controversy over Fundamentalism in the CRC, 1915–66" (Th.D. diss., Concordia Theological Seminary, 1974), pp. 140–55.

5. John E. Kuizenga, who was editor of the *Leader* and professor at and president of Western Theological Seminary, left his posts in 1930 to teach at Princeton Theological Seminary. He was succeeded as editor by Siebe C. Nettinga, John R. Mulder, and Albertus Pieters, who all hailed from the western part of the denomination. Both Nettinga and Mulder had served midwestern parishes and both were professors and presidents of Western Seminary. Pieters had the three elements his denomination valued most highly: the son of a great pioneer pastor of the western RCA, he had been a missionary in Japan for thirty years, and he then served on the Western faculty. The *Intelligencer-Leader's* first solo editor was Bernard M. Mulder; he was succeeded by Louis H. Benes. They too were born in and served pastorates in the West.

6. In 1947, the *Church Herald* had 28,000 readers in the West and 6,000 in the East (see "The *Church Herald* Reports," *Church Herald*, 6 June 1947, p. 7).

7. On the dominant mentality, see the following in the *Christian Intelligencer-Leader:* Raymond B. Drukker, "Religion—The Family Stabilizer," 22 July 1938, p. 9; Simon Blocker, "Religion and Civilization," 16 September 1936, p. 2; and Samuel Zwemer, "Perpetuating Our Heritage," 24 February 1937, p. 5. See also Evert J. Blekkink, "Separatism," *Leader*, 29 April 1931. A good example of Reformed consciousness-raising was Milton J. Hoffman's series, "Why Are We Reformed?" *Church Herald*, 2 March–6 April 1945; on ecumenism and orthodoxy, see notes 19, 24, and 53 to this chapter.

8. Kuiper was *Banner* editor from 1929 to 1956, being reelected to that post by the CRC Synod every two years. For much of his tenure he was also pastor of the Neland Avenue CRC, which had a disproportionate number of Calvin College and Seminary professors in its membership. Colloquially known as "H. J.," he was not related to "B. K.," "R. B.," or any other "Kuiper" named herein.

9. See H. J. Kuiper, "Conservative and Progressive," *Banner*, 11 January 1929, p. 21; and "Our Worst Foe," *Banner*, 1 March 1929, pp. 152–53.

10. H. J. Kuiper, "Conservative and Progressive," *Banner*, 11 January 1929, p. 21.

11. Tanis spent much of his life in more cosmopolitan areas than did his typical ethnic peer. He was born and raised in Paterson, New Jersey, and as a minister in Chicago studied sociology at the University of Chicago. Besides his column (biblically—and typically—titled "The Tumult of the Peoples"), Tanis wrote a book showing his Neo-Calvinism and social concerns: *Calvinism and Social Problems* (Grand Rapids, 1936). For his appreciation of Kuyper, and a classic demonstration of how Kuyper's influence spread in Dutch America, see his column on Kuyper's centennial in the October 1937 *Banner*.

12. The managing editor of the *Forum* was Clarence Bouma, born in the Netherlands in 1891, a Harvard Th.D., and Professor of Apologetics and Ethics at Calvin Seminary.

Bouma first made his appearance as one of the CRC's World War I boosters; he was also the principal author of the 1924 Christian Reformed Synod's declaration on common grace and was appointed to his seminary chair by that Synod. Other leading *Forum* writers included Henry Schultze, professor at Calvin Seminary and ten years president of Calvin College; Henry Ryskamp, Professor of Sociology and Economics and dean of Calvin College; Bastian Kruithof, a graduate of Calvin College, minister in the RCA, and professor at Hope College; and H. J. Van Andel and Jacob Vanden Bosch, both veteran professors at Calvin and former contributors to *Religion and Culture*. In terms of place of birth, the staff was evenly divided: Bouma, Kruithof, and Van Andel were Dutch-born; Schultze, Ryskamp, and Vanden Bosch were American-born.

13. Clarence Bouma, "Allow Us to Introduce Ourselves," *Calvin Forum* 1(May 1935): 5.

14. The novel was Sara E. Gosselink's *Roofs Over Strawtown* (Grand Rapids, 1945). This book had official sanction of sorts; it won a nationwide contest initiated by Calvin College and run by Eerdmans to encourage "Christian fiction" and was subsequently held up by community leaders as an example of a well-written yet morally pure novel, not to mention a cause for ethnic pride. Gosselink took her encouragement to heart, going on to write dozens of stories, most of them with biblical settings.

15. Joan Geisel Gardner, *Desires of the Heart* (Grand Rapids, 1934). The author's name indicates intermarriage in her own case.

16. H. J. Kuiper frequently showed ethnic pride per se, but the connection between ethnicity and religion was far more important to him. It is most obvious in "Should We Preserve the Language of Our Fathers?" *Banner*, 23 March 1939, pp. 268–69; and "Not Ashamed of Our Dutch Blood," *Banner*, 28 April 1933, p. 389, which asked, "What must become of our churches if our ministers cease to read the works of Kuyper and Bavinck?" Clarence Bouma drew the same tie in an editorial in the *Calvin Forum* (7[June–July 1942]: 228), while H. J. Van Andel had it as his driving conviction: "There is no future for Dutch Calvinism in America apart from Dutch culture and Dutch history" ("Folklorism and Calvinism," *Calvin Forum* 3[September 1937]: 34).

17. See, for example, Ralph Stob, "Rethinking Calvinism," *Banner*, 25 May 1939, p. 483; and R. B. Kuiper, "Modernism and We," *Banner*, 14 October 1932, p. 890; and "Fundamentalism and We," *Banner*, 2 December 1932, p. 1048.

18. Nicholas J. Monsma, *The Trial of Denominationalism* (Grand Rapids, 1932), p. 72; Clarence Bouma, "Ecumenicity: Spurious and Genuine," *Calvin Forum* 15 (November 1949): 61–62. Note that the dates of utterance are at the beginning and end of this period; note also the use of quotation marks in Bouma's statement.

19. See John Kuizenga, "What the Liberals Are Driving At," 28 January–18 March 1925; and "What We Can Learn from the Liberals," 6 May–10 June 1925; see also "Our Study of Theology," 18 January–8 February 1922; "Regeneration and Education," 16 August 1922; "Our Double Conflict Today," 11 and 18 October 1922; and "Why We Need a Creed," 22 November 1922—all in the *Leader*. The CRC had a prewar response in F. M. Ten Hoor, "De Moderne Positieve Theologie," *Gereformeerde Amerikaan* 12(October 1908–January 1909).

20. Van Til received his preliminary training at Calvin College and Seminary and was on the junior faculty at Princeton when (in 1929) the conservatives seceded therefrom. He went on to more than forty years of teaching at Westminster. Kuiper left the presidency of Calvin College for a professorship at Westminster in 1933. He eventually became president of that institution and after retiring from his position there assumed the presidency of Calvin Seminary, thus becoming the only Triple Crown winner of twentieth-century orthodox American Calvinism. A typical appreciation of Machen and the orthodox Presbyterian cause can be found in William Masselink's *Professor J. Gresham Machen: His Life and Defense of the Faith* (n.p., 1938).

21. Besides the CRC connections with "old Princeton" noted above (see Chapter 8,

p. 107 and note 5), much of the denomination's most influential leadership in the interwar era had received graduate training there between 1910 and 1929: (in chronological order) Edward J. Tanis, Gerrit Hoeksema, R. B. Kuiper, Henry H. Meeter, Herman Kuiper, J. K. Van Baalen, John Vande Kieft, Clarence Bouma, Watson Groen, George Goris, Henry Schultze, Martin Wyngaarden, Edward J. Masselink, and William Rutgers. In all, sixty-nine CRC ministers/professors graduated from Princeton between 1915 and 1929—more than forty of them in the 1920s, when the liberal-orthodox battle was building to its peak. By contrast, there were only thirteen CRC graduates from 1930 to 1941, one measure of the impact of the 1929 schism. A signal declaration of that impact was that of R. B. Kuiper, "Modernism and We," *Banner*, 14 October 1932, p. 890. For more on this, see pp. 131, 134 herein and Ralph Danhof's *Charles Hodge as Dogmatician* (Goes, 1929), an appreciation of the old "Princeton Theology."

The RCA's helping to fill the gaps left by the CRC-applauded withdrawal only reinforced each side's reputation in the eyes of the other. Samuel Zwemer came from Egypt in 1929 to fill the missions professorship until his retirement in 1936. John Kuizenga taught apologetics, ethics, and systematic theology, retiring in 1947. For evidence of his theological position, see note 24 to this chapter. All data are from the *Biographical Catalogue of Princeton Theological Seminary, 1815–1954*, comp. Orin C. Hopper (Princeton, 1955).

22. They professed the same purpose: to have Christianity respond to the challenges of modern culture neither by subordination nor by separation but by building a distinct Christian framework comprehending all spheres of thought (see Marsden, *Fundamentalism and American Culture* [New York, 1980], pp. 135–38; and Loetscher, *The Broadening Church: A Study of Theological Issues in the Presbyterian Church since 1869* [Philadelphia, 1957], pp. 102–03). But there were subtle—and important—differences between them. Machen did not have Kuyper's total sweep; he was concerned with "all areas of thought" rather than "all areas of life." His conception of the church, as of society, was individualistic (see Loetscher, p. 117); his conception of the state was contractarian and laissez-faire. His tone was "controlled-aristocratic," whereas Kuyper's was "passionate-populistic." Many of these contrasts, in turn, reflected their different philosophical groundings: Kuyper's in Continental dialectical idealism, and Machen's in Scottish commonsense realism. The former was intuitionalist; the latter, intellectualist. Kuyper's concept of competing principial systems "utterly mystified" Machen's mentor, Benjamin B. Warfield, who came close to claiming that *only* Christianity had rationality and coherence and that a neutral mental ground existed where the faith could be proven to anyone's satisfaction (see Marsden, p. 115). Accordingly, Warfield put apologetics at the head of theological labor; Kuyper put it at the tail. As to the increasingly important matter of the veracity of Scripture, Kuyperians stressed the inner testimony of the Holy Spirit, and the Princetonians originated an extreme theory of literalistic inerrancy.

On the Warfield-Princeton train, see Marsden, pp. 109–18; for a Dutch Neo-Calvinist critique thereof, see John Vander Stelt, *Philosophy and Scripture: A Study in Old Princeton and Westminster Theology* (Marlton, N.J., 1978), pp. 202–20, 302–35.

23. Winfield Burggraaff, *The Rise and Development of Liberal Theology in America* (Goes, 1928), p. 210.

24. I have abstracted this argument from dozens of statements. Besides the many parenthetical remarks about Modernism scattered everywhere, there are several comprehensive pronouncements. A convenient catalogue is provided in Burggraaff, *Liberal Theology*, p. 193; a more philosophical summary is provided in Cornelius Van Til, *The New Modernism* (Philadelphia, 1946), pp. viii–ix, 1–8, and 364–79; and Berkhof has contributed a germane collection of lectures, *Aspects of Liberalism*. Typical articles from the *Calvin Forum* include those of Clarence Bouma, "The Supreme Need of the Church," 1(February 1936): 147; and "The Risen Christ Fades Out," 1(April 1936): 195; and of

Louis Berkhof, "Disillusionments of Modernism," 2(October 1936): 57–60. Bouma repeated his charges in "Calvinism in American Theology Today," *Journal of Religion* 27(1947): 43–45. Typical *Banner* articles include those of P. A. Hoekstra, "The Tragedy of a Secularized Church," 26 March 1937, p. 291; and of William Hendriksen, "The Dangerous Silences of Modernism," 2 April 1937, p. 315; and "The Battle about the Book," 9 April 1937, p. 339. Albertus Pieters attacked Modernism on every essential point of doctrine in *The Facts and Mysteries of the Christian Faith* (Grand Rapids, 1926); Louis Berkhof does the same in *Reformed Dogmatics* (3 vols. [Grand Rapids, 1932]) and, concerning the practical applications of theology, in each of the sermons collected in *Riches of Divine Grace* (Grand Rapids, 1948). Another example from sermonic literature is Jacob Bruinooge, "I Believe in God the Father Almighty," in *Sermons on the Apostles' Creed,* ed. H. J. Kuiper (Grand Rapids, 1937), pp. 49–57.

On the RCA side, besides Burggraaff, Pieters, and John Kuizenga's statements cited in note 19 to this chapter, see Kuizenga, "The New Paganism in America," *Christian Intelligencer-Leader,* 16 January 1935, pp. 3–4; "God on the Campus," *Christian Intelligencer-Leader,* 20 June 1941, pp. 32–33; "The Riddle of Oedipus," *Christian Intelligencer-Leader,* 23 June 1939, pp. 8–10; and *Relevancy of the Pivot Points of the Reformed Faith* (Grand Rapids, 1951); Siebe C. Nettinga, "Facing a Pagan World," *Christian Intelligencer-Leader,* 30 April 1937, p. 5; Leonard Greenway, "The Antiquities of Modernism," *Calvin Forum* 1 (April 1936): 205–06; Simon Blocker, "Will the Church Survive?" 22 January 1936; "The Collapse of Liberalism," *Christian Intelligencer-Leader,* 19 February 1936; "The Crisis in Theology," *Christian Intelligencer-Leader,* 4 March 1936; and "Realistic Theology," *Christian Intelligencer-Leader,* 18 March 1936; and the following articles by Louis H. Benes in the *Church Herald:* "What Must the Church Teach?" 25 January 1946; "The Word of the Cross," 29 March 1946; "The Weakness and Strength of Protestantism," 30 August 1946; "The Secularization of the Church," 13 December 1946; and "Christ's Great Commission to His Church," 21 February 1947.

25. Berkhof, *Aspects of Liberalism,* p. 114. Cf. Leonard Greenway, "The Antiquities of Modernism," *Calvin Forum* 1(April 1936): 205–06. Berkhof repeats this point in connection with various articles of doctrine in *Reformed Dogmatics.*

26. See Burggraaff, *Liberal Theology,* p. 210; Louis H. Benes, "The Open and the Closed Mind," *Church Herald,* 29 August 1947, p. 4; Clarence Bouma, "Calvinism and Constructive Scholarship," *Calvin Forum* 5(February 1940): 135–37.

27. Quotation from Edward J. Tanis, "Tumult of the Peoples," *Banner,* 3 January 1930, p. 8. This is a central theme of Bouma, "Calvinism in American Theology Today." See also Kuizenga, *Relevancy of the Reformed Faith,* pp. 12–15; Burggraaff, *Liberal Theology,* pp. 206–08; and Simon Blocker, "The Collapse of Liberalism," *Church Herald,* 19 February 1936, pp. 2–3.

28. See Simon Blocker, "Collapse of Liberalism," *Christian Intelligencer-Leader,* 19 February 1936, p. 2; and Louis H. Benes, "The Word of the Cross," *Church Herald,* 29 March 1946, p. 5. For more on this point, see Chapter 10, pp. 147, 153–54 herein.

29. Berkhof, *Aspects of Liberalism,* pp. 112–13. Cf. John Kuizenga, "What the Liberals Are Driving At," *Leader,* 11 and 18 February and 11 March 1925; and "What We Can Learn From the Liberals," *Leader,* 6 May 1925; Winfield Burggraaff, *Liberal Theology,* p. 193; and William Hendriksen, "The Dangerous Silences of Modernism," *Banner,* 2 April 1937, p. 315.

30. Elizabeth von Maltzahn, *Erich Ohlson* (Grand Rapids, 1932); see pp. 9–19, 179–98, 210–20.

31. Frank Vanden Berg, *Westhaven* (Grand Rapids, 1943); see pp. 123–26, 159–66.

32. Clarence Bouma, "Back to Christian Fundamentals in Education," *Calvin Forum* 1(September 1935): 28. This above all was the lesson of the Princeton-Presbyterian episode. By all accounts, the liberals had been a minority throughout the

struggle, yet with the cooperation of the "moderate" conservatives, the crucial swing vote, they had triumphed over the "maximalist," "positive" conservatives (the Machen camp). To the latter and their CRC sympathizers, the cooperation of the moderates was at most treachery and at least strategic stupidity of the highest order: it fractured the conservative majority and covered the liberals under the moderates' reputation of great personal piety. Regardless of their assessment, the Machenites had the historical facts right (see Loetscher, *Broadening Church*, pp. 102–35). Hence the fear—and contempt—the strictly orthodox had for anyone who spoke of "moderation," "compromise," "toleration," and "irenic" in the same breath with "personal orthodoxy." In reply, however, the moderates had to do no more than point to the results of Machen's strategy. Failing to get the Presbyterian Church to reject extreme liberalism, he first attacked the moderate liberals, then the irenic conservatives, whereupon he seceded (or was ejected), only to have another split in his new church (see Loetscher, p. 103). That the CRC adopted the confrontational strategy may have been something in the way of a tribute to Kuyper, who had used it with more success in the Netherlands.

33. See Cornelius Van Til, *The New Modernism*, subtitled "An Appraisal of the Theology of Barth and Brunner" (e.g., pp. 2–4, 7–8, 244, 372, 376–78). "This enemy comes in the guise of a friend," he writes; "he is all the more dangerous for that . . . a fifth column in orthodox circles" (pp. 3–4). Milder but still very critical are Louis Berkhof, "Disillusionments of Modernism," *Calvin Forum* 2(October 1936): 57–60; Simon Blocker, "The Crisis in Theology" and "Realistic Theology," *Christian Intelligencer-Leader*, 4 and 18 March 1936, pp. 2–3 in each case. Mixed reviews are presented by the following in the *Calvin Forum*: Leonard De Moor, "Calvinism and Revelation," 2(January 1937): 128; D. H. Kromminga, "Theology of Karl Barth," 4(October–December 1938): 55–59, 85–89, 109–12; Edward J. Tanis, "Brunner's Philosophy," 4(March 1939): 174; D. H. Kromminga, "The Christian's Relation to the World according to Barth–Brunner," 13(October 1947): 40–41; and Anthony Hoekema, "Changing Emphases in the Social Gospel," 12(February 1947): 141–45.

34. William Masselink and Ralph Danhof saw their subjects—*J. Gresham Machen and Charles Hodge*, respectively—as valiant but lonely dissenters against the tide of liberalism and infidelity. Ralph Bronkema saw in Puritanism 150 years of degeneration as its inherent flaws came to fruition (see *The Essence of Puritanism* [Goes, 1929]). Peter Y. De Jong traced the decline of one doctrine from the truth of the Puritan fathers to the errors of Horace Bushnell (*The Covenant Idea in New England Theology* [Grand Rapids, 1945]), while Winfield Burggraaff reviewed a longer span and starker horrors, contending that the cancer of liberalism grew from Erasmus to Channing and Emerson, from the Puritans through Edwards to Bushnell, then on to Shailer Mathews and Harry Emerson Fosdick (see *Liberal Theology*).

35. See Kuizenga, "Our Study of Theology," *Leader*, 18 January–8 February 1922.

36. The churches involved were the Wyoming Park Christian Reformed Church and the Calvary Reformed Church (both in Grand Rapids). The Calvary case was more notorious since it involved a full heresy trial and court battle over property and since the schism was led by Martin R. De Haan, a physician-turned-minister who became a leader of the "prophecy" movement in western Michigan. "Undenominationalism" denotes a conservative evangelical movement wishing to dispense with traditional confessions and achieve unity and relevance on the basis of "the Bible alone."

37. Denominational leaders felt compelled to address such speculations repeatedly. See William Hendriksen, *More Than Conquerors: An Interpretation of the Book of Revelation* (Grand Rapids, 1940), pp. 6, 14, 234; Martin J. Wyngaarden, *The Future of the Kingdom in Prophecy and Fulfillment: A Study of the Scope of "Spiritualization" in Scripture* (Grand Rapids, 1934), pp. 70–82, 146, 191–92; and H. J. Kuiper, "The N.R.A. and the Mark of the Beast," *Banner*, 15 September 1933, p. 740.

38. Kuiper, "Fighting on Two Fronts," *Banner*, 6 July 1945, pp. 628–29. Note his

deft placing of Fundamentalism in the worst (for Dutch Calvinists) possible light—as Arminianism. A compendium of all the objections to Fundamentalism is presented in R. B. Kuiper's "Fundamentalism and We," *Banner*, 2 December 1932, p. 1048.

Kuiper's campaigns took place in 1929, the time of the schism, and 1945, when Fundamentalist crusading apparently hit a fever pitch in Grand Rapids. See the following articles he wrote for the *Banner:* "A False Gospel," "The Meaning of the Lordship of Christ," and "What is True Faith?" 1 February 1929, pp. 76–77; "Our Great Problem," 1 March 1929, p. 152; "We Cannot Have Both!" 23 February 1945, pp. 172–73; and "Fighting on Two Fronts," 6 July 1945, pp. 628–29. Other criticisms are noted in the appropriate places in the text. For more extensive treatment, see Hall, "Controversy over Fundamentalism in the CRC."

39. Books devoted to this topic include Hendriksen, *More Than Conquerors;* Wyngaarden, *Future of the Kingdom;* D. H. Kromminga, *The Millennium in the Church: Studies in the History of Christian Chiliasm* (Grand Rapids, 1945); Albertus Pieters, *Studies in the Revelation of St. John* (Grand Rapids, 1954; originally published in 1936 as *The Lamb, the Woman, and the Dragon*); and William Rutgers, "Premillennialism in America" (Th.D. diss., Free University of Amsterdam, 1930). For explication of doctrinal differences, see Hendriksen, *More Than Conquerors,* pp. 48–56, 99–148, 172–88; Pieters, *Studies,* pp. 69, 71, 112, 291–98; Kromminga, *Millennium,* pp. 237–53, 264–66; Jan Karel Van Baalen, *The Heritage of the Fathers* (Grand Rapids, 1948), pp. 328–31; Louis Berkhof, *Reformed Dogmatics,* 3: 309–48.

40. The sense of imminence is pronounced in both Hendriksen (*Conquerors,* pp. 124, 228, 234) and Kromminga (*Millennium,* p. 350); only Pieters demurred (see *Studies,* p. 385).

41. For an account of this case, see Hall, "Controversy over Fundamentalism in the CRC," pp. 39–43; and George Stob, "The Christian Reformed Church and Her Schools" (Th.D. diss., Princeton Theological Seminary, 1955), pp. 445–49. Kromminga had been tending in this direction ever since his first blast against the positive Calvinists immediately after World War I. He published his final position in *The Millennium in the Church* (1945) and *The Millennium: Its Nature, Function, and Relation to the Consummation of the World* (Grand Rapids, 1947). The Seminary Board of Trustees prohibited the publication of two chapters of Kromminga's 1945 book. The Synod of that year began an investigation of his views but vacillated so that the process was still underway at the time of Kromminga's death in 1947. By contrast, Frederick Wezeman, an old student of Ralph Janssen and a teacher at Chicago Christian High School, was brought before the CRC Synod of 1937 on suspicion of "higher critical tendencies." He retained his post only after abject confessions of guilt and repentance. See *CRC Acts of Synod, 1936,* pp. 93–96, 106–15, 146–47; and *Acts of Synod, 1937,* pp. 31–36, 57–61, 68–70, 77–78, 81–82, 90–91, 111–16.

42. On the CRC-NAE relationship, see Hall, "Controversy over Fundamentalism in the CRC," pp. 91–114; for Kuiper's position, see Hall, pp. 101, 114. Interestingly, Clarence Bouma, the regnant champion of principial Calvinism, also backed this venture, and in fact was the CRC's first emissary and negotiator (see Hall, pp. 101–02, 114). Despite such support, CRC membership in the NAE ended in 1951 after eight years (its FCC membership had lasted six). For details on the production of Grand Rapids publishers, see Hall, pp. 140–55. The founder of one of these houses, Zondervan's, was cofounder with H. J. Kuiper of the Reformed Bible Institute.

43. For the Fundamentalist side in this period, see Joel A. Carpenter, "A Shelter in the Time of Storm: Fundamentalist Institutions and the Rise of Evangelical Protestantism, 1929–1942," *Church History* 49(March 1980): 62–75.

44. Quoted matter taken from Daniel Stevick, cited by Marsden in *Fundamentalism and American Culture,* p. 240; see also p. 47; and for J. Gresham Machen's similar reaction, see p. 138.

45. See De Jong, *The Covenant Idea in New England Theology, 1620–1847* (Grand Rapids, 1945), pp. 199–200; Ralph Bronkema, *Essence of Puritanism*, pp. 120–24, 205–07; Clarence Bouma, "Should Preaching Be Theocentric or Christocentric?" *Calvin Forum* 10(February 1945): 132–33; and H. J. Kuiper, "We Cannot Have Both!" *Banner*, 23 February 1945, pp. 172–73; and "Fighting on Two Fronts," *Banner*, 6 July 1945, pp. 628–29.

46. William Hendriksen provides a full statement of this position in *The Covenant of Grace* (Grand Rapids, 1932). See also Leonard Verduin, "Ostrich Nurture," *Banner*, 6 July 1939, p. 627; De Jong, *Covenant Idea;* Van Baalen, *Heritage of the Fathers*, pp. 380–82; Berkhof, *Reformed Dogmatics*, 1: 243–94; Z. J. Sharda, "Revivals," *Banner*, 17 January 1930, p. 57; and H. J. Kuiper, "We Cannot Have Both!" *Banner*, 23 February 1945, pp. 172–73; and "Fighting on Two Fronts," *Banner*, 6 July 1945, pp. 628–29. For a fuller analysis of the theological specifics, see Anthony A. Hoekema, "The CRC and the Covenant," in *Perspectives on the CRC*, ed. De Klerk and De Ridder, pp. 185–201.

47. Bouma, "A Few Questions," *Calvin Forum* 4(March 1939): 173–74. Cf. Henry J. Kuiper's further complaint about "Arminian" Fundamentalism: "We shall also lose [under its spell] our main defense against Modernism. . . . If we yield to Arminianism we have taken the first and a long step to Modernism" ("Fighting on Two Fronts," *Banner*, 6 July 1945, pp. 628–29). This repeated, of course, what B. K. Kuiper and F. M. Ten Hoor had said a generation before regarding the progression from "Methodism" to "Modernism." A historian of the Fundamentalist-Modernist clash in Presbyterianism drew a somewhat similar connection between the "rationalism" of the second party ("seeking the lightest load of faith that reason must bear") and the "pietism" of the first ("satisfied with just enough theology to provide for conversion and holiness"). Both sides sought "the irreducible minimum which can be retained or must be defended. The answers given at such opposite poles were different enough, but there were strange resemblances both in the formulation of the problem and in the method of treating it" (Loetscher, *Broadening Church*, pp. 98–99). For the broader point, see Bastian Kruithof, *The Christ of the Cosmic Road* (Grand Rapids, 1937); H. J. Van Andel, "New Frontier Days," *Calvin Forum* 1(May 1935): 7; Clarence Bouma, "How Dead is Calvinism?" *Calvin Forum* 1(October 1935): 51–52; and "An Educated Minority," *Banner*, 7 June 1933, pp. 534–35; and Ralph Stob, "As to Being Reformed," *Banner*, 1 February and 5 April 1932, pp. 102, 318; "Men of Principle," *Banner*, 29 November 1935, p. 1086; and "Rethinking Calvinism," *Banner*, 25 May 1939, p. 483.

48. Kuizenga, "Why We Need a Creed," *Leader*, 22 November 1922, p. 9. See also his "Shall We Throw Away the Creed?" *Leader*, 16 January–13 February 1918. Kuizenga also saw doctrine as a defensive instrument against Modernism. See also Henry R. Van Til, "Doctrine: A Scriptural Evaluation," *Calvin Forum* 13(March 1948): 160–63; and William T. Radius, "The Creeds, the Bible, and Higher Education," *Calvin Forum* 14(May 1949): 203–05.

49. Berkhof, *Reformed Dogmatics*, 1: 148; on Scripture, see pp. 14–18, 24–30, 138–79. For the place of Scripture in Fundamentalist thought, see Sandeen, *The Roots of Fundamentalism: British and American Millenarianism, 1800–1930* (Chicago, 1970), pp. 103–31.

50. See Berkhof, *Reformed Dogmatics* 1: 18–22, 101–03; 109–10; *The Assurance of Faith* (Grand Rapids, 1939), pp. 34, 75, 77; and *Riches of Divine Grace*, pp. 24–27. Cf. H. J. Kuiper, "What Is First: Emotion or Reason?" *Banner*, 21 October 1932, p. 900. Berkhof consciously followed Bavinck and Geerhardus Vos, but at this point, as with that of Scripture, he shows the "Princetonian" influence of B. B. Warfield.

51. Berkhof, *Manual of Reformed Doctrine* (Grand Rapids, 1933). All told, Berkhof taught at Calvin Seminary for almost four decades, from 1906 to 1944. The first two decades he taught biblical theology and New Testament; he assumed the chair in systematics in 1926 and the presidency in 1931.

52. Berkhof, *Manual of Reformed Doctrine*, p. 5.

53. For detailed accounts of both these proposals, see Herman Harmelink III, *Ecumenism and the Reformed Church* (Grand Rapids, 1968), pp. 58–65, 79–85; and Ernest H. Post, Jr., "A Century of Ecumenical and Unionist Tendencies in the Reformed Church in America: 1850–1950" (Ph.D. diss., Michigan State University, 1966), pp. 169–82, 194–268. Characteristic arguments against the proposals were presented by Albertus Pieters in the following articles in the *Leader:* "Organic Union in General," 27 November 1929, p. 3; "Would General Organic Union Be Desirable?" 4 December 1929, pp. 2–3; "Why Should We Join the Presbyterians?" 18 December 1929, pp. 2–3; and "Editorial Comments," 6 May 1931, p. 8. Both cases generated an RCA West backlash against the Federal Council of Churches, on which, see the following in the *Church Herald:* Albertus Pieters, "The Protestant Apostasy," 25 April 1947, pp. 8–9; and "Let Us Leave the Federal Council," 2 May 1947, pp. 8–9; and Louis Benes, "Infiltration," 14 March 1947, pp. 6–7. Among many articles in favor of both were David Van Strien, "Concerning Our Membership in the Federal Council," *Church Herald,* 28 March 1947, pp. 8–9; John H. Warnshuis, "What I Should Know about the Reformed Church," *Christian Intelligencer-Leader,* 5 July 1935, p. 5; and James Nettinga, "Church Unity," *Christian Intelligencer-Leader,* 13 August 1937, p. 5.

54. Sermons devoted entirely to doctrine can be found in *Sermons on Sin and Grace* and *Sermons on the Apostles' Creed,* ed. Henry J. Kuiper (Grand Rapids, 1937); and Bastian Kruithof, *The High Points of Calvinism* (Grand Rapids, 1949). Louis Berkhof stressed orthodoxy heavily in *The Assurance of Faith* and *Riches of Divine Grace.* Others who emphasized doctrine were Henry Beets, in *The Man of Sorrows* (Grand Rapids, 1935), and Jan Karel Van Baalen, in *The Journey of Man and Other Sermons* (Grand Rapids, 1935) and *The Heritage of the Fathers.*

55. Evert J. Blekkink, *The Fatherhood of God* (Grand Rapids, 1942). Bernard J. Mulder, *The King Came Riding* (Grand Rapids, 1943). A similar pattern appears in Edward H. Tanis, *Behind the Open Hedge: Meditations on the Book of Job* (Grand Rapids, 1941); and Simon Blocker, *When Christ Takes Over* (Grand Rapids, 1945), both RCA authors (along with Blekkink and Mulder). On the CRC side there were Berkhof, *Riches of Divine Grace* and *Assurance of Faith;* Beets, *Man of Sorrows;* and Van Baalen, *Journey of Man.*

56. These motifs are especially strong in Berkhof, *Riches of Divine Grace* and *Assurance of Faith;* Van Baalen, *Journey of Man;* and Tanis, *Behind the Open Hedge.* They are also prominent in eschatological works—especially Hendriksen, *Conquerors,* pp. 34–35, 254–55; and Kromminga, *Millennium,* pp. 235–41, 350.

57. See Beets, *Man of Sorrows;* and Blocker, *When Christ Takes Over.*

58. John A. Dykstra, *Heavenly Days* (Grand Rapids, 1944).

59. Simon Blocker, "The Rebellion of 1937," *Christian Intelligencer-Leader,* 27 August 1937, p. 4. Of course, many sectors of the evangelical complex shared these sentiments and the response detailed in the text following (see Weber, *Living in the Shadow of the Second Coming* [New York, 1939], pp. 61–64, 82–104; Anderson, *Vision of the Disinherited,* pp. 195–222; and Marsden, *Fundamentalism and American Culture,* pp. 85–93). That is not necessarily to suggest that there was increased acculturation on the part of Dutch Americans, however, since this concern grew out of the dynamics of their own tradition and was used to fortify ethno-religious solidarity. Moreover, the different evangelical sectors placed this concern in their own conceptual-behavioral "fields" with pluralistic consequences. "Anti-worldliness" did not "mean" entirely the same thing for, say, dispensationalists, Pentecostalists, Southern Baptists, and the Dutch Reformed.

60. Two collections are William Masselink's *Sermons on the Ten Commandments* (Grand Rapids, 1934), and *Sermons on the Ten Commandments,* ed. H. J. Kuiper (Grand

Rapids, 1951). Preaching such series was mandated by the Heidelberg Catechism, the liturgical base of the CRC.

61. See Kuiper, *Sermons on the Ten Commandments,* pp. 49–57, 79–101; and Masselink, *Sermons on the Ten Commandments,* pp. 66–83, 90–114. Cf. H. J. Kuiper, "Remember the Sabbath Day," *Banner,* 29 April 1932, p. 412.

62. See Masselink, *Sermons on the Ten Commandments,* pp. 153–67; Kuiper, *Sermons on the Ten Commandments,* pp. 129–43; Jacob D. Mulder, "Planned Contraception," *Calvin Forum* 1(March and April 1936): 175–77, 197–99; Synod of the Christian Reformed Church, "A Birth Control Testimony," *Calvin Forum* 1(July 1936): 276. See also Cecil De Boer, *The If's and Ought's of Ethics: A Preface to Moral Philosophy* (Grand Rapids, 1936), pp. 365–66; on sexual ethics, see pp. 339–74; on economic ethics, see pp. 265–327. Eschatological treatises also gave special stress to sexual sin as prime evidence of the world's corruption and a chief means of oppressing the church (see William Hendriksen, *More Than Conquerors,* pp. 200–207; and Albertus Pieters, *Studies in Revelation,* p. 258).

63. These characters appeared in *Westhaven, Desires of the Heart,* and *Erich Ohlson,* respectively.

64. H. J. Kuiper, "Frankly Sensual," *Banner,* 26 July 1929, p. 516. Kuiper's *Banner* editorials on various facets of worldliness include "What Is Wrong with Gambling?" 16 September 1932, p. 780; "Worldliness: The First Stage of Modernism," 26 January 1934, p. 68; "Moral Disintegration," 23 February 1934, p. 165; "When Vileness Is Exalted," 21 September 1934, p. 788; "Moral Lethargy," 10 January 1930, p. 28; "Foolish Song," 5 May 1944, p. 412; "Games of Chance Immoral," 28 February 1930; "Worldlymindedness and Earthlymindedness," 18 October 1940, p. 964. So many activities did Kuiper condemn that it came as a major breakthrough when he allowed that bowling might pass muster, so long as it was not played in "vulgar surroundings" ("The Bowling Craze," 8 May 1942, p. 436).

65. Kuiper, "Sodom and Gomorrah," *Banner,* 12 December 1947, p. 1380. Kuiper made his case against the movies in such *Banner* editorials as "Protecting Our Children," 27 January 1933, pp. 76–77; "Psychology of the Photoplay," 17 February 1933, p. 148; "Crack-Up?" 26 October 1939, p. 988; "The Movie Problem," 26 February, 12 and 26 March, and 23 April 1937, pp. 196, 244, 292, 389; and "The Godless Movies," 27 May 1949, p. 644.

66. H. J. Kuiper, "The Christian Home in Danger," *Banner,* 3 June 1937, p. 532. Several constants of Kuiper's thinking are apparent here: the sense of declension, defensiveness, and near-despair; and the slightly hysterical impression created by the cascading waves of images and parallels, all capped by that memorable "and many other forces besides." Cf. "Our Homes in Peril," *Banner,* 29 September 1933, p. 772; "Time to Wake Up," *Banner,* 11 May 1939, p. 436; "Saving Our Homes," *Banner,* 18 May 1939, p. 460; "The Greatest Sin of the Church," *Banner,* 28 January 1944, p. 76. A similar opinion is presented by Z. J. Sharda in "The Importance of Marriage," *Banner,* 24 January 1930, p. 82.

67. Hendriksen expresses this point succinctly: "God does not save people at random [but] perpetuates his covenant from generation to generation through the families of believers" (*Covenant of Grace,* p. 65). This marked a truncation (quite in keeping with the garrison mentality of the time) of the broad covenant conception the Reformed had postulated against Fundamentalism. It is especially remarkable that Peter Y. De Jong did not question this limitation after studying the Puritans' application of the covenant to a broadly communal, even national context (see his *Covenant Idea*).

68. Bernard Mulder, "Likeness to the World," *Christian Intelligencer-Leader,* 22 October 1943, p. 3. Typical Reformed Church declarations on the subject (all in the *Christian Intelligencer-Leader*) are provided by G. Mennenga, "When Self Is out of Focus," 24 July 1935, pp. 5–6; Nicholas Boer, "How Shall We Keep Sunday?" 9 January

1935, p. 5; John Wesselink, "A Call to Holiness," 2 January 1935, p. 4; John R. Mulder, "Another Birthday for Uncle Sam," 1 July 1936, p. 2; Jean A. Vis, "Moral Anarchy in Perkins Corner," 17 December 1937, p. 7; Richard Jager, "Righteous Indignation," 29 April 1938, pp. 4–5; Henry Steunenberg, "The Church and Social Welfare," 20 October 1939, p. 7; Simon Blocker, "Christ and the American Way of Life," 3 October 1941, p. 3; and "The Rebellion of 1937," 27 August 1937, p. 4; and Bernard Mulder, "Teen Age Girls and Vice," 29 January 1943, pp. 3–4; and "With a United Purpose—Phooey!" 5 March 1943, p. 3.

69. See Samuel Zwemer, "Perpetuating Our Heritage," *Christian Intelligencer-Leader*, 24 February 1937, p. 5; and Jan Karel Van Baalen, *Heritage of the Fathers*, pp. 538–44.

70. Watson Groen, "Thanksgiving Day 1935," *Banner*, 22 November 1935, p. 1062.

CHAPTER TEN

1. Respectively, Berkhof's *Reformed Dogmatics* (3 vols. [Grand Rapids, 1932]), and J. K. Van Baalen's *The Heritage of the Fathers* (Grand Rapids, 1948), a commentary on the Heidelberg Catechism; Cornelius Jaarsma, *The Educational Philosophy of Herman Bavinck: A Textbook in Education* (Grand Rapids, 1935); H. Henry Meeter, *Calvinism: An Interpretation of Its Basic Ideas* (Grand Rapids, 1939); and Edward J. Tanis, *Calvinism and Social Problems* (Grand Rapids, 1936).

2. Jellema generated few publications but a bevy of philosophers and grateful testimony from the many students for whom he redeemed college—and sometimes Christianity. For one instance, see Robert C. Wright, *Frederick Manfred* (Boston, 1979), p. 19. (Manfred dedicated his first novel, *The Golden Bowl* [St. Paul, 1944] to "W.H.J.") A brief, fine assessment is provided in Henry Stob's foreword to Jellema's festschrift, *Faith and Philosophy,* ed. Alvin Plantinga (Grand Rapids, 1964).

3. The novel was *Instead of the Thorn* (New York, 1941). Like Kuyper's *Gemeene Gratie, Christ of the Cosmic Road* (Grand Rapids, 1937) could have had as its subtitle, in parody of Schleiermacher, "On Culture: Speeches to Its Religious Despisers." Interestingly, the quoted material (from p. vii of the book) uses the title of the old positive Calvinist journal.

4. See Van Baalen, *Heritage of the Fathers,* pp. 353, 368, 380–82, 393–96, 454, 569–70, 600–602. See also H. J. Van Andel, "Why Art for the Calvinist?" *Calvin Forum* 6(January 1942): 116–19; and "Calvinism and Precisianism in Dutch Art," 7(May 1943): 211–13. Kruithof identifies these faults implicitly and frequently throughout both his works.

5. See Clarence Bouma, "Calvinism in American Theology Today," *Journal of Religion* 27(1947): 34–35; and any number of his editorials in the *Calvin Forum.* Typical are the first and last articles he wrote: "How Dead Is Calvinism?" 1(October 1935): 51–52; and "Forward in Faith," 15(January 1950): 107–08. This represented quite a different program from the one envisioned by Ralph Janssen, Bouma's early mentor, in congratulatory letters he sent at the height of the "progressive" tide in 1919, as Bouma began his theology studies at Harvard: "the thing most gratifying is the presence at Harvard of a genuine scientific atmosphere and men to sustain it. . . . We are moving progressive rapidly. . . . Harvard may do us a great deal of good [in this regard]" (letter of 26 October 1919, Bouma papers, Calvin College and Seminary Archives, Grand Rapids, Michigan). By the '30s nothing raised Bouma's eyebrows higher or faster than "genuine scientific atmosphere," "rapid progress," or for that matter Harvard Divinity School.

6. John Kuizenga, "The Riddle of Oedipus," *Christian Intelligencer-Leader*, 23 June

1939, p. 10. Watson Groen gave something of the same analysis in "The Threatened Collapse of Civilization: A Blessing or Curse?" *Banner,* 26 October 1939, p. 991. It says much about Groen and his denomination (the CRC) that the question in his title was not at all rhetorical.

7. See Meeter, *Calvinism,* pp. 118–20, 148–56; Kuizenga, *Relevancy of the Pivot Points of the Reformed Faith* (Grand Rapids, 1951), pp. 7–11; E. J. Tanis, "The Enemies of Christian Liberty," *Banner,* 28 August 1942, pp. 762–63; H. J. Kuiper, "Liberty and Authority," *Banner,* 21 April 1933, p. 364; Henry Schultze, "Authority and Liberty," *Calvin Forum* 3(September 1937): 29–30; and "Will Democracies Survive?" *Calvin Forum* 6(June–July 1941): 227; and Jesse De Boer, "The Reformation and Social Authority," *Calvin Forum* 3(January 1938): 126–28.

8. John Kuizenga, "God on Campus," *Christian Intelligencer-Leader,* 20 June 1941, p. 32. Other instances of the argument can be found in Frederick Bronkema, "God or Nihilism," *Christian Intelligencer-Leader,* 1 July 1936, pp. 5–6; Clarence Bouma, "Sweet Land of Liberty," *Calvin Forum* 7(December 1941): 83–86; E. J. Tanis, "The World Today," *Banner,* 6 February 1942, p. 127; H. J. Kuiper, "Fighting Fascism," *Banner,* 28 August 1942, p. 756; Leonard Greenway, "Some Ancestors of Hitlerism," *Calvin Forum* 7(March 1942): 161–62; and Leonard Verduin, "The New Minister," *Calvin Forum* 9(April 1944): 188–91. Henry Schultze put it in an epigram: "Men have ceased to think much about God. They are thinking less and less about man" ("The Depreciation of Human Personality," *Calvin Forum* 2[October 1936]: 52). Verduin preferred the following screaming indictment: "The liberal church has taken an active part in issuing the pagan manifesto that has . . . prepared the way for just such a course of events [as that which occurred in Germany]. . . . The theology of our liberal theologians is closely akin to that of the Storm Troopers. . . . Those who are lying in anguish today are there because of a faith that the Nazis hate. It is the same faith that our liberal theologians would fain consign to oblivion!" ("The New Minister," pp. 188, 191).

9. See Jacob Vanden Bosch, "Art and Morality," *Calvin Forum* 7(November 1941): 189–92. See also H. J. Van Andel, "Schools of Nineteenth-Century Painting," *Calvin Forum* 3(June 1938): 251–53; "Ultra-Modern Painting," *Calvin Forum* 4(January and February 1939): 128–30, 153–54; and "A Chronicle of Art," *Calvin Forum* 7(June–July 1942): 234. According to Van Andel, with the Fauves in 1905, "modern art lost its balance. It went mad. . . . [Yet,] the beginning of this modern chaos and misery is not simply of 1905, but of a century earlier. . . . Already nineteenth-century art plainly shows that mankind in 1789 set its feet on the path of unbelief and revolution. . . . Rousseau and Kant have sown the storms. We reap the whirlwind" ("Nineteenth-Century Painting," pp. 251, 253). Van Andel was one of the few (E. J. Tanis being one other) to use the Groen-Kuyper rhetoric exactly.

10. See the *Forum*'s special issue on education, 2(June 1937): 243–53. See also the following articles in that journal: Henry Van Zyl, "Present-Day Teaching in the United States," 3(December 1937): 110–12; "More Lost Provinces in Education?" 4(September 1938): 31–34; Clarence Bouma, "Rudderless Rabbits," 7(October 1941): 35–36; and Lambert Flokstra, "Education for Democracy," 13(January 1948): 107–08. In this connection, one of the *Forum*'s favorite "outsiders" was Robert Hutchins, who was frequently championed against John Dewey.

11. See Schultze, "Planning for Higher Education," *Calvin Forum* 8(April 1943): 185–87; "Liberal Arts in the Balances," *Calvin Forum* 8(February 1943): 132–35; and "Will the Liberal Arts Come Back?" *Calvin Forum* 11(August–September 1945): 13–15.

12. CRC statements can be found in the following *Calvin Forum* articles: Clarence Bouma, "Back to Christian Fundamentals in Education," 1(September 1935): 28; "Calvinism and Constructive Scholarship," 5(February 1940): 135–37; and "Christian Principles and Scientific Study," 6(August–September 1940): 3–4; and Jacob Vanden Bosch, "Freedom in Education," 5(May 1940): 213–17. Reformed Church statements can be

found in the following *Christian Intelligencer-Leader* articles: Anthony Te Paske, "Education Sunday," 27 January 1939, pp. 3–4; John R. Mulder, "The Reformed Church Believes in Education," 15 January 1936, p. 2; and Bernard Mulder, "College—For What?" 26 January 1940, pp. 3–4.

13. Clarence Bouma, "Can Science Save Us?" *Calvin Forum* 4(June–July 1939): 243. Typical *Forum* articles on philosophy include Bouma, "Philosophy Teaching and the Christian Faith," 4(September 1938): 28–29; Cornelius Jaarsma, "A Quest for Certainty amidst Modern Perplexity," 1(December 1935): 107–09; and Cecil De Boer, *Responsible Protestantism,* a collection of essays originally written for the *Forum* (Grand Rapids, 1957), pp. 77–84. (De Boer also examines popular materialism in this volume, on pp. 116–32, 177–91, 230–34.)

14. See Clarence Bouma, "God and Your College Diploma," *Calvin Forum* 13(August–September 1947): 7–11; and John van Lonkhuyzen, "The Scientific Mission," *Calvin Forum* 13(February 1948): 136–40.

15. See De Vries, *Beyond the Atom* (Grand Rapids, 1948), pp. 78, 81–83, 158. For the entire argument, see pp. 14–34. See also De Boer, *Responsible Protestantism,* pp. 13–17, 239–43. Pertinent *Forum* articles include Cornelius Jaarsma, "Christian Theories and the Scientific Method," 5(March 1940): 167–70; Edwin Y. Monsma, "Two Approaches in Teaching Organic Sciences," 8(April 1943): 192–93; and "Some Presuppositions of Evolutionary Thinking," 14(October 1948): 45–48; and William Radius, "Science, Evolution, and Christianity," 10(March 1945): 165–69.

16. De Boer, *Responsible Protestantism,* p. 24. The entire argument is found on pp. 2–37, 239–43.

17. See H. J. Kuiper, "Where We Stand on Prohibition," *Banner,* 4 November 1932, p. 948.

18. Geerlings, "People Out of Work," *Leader,* 19 March 1930, p. 5.

19. Some expressions of this mood found in the *Christian Intelligencer-Leader* include the following articles by Siebe C. Nettinga: "Uncompromising Christianity," 6 September 1933, pp. 2–3; "Is There a Revival of Calvinism?" 23 October 1935, pp. 4–5; "The Doctrinal Emphasis in Christianity," 23 January 1935, pp. 5–6; "Facing a Pagan World," 6 April 1936, pp. 5–6; and John R. Mulder, "Another Birthday for Uncle Sam," 1 July 1936, pp. 5–6.

20. See Henry Geerlings, "Too Much Government," *Leader,* 16 December 1931, p. 4; John R. Mulder, "The Christian and the Dole," *Christian Intelligencer-Leader,* 2 January 1935, p. 3; Lambertus Hekhuis, "The Christian and the Economic Situation," *Christian Intelligencer-Leader,* 29 May 1935, pp. 3–4; and Simon Blocker, "Christianity and Industry," *Christian Intelligencer-Leader,* 2 September 1936, p. 3.

21. See the following articles by H. J. Kuiper in the *Banner:* "Depression Psychology," 13 May 1932, p. 460; "Review of 1932," 30 December 1932, pp. 1140–41; "Is There No Remedy?" 10 March 1933, p. 220; and "A Forgotten Factor," 21 September 1934, p. 788.

22. Kuiper, "The Ethical Note," *Banner,* 12 January 1934, pp. 20–21. Although attacks on "Wall Street" could have an anti-Semitic aspect, there is no evidence of such in this case.

23. Kuiper, "Government in Business," *Banner,* 8 March 1935, p. 220. See also the following of his articles in the *Banner:* "The Position of the Christian on Present Economic Issues," 2 November–14 December 1934, pp. 932, 980, 1004, 1052, 1076; "Is Socialism Good?" 12 April 1935; and "A Few Observations on This Political Campaign," 23 October 1936, p. 988.

24. Kuiper, "The Ethical Note," *Banner,* 12 January 1934, p. 21.

25. Kuiper detailed this view most completely in his series "The Position of the Christian on Present Economic Issues," *Banner,* 2 November–14 December 1934, pp. 932, 980, 1004, 1052, 1076; he repeated it in "Socialism and Orthodox Christianity,"

Banner, 25 January 1935, pp. 76–77. Significantly, old Antithetical Kuyperian Klaas Schoolland wrote his swan song on the occasion of the 1936 elections, condemning the "principle" of "state-absolutism" and America's drift toward it ("Society, State, and Government," *Banner,* 30 October 1936, pp. 1022–23).

Two notes as to the sources of such sentiment. On January 1, 1915 H. J. Kuiper had written B. K. Kuiper, then a Calvin professor, about the recent assignment of the "sociological department" in the *Banner* to him (H. J.). "I have never made a systematic study of the subject," he said, "and confess that I know very little about it." Would B. K. therefore be so kind as to recommend some college textbooks and "a few good works." Later, after H. J. had succeeded in getting B. K. ousted from the faculty, the latter received some money from his brother Anton to have his house painted. The words that came with the check (dated August 21, 1936) might have been expected from one in Anton's position (he was an assistant manager for Prudential Life) given the circumstances (the Roosevelt-Landon presidential campaign was on), but nonetheless show that reactionary politics were by no means the monopoly of the clergy: "You can tell these fellows that are going to do the work that they are getting these jobs not because Roosevelt and his crowd are responsible for any prosperity . . . because I am spending my money out of fear and nothing else. Fear that if Roosevelt and his crowd of nuts get in there another four years, in a short time any money I or anyone else has won't be worth much more than a plugged nickel." B. K. was to make certain that the painters were not going to vote for F. D. R. and that he and his wife were soliciting their acquaintances diligently for Landon. (Both letters in B. K. Kuipers papers, Calvin College and Seminary Archives.)

26. Typical overall appraisals from the *Forum* are provided by Peter Hoekstra, "Our Two Major Parties—An Interpretation," 2(September 1936): 42–44; and Henry J. Ryskamp, "Recent Trends," 8(January 1943): 113–16. See also Clarence Bouma, "The New Deal at Its Best," *Calvin Forum* 3(September 1937): 27–28.

27. H. J. Van Andel, "Four 'Republican' Principles," *Calvin Forum* 4(August 1938): 5–6. Concerning Kuiper and other "reactionaries," see Clarence Bouma, "Wilson and Roosevelt Vindicated," *Calvin Forum* 9(December 1943): 84–85. Bouma eulogized Roosevelt in "The Passing of a Great Leader," *Calvin Forum* 10(May 1945): 203–05.

28. H. J. Van Andel, "Four 'Republican' Principles," *Calvin Forum* 4(August 1938): 5–6. See also C. J. Smit, "Adam Smith and the Doctrine of Original Sin," *Calvin Forum* 6(October 1940): 37–40. And see Clarence Bouma, "Sham Liberty and Real Liberty," *Calvin Forum* 2(December 1936): 100; and Tanis, *Calvinism and Social Problems,* p. 57.

29. See E. J. Tanis, *Calvinism and Social Problems,* pp. 30–40, 61–67, 72–78, and especially 83–86. See also Meeter, *Calvinism,* pp. 102–03, 128–37.

30. See Meeter, *Calvinism,* pp. 104–16, 118–24, 129–31; Tanis, *Calvinism and Social Problems,* pp. 78–93; and Clarence Bouma, "Sham Liberty and Real Liberty," *Calvin Forum* 2(December 1936): "The government . . . must not rule a bit more than is strictly necessary for the common good. There is no room for a paternalistic, autocratic or dictatorial government" (p. 100). See also Bouma, "Sitting Down on Law and Order," *Calvin Forum* 2(April 1937): 195. During the Depression, sympathies toward labor naturally increased; yet such organizing tactics as sit-down strikes seemed a challenge to lawful authority and therefore were sharply criticized. Because both denominations had formed positions on union membership earlier, there was comparatively little discussion of that issue during this period.

31. See, for instance, Henry J. Ryskamp, "Recent Trends," *Calvin Forum:* 8(January 1943): "In a world in which men are as interdependent as they are now we may not ignore or shirk our common responsibility for the security of all. . . . When capital becomes collectivized labor must also be. . . . Recognition of such facts and the translation of them into legislation for the common good is necessary" (p. 115).

32. De Boer, *The If's and Ought's of Ethics: A Preface to Moral Philosophy* (Grand Rapids, 1936), p. 292. For his broader treatment of economic ethics, see pp. 265–327.

33. Henry J. Ryskamp, "A Declining World?" *Calvin Forum* 5(May 1940): 221. Ryskamp's argument is evident in the following articles in the *Calvin Forum:* "An Approach to the New Deal," 2(September 1936): 40–41; "The New Deal," 2(October 1936): 65–67; "Chains of Our Own Forging," 3(April 1938): 204–06; "Toward Understanding," 3(June 1938): 256–57; "The American Way," 4(August 1938): 12–13; "Disturbing Economic Reflections," 5(August–September 1939): 14–16; "This Is My Father's World," 5(November 1939): 62–63; "A Declining World?" 5(May 1940): 220–22; "Economic Freedom and War," 6(November 1940): 61–62; "Recovery, Reform, and Defense," 6(January 1941): 111–14; and "A World of Paradoxes," 8(November 1942): 61–63. The resonances with Reinhold Niebuhr's contemporary critique are obvious but the evidence concerning precise influence is lacking.

34. Ryskamp's perspective is made nicely evident in his article titles: "This Is My Father's World," for instance, "A Declining World?" and "A World of Paradoxes." Examples of his self-criticism can be found in "Economics and Ethics," *Calvin Forum* 2(March 1937): 171–72; and "Chains of Our Own Forging," *Calvin Forum* 3(April 1938): 204–06.

35. Victor J. Blekkink, "The Olive Branch and the Bayonet," *Christian Intelligencer-Leader,* 18 November 1936, p. 3. Mulder made his case in "The Church and Peace," *Calvin Forum* 1(October 1935): 53–55, and in such editorials in the *Christian Intelligencer-Leader* as "Disillusionment," 30 April 1937, p. 3; "Roping in America," 18 February 1938, p. 3; "A Christian Philosophy of Peace," 5 May 1939, p. 3; "Along the Road to War," 22 September 1939, p. 3; and "The Same Old War," 2 August 1940, p. 3.

36. Kuiper, "Some Thoughts about Pacifism," *Banner,* 8 June 1934, p. 509. This was the last in a series (running from 16 March to 8 June 1934) in which Kuiper laid out the antipacifist case. That case was best made by *Leader* editor Albertus Pieters in *The Christian Attitude towards War* (Grand Rapids, 1932). Another Christian Reformed opponent was Jacob Bruinooge (see "The View of Obedience without Reservations," *Calvin Forum* 1[May 1935]: 13–14). And an incendiary RCA attack was made by John Bovenkerk in "The Modern Pacifist Movement," *Calvin Forum* 1(October 1935): 55–57.

37. See, for example, Meeter, *Calvinism,* pp. 104–06, 198–226.

38. See H. J. Kuiper, "Some Thoughts about Pacifism," *Banner,* 27 April 1934, p. 364; and Raymond Van Heukelom, "A Critique of Pacifism," *Calvin Forum* 7(April 1942): 191–94.

39. Bouma, "War, Peace, and the Christian," *Calvin Forum* 1(December 1935): 99–102. This received the largest response of any *Forum* editorial. Over ten thousand copies were sent out.

40. See Tanis, "The World Today," *Banner,* 7 September 1939, p. 819; 5 October 1939, p. 920; and 4 July 1941, p. 630. See also Mulder, "The Church and War," *Christian Intelligencer-Leader,* 15 September 1939, pp. 3–4; "Along the Road to War," *Christian Intelligencer-Leader,* 22 September 1939, p. 3; and "The Same Old War," *Christian Intelligencer-Leader,* 2 August 1940, p. 3. And see Kuiper, "From Mammon to Mars," *Banner,* 21 September 1939, p. 869; "The Attitude of Our Churches toward the Present European War," *Banner,* 5 October 1939, p. 916; and "No Right to Go to War!" *Banner,* 31 January 1940, p. 100.

41. Tanis, *Banner,* 4 July 1941, p. 630. See also Tanis, "A Difficult Decision," *Banner,* 13 September 1940, p. 848; H. J. Kuiper, "The International Situation," *Banner,* 25 October 1940, pp. 988–89; and Bernard Mulder, "Danger to Christianity," *Christian Intelligencer-Leader,* 22 November 1940, p. 4.

42. See Mulder, "Is This a Righteous War?" *Christian Intelligencer-Leader,* 26 December 1941, pp. 3–4; "What Are You?" *Christian Intelligencer-Leader,* 9 October 1942, pp. 3–4; and "I Am Sorry for Japan," *Christian Intelligencer-Leader,* 19 December 1941, pp. 12–13; H. J. Kuiper, "If This Be War . . . !" *Banner,* 4 June 1943, p.

508; and B. D. Dykstra, "Saving Minorities," *Christian Intelligencer-Leader,* 10 September 1943. Dykstra, an old Bryanite Prohibition-and-Peace type from northwest Iowa, was referring to conscientious objectors in his title.

43. See the following in the *Christian Intelligencer-Leader:* Bernard Mulder, "Time To Think about It Again," 5 March 1943, p. 3; "D-Day Praying," 21 July 1944, p. 3; "The United Nations Charter: What Can the Church Do Now?" 24 August 1945, pp. 8–9. Vernon Kooy articulated the battle of the two wills in "Not a Crown, but a Cross!" 15 May 1942, pp. 4–5.

44. See Kuiper, "The Sin of Our Military Unpreparedness," *Banner,* 13 March 1942, p. 244; and "The Christian College Graduate in Time of War," *Calvin Forum* 7(June–July 1942): 220–23; and J. J. Steigenga, *Banner,* 25 July 1941, p. 702.

45. See the following in the *Banner:* H. J. Kuiper, "Shall We Pray for Victory?" 23 January 1942, p. 76; and "Retribution," 18 September 1942, p. 828; J. J. Steigenga, "The Raging of the Nations," 6 February 1942, p. 128; John Vander Ploeg, "To US Belongeth Confusion of Face," 18 September 1942, pp. 832–33. The first thing both denominations did after the war came was pass resolutions imploring the government to clean up military bases; they spent months thereafter discussing measures they could take to help that cause. One effort was James Putt's *A Good Soldier of the Lord Jesus Christ* (Fulton, Illinois, 1943), a handbook for young soldiers. Putt, a CRC minister, declared the soldier's three prime duties to be daily religious devotions, moral cleanliness, and obedience to officers.

46. See Kuiper, "Fighting Fascism," *Banner,* 28 August 1942, p. 756. See also Vander Ploeg, "To US Belongeth Confusion of Face," *Banner,* 18 September 1942, pp. 832–33; and "The Bright Side of the War," *Banner,* 5 February 1943, pp. 129–30.

47. Bouma articles (all in the *Calvin Forum*) at crucial dates include the following: "The Statue of Liberty Assumes New Meaning," 2(December 1936): 99–100; "The Nazi Juggernaut Rolls On," 3(April 1938): 195–96; "The World Struggle and the Christian Church," 5(October 1939): 36; "Sweet Land of Liberty," 7(December 1941): 83–87; and "The Dry Rot of Pacifism," "Hold Your Civil Tongues for the Duration!" and "Some Plain Forthright Duties to Observe," all 7(March 1942): 155–57.

48. See the following *Forum* articles: Leonard De Moor, "Rosenberg's Myth and Nazi Paganism," 3(April 1938): 200–203; and Clarence Bouma, "Armistice Day, 1938," 4(November 1938): 75–76; "The Deeper Issue—Democracy versus Autocracy" and "The World Struggle and the Christian Church," both 5(October 1939): 35–37; "The Demon of Totalitarianism" and "At Last America Is Waking Up!" both 5(June–July 1940): 235–37; and "Brave Little Holland" and "Thank God for the British," both 6(December 1940): 84–86. Bouma's papers include copies of the large Grand Rapids newspaper advertisements he (and H. J. Ryskamp) signed in 1939 and '40 urging American support of the Allies, and notices of the internationalist rallies at which he presided ("Political and Civic Activities" folder, Bouma papers, Calvin College and Seminary Archives).

49. See the following *Forum* articles: Clarence Bouma, "The World Struggle and the Christian Church," 5(October 1939): 36; "The War in Europe," 5(November 1939): 59–60; and "Sweet Land of Liberty," 7(December 1941): 83–87; Henry J. Ryskamp, "Contemporary Economic Survey," 4(April 1939): 207–08; and "A Declining World?" 5(May 1940): 220–22; and Henry Schultze, "Christianity and Democracy," 6(April 1941): 203.

50. See the following *Forum* articles: Clarence Bouma, "The Christmas of the Atomic Bomb," 11(December 1945): 83–84; and "The Fade-Out of God" and "Our Godless Education," both 12(February 1947): 131–32; and Henry Schultze, "Humanity Discredited," 13(January 1948): 107. See also Cecil De Boer, *Responsible Protestantism,* pp. 116–32, 177–91, 230–34.

51. See Kuiper, "Thoughts on Victory," *Banner,* 18 May 1945, p. 460. This

thought had already formed before the war's end: see John Verbrugge, "Do We Deserve Peace?" *Banner*, 23 June 1944, p. 584; and G. Hoeksema, "A Different World?" *Banner*, 4 August 1944, p. 728.

52. See the following articles by Benes in the *Church Herald:* "The Weakness and Strength of Protestantism," 30 August 1946, p. 5; "The Secularization of the Church," 21 February 1947, pp. 6–7; "Has the Church Failed?" 19 September 1947, pp. 6–7; and "The Christian Faith and the Social Order," 26 September 1947, pp. 6–7. See also Harold J. Hoffman, "Whither America?" 12 April 1946, p. 9; and Jacob Blaauw, "The Christian Answer to Our Moral Decay," 9 May 1947, pp. 4–5.

53. See Bernard Mulder, "The United Nations Charter: What Can the Church Do Now?" *Church Herald*, 24 August 1945, pp. 8–9; Clarence Bouma, "The Problems of Peace," *Calvin Forum* 10(June–July 1945): 227–29; Edward J. Tanis, "The War against Communism," *Banner*, 28 March 1947, p. 390; and "U.S. Plans to Beat Russia," *Banner*, 9 September 1949, p. 1062.

54. Kuiper, "Our Church and the Labor Union," *Banner*, 18 June 1943, p. 540. Also on labor, see Kuiper, "Labor Union Problem," *Banner*, 4 March 1949, p. 260; Clarence Bouma, "The Recent Labor Crisis," *Calvin Forum* 11(June–July 1946): 231–32; and Cecil De Boer, *Responsible Protestantism*, pp. 177–91, 207–22. On "Statism," see H. J. Kuiper, "What About the Post-War World?" *Banner*, 14 July 1944, p. 652; and De Boer, *Responsible Protestantism*, pp. 177–78, 190–91.

CHAPTER ELEVEN

1. Bernard H. M. Vlekke and Henry Beets's *Hollanders Who Helped Build America* (New York, 1942) catalogues many of these individuals (see pp. 59–323), and Arnold Mulder sketches some of the more famous in *Americans from Holland* (New York, 1947), pp. 233–42, 291–302.

2. Naturally, substantial differences exist between, and sometimes within, each novelist's corpus; and together they have concerns beyond that of confronting their origins. This study focuses, however, on the very considerable part the ethno-religious factor does play in shaping their work. Since the criticism they have received has sometimes underplayed or misconstrued the influence of their origins upon these writers, I am here offering a supplementary—and I hope fructifying—approach. One unpublished study has examined De Jong, De Vries, and Manfred in this light: Cornelius J. Ter Maat's "Three Novelists and a Community: A Study of American Novelists with Dutch Calvinist Origins" (Ed.D. diss., University of Michigan, 1963). This study (which appeared too early to cover much of De Vries) emphasizes the disjunctions between origins and work and barely touches on non-ethnic materials, whereas I stress the continuities and lasting influences, positive and negative, in ethnic and non-ethnic works alike. The *Reformed Journal* devoted an issue to these three authors, also two decades ago (13[April 1963]); and John J. Timmerman, a classmate of the three and later professor of English at Calvin College, gives personal and literary commentary in *Markings on a Long Journey*, ed. Rodney J. Mulder and John H. Timmerman (Grand Rapids, 1982), pp. 111–31.

3. The coincidence extended even further. In 1936, the three finished one-two-three in a writing contest sponsored by Eerdmans Publishing Company. Contrary to prior arrangements, H. J. Kuiper, seeing the winning entries, refused to print them in the *Banner* (according to Frederick Manfred in *Conversations with Frederick Manfred*, John R. Milton, moderator [Salt Lake City: University of Utah Press, 1974], p. 103).

4. The cultural collision of the 1960s produced another set of fugitives from Dutch America, preeminent among them being Paul Schrader, Hollywood screenwriter and director (see pp. 321–22 herein).

5. Arnold Mulder, *Bram of the Five Corners* (Chicago, 1915), p. 160.

6. See the chapter "Dutch Domestic Mores" in *Americans from Holland*. The sections on "The Romantic Movement on the Dutch Frontier" and "Bilingual Culture" also have good moments. The villains noted in the text appear in *The Dominie of Harlem* (1913) and *Bram of the Five Corners*, respectively. *The Outbound Road* (1919) and *The Sand Doctor* (1921) target groups rather than individuals—the malicious denominational college faculty in the first, and small-town speculators in the second.

7. A similar figure in *The Outboard Road* is more timorous. He disobeys his heart's commands out of hope for the presidency of the denominational college, but finally regains his integrity by joining Teunis the Great Artist (and also his son by a Latin opera singer, as it turns out) in New York glory. The young protagonist of *The Sand Doctor* rejects the mercenary practices of his profession, takes to brooding walks on the dunes and clinical researches on the local schizophrenic (as it happens, the son of a magnate who provides, in the backwoods of Michigan, "the most advanced laboratory in the world" for the project), endures the scorn of the locals, and reaches an earthshaking discovery that guarantees his place in the history of science.

8. Mulder, *The Dominie of Harlem* (Chicago, 1913), pp. 125–26, 136–37.

9. See, for example, *Americans from Holland* (Philadelphia, 1947), p. 254.

10. *Bram of the Five Corners*, p. 307.

11. Mulder wrote one more book after this period, the Dutch title in Louis Adamic's immigrant history series, *Americans from Holland* (1947). Much read and regarded, this work presents the same assimilationist values as the novels, though with a better touch. Mulder reproves at every point the "clannish" elements in Dutch America but concludes that, happily, these were few. "The vast majority believes [it] their duty to adapt themselves to the political and cultural institutions they find here" (p. 277). Again autobiographically, Mulder gives special weight to "the lost generation" who pioneered in this process. He seems unaware of the ambiguity of the label, but, perhaps recognizing the problems with his earlier fiction, he adds, "an adequate conception of the 'lost generation' . . . is a subject for a future great novelist" (p. 273).

As for the ethnic masses, Mulder praises their "healthy blood," the hard work and thrift by which they won a good share of the new land's riches, and their political disposition: "They are inclined to feel that the very essence of American civilization is progressive change" (p. 277). With these advantages, Mulder was certain, the Dutch would soon realize their historical destiny of "pumping rich new blood through the pulses of American institutions" (p. 278).

12. David Cornel De Jong, *Outside the Four Walls of Everything* (Baltimore, 1961), p. 19.

13. Comparing the autobiography to the fiction shows how closely De Jong relied on immediate personal experience in his novels. That De Jong gave his hometown, Wierum, the name "Old Haven" is some indication of his affections. As to the quality and themes of the novel, Howard Mumford Jones called *Old Haven* "an extraordinary novel which makes most current fiction in comparison thin and pale . . . almost the only new book concerning which I can honestly say that it seems to me touched with genius" ("You Can't Beat the Dutch," *Saturday Review*, 24 September 1938, p. 5).

14. Compare, for example, the European and American sections of *With a Dutch Accent* (pp. 1–186 and 187–306) to those of *Belly Fulla Straw* (pp. 16–36 with pp. 50–59). The European adolescent rebel is Renzel in *Day of the Trumpet* (1941).

15. *Belly Fulla Straw* (New York, 1934), p. 5; *With a Dutch Accent*, p. 171.

16. *With a Dutch Accent*, pp. 208–9. Regarding De Jong's treatment of the house and neighbors, compare *With a Dutch Accent*, pp. 200–209, to *Belly Fulla Straw*, pp. 50–60, and *Two Sofas in the Parlor*, pp. 11–12. Regarding the ghetto-dwellers' particular offenses, see *Two Sofas in the Parlor*, p. 201, and *Belly Fulla Straw*, pp. 60, 110. Constance Rourke noted De Jong's bias in "Eastward of Lake Michigan," rev. of *Belly*

Fulla Straw, New York *Herald Tribune Book Review*, 1 April 1934, p. 7. De Jong's grudges were pronounced enough in his college years to keep even so genteel an observer as John J. Timmerman in rather bad temper for fifty years (see *Markings*, pp. 111–13, 126). Characteristically, De Jong responded to the *Reformed Journal*'s review of his work by downplaying his best (ethnic) books and exaggerating the worst (non-ethnic) in a letter to the editor (*Reformed Journal* 13[May–June 1963]: 2, 24).

17. *Two Sofas in the Parlor* (Garden City, N.Y., 1952), p. 111. Cf. *Belly Fulla Straw*, p. 178.

18. *Belly Fulla Straw*, p. 105. The mother's "sudden religiosity" was "all for the neighbors' sake" (p. 112) and was the first, most important, step of total conformity to the neighborhood (see pp. 124, 149). *Two Sofas in the Parlor* opens with the mother enjoining her son to "remember first of all you are a covenant child, a Calvinist boy, here in this uncouth land, where virtue and worth seem to be measured by dollars only. . . . It is a land wholly without pattern, and I am not going to sit meekly by and see my children lose their souls in it" (p. 11).

19. *With a Dutch Accent*, p. 252.

20. Cf. *With a Dutch Accent*, pp. 262, 277, 299–306. *Day of the Trumpet* confirms his point of view, showing a bloated, complacent Netherlands purged in the fires of war (the Nazi invasion).

21. Confirming this judgment is the way De Jong presents his decisive moment, the adolescent crisis of self-discovery, in an Old-World context (the case of Renzel in *Day of the Trumpet*): the rebel has inherited resources to bring to the struggle and the community, secure in its sense of self and ties to times past, can tolerate more diversity.

22. *Light Sons and Dark* (New York, 1940) describes the hostility of one pair of sons and their mother toward another pair of sons and their father in the context of a bleak Kansas farm. *The Desperate Children* (Garden City, N.Y., 1949), encompassing a small New England city and a nearby farm, pits two boys and a kindly matron teacher against a venomous school principal. (Both these novels have counterparts among De Jong's short stories.) *Benefit Street* (New York, 1942) has the clearest autobiographical overtones as it tells the interlocking stories of the inhabitants of a Providence, Rhode Island, boardinghouse. *Somewhat Angels* (New York, 1945) concerns the relationships of a mother and her daughters-in-law, again in a New England city, during the forced separations of wartime.

23. Grace Frank, rev. of *Somewhat Angels*, *Saturday Review*, 17 November 1945, p. 52.

24. "Sitting in the Sun," in *Snow-on-the-Mountain and Other Stories* (New York, 1946), p. 28. Many of his short stories explore this "unholy trinity": "Those Who Eat Dragonflies" (also in *Snow-on-the-Mountain and Other Stories*) and "Beneath a Still Sky," "The Unfairness of Easter," "The Funeral of Papje," and "The Pigeons," in *The Unfairness of Easter and Other Stories* (San Jose, 1959).

25. See *Somewhat Angels* (New York, 1945), pp. 176–77.

26. *Old Haven*, pp. 126–32, 155; *Day of the Trumpet*, pp. 53–63.

27. Wallace Fowlie, "The Cogent Land," rev. of *Across the Board*, in *Poetry* 62(June 1943): 171.

28. From "In Due Season," p. 19, and "The Time Has Come," p. 53, in *Across the Board: Poems by David Cornel De Jong* (New York, 1943), p. 19.

29. Fowlie, "The Cogent Land," p. 172.

30. Frederick Manfred, *This Is the Year* (Garden City, N.Y., 1947), p. 26.

31. In "Sinclair Lewis' Funeral" (*South Dakota Review* 7[Winter 1969–70]: 60) Manfred speaks of his mother's wish. The literary creations of his college years indicate that his crises were romantic (see, for instance, "To—" and "Broken Prism," Calvin College *Chimes*, 12 April 1934, pp. 13–16; "A Lyric from a Deathbed . . . ," *Chimes*, 10 May 1934, p. 13; and "Sonnet," Calvin College *Prism 1934*, p. 91). The conjunction

of these romantic crises with religious difficulties is abundantly reflected in *The Primitive* (1949), which is based on Manfred's experience at Calvin College.

32. See Feike Feikema, "Report from Minnesota," *New Republic,* 11 October 1943, pp. 480–81.

33. For a good description of Manfred's personality ("an elemental force"), see Wallace Stegner's foreword in *Conversations with Frederick Manfred,* moderated by John R. Milton, pp. xi–xvi. These conversations contain a wealth of information about Manfred's life and work. Robert C. Wright's *Frederick Manfred* (Twayne United States Authors Series, no. 336 [Boston, 1979]) is a comprehensive survey. It, along with the critical titles listed in its bibliography (pp. 172–76), shows that almost all commentary has been on Manfred as a Western writer. My concern here, of course, is to demonstrate the ethno-religious roots and purpose of his writing.

Manfred became reconciled with Calvin College at his class's twenty-five-year reunion, when he was adulated by the student body. "That was a great day. I was so excited I couldn't sleep for about two days afterwards. . . . The Old Mother . . . had allowed me to come back and had treated me warmly" (*Conversations,* p. 170); significantly, the book closes with these words).

34. *Wanderlust* (Denver, 1962) is a revised one-volume edition of the trilogy originally published by Doubleday (as *World's Wanderer*) in three separate volumes: *The Primitive,* 1949; *The Brother,* 1950; and *The Giant,* 1951. Quotations have been taken from the 1962 edition. My use of the term "autobiography" in regard to Manfred's work denotes lightly fictionalized autobiography rather than literal autobiography.

35. In *Conversations with Frederick Manfred,* the author recalls, "I said that literature was a world-and-life view. . . . We [authors] are producing universal things." Other instances of sermonizing occur in *Boy Almighty* (pp. 274–75), *This Is the Year* (pp. 478–82), *Eden Prairie* (pp. 335–36), *Riders of Judgment* (pp. 366–68), *Morning Red* (pp. 561–65), and *The Chokecherry Tree* (pp. 189–93).

36. The most extreme cases in the autobiographical series are *Morning Red* and *Eden Prairie,* the latter featuring schoolchildren copulating, an offensive human stud, female prudery, repressed sexual feelings of one brother for another, and a woman's memories of her brother's sexual advances. In *The Golden Bowl* (1944) sex is decisive in the working out of the plot; *Boy Almighty* shows its capacity to produce both frustration and fulfillment; *This Is the Year* (1947) explores the abuse of sex and its broader symbolism. Sexuality also provides major themes and subplots in all the others except *Lord Grizzly* (1954). Cf. "The Mink Coat," "High Tenor," "Wild Land," and the title story in *Apples of Paradise and Other Stories* (1968).

37. In Manfred's use of the setting, "Siouxland" centers on the juncture of Iowa, Minnesota, and South Dakota but extends well into the high plains. For his remark about Siouxland being his spiritual region, see "West of the Mississippi: An Interview with Frederick Manfred," *Critique* 2(Winter 1959): 54. In this interview he also recounts his discovery of the West as a mythic region and his personal links with it (pp. 35–41) as well as its aesthetic uses: "I began to feel a thinness in my own heroes. No matter how hard I worked . . . somehow they did not have all the dimensions for me. They lacked something . . . a 'usable past' within themselves; there wasn't enough history or country or culture to use as a background" (p. 39). Cf. Ter Maat: "Unlike the Dutch-American community, it [Siouxland] gives the space and freedom necessary . . . to his work" ("Three Novelists," p. 133).

38. *Conquering Horse* centers on rites of passage; *Lord Grizzly* on man vs. nature and charity vs. vengeance. *Scarlet Plume* redoes Romeo and Juliet, *King of Spades* Oedipus, and *Riders of Judgment* Jesus. Critical analyses of these works include Russell Roth, "The Inception of a Saga: Frederick Manfred's 'Buckskin Man,'" *South Dakota Review* 7(Winter 1969–70): 87–99; D. E. Eylder, "Manfred's Indian Novel," *South Dakota Review* 7(Winter 1969–70), pp. 100–109; and James C. Austin, "Legend,

Myth, and Symbol in Frederick Manfred's *Lord Grizzly*," *Critique* 6(Winter 1963): 122–30. Manfred himself indicated the importance of *This Is the Year* to the series: "The concept of Siouxland came to me when I was writing *This Is the Year*—that would be my core, my center from which all other novels would gradually work out. . . . I decided . . . I would write a whole series of books . . . so that when I was through I'd have something all the way from 1800 on to the day I die" ("West of the Mississippi," *Critique*, p. 40).

39. Some of the most eloquent passages in this regard can be found in *Scarlet Plume* (pp. 249–52, 291–98) and *King of Spades* (pp. 157–61, 180–84). For his own statement on this score see "Interview," *South Dakota Review* 7(Winter 1969–70): 114.

40. So suggested a reviewer in the *New York Herald Tribune Book Review*, 28 November 1954, p. 14.

41. *King of Spades*, set at the end of the frontier, is the weakest book of regional history. *Eden Prairie* (1968), *Milk of Wolves* (1976), and *Sons of Adam* (1980) are set in modern Siouxland and suffer the "thinness" Manfred sensed in their earlier counterparts (see note 37 to this chapter). Manfred's turn (especially in the first two) to sexual reminiscence for substance does not rescue them; family and religion prove much stronger.

42. Pertinent passages can be found on pp. 9, 17–20, 31–33, 40–51, 180–90. His early assimilationist stance is manifest in "West of the Mississippi," *Critique*, pp. 50–51. Cf. Ter Maat, "Three Novelists," pp. 88–95.

43. The whole first session of *Conversations with Frederick Manfred* is devoted to Manfred's Frisian past (pp. 1–13), the Anglo-Saxon and anti–"Hollander" themes being pronounced (pp. 4–5, 8–9). Cf. *Green Earth*, p. 2.

44. James Austin, "Legend, Myth, and Symbol," *Critique*, pp. 126–30. The King James Bible was one of three books he took on his journeys, one of four he deemed most influential on his style (see "West of the Mississippi," *Critique*, pp. 47–48).

45. Peter De Vries, *Reuben, Reuben* (Boston, 1964), p. 432.

46. De Vries, *The Blood of the Lamb* (Boston, 1962), pp. 48–53.

47. Peter De Vries, "The Curatorium Pigeon-Hole," Calvin College *Chimes*, 17 October 1930, p. 2; this is one of the premier moments in Dutch-American folklore. For De Vries' oratorical skill and political stance, see his prize-winning speech, "Bolshevism or Vaccinate," Calvin College *Prism, 1931,* pp. 124–26; for a collegiate attack on Calvinistic orthodoxy, see "Gifts for the Christ," *Chimes*, 18 December 1930, p. 2. His politics settled into liberalism by the '40s: see "On Being Thirty," *Poetry* 61(October 1942): 382–83, and "A Note on This Issue," *Poetry* 62(August 1943): 272–77; and in the '70s he described himself as being "rather stodgily involved" in Democratic politics in Westport (see *World Authors, 1950–1970*, ed. John Wakeman [New York, 1975], p. 388). His novels target such positions, however: see *The Glory of the Hummingbird* (1974), pp. 235–36; and *Through Fields of Clover* (1961), pp. 237–39.

48. The essay was "James Thurber: The Comic Prufrock," *Poetry* 62(December 1943): 150–59. Cf. Burton Bernstein, *Thurber: A Biography* (New York, 1975), pp. 360–63. In an interesting ethnic connection, De Vries published some of David De Jong's poetry (*Poetry* 62[June 1943]) and reviewed *With a Dutch Accent* for the Chicago *Sun Book Week* (27 February 1944, p. 9).

49. Roderick Jellema, *Peter De Vries*, Contemporary Writers in Christian Perspective (Grand Rapids, 1966), p. 15. Jellema covers the first half of the corpus thoroughly and well. I agree with him on most points, although my focus is somewhat different. Besides the ethno-religious dimension, Jellema analyzes De Vries's use of comic conventions. Other scholarship treats the latter more heavily (see, for instance, Jack K. Boyd, "The Novels of Peter De Vries: A Critical Introduction" [Ph.D. diss., University of Arkansas, 1971]). I take here the other focus.

50. Perhaps this accounts for columnist George Will's occasional remark that De Vries is his favorite novelist. De Vries's dual self-alienation is expressed with neat

inelegance by his character Frank Spofford in *Reuben, Reuben:* "For now I am displaced indeed, belonging neither to that world I stole briefly out of to explore another nor in that other I skipped out to explore" (p. 180).

51. Another representative of this type is Alma Marvel, the matriarch of *Through Fields of Clover.* In a slightly different vein, Pete and Tillie of *The Cat's Pajamas & Witch's Milk* (1968), the ordinary couple supreme, have a sure sense of their own and life's limitations; Pete mixes healthy self-deprecation with ridicule of "everything and nobody." Confronted by the death of their son Charlie, they manage as well as humanly possible; that is, they compound their suffering by wounding each other, but eventually endure tragedy with love and grace.

52. Tickler's (his name is Anglicized from the Dutch Tigchelaar) participation in a fixed gameshow finally brings him before a Senate investigating committee, allowing De Vries to parody the Watergate hearings being aired while he was writing the book.

53. For the central place of "worldliness" in De Vries's own memory, see *World Authors,* p. 387. Don Wanderhope later calls his odyssey a "reverse pilgrimage" (p. 66), which concept Jellema uses as the title of the biographical portion of *De Vries* and as a unifying theme of his whole critique. Cf. Jim Tickler's similar characterization of the process ("sanctity renounced for the world") in *Glory of the Hummingbird,* p. 137.

54. Don "casts his cares" by throwing the cake meant for his daughter's birthday party into the face of a statue of the crucified Christ (Jellema perceptively discusses this act as a ritual of atonement [*De Vries,* pp. 38–39]), then falls at the foot of the statue partly out of grief, partly in a drunken stupor.

55. Jellema, for instance, maintains that Don Wanderhope's final position is ambivalence (*De Vries,* pp. 38–40), whereas John J. Timmerman emphasizes De Vries's distance from Christian commitments (*Markings,* pp. 116–20).

56. De Vries, *Mrs. Wallop* (Boston, 1970), p. 115.

57. See Jellema, *De Vries,* p. 10. This class of characters falls into two types: those who try the game but fail, and those who succeed, thereby casting their flaws into bolder relief. Examples of the first are Dick and Augie of *The Tunnel of Love* (1954), and Chick Swallow and Nickie Sherman of *Comfort Me With Apples* (1956) and *The Tents of Wickedness* (1959). Examples of the second are Andrew Mackerel of *The Mackerel Plaza* (1958) and Geneva Mopworth and Nector Schmidt in *Reuben, Reuben.*

58. In *Forever Panting* (1973), says Penelope Gilliatt's review ("The Unbudgeable Blodgett," *New Yorker,* 16 July 1973, p. 76), "De Vries embalms . . . the modern psychiatric version of man against himself." The critique is also pronounced in *Reuben, Reuben.* For an early parody of psychoanalysis and its literary derivations, see De Vries's "My Hear is A (After Reading Delmore Schwartz's *Genesis*)," *Poetry* 62(June 1943): 142–44.

59. A. C. Spectorsky, "In Decency, Conn.," rev. of *The Tents of Wickedness, New York Times Book Review,* 19 July 1959, p. 5. This is one source of De Vries's penchant for parody, conducted unwittingly by his sophisticates in their discourse and perfected in his own manipulations of sundry literary styles. *The Tents of Wickedness* is a tour de force of literary parody: De Vries has Chick Swallow search for the path out of his maze by adopting the visions, in turn, of Marquand, Faulkner, Kafka, and Joyce, with bits of Fitzgerald, Dreiser, Greene, Auden, and Proust on the side. Nicely enough, Chick ultimately finds "the answer" in a poem from the *Home Book of Verse,* "Jest A-Wearying for You" (p. 264).

60. De Vries emphasized his affectionate motivation in an interview: "The satirist shoots to kill while the humorist brings his prey back alive—often to release him again for another chance. . . . Humor is more charitable, and, like charity, suffereth long and is kind. Well, I don't think I shoot to kill" (Douglas M. Davies, "Interview with Peter De Vries," *College English* 29[1967]: 525). Yet many of his works have flirtations with destruction (e.g., *Glory of the Hummingbird,* pp. 88–95, 113). The deeper spiral begins with the derangements of *The Tents of Wickedness,* builds through "The Slaughter of

the Innocents" in *Blood of the Lamb*, the familial bitterness of *Fields of Clover* and *Reuben, Reuben*, and Stan's everlasting hangover in *Let Me Count the Ways*. It climaxes in *The Vale of Laughter* and *The Cat's Pajamas & Witch's Milk*.

61. The most extreme example, perhaps, is *I Hear America Swinging* (1976), but A. C. Spectorsky had noted that adultery was a "preoccupation," "a kind of compulsion" in De Vries's writing as early as 1959 ("In Decency, Conn.," p. 5).

62. De Vries, *Reuben, Reuben*, p. 197.

63. The trend is especially noticeable in *I Hear America Swinging* and subsequent works: *Madder Music* (1977), *Consenting Adults; or, The Duchess Will be Furious* (1980), *Sauce for the Goose* (1981), and *Slouching Towards Kalamazoo* (1983).

64. See *The Vale of Laughter* (Boston, 1967), p. 215, and *The Mackerel Plaza* (Boston, 1958), p. 260.

65. See *The Blood of the Lamb*, p. 243.

66. *Let Me Count the Ways*, pp. 123–24.

67. De Vries, *Mrs. Wallop*, p. 306. See also *Reuben, Reuben*, pp. 212–13; *Let Me Count the Ways*, pp. 306–07; and *Forever Panting*, pp. 272–74.

68. De Vries, *The Blood of the Lamb*, p. 246.

69. A point made by John Wain in his review of *Through Fields of Clover* ("Home Truths," *New Yorker*, 25 February 1961, pp. 130–31).

70. De Vries, *The Vale of Laughter*, p. 216.

CHAPTER TWELVE

1. Bouma, in a letter to Boer, 20 July 1948. Bouma papers, Calvin College and Seminary Archives, Grand Rapids, Michigan.

2. I have relied on an unpublished paper by Marvin Ouwinga, "The Home Front and the Struggle Against Frank McKay" (unpublished paper, Calvin College and Seminary Archives), for information on the "Home Front." For its role in Ford's career, see Jerald F. ter Horst, *Gerald Ford and the Future of the American Presidency* (New York, 1974), pp. 4–25. The originating and culminating episodes of Ford's career provide a fine counterpoint pertinent to our subject group—the white knight of clean government pardoning Richard Nixon for all Watergate crimes, the pardon's patriotic cloak being the consistent feature.

3. There has been much discussion of the definition and even propriety of the concept of civil religion (see *American Civil Religion*, ed. Russell E. Richey and Donald G. Jones [New York, 1974]). I use the term here somewhat as John F. Wilson uses "public religion" in *Public Religion in American Culture* (Philadelphia, 1979)—that is, referring not to a formal cult of the state so much as to a web of values and rhetoric serving to idolize various aspects of American culture and its normative "way of life" as a whole.

4. Again, there were assorted harbingers (e.g., H. J. Kuiper, "The Christ and the Red Dragon," *Banner*, 22 December 1944, p. 1204), but it was in 1949–50 that the periodicals shifted markedly toward the crusading, totalistic cold war mentality at issue here. See Louis Benes, "The Communist Menace," *Church Herald*, 29 July 1949, p. 65; and "Communism—A World Threat," *Church Herald*, 2 September 1949, p. 4; H. J. Kuiper, "Let Us Have a Day of Prayer!" *Banner*, 8 September 1950, p. 1092; and E. J. Tanis, "Russian Strength," *Banner*, 24 November 1950, p. 1446.

5. See Tanis, "The War against Communism," *Banner*, 28 March 1948, p. 390; "U.S. Plans to Beat Russia," *Banner*, 9 September 1949, p. 1062; and "Enemies Within," *Banner*, 4 September 1953, p. 1062. And see Louis Benes, "The Communist Menace," *Church Herald*, 29 July 1949, p. 6; and "Congress and Communism," *Church Herald*, 6 November 1953, p. 6.

6. Bouma, "Is Free Enterprise Anti-Christian?" *Calvin Forum* 14(February 1949): 137; see the full article on pp. 120–22 of the January issue and pp. 134–37 of the February issue. See also H. J. Ryskamp, "Retrospect and Prospect," *Calvin Forum* 15(January 1950): 109–11; and William Harry Jellema, "Christianity, Capitalism, and Socialism," *Calvin Forum* 15(January 1950): 108–12, the latter being part of a symposium including Norman Thomas. The citation of anti-Communist pieces could go on for pages. A sampling covering the spectrum from "left" to "right" can be found in Harry Boer, "The Second Islam," *Calvin Forum* 16(February 1951): 138–39; Lester De Koster, "Communist Faith and Christian Witness," *Reformed Journal* 4(June 1954): 1–5; and *"Christian* Anti-Communism," *Reformed Journal* 11(September 1961): 3–4; Louis Benes, "The Front Battle Line," *Church Herald,* 18 February 1955, p. 6; Henry R. Van Til, "Christian Communism or Christian Charity?" *Torch and Trumpet* 1(October 1951): 14; Albert Bosscher, "Communism: A New Religion," *Torch and Trumpet* 3(June and December 1953): 1–5, 8–10; and 4(April 1954): 23–25; and Harold Sonnema, "The Need for an Awakening to the Danger of Communism," *Banner,* 30 June 1961, p. 22.

7. The entire incident is detailed by John J. Timmerman in *Promises to Keep* (Grand Rapids, 1975), pp. 185–90. For Kuiper's position, see the following articles, all in 1950 issues of the *Banner:* "Some Observations on Flynn's 'The Road Ahead,'" 25 August, p. 1028; "Our Answer to Mr. De Koster," 22 and 29 September, pp. 1157, 1189; "Our Church's Stand on Socialism," 20 October, p. 1284; "Thoughts on Economic Freedom," 3 November, p. 1348; and "We Conclude a Debate," 24 November, p. 1444. De Koster's statements appeared in "John T. Flynn Looks Ahead," *Calvin Forum* 15(August 1950): 15–18; in a letter printed in the 18 August 1950 issue of the *Banner,* p. 1020; and in "Mr. De Koster Again States His Case," *Banner,* 24 November, p. 1460. Other faculty joined De Koster in publishing the declaration "Eighteen Professors Disown Flynn's Line of Thought," *Banner,* 15 September 1950, p. 1124.

The coincidence in time between this incident (and its surrounding aura of suspicion) and "McCarthyism" in the American world deserves some comment. Perhaps the first drew some inspiration from the second, or at least drew from the same pressures and events. But it is probably more instructive to view the Dutch-American case in terms of the dynamics of group development. Mary Douglas's "group-grid" concept (outlined in *Natural Symbols: Explorations in Cosmology* [New York, 1970]) provides a suitable analytic tool. Societies—and subcultures—located on the "group" end of the spectrum have a strong idea of the social body as a whole but little of internal differentiation or any complex of impersonal rules ("grid") regulating behavior. Such groups divide the world between "inside" and "outside," are highly concerned with maintaining the boundary between the two, and articulate their defense of that boundary in rhetoric/rituals of "purification" against "infection." Specific "sins" often serve as crucial litmus tests in the process, "witchhunting" episodes are common as symbolic modes of purification, and internal conflicts are settled by fission or expulsion.

Translating "sin" into "heresy" as well as "worldliness," we can see how well the CRC of the previous thirty years fit this model. The conflict of the '20s brought simple group unity into jeopardy; it was restored via extensive fission and expulsion, and maintained thereafter through strong consciousness of insider/outsider status and boundaries. H. J. Kuiper's surveillance of these tended strikingly toward infection-purification rhetoric, and litmus tests of orthodoxy and behavior were unmistakable. The early-'50s episode turned out to be his last offensive, the first to fail. Factional plurality persisted, with a resulting shift toward "grid" structure predicted by Douglas's model: the late '50s were the "take-off" point of CRC bureaucratization. The RCA had held a higher "grid" and lower "group" consciousness all along, which corresponds to their lower intensity on everything from group mores to theological precision to group/world differentiation. For all its elimination of "witchhunting," of course, "grid" structure brings its own set of problems, long familiar to the RCA and hereafter increasingly problematic in the CRC, as we shall see.

8. The minutes, protests, appeals, apologias, and certain personal letters are collected in files on "Seminary Situation: 1950–1952" in the Calvin College and Seminary Archives. Cf. the Clarence Bouma papers for those years. A sanitized account of the background and resolution of the case is available in the CRC *Acts of Synod, 1952* (Grand Rapids, 1952), pp. 95–104, 115–18.

9. Kuiper, "The Seminary Situation," *Banner,* 25 July 1952, p. 932.

10. See p. 131 herein. A popular biography is William White, Jr.'s *Van Til, Defender of the Faith: An Authorized Biography* (Nashville, 1971). A detailed analysis of important facets of Van Til's thought is available in John Vander Stelt's *Philosophy and Scripture: A Study in Old Princeton and Westminster Theology* (Marlton, N.J., 1978), pp. 220–70, 303–14. Comment from eminent critics and Van Til's replies can be found in *Jerusalem and Athens: Critical Discussions on the Theology and Apologetics of Cornelius Van Til,* ed. E. R. Geehan (Phillipsburg, N.J., 1971).

11. In *Common Grace* (Philadelphia, 1947) Van Til spells out his entire position; see especially pp. 82–89. For his disposal of Kuyper and Bavinck on the matter, see pp. 34–58. Specific to the Dutch-American controversy was his article "Common Grace and Witness-Bearing," *Torch and Trumpet* 4(December 1954): 1–10.

12. See Van Til, *Common Grace,* pp. 43–44, 62–63, 68. Cf. Vander Stelt, *Philosophy and Scripture,* pp. 226–33; on the Jellema connection, see pp. 226–27.

13. See, for instance, Leonard Greenway, et al., "Introducing 'Common Grace,'" *Torch and Trumpet* 3(August 1953): 1–3; William Rutgers, "Common Grace: The Accepted View," *Torch and Trumpet* 3(December 1953): 13–17; Adam Persenaire, "The Antithesis and Common Grace," *Banner,* 20 March 1953, pp. 356–57; and "Review: General Revelation and Common Grace," *Torch and Trumpet* 3(December 1953): 1–5, 12; and R. B. Kuiper, *To Be or Not To Be Reformed: Whither the Christian Reformed Church?* (Grand Rapids, 1959), pp. 117–26.

14. Henry R. Van Til, *The Calvinistic Concept of Culture* (Grand Rapids, 1959), pp. 148, 181, 141, 237.

15. In *General Revelation and Common Grace* (Grand Rapids, 1953) Masselink gives his whole critique. The quoted characterization is John Timmerman's, in *Promises to Keep,* p. 189.

16. The issue hit its peak in 1953–54. In favor of Van Til were his own "Religious Philosophy," February 1953, pp. 124–28; and Edwin Palmer, "Caricature," November 1954, pp. 62–65. Opposed were Cecil De Boer, "The New Apologetic," August 1953, pp. 3–7; Jesse De Boer, "Professor Van Til's Apologetics," August–November 1953, pp. 7–12, 27–34, 51–57; Franklin Van Halsema, "Van Til in Review," December 1953, pp. 82–85; Thedford Dirkse, "The Extent of the Antithesis," March 1954, pp. 147–49; and Dirk Jellema, "The Philosophy of Vollenhoven and Dooyeweerd," April, May, and October 1954, pp. 169–71, 192–94, 31–33. The entire April 1955 issue was given to a symposium on James Daane's critique of Van Til and others, *A Theology of Grace.*

17. Cecil De Boer, "The New Apologetic," *Calvin Forum* 19(August 1953): 3; *Responsible Protestantism* (Grand Rapids, 1957), pp. 246–47.

18. Quoted matter taken from James Daane, "A Progressive Theology," *Reformed Journal* 1(September 1951): 11. See similarly his inaugural statement, "Self-Examination Expanded," *Reformed Journal* 1(March 1951): 3–4; and "The State of Theology in the Church," *Reformed Journal* 7(September 1957): 3–17 (a CRC centennial article). Representative pieces from other contributors include Harry R. Boer, "Perspectives for Reformed Advance," *Calvin Forum* 13(January 1948): 109–13, and his attack on CRC home missions policy, *That My House May Be Filled* (Grand Rapids, 1957); George

Stob, "The CRC and the Problem of Divorce," *Reformed Journal* 6(April 1956): 9–23; and Simon J. De Vries's series "The Distortion of Denominational Ideals," *Reformed Journal* 9(September–December 1959) and 10(April 1960).

19. Quoted matter taken from Daane, "The Principle of the Equal Ultimacy of Election and Reprobation," *Reformed Journal* 3(November 1953): 15. It would be redundant to cite all of Daane's pieces on these matters; he addressed them in the *Reformed Journal* in April and May 1951; May and June 1953; November 1953–February 1954; March, June, and October 1960–January 1961; and various times thereafter. His comprehensive presentations can be found in *A Theology of Grace* (Grand Rapids, 1954) (summarized under the same title in the *Reformed Journal* 5[March, April 1955]: 10–12, 9–11); and *The Freedom of God: A Study of Election and Pulpit* (Grand Rapids, 1973). Concerning common grace in particular, see "Common Grace and Individualism," *Reformed Journal* 1(April 1951): 11–12; and "Reflections on Common Grace," *Reformed Journal* 3(May 1953): 13–15. For Barthian sympathies, see for example "Can We LEARN From Karl Barth?" *Reformed Journal* 12(April 1962): 7–9. Although he served several CRC parishes, Daane was never given a teaching position in the denomination, although he did hold major posts in the "neo-evangelical" network—as associate editor of *Christianity Today* (1961–65) and Professor of Pastoral Theology at Fuller Seminary (1965–79).

20. A point noted by reviewers sympathetic to his position such as S. J. Ridderbos, "Daane on Van Til," *Reformed Journal* 5(February 1955): 9–11; and M. Eugene Osterhaven, rev. of *The Freedom of God, Reformed Review* 27(Spring 1974): 151–54.

21. Good examples are Henry Stob's series on "Faith and Science," *Reformed Journal* 5(April–September 1955), and *The Christian Conception of Freedom* (Grand Rapids, 1957); and Henry Zylstra, *Testament of Vision* (Grand Rapids, 1958), pp. 5–14, 90–101, 141–44.

22. See Zylstra, *Testament of Vision,* pp. 15–28, 60–72, 77–89, 102–12. Zylstra's elegance of style, taste, and standards represented the end product of a long ascent from his Platte, South Dakota, origins to a Harvard Ph.D. The climb in many ways mirrored the one so often recounted by his college classmate Peter De Vries. Zylstra was also a veteran, however, which doubtless exposed him to the seamier side of things.

23. Stob, "Note to a College Freshman," *Reformed Journal* 2(September 1952): 7. Regarding limitations on Christian approaches to research, see "Religion in Science," *Reformed Journal* 5(September 1955): 12–14. Stob was also a World War II veteran and a peer of Peter De Vries not only in college but in childhood. He and his cousin, fellow *Journal* editor George Stob, grew up in the Dutch community in Chicago.

24. See the following articles by Stob in the *Reformed Journal*: "The Mind of the Church," 7(March 1957): 3–6; "The Mind of Safety," 7(April 1957): 4–9; "The Militant Mind," 7(June, July, and October 1957): 3–7, 3–6, 13–17; and "The Positive Mind," 11(March 1961): 5–9. Like his "Note to a College Freshman," this series became a lightning rod attracting the bolts of the opposition's anger. H. J. Kuiper said he could not recall "any article with which we disagree so completely" as "The Mind of Safety" ("Safety First," *Torch and Trumpet* 7[May 1957]: 3–6).

25. Stob, "Academic Freedom at Calvin," *Reformed Journal* 2(August 1952): 6.

26. Kuiper, *To Be or Not To Be Reformed,* p. 37. Similar quotations appear throughout this book, which is one large elaboration of this theme. On Henry Van Til's sentiments, see for instance "Road to Modernism—Signposts!" *Torch and Trumpet* 3(June and October 1953): 25–30, 15–17.

27. A good sampling of its sentiments is provided in the *Torch and Trumpet*'s nine-part CRC centennial series, "The Pillars of Our Church," beginning October 1956.

28. R. B. Kuiper, *To Be or Not To Be Reformed,* p. 194. Exemplary H. J. Kuiper pieces in *Torch and Trumpet* (of which he became editor upon his mandatory retirement from the *Banner*) include "At the Turn of the Year," 8(January 1959): 4–5; and "What Is Happening to the CRC?" 9(April 1959): 7–9. Berkhof's lectures were published as

The Kingdom of God (Grand Rapids, 1951). The book did contain two chapters on neo-orthodoxy added subsequent to the lectures, but presented the other materials unchanged. Both Berkhof and R. B. Kuiper thus showed their party's establishment position: "balance" was their favorite description of Calvinism, a balance that had been achieved and that was only threatened by change. Appropriately, James Daane often disparaged the idea, its realization, and/or the lack thereof.

29. Immigration figures are taken from Gordon Osterman, et al., *To Find a Better Life: Aspects of Dutch Immigration to Canada . . . 1920–1970* (Grand Rapids, 1975), pp. 94, 97. Total Dutch-Canadian immigration from 1945 to 1966 was 149,000; the Calvinist (*Gereformeerde*) total during that period was 47,000. Canadians totaled twenty percent of CRC communicant membership by 1965; of the total membership (baptized children included), they constituted twenty-four percent. See Appendix, Table III.

30. An autobiographical account is provided in an interview with Runner that concludes his festschrift, *Hearing and Doing: Philosophical Essays Dedicated to H. Evan Runner*, ed. John Kraay and Anthony Tol (Toronto, 1979), pp. 333–61; on his early years and education, see pp. 334–39. Interestingly, while studying in Amsterdam, Runner was a neighbor of Harry Boer (see pp. 337, 348). For a fine overview of his life and purpose, see Bernard Zylstra, "H. Evan Runner: An Assessment of His Mission," in *Life is Religion: Essays in Honor of H. Evan Runner*, ed. Henry Vander Goot (St. Catharines, Ontario, 1981), pp. 1–14.

31. Bernard Zylstra, "Runner: An Assessment," p. 13. Runner's academic style and substance are evident in the lecture series he gave in Canada in 1960–61, recorded in *The Relation of the Bible to Learning* (Beaver Falls, Pa., 1974).

32. A classic speech was "Het Roer Om!" ("Rudder Hard Over!"; note Runner's use of a Dutch title), *Torch and Trumpet* 3(April 1953): 1–4. See also "Does Christian Witness Demand an Absolute Break?" *Torch and Trumpet* 3(August 1953): 8; and under similar title, 4(June 1954): 1–8. His series in *Torch and Trumpet* of April to October 1955 gives commentary on the common grace issue. Years before, Runner had written a very cordial letter to Herman Hoeksema, endorsing his views over those of the *Calvin Forum* (letter of 15 May 1942; Clarence Bouma papers, Calvin College and Seminary Archives). One example of the socio-cultural hostilities felt—and returned—by Runner's followers can be found in a Groen Club speech of 1965 in which Canadian Calvinist leaders were cast as latter-day John the Baptists and their Grand Rapids adversaries as "sons of vipers," Pharisees and Sadducees proud of their family pedigree. "The Word of God says that the Lord can raise up sons of Calvin out of the stones, the blockheads of Canada. It is not who your father is or how successful your deeds are that count with God." That the speaker was himself an American of more than one generation's standing was a telling, though not unique, instance in this circle. (See Calvin Seerveld, "Christian Camel Drivers, Unite?" *Torch and Trumpet* 15[September 1965]: 8–12.)

33. The *Western Seminary Bulletin* had its debut in May 1947. Typical reviews of Niebuhr appeared in the *Bulletin* 4(June 1950): 13–14; and in the *Reformed Review* 9(October 1955): 50–52. Reviews of Brunner appeared in the *Bulletin* 1(May 1947): 10–11; and 3(March 1950): 13–15. For neo-orthodox themes, see D. Ivan Dykstra, "Theological Approach to World Crisis," *Western Seminary Bulletin* 4(March 1951): 1–5; and I. John Hesselink, "Encounter in Japan: Emil Brunner," *Reformed Review* 9(January 1956): 12–31.

34. In the *Western Seminary Bulletin,* see W. L. Ietswaart, "Church Life and Theology in the Netherlands," 1(March 1948): 7–11; and Isaac C. Rottenberg, "Nederlandse Hervormde Kerk," 6(March 1953): 4–7. In the *Reformed Review*, see Eugene Heideman, "The Confession of Our Fathers," 9(January 1956): 34–41; James

C. Eelman, "Philippus Jacobus Hoedemaker, 1839–1910," 10(January 1957): 17–31; and Lester J. Kuyper, "The Netherlands Reformed Church: Her Faith and Life," 13(May 1960): 18–31.

35. Henry Bast, *An Appeal to the Ministers and Laymen of the Chicago and Iowa Synods* (Grand Rapids, 1946), p. 11. Bast's mention of contributions refers to his finding that the RCA East's giving had fallen during the period from 1931 to 1946 by $50,000 to $438,000, while Western giving had risen by $540,000 to $1,000,000 (p. 8).

36. Henry Bast, *The Authority of the Bible* (Grand Rapids, 1951), and *The Ordination Vows of Ministers and Elders* (Grand Rapids, 1947); Joint Committee of the Particular Synods of Chicago and Michigan, *Marriage-Divorce-Remarriage* (Grand Rapids, 1957); and Harry Buis, *The Doctrine of Eternal Punishment* (Philadelphia, 1957). A perennial concern of this party is evident in Henry Kik's "The Federal Council of Churches and the Reformed Faith" (n.p., n.d.). The type of spirituality is well portrayed in Henry Bast, *The Lord's Prayer* (Grand Rapids, 1957); Gordon Girod, *The Deeper Faith* (Grand Rapids, 1958); and various sermons in *The Reformed Pulpit* (Grand Rapids, 1956).

37. As the Appendix shows, RCA membership grew in the 1950s from 250,000 to 325,000 and peaked in 1965 at 385,000. Most of the gains came then and thereafter in the Western sector, offsetting substantial absolute losses in the East after 1965. (In the period from 1955 to 1965, the West's percentage of total communicant membership rose from 44 to 50; in the period from 1965 to 1975, from 50 to 61.) Classis California's communicant membership grew by over 13,000 (500 percent) from 1955 to 1975, more than the denominational total (8,095) and almost one-third of the Western sector's 40,000 expansion. See Appendix, Table II.

38. See, for example, George Stob, "Trained for Tragedy," *Calvin Forum* 13(June 1948): 242–45; Harry R. Boer, "The Second Islam," *Calvin Forum* 16(February 1951): 138–39; E. J. Tanis, "Democracy Is Sick," *Banner*, 13 May 1955, p. 586; Richard J. Frens, "The Church and Social Programs," *Banner*, 24 October 1958, p. 6; John Vander Ploeg, "Christianity's Antidote to Communist Appeal," *Banner*, 4 March 1960, p. 5; Louis H. Benes, "Hopes for World Peace," *Church Herald*, 8 May 1953, p. 6, and "God in Our World Crisis," *Church Herald*, 20 October 1961, p. 6; and the items by Lester De Koster in note 53 to this chapter.

39. See the following *Church Herald* articles by Benes (all on pp. 6ff.): "Has the Church Failed?" 19 September 1947; "The Christian Faith and the Social Order," 26 September 1947; "The Christianity of Main Street," 24 April 1953; "Moral Decay and the Christian Faith," 29 February 1952; "Alcohol's Harvest," 8 January 1954; "The Kinsey Attack on Morals," 11 September 1953.

40. See Benes, "The Christian Faith and the Social Order," *Church Herald*, 26 September 1947, pp. 6–7, 22.

41. Of very many statements on liquor, see Benes, "Alcohol's Harvest," *Church Herald*, 8 January 1954, p. 6; and "About Alcohol and Authority," *Church Herald*, 19 February 1960, p. 7. His anti-Catholicism peaked in the 1960 presidential campaign; see his weekly editorials in the *Church Herald* from August to November of that year. Another tack was to assert that Catholicism was not the final bulwark against Communism it claimed to be, but its mate and ally: see, for example, "Our Bulwark against Communism," *Church Herald*, 1 April 1949, p. 6; and "Congress and Communism," *Church Herald*, 6 November 1953, p. 6. Benes also campaigned vigorously against tax funding for parochial schools (see the *Church Herald*, 10 February, 17 March, and 14–21 April 1961, p. 6 each issue). The Christian Reformed opposed him on the latter, of course, but—one sign of "Americanization" in this period—some joined him on the other points. A new antiliquor note appeared with the appointment of John Vander Ploeg as *Banner* editor, and CRC periodicals also editorialized against Kennedy (see Henry James Huisjen, "A Catholic for President? Three CRC Publications and the 1960

Election," M.A. Thesis, Michigan State Univeristy, 1976), though not as ardently as the *Church Herald*. For CRC *pro*-Catholic declarations, see Cecil De Boer, *Responsible Protestantism*, pp. 106–15.

42. This line is exemplified in H. J. Kuiper, "Authority in the Home," *Banner*, 9 and 16 September 1955, pp. 1060, 1092; John Vander Ploeg, "High Time to Protest," *Banner*, 28 February 1958, p. 4; and "Materialism—The Road to Ruin," *Banner*, 6 November 1959, p. 4; and Gordon Girod, *The Deeper Faith*.

43. John Vander Ploeg, "Norman Vincent Peale," *Banner*, 3 January 1958, pp. 4–5. See also H. J. Kuiper, "More Religion, Less Morality," *Banner*, 4 March 1955, p. 260.

44. The episode is recounted by Joseph H. Hall, "The Controversy over Fundamentalism in the CRC, 1915–66" (Th.D. diss., Concordia Theological Seminary, 1974), pp. 101–40. Kuiper quoted by Hall, p. 114. The Stob quotation is taken from his article "Our NAE Dilemma," *Reformed Journal* 1(May 1951): 4–5.

45. Harry Boer coined the term in "Perspectives for Reformed Advance," *Calvin Forum* 13(January 1948): 13; various young CRC critics repeated it in *Youth Speaks on Calvinism* (Grand Rapids, 1948); see, for example, pp. 27–37 therein.

46. See the Christian Labor Association's "Program for Christian Social Action," *Reformed Journal* 3(August 1953): 14–16; and H. Evan Runner, "Het Roer Om!" *Torch and Trumpet* 3(April 1953): 1–4.

47. In the *Torch and Trumpet*, see Henry R. Van Til, 2(December 1952): 32; John De Jong, "Calvinists—Worthy of the Name?" 4(August 1954): 12–13; and H. Evan Runner, "Christian Witness Requires Christian Organization," 4(June 1954): 1–8. In the *Reformed Journal*, see Gerald Vandezande and Harry Antonides, "Christian Political Action and Separate Organization," 14(May 1964): 26–28.

48. See Lester De Koster, "Is Separate Christian Organization Mandatory?" *Reformed Journal*, 7(May 1957): 12–22. See also Calvinistic Culture Association, "Principles and Work Program," *Torch and Trumpet* 3(April 1953): 31–32. Runner's "Het Roer Om!" was the organization's opening address.

49. See James Daane, "For Prayer and Breakfast," *Reformed Journal* 12(March 1962): 3. The two professors were Lester De Koster (see his "Calvinists and Democrats," *Reformed Journal* 8[October 1958]: 4–10) and Tony Brouwer (see his "Political Impact or Paralysis?" *Reformed Journal* 12[October 1962]: 5–7). Typically, these precipitated the Antitheticals' principal reply (see letters and articles in the *Reformed Journal* 13[March and October 1963] and 14[May and July 1964]) and the Confessionalists' voiced but unpublished partisan (i.e., Republican) objections.

50. See Harry R. Boer, "It Can Be Done," *Reformed Journal* 2(March 1952): 1–2; and Calvinistic Action Committee, *God-Centered Living; or, Calvinism in Action* (Grand Rapids, 1951), pp. 143–54, 201–25.

51. George Stob, "The Christian Duty toward Society," *Reformed Journal* 4(February 1954): 8–10; quotations are taken from pp. 9 and 8, respectively.

52. Verduin, "Biblical Christianity and Cultural Composition," *Reformed Journal* 3(October 1953): 1–5 (quoted matter taken from p. 5). See also "Which Belgic Confession?" *Reformed Journal* 11(August 1961)–12(January 1962); on the U.S. Constitution, see the January issue, p. 18. And see "The Church's Return to the Womb," *Reformed Journal* 13(February 1963): 6–9. Verduin's position is elaborated in book form in *The Reformers and Their Stepchildren* (Grand Rapids, 1964).

53. Quotations taken from "*Christian* Anti-Communism," *Reformed Journal* 11(September 1961): 4; and "Anti-Communist Book List," *Reformed Journal* 11(October 1961): 8. On Kennedy, see De Koster's comment on a letter to the *Journal* sent by G. Vandezande and H. Antonides, *Reformed Journal* 14(May–June 1964): 29; on Dutch precedents, see "Calvinists and Democrats," *Reformed Journal* 8(October 1958): 7. De Koster's book-length presentation of these views is *All Ye That Labor* (Grand Rapids, 1956; rev. ed., *Communism and Christian Faith*, 1962).

54. Dirk Jellema, "Groen Van Prinsterer," *Calvin Forum* 19(January 1954): 116. *Youth Speaks on Calvinism* (1948) and *Youth Speaks on Christianity and Civilization* (Grand Rapids, 1950) are collections of essays written by Calvin College students who would be leading lights of its faculty in later years; among them are Nicholas Wolterstorff, Lewis Smedes, Dirk Jellema, George Harper, and Clifton Orlebeke. For Kuiper's response, see his series of articles in 21 January to 4 February 1949 issues of the *Banner*. Specific appropriations of the Kuyperian tradition can be found in the following articles by Dirk Jellema: "Abraham Kuyper: Forgotten Radical?" *Calvin Forum* 15(May 1950): 211–13; "The Dutch Calvinist Labor Movement," *Reformed Journal* 7(October 1957): 10–13; and "Some Thoughts on Christian Social Action" (an answer to Leonard Verduin), *Reformed Journal* 4(January 1954): 13–15. Application of the tradition to the American scene can be found in Lewis Smedes, "The Tyranny of Things," *Reformed Journal* 5(July 1955): 1–2; and Dirk Jellema, "Zeitgeist," *Reformed Journal* 5(March–May 1955): 1–3, 7–9, 8–10.

55. The *Reformed Journal*'s patron was G. C. Berkouwer; the *Reformed Review*'s was A. A. van Ruler; and the Antitheticals' was H. Th. Vollenhoven and especially Herman Dooyeweerd—on each of whom there is more in Chapter 13 herein. Such Confessionalists as Henry R. Van Til drew off Klaas Schilder (Van Til's *Calvinistic Concept of Culture* is replete with references to him, and Cornelius Van Til studied under him in the Netherlands). Most Confessionalists would have no figure more recent than the Secession of 1834 and would insist that they drew off the Synod of Dort directly.

56. The events recounted in this chapter thus round off the CRC's neat fit with Martin Marty's three-stage model of ethnic church progression (summarized in *The Public Church,* p. 57). The first, "familial" stage, characterized by natural primary associations, ended for the CRC with the strife of the 1920s. In the second, "military" phase, the faction that emerges triumphant from the "familial" break-up imposes an abstract ideal upon its rivals to the ends of total control and uniformity of opinion—which describes the era of H. J. Kuiper's tenure (1925–55). Marty's third, "political" stage, which begins with the pluralization noted here, requires compromise among several coexisting groups that does not jeopardize the integrity of the whole or any component part. The CRC showed some of the strain of that strategy in the '50s, but more in subsequent decades.

57. On the 1960 election, see note 41 to this chapter. On the Cuban missile crisis and its aftermath, see Lester De Koster, "The Challenge of the Collective," *Reformed Journal* 12(July 1962): 7–10 (an interesting anticipation); R. J. Frens's current events column, *Banner,* 19 October and 30 November–14 December 1962; and John Vander Ploeg, "Christ in the Crisis," *Banner,* 30 November 1962, p. 8. On the assassination, see John Vander Ploeg, "Worship Christ the New-Born King," *Banner,* 20 December 1963, pp. 8–10; and Louis Benes, *Church Herald,* 6–13 December 1963, p. 6 each issue.

CHAPTER THIRTEEN

1. Background and context are provided—with heavy pro-merger bias—in Harmelink, *Ecumenism and the Reformed Church* (Grand Rapids, 1968), pp. 79–94. Representative statements favoring merger can be found in the following *Church Herald* articles: M. Verne Oggel, "Report on the State of Religion," 5 June 1964, pp. 8–11; Norman Vincent Peale, "Thoughts on the Plan of Union," 29 November 1968, p. 12; and Norman Thomas, "Why I Favor Union . . . ," 27 December 1968, pp. 12–14. Statements against merger can be found in the following *Church Herald* articles: Abraham Rynbrandt, "Is Church Merger Wise?" 10 April 1963, p. 10; Henry Bast, "The Issues in Church Union," 13 December 1968, p. 12; and Jerome De Jong, "For Renewal in the Reformed Church," 30 May 1969, p. 10.

2. See the *Church Herald,* 4 April 1969, p. 26. The PCUS presbyteries gave exactly the majority needed for approval: 58–18. The RCA's congregational count against the merger (975–935) and the Synodical delegate rejection of COCU (148–128) were of roughly the same proportions.

3. See the report on the General Synod meetings in the *Church Herald* of 27 June 1969 (p. 13) and 25 July 1969 (p. 6). For role reversals, see Gordon Girod, "What about CRC-RCA Merger?" *Torch and Trumpet* 19(October 1969): 2–6.

4. See Donald Luidens, "The RCA Today," *Church Herald,* 8 September 1978, p. 4. Ethnicity percentages per Particular Synod were as follows: Albany, 24; New Jersey, 26; New York, 12; Chicago, 66; Michigan, 78; West, 58. Overall sectional rates may vary a bit from those in the text because the Particular Synods differ in size. Luidens also discovered substantial behavioral differences between the two sections, the West scoring much higher on frequency of church attendance (with 87 percent attendance, compared to the East's 58 percent) and double on *Church Herald* readership (with 74 percent, compared to the East's 36 percent). See the *Church Herald,* 22 September 1978, pp. 10–12.

5. See Girod, "What about a CRC-RCA Merger?" *Torch and Trumpet* 19(October 1969): 2–6.

6. See Gordon Girod, "Evaluating the General Synod," *Torch and Trumpet* 16(January 1966): 14–17; Ronald Brown, "The 1966 Synod of the RCA," *Torch and Trumpet* 16(October 1966): 2–4; and "A Chart for the Future," *Church Herald,* 16 May 1969, p. 10; and Jerome De Jong, "For Renewal in the Reformed Church," *Church Herald,* 30 May 1969, p. 10.

7. On the "Festival of Evangelism," held in Detroit in 1970, see the reflections of Carl Schroeder and Donald Van Hoeven in the *Reformed Review* 24(Autumn 1970): 4–16; on a "mission festival" held in Milwaukee in 1971, see the reflections of Charles Wissink and I. John Hesselink in the *Reformed Review* 25(Winter 1972): 81–88, 105–07. A whole issue of the *Reformed Review* (23[Winter 1970]) was devoted to the topic of "Reconciliation within the Church," and showed its contributors, strong supporters of union, a bit at a loss for direction and formulas. The festivals served to reverse that uncertainty.

8. See Harold Dekker, "God So Loved All Men," *Reformed Journal* 12(December 1962): 5–7, and 13(February 1963): 13–16; quoted matter taken from p. 16. See also Dekker, "God's Love to Sinners, One or Two?" *Reformed Journal* 13(March 1963): 12–16; and Henry Stob, "Does God Hate Some Men?" *Reformed Journal* 13(February 1963): 9–13. James Daane and Harry Boer wrote frequently on the matter until its final resolution; see, for instance, their series in the *Journal* running from October 1964 to March 1965 (with bibliography on p. 17 in the concluding issue).

9. On the case as a whole, the best presentation is provided by R. B. Kuiper, "Professor Dekker on God's Universal Love," *Torch and Trumpet* 13(March 1963): 4–9; on imposition of logic, see Kuiper, "Is the Glory Departing?" *Torch and Trumpet* 13(May 1963): 8–15. Kuiper had been particularly irritated by Daane's critique of his *God-Centered Evangelism* (Grand Rapids, 1957), a book also pertinent to the present controversy inasmuch as it presents a strong Confessionalist call for "outreach" (in contradistinction to Harry Boer, *That My House May Be Filled* [Grand Rapids, 1957]).

10. See CRC *Acts of Synod, 1967,* pp. 486–607, 727–38; quoted matter taken from p. 736. A digest can be found in John B. Hulst, "After Four and a Half Years—A Decision," *Torch and Trumpet* 17(September 1967): 2–6. Some indication of the degree of the Confessionalists' anxiety is evident in their devotion of the April and May 1967 issues of *Torch and Trumpet* almost entirely to the case (see, for instance, Edward Heerema, "The CRC on Trial" in the May issue, pp. 2–8).

11. For information on this issue I have relied on Norman Rozenboom, "The 'Infallibility' Dispute," unpublished paper, 1971, Calvin College and Seminary Archives. The 1959 decision led to a two-year study of the question, the results of which were presented to and approved by the 1961 Synod.

12. The 1951 Synod had removed some of the legalistic character of the old prohibitions (one added element in the factional battle of that time), and the 1966 decision took a positive Calvinist approach of permeating all areas of culture with Christianity (see *CRC Acts of Synod, 1966*, pp. 316–61).

13. See William R. Hutchison, *The Modernist Impulse in American Protestantism* (New York, 1976), pp. 41–110. Other similarities are those of socio-cultural class, as we shall see, and the project of "de-culturating" (i.e., de-Westernizing) foreign missions, a favorite theme of Harry Boer in the CRC and of late-nineteenth-century liberals (see Hutchison, pp. 111–44).

14. See Merle Meeter, "The Winds of Change," *Torch and Trumpet* 17(January 1967): 11–13; and Alexander De Jong, "'God Loves All Men'—Continuing the Discussion," *Reformed Journal* 13(May 1963): 14–17.

15. On Kennedy, see Vander Ploeg, "Worship Christ the New-Born King," *Banner*, 20 December 1963, pp. 8–10. On domestic politics, see Vander Ploeg, "A.D. 1966," *Banner*, 30 December 1966, p. 8; and "Riot Prevention Is Everybody's Business," *Banner*, 15 March 1968, p. 8; and Edwin Palmer, "The Free and Dr. King," *Torch and Trumpet* 15(February 1966): 8 (in which Palmer deplores the Amsterdam university's award of an honorary degree to Martin Luther King, Jr.); "Civil Disobedience," *Torch and Trumpet* 18(March 1968): 2–7; and a harsh response to King's assassination, also in *Torch and Trumpet* ("Martin Luther King," 18[May 1968]: 1–3). On the White House briefing, see Vander Ploeg, "And So We Went to Washington," *Banner*, 26 April 1968, p. 8; cf. the *Banner*, 10 May 1968, p. 8.

16. See Louis Benes's editorial in the *Church Herald* of 17 January 1964, p. 9; and see Arie Brouwer, "Is There Room for Christ in the Classroom?" *Church Herald*, 20 March 1964, p. 5. Cf. (on the CRC side) Nicholas Wolterstorff, "Religion and the Schools," *Reformed Journal* 16(February–April 1966).

17. On civil rights, see Louis Benes, "The March on Washington," *Church Herald*, 20 September 1963, p. 6; and "I Could Cry" (an editorial on the King assassination), *Church Herald*, 24 April 1968, p. 6. On Vietnam, Benes moved from support in the 24 September 1965 issue of the *Church Herald* (p. 8) to disavowal in the 16 February 1968 issue (p. 8), while John Vander Ploeg remained "True Blue to Our Boys in Vietnam" (*Banner*, 4 February 1966, p. 8). A telling expression of bi-denominational support for the war cause was "Project Thank You" (thanking the American troops, that is, not the Vietnamese) in western Michigan, which sent servicemen packets containing towelettes, socks, and soft-drink mix "for the body" and the Gospel of Mark "for the soul" (see the *Banner*, 27 December 1967, p. 9).

18. This was a particularly strong theme of Benes: see "Renewal and Revolution," *Church Herald*, 4 October 1968, p. 6; and "More Thoughts on Watergate," *Church Herald*, 24 August 1973, p. 6. On the CRC side, see John Vander Ploeg, "A.D. 1966," *Banner*, 30 December 1966, p. 8; Andrew Kuyvenhoven, "Freedom and Obedience," *Banner*, 29 December 1967, p. 16; and Joel Nederhood, "Grace for Black and White," *Banner*, 3 May 1968, pp. 4–6.

19. See Benes, "Renewal and Revolution," *Church Herald*, 4 October 1968, p. 6. The citation of Wesley was repeated throughout Benes's 1969 editorials.

20. Their manifesto, *Out of Concern for the Church* (Toronto, 1970), featured the school's leading new lights: Hendrik Hart, James Olthuis, Calvin Seerveld, and Bernard Zylstra. Although first recruited by H. Evan Runner, they had gone beyond him, particularly in the radicalizing environment of the Free University in the 1960s. They were shortly joined by C. T. McIntire, son of the famous American Fundamentalist, whose political and religious views were the opposite of his father's.

21. According to Hendrik Hart, in *Out of Concern for the Church*, pp. 32–33.

22. The five essays in the manifesto all sounded these themes in one way or another; see, for example, pp. 10–14, 21–25, 31–33, 37–39, 77–81, 99, 103.

23. Confessionalist overtures are evident in the April, May, and September 1969

issues of *Torch and Trumpet,* which are given over largely to this project. The first turnabout appears in Peter Y. De Jong, "Reply to My Friend," *Torch and Trumpet* 20(July 1970): 17–20, which was very mild compared to later, mounting attacks (see note 38 to this chapter). On the progressive side, James Daane's review gives evidence of just the sort of ecclesiasticism and mild reformist strategy the manifesto had decried (see the *Reformed Journal* 21[January 1971]), though earlier he had engaged in "church-as-revolutionary" talk himself (see "The Church and Our Social Crisis," *Reformed Journal* 19[February 1969]: 4–5). More stridently, a CRC bureaucrat attacked the Canadians for having unsettled a national missions festival of young people with calls for radical transformation of the U.S. first and any overhaul of mission purpose thereafter (see Eugene Rubingh, "Sabotage at Urbana," *Reformed Journal* 21[February 1971]: 14–16). A keen and better balanced assessment is provided by Nicholas Wolterstorff in "The AACS in the CRC," *Reformed Journal* 24(December 1974): 9–15, in which he applauds various Kuyperian elements in the movement but criticizes its "movementism," triumphalism, its constant "proclamation" without requisite scholarly discussion, and so on.

24. See Leonard Verduin's review of *The New Left and Christian Radicalism,* by Arthur Gish, *Reformed Journal* 21(January 1971): 23–25. See also Lester De Koster, "Viet Nam," *Reformed Journal* 15(October 1965): 3 (from which the quotation is taken); "Daystar for Vietnam," *Reformed Journal* 16(March 1966): 7–9; "Tet Paid Off," *Reformed Journal* 18(April 1968): 5; and "First War the U.S. Has Lost," *Banner,* 11 April 1975, p. 6. De Koster mounted two campaigns against the Far Right in the *Reformed Journal,* in September–December 1965 and January–May 1968. He brought both themes together in a centrist expostulation ("The New Left, the Old Right, and the Rest of Us," *Reformed Journal* 19 [February 1969]: 5) and in his paean to Lyndon Johnson (over against Eugene McCarthy), "Liberals Lack Mirrors," *Reformed Journal* 19(April 1969): 4. De Koster would later issue an edition of the Federalist Papers for the American bicentennial, stressing American-Christian compatibilities.

25. A good sampling of such reversals can be found in the January, March, and May 1968 issues of the *Reformed Journal,* the last giving reactions to the King assassination, the first being a special issue on "Poverty in America," and the second giving evidence of concern over both the Tet offensive and prospects for summer rioting. The Vietnam protest climaxed in the December 1969 issue (pp. 2–10) and in Richard Mouw's assessment of the Vietnam Moratorium (*Reformed Journal* 20[January 1970]: 6–8).

26. See the following in the *Reformed Journal:* Dirk Jellema, "Abraham Kuyper's Answer to 'Liberalism,'" 15(May 1965): 10–14; Richard Mouw, "Calvinist—What's in a Name?" 21(February 1971): 3–4; and Howard Hageman, "Complaint of a Conservative," 22(July 1972): 3. A few examples among many of Kuyperian social analysis can be found in the following: Lewis Smedes, "Evangelicals and the Social Question" and "Where Do We Differ?" *Reformed Journal* 16(February and May 1966): 9–13, 8–10; on ideology in society, see Nicholas Wolterstorff, "Religion and the Schools," *Reformed Journal* 16(February–April 1966); on ideology in scholarship, see Wolterstorff, *Reason within the Bounds of Religion* (Grand Rapids, 1976).

27. See the following in the *Reformed Journal:* Roderick Jellema, "In Defense of Being Modern," 15(November 1965): 12–17; and "Who Is Twentieth Century Man?" 16(December 1966): 11 (from which the quotation is taken); Wesley Kort, "Recent Fiction and the Christian Reader," 16(September 1966): 17–19; Stanley Wiersma, "Flannery O'Connor and the Heidelberg Catechism," 20(October 1970): 14–17; Nicholas Wolterstorff, "The New Student," 19(April 1969): 11–15; Harry Boer, "Insecticides and Flower People," 19(October 1969): 3; and Gordon Van Harn, "God's Glory and Man's Smog," 21(January 1971): 11–14.

28. See the following in the *Reformed Journal:* on the New left, Lewis Smedes,

"To Cry for Old Gods," 20(December 1970): 3–4; and on secular theology, Alvin Plantinga, "On Being Honest to God," 14(April 1964): 11–15; Henry Stob, 16(March, September, and November 1966); and Lewis Smedes, "Signals From God," 20(February–April 1970), especially April, pp. 10–12.

29. See Richard Mouw, "Calvinist–What's in a Name?" *Reformed Journal* 21(February 1971): 3–4. Mouw presents a good example of the Calvinist-Anabaptist exchange in *Politics and the Biblical Drama* (Grand Rapids, 1976), pp. 85–116.

30. Lewis Smedes, "From Hartford to Boston," *Reformed Journal* 26(April 1976): 2–3. See also the self-designated "realist" approach of Smedes's *Love within Limits* (Grand Rapids, 1978); Richard Mouw's *Politics and the Biblical Drama* (wherein he cites H. Richard Niebuhr as having formulated "well . . . the thesis we have been developing . . . throughout this book" [pp. 132–33]); George Marsden's citation of Reinhold Niebuhr in the introduction to *Fundamentalism and American Culture* (p. vii); and Ronald Wells's likewise in *The Wars of America: Christian Views* (Grand Rapids, 1981), pp. 2–7.

31. See Berkouwer's autobiographical *A Half Century of Theology* (E.T., Grand Rapids, 1977). Kuitert's publications in translation include *The Reality of Faith* (Grand Rapids, 1968) and, on biblical hermeneutics, *Do You Understand What You Read?* (Grand Rapids, 1970), which is dedicated to Berkouwer and translated by Lewis Smedes. Kuitert's very controversial address to the 1968 CRC Synod was defended by Smedes (see the *Reformed Journal* 18[July 1968]: 15–17). For signs of subsequent influence, see Jack Rogers's review of *Do You Understand What You Read?* in the *Reformed Journal* 21(January 1971): 28; see also note 37 to this chapter.

32. Some description of Netherlandic developments is available in Shetter, *Pillars of Society* (The Hague, 1971). On the Calvinist side in particular, see Thijs Booy, *Gereformeerd: hoe lang nog?* and B. Rietveld, *Wat is er aan de hand met de Gereformeerde Kerken in Nederland?* (Kampen, 1976). The '60s were severe also in the Netherlands, sparking the formation of a "New Left" political party, the radicalization of the Free University, sexual liberation, and gender-role flexibility, to all of which and more the confessional parties' convergence was in part a response. The similarity of American and Netherlandic patterns and problems at this point corroborates an underlying assumption of this study, namely, that "Americanization" can well be treated as a species of "modernization," also in its intellectual developments.

33. A fine introduction to Dooyeweerd's thought is provided in L. Kalsbeek's *Contours of a Christian Philosophy* (Toronto, 1975); a briefer introduction is provided by Jacob Klapwijk's two articles in the *Reformed Journal* 30(February and March 1980). Dooyeweerd's principal works in English translation are *New Critique of Theoretical Thought*, 4 vols. (Philadelphia, 1953–58); *In the Twilight of Western Thought* (Nutley, N.J., 1968); and *Roots of Western Culture: Pagan, Secular, and Christian Options* (Toronto, 1979). Explicit statements of solutions are provided by James Olthuis and Calvin Seerveld in *Out of Concern for the Church*, pp. 107–22 and 56–68, respectively. The "Law-Word" conception is evident in Dooyeweerd (the title of his project being "Philosophy of the Law-Idea"), Runner (see Theodore Plantinga, "The Christian Philosophy of H. Evan Runner," in *Life Is Religion: Essays in Honor of H. Evan Runner*. ed. Henry Vander Goot [St. Catharines, Ontario, 1981], pp. 15–28), and—in theological application—Gordon Spykman, "A New Look at Election and Reprobation," in *Life Is Religion*, pp. 171–91.

34. Heideman, *Our Song of Hope: A Provisional Confession of Faith of the RCA* (Grand Rapids, 1975); the document was awarded secondary status by the denomination's General Synod in 1978. I have relied on the three articles by Tjaard Hommes, Paul Fries, and Heideman in the special van Ruler issue of the *Reformed Review* (26[Winter 1973]) and I. John Hesselink's introduction to that issue ("Contemporary Protestant Dutch Theology") for background on van Ruler. His critique of Kuyper is presented in

Kuypers Idee eener Christelijke Cultuur (Nijkerk, 1940). My comment about "optimism" stems from comparing the tone of the sources cited here to that of the statement Lewis Smedes made in "From Hartford to Boston" (*Reformed Journal* 26[April 1976]: 2–3), quoted on p. 212 herein. Both would agree that "already but not yet" describes the present status of the Kingdom of God, but van Ruler would seem to stress the first, Smedes the second; van Ruler the joyful reception of God's "signals," Smedes the human—Christian—corruption thereof. For documentation of RCA Calvin scholarship, see Hesselink, "The Future of a Distinctive Dutch-American Theology," in *Perspectives on the Christian Reformed Church: Studies in Its History, Theology, and Ecumenicity,* ed. Peter De Klerk and Richard R. De Ridder (Grand Rapids, 1983), pp. 289–90; on the influence of Bavinck, see pp. 286–87; and on the RCA's general confessional revitalization, see p. 278.

35. Osterhaven, *The Spirit of the Reformed Tradition* (Grand Rapids, 1971); on social mandate, see pp. 149–63. Osterhaven, Professor of Theology at Western Seminary, also echoed some van Ruler themes in *The Faith of the Church* (Grand Rapids, 1982)—for example, in the central chapter, "John Calvin: Order and the Holy Spirit." See also Donald Bruggink, *Christ and Architecture* (Grand Rapids, 1963) and *When Faith Takes Form* (Grand Rapids, 1971); and Howard G. Hageman, *Pulpit and Table* (Richmond, 1962; originally presented as the Stone Lectures, Princeton). The Heidelberg memorial volume is *Guilt, Grace, and Gratitude,* ed. Donald Bruggink (New York, 1963), which features an introductory essay by Hageman. It is only fair to say that the CRC can lay claim to a monumental commentary on the Catechism in J. K. Van Baalen's *The Heritage of the Fathers* (Grand Rapids, 1948).

36. Besides the works cited in the preceding note, see Hageman's many columns in the *Church Herald* and periodic contributions to the *Reformed Journal,* including "Complaint of a Conservative," 22(July 1972): 3; and "Does the Reformed Tradition in 1975 Have Anything to Offer American Life?" 25(March 1975): 10–18 (the quotations in the text being taken from the latter, pp. 12–14). See also *Pulpit and Table,* p. 30.

37. Examples of their '60s attitudes can be found in the following *Torch and Trumpet* articles: H. J. Kuiper, "Doctrinal Disturbances in a Sister Church," 12(November 1962): 8–10; Edwin Palmer, "The Free and Dr. King," 15(February 1966): 8; "Civil Disobedience" 18(March 1968): 2–7; and 18(May 1968): 1–3; and Louis Praamsma, "What's Happening in the Netherlands?" 18(February–April 1968). The *Banner* carried a constant stream of remarks criticizing Harry Kuitert and Jan Lever, the two Free University faculty in question. On the other side, see the series by John Timmer and Nicholas Wolterstorff on hermeneutics and the Dutch case in particular, in the *Reformed Journal* 19(July–December 1969); and Harry Boer, *Above the Battle? The Bible and Its Critics* (Grand Rapids, 1977), a volume based on many of Boer's contributions to the *Reformed Journal* in previous years. The Synodical examination was commissioned in 1969, returned (as "Report 36") in 1971, and presented in final form (as "Report 44") in 1972 (see the CRC *Acts of Synod, 1972,* pp. 493–546).

38. Vander Ploeg, "The Social Dance at Calvin College," *Outlook* 27(September 1977): 2–5; the quotation is taken from p. 4. The hopeful assessment of Report 44 was that of Henry Vanden Heuvel, "Report on Synod 1972," *Outlook* 22(July 1972): 9–10, but the report did not meet the rigorous standards set beforehand: see John Vander Ploeg, "The Most Critical Issue Facing Synod 1971," *Outlook* 21(August 1971): 2–5; and Peter De Jong, *Outlook* 21(June 1971): 19–21. The professors charged were Willis De Boer and John Stek, of Calvin College and Calvin Seminary, respectively, and Allen Verhey, an ordained CRC minister teaching at Hope College. The issue of biblical authority also separated the Confessionalists further than ever from the "Toronto" school (see John Vander Ploeg, "One 'Word of God' or Three?" *Outlook* 22[February 1972]: 5–8).

39. Vander Ploeg's series on this question ran in *Outlook* from January to May of

1974 (the quotation is taken from the March issue, p. 17); the May article constitutes an example of traditionalistic ecumenicity. Vander Ploeg's strategy was contrary to that of his predecessor, Peter Y. De Jong (editor from 1964 to 1970): De Jong pleaded for conciliation in one of his last editorials, "Have We Written Each Other Off?" *Torch and Trumpet* 19[March 1970]: 14. Vander Ploeg's inaugural was "Polarization—With No Apology," *Torch and Trumpet* (soon renamed *Outlook*) 20(October 1970): 8. In De Jong's regime, the journal had a respectable academic tone and a national network of contributors, both of which lapsed under the new management, to be replaced by strict and narrow denominational concerns.

40. See John Vander Ploeg, "It's Our Battle Too," *Outlook* 26(June 1976): 4–5; and cf. similar articles throughout 1977 triggered by *Banner* editor Lester De Koster's retort to Lindsell. Among the evangelicals appearing in the *Church Herald* over the years were Billy Graham, Leighton Ford, Carl Henry, Mark Hatfield, Ronald Sider, John Stott, and Tom Skinner. *Reformed Review* ambivalence is evident in that publication's reprint of I. John Hesselink's inaugural speech as president of Western Seminary—"Toward a Seminary that is Catholic, Evangelical, and Reformed," 27(Winter 1974): 103–11—in which doubts are expressed concerning the middle term only.

41. See Lewis Smedes, "Evangelicals, What Next?" *Reformed Journal* 19(November 1969): 4. On the Chicago Declaration (signed by Smedes, Mouw, and *Journal* managing editor Marlin Van Elderen), see the entire January 1974 issue. The Hartford Affirmation (signed by Mouw and Smedes among twenty-two others) is reprinted in the March 1975 *Journal* (pp. 8–9); cf. Mouw's contribution to the follow-up book, *Against the World For the World: The Hartford Appeal and the Future of American Religion*, ed. Peter L. Berger and Richard J. Neuhaus (New York, 1976), pp. 99–125. The April and July 1974 issues of the *Journal* contain a significant proportion of "outside" evangelical contributions, but the fact that at Hartford Smedes and Mouw were the only evangelicals in a very elite assembly says much about Dutch Reformed sophistication and influence in American evangelical circles.

42. Mouw, *Called to Holy Worldliness* (Philadelphia, 1980). The phrase "Fundamental American perspective" is taken from I. John Hesselink's discussion of Herbert W. Richardson's book *Toward an American Theology* (1967) in *Reformed Review* (Summer 1970): 202, but it has appeared in a great number of studies on American religion.

43. See the series by John Vander Ploeg in *Outlook* 21(August–November 1971). See also the following articles in the *Reformed Journal:* Marlin Van Elderen, "Explo '72 and Campus Crusade," 22(July–August 1972): 8–9, 15–20, and "The Jesus Freaks," 21(May 1971): 16–20; Lewis Smedes, "Only a Sinner?" 22(December 1972): 6–7; and James Daane, "Pentecostalism and Reformation Faith," 24(April 1974): 17–20. And see Anthony Hoekema, *Holy Spirit Baptism* (Grand Rapids, 1972); and David Holwerda, *Neo-Pentecostalism Hits the Church* (Grand Rapids, 1974), the latter a booklet growing out of the 1973 CRC Synod's strictures against the movement.

44. "Folk poet" is the designation on the cover copy of *Purpaleanie and Other Permutations* (Orange City, Iowa, 1978), by Wiersma persona Sietze Buning. On ecumenicity, see Wiersma, "Flannery O'Connor and the Heidelberg Catechism," *Reformed Journal* 20(October 1970): 10; on ethno-religious culture itself, see his "Confessions of an Ex-WASP," *Reformed Journal* 23(April 1973): 27–30; and his letters on the death of an old friend, *Journal* managing editor Calvin Bulthuis ("'Choose What Is Difficult'") 22[May–June 1972]: 18–23). The death of Bulthuis also brought from Lewis Smedes a profound personal ode to "a definable community where tradition and mission and life-perspective all merge in a communal experience [in which alone] will authentic friendship be possible" ("A Word of Thanks for a Friend," *Reformed Journal* 22[February 1972]: 6).

45. Good examples are "Barnyard Miracle," "The Valleys Stand So Thick with Corn," "Obedience," "Calvinist Farming," "Calvinist Sunday Dinner," and the title

poem, all in *Purpaleanie*. Vis-à-vis the renegade novelists discussed above, Wiersma works the same region and clans as Manfred, observes the same discrepancies as De Jong, and achieves the same (comic) resolution as De Vries, though very much in his own way.

Of the youngest generation of "rebels," a few comments are possible. James Den Boer (Calvin College, 1960) has published two volumes of poetry, *Learning the Way* (Pittsburgh, 1968) and *Trying to Come Apart* (Pittsburgh, 1971), in which there are explicit treatments of the ethnic and religious elements of his past and a general sense of loss, human frailty, and tough-mindedness clearly connected with that past. William Brashler, a Calvin College exile of 1968 and Chicago-based novelist best known for works on black baseball history, shows the least effects of and affection for his upbringing. The most famous of this set is Paul Schrader (Calvin College, 1968), Hollywood screenwriter and director (*Obsession, Taxi Driver, Blue Collar, Hardcore, Raging Bull, Cat People*). Schrader has traded hard and well upon his background (e.g., posing in *Esquire* in a Calvin sweatshirt). As critics found in the case of *Taxi Driver*, there is a measure of substance as well as image in this "Calvinism," although as they determined of *Hardcore* (which follows a CRC businessman's search for his runaway daughter in the Hollywood pornography network), Schrader has not escaped the earlier renegades' difficulties in handling native materials.

46. Roderick Jellema, "The Work of Our Hands" [dedicated to W. Harry Jellema], *The Lost Faces* (Washington, D.C., 1979), p. 17; "Poem Beginning with a Line Memorized at School," *Something Tugging at the Line* (Washington, D.C., 1974), p. 8. Jellema is Professor of English at the University of Maryland.

47. Roderick Jellema, "Hearing My Teeth Snap the Skin of an Apple . . . ," *Something Tugging*, p. 41; "Heading In," *Lost Faces*, p. 18; "First Climb up Three Surfers' Peak," *Lost Faces*, pp. 77–78; "Incarnation," *Something Tugging*, pp. 14–15.

48. Besides the extension of the Christian school movement, a new sophistication in political critique, and the other changes we have considered, a striking example is provided by Jack Rogers, *The Authority and Interpretation of the Bible: An Historical Approach* (San Francisco, 1979), which offers the "middle way between liberalism and the Reformed scholastic [inerrancist] approach typified by the old Princeton school" called for by I. John Hesselink (see "Dutch-American Theology," p. 288). Rogers, from an American Presbyterian background, turned to Dutch sources, particularly Herman Bavinck, for this hermeneutic. For a personal statement showing the socio-political connections therewith, see Rogers, "Confessions of a Post-conservative Evangelical," *Reformed Journal* 23(February 1973): 10–13.

49. Perhaps this is simply another part of the wages of the "success" that are alleged to come to every American ethnic group. Richard Quebedeaux has applied the idea to evangelicals more widely, with several points pertinent to the present case. The *Reformed Journal*'s evolution reflects an increase in wealth, social status, and especially educational attainment—altogether, a new respectability—that characterizes the evangelical "left" in general. The *Outlook*'s new role as voice for a dissenting conservative caucus has counterparts in other evangelical sectors. Both, to Quebedeaux, represent accommodations to the larger culture that make survival problematic, particularly since they have coincided (among Reformed and evangelicals alike) with a loosening of the subculture's institutional apparatus (see *Worldly Evangelicals*, pp. 10–24, 44–51). The clearest display of these developments and of their very mixed consequences belongs to a third—and suitably ethnic—body, the American Catholic Church since Vatican II.

50. See the testament of an Amway founder, Richard M. De Vos, *Believe!* (Old Tappan, N.J., 1975). That this lies as far from traditional Dutch spirituality as it does close to the American popular version can be seen in a typical sketch of the latter (Richard Quebedeaux, *By What Authority?* [San Francisco, 1982], pp. 1–16), where pop faith is described as being oriented toward anonymous mass consumption rather

than issuing from a coherent community; as gauging status by "sales" rather than by mastery of knowledge or conduct; as lauding celebrities rather than leaders; as rendering all things understandable and remediable, with no paradoxical or inscrutable remainder; as "mentalizing" the Protestant ethic and "instrumentalizing" God and faith to practical, daily, psychic-material ends; and as shifting social ethics to either individualism, apathy, or right-wing restoratives. Quebedeaux also corroborates an insight of earlier Dutch-American leaders by noting the Methodist background of Norman Vincent Peale, whose gospel of success lies at the source of Schuller and Amway empires alike (pp. 81–82).

51. This is another consequence, in terms of Mary Douglas's model, of the move from "group" to "grid." Several apparent anomalies are clarified by this construct, the most obvious of which is the coincidence of communal diffusion and bureaucratic multiplication, but also the Amway-*Reformed Journal* connection. As "grid" displaces "group," religion will shift from "ritual"-"communal" to "ethical"-"individual," and the latter will flow in either a "service" (*Reformed Journal*) or "success" (Amway) direction (see Mary Douglas, *Natural Symbols*, pp. 12–14, 36).

Selected Bibliography

AMERICAN HISTORY

Political and Social

Formisano, Ronald P. *The Birth of Mass Political Parties: Michigan, 1827–1861*. Princeton: Princeton University Press, 1971.

Hays, Samuel P. *American Political History as Social Analysis*. Knoxville: University of Tennessee Press, 1980.

Higham, John. "Hanging Together: Divergent Unities in American History." *Journal of American History* 61(June 1974): 5–28.

Jensen, Richard. *The Winning of the Midwest*. Chicago: University of Chicago Press, 1971.

Kennedy, David M. *Over Here: The First World War and American Society*. New York: Oxford University Press, 1980.

Kleppner, Paul J. *The Cross of Culture: A Social Analysis of Midwestern Politics, 1850–1900*. New York: Free Press, 1970.

O'Neill, William L. *The Progressive Years: America Comes of Age*. New York: Dodd, Mead, 1975.

Wiebe, Robert. *The Search for Order, 1877–1920*. New York: Hill and Wang, 1967.

Religious

Ahlstrom, Sydney E. *A Religious History of the American People*. New Haven: Yale University Press, 1972.

Albanese, Catherine. *America: Religions and Religion*. Belmont, Cal.: Wadsworth Publishing Co., 1981.

Handy, Robert. *A Christian America: Protestant Hopes and Historical Realities*. New York: Oxford University Press, 1971.

Hutchison, William R. *The Modernist Impulse in American Protestantism*. New York: Oxford University Press, 1976.

Marsden, George M. *Fundamentalism and American Culture: The Shaping of Twentieth Century Evangelicalism, 1870–1925*. New York: Oxford University Press, 1980.

Marty, Martin. *The Public Church: Mainline, Evangelical, Catholic*. New York: Crossroad, 1981.

————. *Righteous Empire: The Protestant Experience in America.* New York: Dial Press, 1970.

Quebedeaux, Richard. *The Worldly Evangelicals.* New York: Harper and Row, 1978.

Sandeen, Ernest. *The Roots of Fundamentalism: British and American Millenarianism, 1800–1930.* Chicago: University of Chicago Press, 1970.

Weber, Timothy P. *Living in the Shadow of the Second Coming: American Premillennialism, 1875–1925.* New York: Oxford University Press, 1979.

Immigration and Ethnic Religion

Abramson, Harold J. *Ethnic Diversity in Catholic America.* New York: John Wiley and Sons, 1973.

Barton, Josef J. *Peasants and Strangers: Italians, Rumanians, and Slovaks in an American City, 1890–1950.* Cambridge: Harvard University Press, 1975.

Blegen, Theodore. *Norwegian Migration to America: The American Transition.* Northfield, Minn.: The Norwegian-American Historical Association, 1940.

Dinnerstein, Leonard, and David Reimers. *Ethnic Americans: A History of Immigration and Assimilation.* New York: Harper and Row, 1975.

Dolan, Jay P. *The Immigrant Church: New York's Irish and German Catholics, 1815–1865.* Baltimore: Johns Hopkins University Press, 1975.

Gambino, Richard. *Blood of My Blood: The Dilemma of the Italian Americans.* Garden City, N.Y.: Doubleday, 1974.

Gleason, Philip. *The Conservative Reformers: German-American Catholics and the Social Order.* Notre Dame, Ind.: University of Notre Dame Press, 1968.

Gordon, Milton M. *Assimilation in American Life: The Role of Race, Religion, and National Origins.* New York: Oxford University Press, 1964.

Greeley, Andrew. *Ethnicity in the United States: A Preliminary Reconnaissance.* New York: John Wiley and Sons, 1974.

Greene, Victor. *For God and Country: The Rise of Polish and Lithuanian Ethnic Consciousness in America, 1860–1910.* Madison, Wisc.: State Historical Association of Wisconsin, 1975.

Handlin, Oscar. *The Uprooted: The Epic Story of the Great Migrations That Made the American People.* New York: Grosset and Dunlap Publishers, 1951.

Herberg, Will. *Protestant-Catholic-Jew: An Essay in American Religious Sociology.* Garden City, N.Y.: Doubleday, 1955.

Howe, Irving. *World of Our Fathers.* New York: Harcourt Brace Jovanovich, 1976.

Jones, Maldwyn. *American Immigration.* Chicago: University of Chicago Press, 1960.

Luebke, Frederick A. *Bonds of Loyalty: German-Americans and World War I.* DeKalb, Ill.: Northern Illinois University Press, 1974.

McLaughlin, Virginia Y. "Patterns of Work and Family Organization: Buffalo's Italians." *Journal of Interdisciplinary History* 2(Fall 1971): 299–314.

Marty, Martin. "Ethnicity: The Skeleton of Religion in America." *Church History* 41(March 1972): 5–21.

Mauelshagen, Carl. *The Effect of German Immigration Upon the Lutheran Church in America, 1820–1870.* Athens, Ga.: University of Georgia Press, 1936.

Miller, Randall M., and Thomas D. Marzik, eds. *Immigration and Religion in Urban America.* Philadelphia: Temple University Press, 1977.

Novak, Michael. *The Rise of the Unmeltable Ethnics: Politics and Culture in the Seventies.* New York: Macmillan, 1972.

Passi, Michael M. "Immigrants and the City: Problems of Interpretation and Synthesis in Recent White Ethnic History." *Journal of Ethnic Studies* 4(Summer 1976): 61–72.

Polenberg, Richard. *One Nation Divisible: Race, Class, and Ethnicity in the United States since 1938.* New York: Viking Press, 1980.

Smith, Timothy L. "Religion and Ethnicity in America." *American Historical Review* 83(December 1978): 1155–85.

———. "Religious Denominations as Ethnic Communities: A Regional Case Study." *Church History* 35(1966): 207–26.

Stephenson, George M. *The Religious Aspects of Swedish Immigration: A Study of Immigrant Churches.* Minneapolis: The University of Minnesota Press, 1932.

Stout, Harry S. "Ethnicity: The Vital Center of Religion in America." *Ethnicity* 2(June 1975): 204–20.

Taylor, Philip A. M. *The Distant Magnet: European Migration to the U.S.A.* London: Eyre and Spottiswoode, 1971.

Tomasi, Silvio M. *Piety and Power: The Role of the Italian Parishes in the New York Metropolitan Area.* New York: Center for Migration Studies, 1975.

Vecoli, Rudolph J. "Contandini in Chicago: A Critique of *The Uprooted.*" *Journal of American History* 51(1964): 404–17.

Wrobel, Paul. *Our Way: Family, Parish and Neighborhood in a Polish-American Community.* Notre Dame, Ind.: University of Notre Dame Press, 1979.

SOCIAL SCIENCE THEORY

Berger, Peter L. *Facing Up to Modernity: Excursions in Society, Politics, and Religion.* New York: Basic Books, 1977.

———. *The Heretical Imperative: Contemporary Possibilities of Religious Affirmation.* Garden City, N.Y.: Doubleday, 1979.

———. *A Rumor of Angels: Modern Society and the Rediscovery of the Supernatural.* Garden City, N.Y.: Doubleday, 1969.

———. *The Sacred Canopy: Elements of a Sociological Theory of Religion.* Garden City, N.Y.: Doubleday, 1967.

Berger, Peter L., and Richard J. Neuhaus. *To Empower People: The Role of Mediating Structures in Public Policy.* Washington: American Enterprise Institute, 1977.

Douglas, Mary. *Natural Symbols: Explorations in Cosmology.* New York: Pantheon Books, 1970.

Robertson, Roland. *The Sociological Interpretation of Religion.* New York: Schocken, 1970.

Wallace, Anthony F. C. "Paradigmatic Processes in Cultural Change." In *Rockdale: The Growth of an American Village in the Early Industrial Revolution.* New York: Knopf, 1978. Pp. 477–85.

———. *Religion: An Anthropological View.* New York: Random House, 1966.

Wilson, John F. *Religion in American Society: The Effective Presence.* Englewood Cliffs, N.J.: Prentice Hall, 1978.

DUTCH-AMERICAN HISTORY

Beets, Henry. *De Christelijke Gereformeerde Kerk in Noord Amerika: Zestig Jaren van Strijd en Zegen.* Grand Rapids: Grand Rapids Printing Company, 1918.

Bratt, John H. "The Missionary Enterprise of the Christian Reformed Church of America." Th.D. diss., Union Theological Seminary, 1955.

Brinks, Herbert J. "The CRC and RCA: A Study of Comparative Cultural Adaptation in America." Paper presented at the Great Lakes History Conference, Grand Rapids, May, 1979.

———, ed. "Guide to the Dutch-American Historical Collections of Western Michigan." Grand Rapids and Holland, Mich.: Dutch-American Historical Commission, 1967.

Bruins, Elton J. *The Americanization of a Congregation.* Grand Rapids: Wm. B. Eerdmans Publishing Co., 1970.

_____. "The Church at the West: A Brief Survey of the Origin and Development of the Dutch Reformed Church in the Middle West." *Reformed Review* 20(December 1966): 2–20.

_____. "The Dutch in America: A Bibliographical Guide for Students." Holland, Mich.: Hope College, 1975.

De Jong, Gerald F. *The Dutch in America, 1609–1974.* Boston: Twayne Publishers, 1975.

De Klerk, Peter, and Richard De Ridder, eds. *Perspectives on the Christian Reformed Church: Studies in Its History, Theology, and Ecumenicity.* Grand Rapids: Baker Book House, 1983.

Eenigenburg, Elton M. *A Brief History of the Reformed Church in America.* Grand Rapids: Douma Publications, n.d.

Ganzevoort, Herman, and Mark Boekelman, eds. *Dutch Immigration to North America.* Toronto: Multicultural History Society of Ontario, 1983.

Hall, Joseph. "The Controversy Over Fundamentalism in the Christian Reformed Church." Th.D. diss., Concordia Theological Seminary, 1974.

Harmelink, Herman, III. *Ecumenism and the Reformed Church.* Grand Rapids: Wm. B. Eerdmans Publishing Co., 1968.

Heideman, Eugene. "The Descendants of Van Raalte." *Reformed Review* 12(March 1959): 33–42.

Kirk, Gordon W., Jr. *The Promise of American Life: Social Mobility in a Nineteenth Century Immigrant Community: Holland, Michigan.* Philadelphia: American Philosophical Society, 1978.

Kromminga, Dietrich H. *The Christian Reformed Tradition: From the Reformation to the Present.* Grand Rapids: Wm. B. Eerdmans Publishing Company, 1943.

Kromminga, John H. *The Christian Reformed Church: A Study in Orthodoxy.* Grand Rapids: Baker Book House, 1949.

Lucas, Henry S., ed. *Dutch Immigrant Memoirs and Related Writings.* 2 vols. Assen, the Netherlands: Van Gorcum Press, 1955.

_____. *Netherlanders in America.* Ann Arbor: University of Michigan Press, 1955.

Luidens, John P. "The Americanization of the Dutch Reformed Church." Ph.D. diss., University of Oklahoma, 1969.

Mol, Johannes J. *The Breaking of Traditions: Theological Convictions in Colonial America.* Berkeley: Glendessary Press, 1968.

Mulder, Arnold. *Americans From Holland.* The Peoples of America Series, ed. Louis Adamic. Philadelphia: J. B. Lippincott Company, 1947.

Post, Ernest H., Jr. "A Century of Ecumenical and Unionist Tendencies in the Reformed Church in America: 1850–1950." Ph.D. diss., Michigan State University, 1966.

Reformed Church in America. *Tercentenary Studies, 1928.* N.p., 1928.

Stob, George. "The Christian Reformed Church and Her Schools." Th.D. diss., Princeton Theological Seminary, 1955.

Swierenga, Robert P. "The Impact of Reformed Dutch Immigrants on the American Reformed Churches in the Nineteenth Century." Paper presented to the American Society of Church History, Toronto, Canada, 18 April 1975.

_____. "Local-Cosmopolitan Theory and Immigrant Religion: The Social Bases of the Antebellum Dutch Reformed Schism." *Journal of Social History* 14(Fall 1980): 113–35.

_____, ed. *They Came to Stay: Dutch Immigration to North America, 1782–1982.* New Brunswick, N.J.: Rutgers University Press, 1984.

Swierenga, Robert P., and Harry S. Stout. "Dutch Immigration in the Nineteenth Century, 1820–1877: A Quantitative Overview." *Indiana Social Studies Quarterly* 28(Autumn 1975): 7–34.

Tanis, James. *Dutch Calvinistic Pietism in the Middle Colonies.* The Hague: Martinus Nijhoff, 1968.

Timmerman, John J. *Markings on a Long Journey.* Ed. Rodney J. Mulder and John H. Timmerman. Grand Rapids: Baker Book House, 1982.

_____. *Promises to Keep: A Centennial History of Calvin College.* Grand Rapids: Calvin College and Wm. B. Eerdmans Publishing Co., 1975.

Vanden Berge, Peter, ed. *Historical Directory of the Reformed Church in America, 1628–1965.* New Brunswick, N.J.: Commission on History, Reformed Church in America, 1966.

Vander Stelt, John. *Philosophy and Scripture: A Study in Old Princeton and Westminster Theology.* Marlton, N.J.: Mack Publishing Co., 1978.

Van Halsema, Dick L. "The Rise of Home Missions in the Christian Reformed Church (1857 to the Present)." S.T.M. diss., Union Theological Seminary, 1953.

Van Hinte, Jacob. *Nederlanders in Amerika: Eene Studie over Landverhuizers en Volkplanters in de 19de en 20ste Eeuw in de Vereenigde Staten van Amerika.* Groningen: P. Noordhoff, 1928.

Van Hoeven, James W., ed. *Piety and Patriotism: Bicentennial Studies of the Reformed Church in America, 1776–1976.* Grand Rapids: Wm. B. Eerdmans Publishing Co., 1976.

Vlekke, Bernard H. M., and Henry Beets. *Hollanders Who Helped Build America.* New York: American Biographical Company, 1942.

Zwaanstra, Henry. *Reformed Thought and Experience in a New World: A Study of the Christian Reformed Church and Its American Environment, 1890–1918.* Kampen, the Netherlands: J. H. Kok, 1973.

PERIODICALS

The Banner. Grand Rapids. Vols. 39–115 (1904–1980). Official weekly of the Christian Reformed Church.

The Leader. Holland, Michigan. Vols. 1–27 (1907–1934). Weekly of the western section of the Reformed Church in America.
Superseded by *The Christian Intelligencer-Leader.*

The Christian Intelligencer-Leader. Holland, Michigan. Vols. 28–36 (1934–1943). Official weekly of the Reformed Church in America.
Superseded by *The Church Herald.*

The Church Herald. Holland, Michigan. Vols. 1–37 (1944–1980). Official weekly of the Reformed Church in America.

De Gereformeerde Amerikaan. Holland, Michigan. Vols. 1–20 (1897–1916).

De Gids. Grand Rapids. Vols. 14–18 (January 1906–February 1911).
Superseded by *De Calvinist.*

De Calvinist. Grand Rapids. Vol. 1 (February 1911–February 1912), vols. 4–5 (November 1914–June 1915), vols. 6–8 (January 1916–August 1918).
Superseded by *The Christian Journal.*

The Christian Journal. Grand Rapids. Vols. 8–10 (September 1918–November 1920).

Religion and Culture. Grand Rapids. Vols. 1–6 (May 1919–May 1925).
Superseded by *The Reformed Herald.*

The Witness. Grand Rapids. Vols. 1–4 (December 1921–May 1925).
Superseded by *The Reformed Herald.*

The Reformed Herald. Grand Rapids. Vol. 1 (June 1925–May 1926).

The Calvin Forum. Grand Rapids. Vols. 1–20 (1935–1956).

The Western Seminary Bulletin. Holland, Michigan. Vols. 1–8 (1947–1955).
Superseded by *The Reformed Review.*

The Reformed Review. Holland, Michigan. Vols. 9–33 (1955–1980).

The Reformed Journal. Grand Rapids. Vols. 1–30 (1951–1980).

Torch and Trumpet. Grand Rapids. Vols. 1–20 (1951–1970).
Superseded by *The Outlook.*

The Outlook. Grand Rapids. Vols. 21–30 (1971–1980).

PART ONE: THE NETHERLANDIC BACKGROUND

Secession and Immigration

Algra, H. *Het Wonder van de 19e Eeuw: van vrije kerken en kleine luyden.* Franeker: T. Wever, 1966.

Bosch, J. *Figuren en Aspecten uit de Eeuw der Afscheiding.* Goes: Oosterbaan & Le Cointre, 1952.

Knappert, Laurentius. *Geschiedenis der Nederlandsche Hervormde Kerk Gedurende de 18e en 19e Eeuw.* Vol. II. Amsterdam: Meulenhoff & Co., 1912.

Mulder, Lambert A. *Revolte der Fijnen: De Afscheiding van 1834 als Sociaal Conflict en Sociale Beweging.* Meppel: Boom, 1973.
A sociological study with special attention given to the province of Friesland.

Petersen, William. *Planned Migration: The Social Determinants of the Dutch-Canadian Movement.* University of California Publications in Sociology and Social Institutions, Vol. II. Berkeley and Los Angeles: University of California Press, 1955.
Study of post–World War II Dutch emigration with implications for the earlier movements.

Stoeffler, F. Ernest. *The Rise of Evangelical Pietism.* Leiden: E. J. Brill, 1965.

Stokvis, Pieter R. D. *De Nederlandse Trek Naar Amerika, 1846–1847.* Leiden: Universitaire Pers, 1977.

Ten Zijthoff, G. J. "Het Reveil en de Christelijke Gereformeerde Amerikaanse Nederlanders: Mythe en Realiteit." *Nederlandse Theologisch Tijdschrift* 21(1966): 19–42.

Vries, Ph. de. "De Nederlandse cultuur in de eerste helft van de 18e eeuw." In *Algemeene Geschiedenis der Nederlanden,* vol. 7, ed. J. A. van Houtte, et al. Utrecht: W. De Haan, 1964.

Weerden, J. S. van. *Spanningen en Konflicten: Verkenningen rondom de Afscheiding van 1834.* Groningen: Sasland, 1967.

Weiler, A. G., Otto J. de Jong, L. J. Rogier, and C. W. Mönnich. *Geschiedenis van de Kerk in Nederland.* Utrecht and Antwerp: Aula-Boeken, 1963.

The Reveil

Capadose, Abraham. *Le Despotisme Consideré Comme le Developpement Natural du Système Liberal. . . .* Amsterdam: J. H. den Ouden, 1830.

Costa, Isaac da. *Bezwaren tegen den Geest der Eeuw.* Leiden: L. Herdingh en Zoon, 1823.

Groen van Prinsterer, Guillaume. "The Anti-Revolutionary Principle." In *La Partie Anti-Revolutionaire et Confessionale dans l'Eglise Reformeé des Pays Bas* (1860). Trans. J. Faber. Grand Rapids, 1956. (Mimeographed.)

————. *Ongeloof en Revolutie: Een Reeks van Historische Voorlezingen.* Ed. by P. A. Diepenhorst. Kampen: J. H. Kok, 1922.
A series of historical lectures originally delivered in 1848.

Does, J. C. van der. *Bijdrage tot de Geschiedenis der Wording van de Anti-Revolutionaire of Christelijk-Historische Staatspartij.* Amsterdam: W. Ten Have, 1925.

Kluit, M. Elizabeth. *Het Protestantse Reveil in Nederland en Daarbuiten, 1815–1865.* Amsterdam: Paris, 1970.

Neo-Calvinism: Primary Works

Bavinck, Herman. *De Algemeene Genade.* Kampen: G. Ph. Zalsman, 1894.
Rectoral address at the Theological School at Kampen.

_____. *Christelijke Wereldbeschouwing*. Kampen: J. H. Bos, 1904.
Rectoral address at the Vrije Universiteit at Amsterdam.
_____. "Christendom en Natuurwetenschap" and "De Navolging van Christus en het Moderne Leven." In *Kennis en Leven: opstellen en artikelen uit vroegere jaren.* Kampen: J. H. Kok, 1922.
_____. *The Philosophy of Revelation*. New York: Longmans, Green, and Co., 1909. The Stone Lectures at Princeton University, 1908.
Kuyper, Abraham. *Antirevolutionaire Staatkunde: Met Nadere Toelichting op Ons Program.* 2 vols. Kampen: J. H. Kok, 1916–1917.
_____. "Calvinism: The Origin and Safeguard of Our Constitutional Liberties." *Bibliotheca Sacra* 52(1895): 385–410, 646–75.
_____. *Christianity and the Class Struggle*. Trans. Dirk Jellema. Grand Rapids: Piet Hein Publishers, 1950.
_____. *De Christus en de Sociale Nooden en Demokratische Klippen*. Amsterdam: J. A. Wormser, 1895.
_____. *Conservatisme en Orthodoxie: Valsche en Ware Behoudzucht*. Amsterdam: H. De Hoogh & Co., 1870.
Kuyper's stinging farewell address to his congregation in Utrecht.
_____. *Eenvormigheid, de Vloek van het Moderne Leven*. Amsterdam: H. De Hoogh, 1869.
_____. *De Gemeene Gratie*. 3 vols. Amsterdam: Höveker & Wormser, 1902–1904.
_____. *Lectures on Calvinism*. Grand Rapids: Wm. B. Eerdmans Publishing Co., 1961. The Stone Lectures at Princeton University, 1898.
_____. *Het Modernisme een Fata Morgana op Christelijk Gebied*. Amsterdam: H. de Hoogh & Co., 1871.
_____. *Niet de Vrijheidsboom maar het Kruis*. Amsterdam: J. A. Wormser, 1889.
_____. *Ons Instinctieve Leven*. Amsterdam: W. Kirchner, 1908.
_____. *The Practice of Godliness*. Trans. and ed. Marian M. Schoolland. Grand Rapids: Wm. B. Eerdmans Publishing Co., 1945.
Gleaned from Kuyper's devotional column in the church weekly, *De Heraut.*
_____. *Pro Rege, of Het Koningschap van Christus*. 3 vols. Kampen: J. H. Kok, 1911–1912.
_____. *Souvereiniteit in Eigen Kring*. Amsterdam: J. H. Kruyt, 1880.
Address at the founding of the Vrije Universiteit.
_____. *To Be Near unto God*. Trans. John Hendrik de Vries. Grand Rapids: Wm. B. Eerdmans Publishing Co., 1924.
_____. *De Verflauwing der Grenzen*. Amsterdam: J. A. Wormser, 1892.
Rectoral address at the Vrije Universiteit.

Neo-Calvinism: Secondary Works

Bremmer, R. H. *Herman Bavinck als Dogmaticus*. Kampen: J. H. Kok, 1961.
_____. *Herman Bavinck en zijn Tijdgenooten*. Kampen: J. H. Kok, 1966.
Abundant insights into his life and times.
Bulhof, Ilse. "The Netherlands," in Thomas F. Glick, ed., *The Comparative Reception of Darwinism*. Austin: University of Texas Press, 1972.
Fogarty, Michael P. *Christian Democracy in Western Europe: 1820–1953*. Notre Dame, Ind.: University of Notre Dame Press, 1957.
Haitjema, Theodorus Lambertus. "Abraham Kuyper und die Theologie des Holländischen Neucalvinismus." *Zwischen den Zeiten* 9(1931): 331–54.
A Neo-Orthodox critique.
Jellema, Dirk. "Abraham Kuyper's Attack on Liberalism." *Review of Politics* 19(October 1957): 472–85.
The best English introduction.

————. "Abraham Kuyper: Forgotten Radical?" *Calvin Forum* 15(May 1950): 211–13.

Kasteel, P. *Abraham Kuyper.* Kampen: J. H. Kok, 1938.
The standard biography, written by a Catholic.

Ridderbos, Simon Jan. *De Theologische Cultuurbeschouwing van Abraham Kuyper.* Kampen: J. H. Kok, 1947.
An "insider's" distillation and commentary.

Romein, Jan. "Abraham Kuyper: De Klokkenist der Kleine Luyden." In *Erflaters van Onze Beschaving,* by Jan and Annie Romein. Amsterdam: Em. Queridos, 1971.
The finest short study in Dutch; again, written by an "outsider."

Shetter, William Z. *The Pillars of Society: Six Centuries of Civilization in the Netherlands.* The Hague: Nijhoff, 1971.

Westra, Johan. "Confessional Parties in the Netherlands, 1813–1946." Ph.D. diss., University of Michigan, 1972.

Zuidema, S. U. "Common Grace and Christian Action in Abraham Kuyper." In *Communication and Confrontation.* Assen/Kampen: Van Gorcum/Kok, 1972. Pp. 52–105.

PART TWO: DUTCH, REFORMED, AND AMERICAN: DEFINITIONS, 1900–1916

Sermons

Beuker, Hendericus. *Leerredenen.* Holland, Mich.: H. Holkeboer and H. Brink, 1901.

Ministers of the Reformed Church in America. *Messages from the Word.* Holland, Mich.: Holland Printing Company, 1912.

Predikanten der Christelijke Gereformeerde Kerk in Noord Amerika. *Tot de Volmaking der Heiligen: Achttiental Leerredenen.* . . . Holland, Mich.: Holland Printing Co., 1911.

————. *Uit Eigen Kring: Twee-en-vijftig Leerredenen.* Grand Rapids: J. B. Hulst, 1903.

————. *Van de Onzen: Eerste Twaalftal Leerredenen.* Grand Rapids: B. Sevensma, 1910.

Predikanten der Gereformeerde Kerk in Amerika. *Leerredenen.* Holland, Mich.: Holland Printing Company, 1912.

Van Lonkhuyzen, John. "De Fundamenten Omgestooten." Grand Rapids: L. Kregel, Uitgever, 1913.

————. *Koop de Waarheid en Verkoop Ze Niet.* Den Haag: J. Bootsma, [1909].

Books and Pamphlets

Beets, Henry. *Abraham Lincoln: zijn tijd en leven.* Grand Rapids: J. B. Hulst and B. Sevensma, 1909.

————. *Het Leven van William McKinley.* Holland, Mich.: H. Holkeboer, 1901.

Berkhof, Louis. *Christendom en Leven.* Grand Rapids: Eerdmans-Sevensma Co., 1916.

————. *The Christian Laborer in the Industrial Struggle.* Grand Rapids: Eerdmans-Sevensma Co., 1916.

————. *The Church and Social Problems.* Grand Rapids: Eerdmans-Sevensma Co., 1913.

Diekema, Gerrit Jan. Speeches. Archives, Netherlands Museum, Holland, Mich.

Engelmann, Larry. "Dry Renaissance: The Local Option Years, 1889–1917." *Michigan History* 59(1975): 69–90.

Gaffin, Richard B., Jr., ed. *Redemptive History and Biblical Interpretation: The Shorter Writings of Geerhardus Vos*. Phillipsburg, N.J.: Presbyterian and Reformed Publishing Co., 1980.

Hulst, Lammert J., and Gerrit K. Hemkes. *Oud- en Nieuw-Calvinisme: Tweeledige inlichting voor ons Hollandsche Volk. . . .* Grand Rapids: Eerdmans-Sevensma Co., 1913.

Kuiper, Barend Klaas. *Ons Opmaken en Bouwen*. Grand Rapids: Eerdmans-Sevensma, 1918.

   Originally a series of articles on Americanization published in the *Banner*, 1911–1914.

————. "Orthodoxy and Christianity." Calvin College *Chimes*, June 1910 (supplement).

————. *The Proposed Calvinistic College at Grand Rapids*. Grand Rapids: B. Sevensma, 1903.

Kuiper, Rienck Bouke. *Christian Liberty*. Grand Rapids: Eerdmans-Sevensma Co., 1914.

Kuyper, Abraham. *Varia Americana*. Amsterdam: Höveker & Wormser, 1899.

Semi-Centennial Committee of the Christian Reformed Church. *Gedenkboek van het Vijftigjarig Jubileum der Christelijke Gereformeerde Kerk: A.D. 1857–1907*. Grand Rapids: Hulst-Sevensma, 1907.

Steffens, Nicholas M. "Calvinism and the Theological Crisis." *Presbyterian and Reformed Review* 12(April 1901): 211–25.

————. "The Christian View with Regard to the Sins and Disorders of the World." Holland, Mich.: Western Social Conference of the Reformed Church in America, 1910.

Vander Hill, C. Warren. *Gerrit J. Diekema*. Grand Rapids: William B. Eerdmans, Publisher, 1970.

Van Lonkhuyzen, John. "Abraham Kuyper: A Modern Calvinist." *Princeton Theological Review* 19(January 1921): 131–47.

————. *Billy Sunday: Een Beeld uit het Tegenwoordige Amerikaansche Godsdienstige Leven*. Grand Rapids: Eerdmans-Sevensma, 1916.

————. "Het Recht van Werkstaking." Grand Rapids: J. C. Smit, 1913.

Ziewacz, Lawrence E. "The Progress of Woman Suffrage in Nineteenth Century Michigan." *Journal of the Great Lakes History Conference* 2(1979): 29–39.

PART THREE: WARS WITHOUT AND WITHIN, 1917–1928

The Dutch and World War I

De Jong, Ymen P. *Daden des Heeren: Drie Leerredenen Gehouden in verband met den Wereld Oorlog 1914–1919*. Grand Rapids: n.p., 1919.

Kuiper, Barend K. *De Groote Oorlog*. Grand Rapids: Eerdmans-Sevensma Co., 1919.

————. *De Vier Paarden uit Openbaring*. Grand Rapids: Eerdmans-Sevensma Co., 1918.

Kuiper, Rienck B. *While the Bridegroom Tarries: Ten After-the-War Sermons on the Signs of the Times*. Grand Rapids: The Van Noord Book and Publishing Co., 1919.

Tanis, Edward J. "The Church, the Christian, and the War." Grand Rapids: Louis Kregel, Publisher, 1917.

The Bultema Case

Acta der Synode 1918 van de Christelijke Gereformeerde Kerk.
Berkhof, Louis. *Premillennialisme: Zijn Schriftuurlijke Basis en Enkele van zijn Prac-tische Gevolgtrekkingen.* Grand Rapids: Eerdmans-Sevensma Co., 1918.
Bultema, Harry. *Maranatha! Eene Studie over de Onvervulde Profetie.* Grand Rapids: Eerdmans-Sevensma Co., Publishers, [1917].
De Jong, Ymen P. *De Komende Christus: Eene Studie ter Weerlegging van de Grond-stellingen van het Pre-Millennialisme.* Grand Rapids: The Van Noord Book and Publishing Co., 1920.

The Janssen Case

Acta der Synode 1922 van de Christelijke Gereformeerde Kerk.
Berkhof, Louis, et al. *Waar Het in de Zaak Janssen Om Gaat.* N.p., [March 1922].
    Reply to Janssen's self-defense.
Boer, Harry R. "Ralph Janssen After Fifty Years . . ." *Reformed Journal* 22(December 1972): 17–22.
————. "Ralph Janssen: The 1922 Loaded Court." *Reformed Journal* 23(January 1973): 22–28.
————. "The Janssen Case: Aftermath." *Reformed Journal* 23(November 1973): 21–24.
    The pro-Janssen case.
Janssen, Ralph. *De Crisis in de Christelijke Gereformeerde Kerk in Amerika: Een Strijdschrift.* Grand Rapids: n.p., 1922 (February).
————. *De Synodale Conclusies.* Grand Rapids: n.p., 1923.
————. *Het Synodal Vonnis en zijn Voorgeschedenis Kerkrechtelijk Beoordeeld.* Grand Rapids: n.p., 1922 (November).
————. *Voorzetting van de Strijd.* Grand Rapids: n.p., 1922 (June).
Kuiper, Barend K. *De Janssen Kwestie en Nog Iets.* Grand Rapids: Eerdmans-Sevensma Co., 1922.
Manni, Jacob, Henry J. Kuiper, Henry Danhof, and Herman Hoeksema. "Report of the Majority Section of the Janssen Investigating Committee." *Reports and Decisions in the Case of Dr. R. Janssen.* Synod of Orange City, Ia., 1922.
Ten Hoor, Foppe M., William Heyns, Louis Berkhof, and Samuel Volbeda. *Nadere Toelichting omtrent de Zaak Janssen.* Holland, Mich.: Holland Printing Company, [1920].
    The opening public attack on Janssen.
Van Lonkhuyzen, John, Gerrit Hoeksema, and Dietrich H. KrOmminga. "Report of the Minority Section of the Janssen Investigating Committee." *Reports and Decisions in the Case of Dr. R. Janssen.* Synod of Orange City, Ia., 1922.

The Hoeksema Case

Acta der Synode 1924 der Christelijke Gereformeerde Kerk.
Berkhof, Louis. *De Drie Punten in Alle Deelen Gereformeerd.* Grand Rapids: Wm. B. Eerdmans Publishing Co., 1925.
    The Establishment defense against Hoeksema.
Bronkema, Fred. "The Doctrine of Common Grace in Reformed Theology, or New Calvinism and the Doctrine of Common Grace." Th.D. diss., Harvard University, 1928.
    Pronouncedly anti-Hoeksema.
Bultema, Harry. *Wat zegt de Schrift van de Algemeene Gratie?* Muskegon, Mich.: Bereer Publication Committee, 1925.

Danhof, Henry. *De Idee van het Genadeverbond.* Grand Rapids: The Van Noord Book and Publishing Company, 1920.
An early attack on common grace.
Hoeksema, Gertrude. *Therefore Have I Spoken: A Biography of Herman Hoeksema.* Grand Rapids: Reformed Free Publishing Association, 1969.
Hoeksema, Herman. *The Protestant Reformed Churches in America: Their Origin, Early History, and Doctrine.* Grand Rapids: First Protestant Reformed Church, [1936].
_____. *Van Zonde en Genade.* Kalamazoo, Mich.: n.p., [1923].
Hoeksema, Herman, and Henry Danhof. *Niet Doopersch Maar Gereformeerd.* N.p., [1922].
Kuiper, Henry J. *The Three Points of Common Grace: Three Sermons. . . .* Grand Rapids: Wm. B. Eerdmans Publishing Co., 1925.
Another Establishment defense against Hoeksema.
Kuiper, Herman. *Calvin on Common Grace.* Goes, the Netherlands: Oosterbaan & Le Cointre, 1928.
An academic treatise tending against Hoeksema.
Van Baalen, Jan Karel. *De Loochening der Gemeene Gratie: Gereformeerd of Doopersch?* Grand Rapids: Eerdmans-Sevensma Co., 1922.
_____. *Nieuwigheid en Dwaling: De Loochening der Gemeene Gratie Nogmaals Gewogen en te Licht Bevonden.* Grand Rapids: Eerdmans-Sevensma Co., 1923.
The foremost anti-Hoeksema tracts.

Pronouncements on Worldliness

Agenda of the Synod of the Christian Reformed Church, 1928.
Kuiper, Rienck B. *"Not of the World": Discourses on the Christian's Relation to the World.* Grand Rapids: Wm. B. Eerdmans Publishing Company, 1929.
Tuuk, Edward J. *As To Being Worldly.* Grand Rapids: Wm. B. Eerdmans Publishing Co., 1927.

PART FOUR: THE CONSOLIDATED COMMUNITY, 1928–1948

Sermons and Commentaries

Beets, Henry. *The Man of Sorrows: A Series of Lenten Sermons.* Grand Rapids: Wm. B. Eerdmans Publishing Company, 1935.
Berkhof, Louis. *The Assurance of Faith.* Grand Rapids: Wm. B. Eerdmans Publishing Co., 1939.
_____. *Riches of Divine Grace: Ten Expository Sermons.* Grand Rapids: Wm. B. Eerdmans Publishing Co., 1948.
Blekkink, Evert J. *The Fatherhood of God.* Grand Rapids: Wm. B. Eerdmans Publishing Co., 1942.
Blocker, Simon. *When Christ Takes Over.* Grand Rapids: Wm. B. Eerdmans Publishing Co., 1945.
Dykstra, John A. *Heavenly Days.* Grand Rapids: Wm. B. Eerdmans Publishing Co., 1944.
Kruithof, Bastian. *The High Points of Calvinism.* Grand Rapids: Baker Book House, 1949.
Kuiper, Henry J., ed. *Sermons on Sin and Grace.* Grand Rapids: Zondervan Publishing House, 1937.

————. *Sermons on the Apostles' Creed*. Grand Rapids: Zondervan Publishing House, 1937.

————. *Sermons on the Ten Commandments*. Grand Rapids: Zondervan Publishing House, 1951.

Masselink, William. *Sermons on the Ten Commandments*. Grand Rapids: Zondervan Publishing House, 1934.

Mulder, Bernard J. *The King Came Riding: The Challenge of Holy Week*. Grand Rapids: Wm. B. Eerdmans Publishing Co., 1943.

Tanis, Edward H. *Behind the Opened Hedge: Meditations on the Book of Job*. Grand Rapids: Zondervan Publishing House, 1941.

Van Baalen, Jan Karel. *The Heritage of the Fathers*. Grand Rapids: Wm. B. Eerdmans Publishing Co., 1948.
    A commentary on the Heidelberg Catechism.

————. *The Journey of Man and Other Sermons*. Grand Rapids: Wm. B. Eerdmans Publishing Co., 1935.

Popular Novels

Gardner, Joan Geisel. *Desires of the Heart*. Grand Rapids: Zondervan Publishing House, 1934.

Gosselink, Sara E. *Roofs Over Strawtown*. Grand Rapids: Wm. B. Eerdmans Publishing Co., 1945.

Kruithof, Bastian. *Instead of the Thorn*. New York: Half-Moon Press, 1941.

Kuipers, Cornelius. *Deep Snow: An Indian Story*. Grand Rapids: Zondervan Publishing House, 1934.

Maltzahn, Elizabeth von. *Erich Ohlson*. Grand Rapids: Wm. B. Eerdmans Publishing Co., 1932.
    Translation of German novel long popular in Dutch as *Op Vasten Grond*.

Vanden Berg, Frank. *Westhaven*. Grand Rapids: Wm. B. Eerdmans Publishing Co., 1943.

Doctrinal and Controversial Works

Berkhof, Louis. *Manual of Reformed Doctrine*. Grand Rapids: Wm. B. Eerdmans Publishing Co., 1933.

————. *Reformed Dogmatics*. 3 vols. Grand Rapids: Wm. B. Eerdmans Publishing Co., 1932.

Bouma, Clarence. "Calvinism in American Theology Today." *Journal of Religion* 27(1947): 34–45.

Hendriksen, William. *The Covenant of Grace*. Grand Rapids: Wm. B. Eerdmans Publishing Co., 1932.

————. *More Than Conquerors: An Interpretation of the Book of Revelation*. Grand Rapids: Baker's Book Store, 1940.

Kromminga, Dietrich H. *The Millennium in the Church: Studies in the History of Christian Chiliasm*. Grand Rapids: Wm. B. Eerdmans Publishing Co., 1945.

Pieters, Albertus. *The Facts and Mysteries of the Christian Faith*. Grand Rapids: Wm. B. Eerdmans Publishing Co., 1926.

————. *Studies in the Revelation of St. John*. Grand Rapids: Wm. B. Eerdmans Publishing Co., 1954.
    Originally published in 1936 as *The Lamb, the Woman, and the Dragon*.

Van Til, Cornelius. *The New Modernism: An Appraisal of the Theology of Barth and Brunner*. Philadelphia: The Presbyterian and Reformed Publishing Co., 1946.

Wyngaarden, Martin J. *The Future of the Kingdom in Prophecy and Fulfillment: A*

Study of the Scope of "Spiritualization" in Scripture. Grand Rapids: Zondervan Publishing House, 1934.

Historical Studies

Bronkema, Ralph. *The Essence of Puritanism.* Goes: Oosterbaan & Le Cointre, [1929].

Burggraaff, Winfield. *The Rise and Development of Liberal Theology in America.* Goes: Oosterbaan and Le Cointre, 1928.

Danhof, Ralph J. *Charles Hodge as a Dogmatician.* Goes: Oosterbaan and Le Cointre, [1929].

De Jong, Peter Y. *The Covenant Idea in New England Theology, 1620–1847.* Grand Rapids: Wm. B. Eerdmans Publishing Co., 1945.

Masselink, William. *Professor J. Gresham Machen: His Life and Defense of the Faith.* Published by the author, [1938].

Cultural and Social Affairs

Berkhof, Louis. *Aspects of Liberalism.* Grand Rapids: Wm. B. Eerdmans Publishing Co., 1951.
    Distillation of earlier speeches and articles.

De Boer, Cecil. *The If's and Ought's of Ethics: A Preface to Moral Philosophy.* Grand Rapids: Wm. B. Eerdmans Publishing Co., 1936.

_____. *Responsible Protestantism.* Grand Rapids: Wm. B. Eerdmans Publishing Co., 1957.
    Largely composed of articles written several years before in the *Calvin Forum.*

De Vries, John. *Beyond the Atom: An Appraisal of Our Christian Faith in This Age of Atomic Science.* Grand Rapids: Wm. B. Eerdmans Publishing Co., 1948.

Jaarsma, Cornelius. *The Educational Philosophy of Herman Bavinck: A Textbook in Education.* Grand Rapids: Wm. B. Eerdmans Publishing Co., 1935.

Kruithof, Bastian. *The Christ of the Cosmic Road: The Significance of the Incarnation.* Grand Rapids: Wm. B. Eerdmans Publishing Co., 1937.

Kuizenga, John E. *Relevancy of the Pivot Points of the Reformed Faith.* Grand Rapids: Society for Reformed Publications, 1951.
    A speech originally delivered in 1941.

Meeter, H. Henry. *Calvinism: An Interpretation of Its Basic Ideas.* Grand Rapids: Zondervan Publishing House, 1939.
    A mild summary of the political and theological ideas of Neo-Calvinism.

Monsma, Nicholas J. *The Trial of Denominationalism.* Grand Rapids: Wm. B. Eerdmans Publishing Co., 1932.

Pieters, Albertus. *The Christian Attitude Toward War.* Grand Rapids: Wm. B. Eerdmans Publishing Co., 1932.

Putt, James. *A Good Soldier of the Lord Jesus Christ.* Published by the author, 1943.

Tanis, Edward J. *Calvinism and Social Problems.* Grand Rapids: Zondervan Publishing House, [1936].

PART FIVE: REBELLION AND REFRACTION

Arnold Mulder

1913 *The Dominie of Harlem.* Chicago: A. C. McClurg & Co.

1915 *Bram of the Five Corners.* Chicago: A. C. McClurg & Co.

1919 *The Outbound Road*. Boston and New York: Houghton Mifflin.
1921 *The Sand Doctor*. Boston and New York: Houghton Mifflin.
1947 *Americans From Holland*. Philadelphia: J. B. Lippincott.

David Cornel De Jong

1934 *Belly Fulla Straw*. New York: Alfred A. Knopf.
1938 *Old Haven*. Boston: Houghton Mifflin.
1940 *Light Sons and Dark*. New York: Harper and Brothers.
1941 *Day of the Trumpet*. New York: Harper and Brothers.
1942 *Benefit Street*. New York: Harper and Brothers.
1943 *Across the Board: Poems*. New York: Harper and Brothers.
1944 *With a Dutch Accent: How a Hollander Became an American*. New York: Harper
     and Brothers.
1945 *Somewhat Angels*. New York: Reynal and Hitchcock.
1946 *Snow-on-the-Mountain and Other Stories*. New York: Reynal and Hitchcock.
1949 *The Desperate Children*. Garden City, N.Y.: Doubleday.
1952 *Two Sofas in the Parlor*. Garden City, N.Y.: Doubleday.
1959 *The Unfairness of Easter and Other Stories*. San Jose: The Talisman Press.
1961 *Outside the Four Walls of Everything*. Baltimore: Linden Press.

Frederick F. Manfred

1944 *The Golden Bowl*. St. Paul: The Webb Publishing Company.
1945 *Boy Almighty*. St. Paul: The Itasca Press.
1947 *This is the Year*. Garden City, N.Y.: Doubleday.
1948 *The Chokecherry Tree*. Garden City, N.Y.: Doubleday.
1954 *Lord Grizzly*. New York: Random House.
1956 *Morning Red: A Romance*. Denver: Alan Swallow.
1957 *Riders of Judgment*. New York: Random House.
1959 *Conquering Horse*. New York: McDowell, Oblonsky.
1961 *Arrow of Love*. Denver: Alan Swallow.
1962 *Wanderlust*. Denver: Alan Swallow.Originally published as the trilogy *World's
     Wanderer: The Primitive* (1949), *The Brother* (1950), and *The Giant* (1951).
     Garden City, N.Y.: Doubleday.
1964 *Scarlet Plume*. New York: Trident Press.
1966 *King of Spades*. New York: Trident Press.
1967 *Apples of Paradise and Other Stories*. New York: Trident Press.
1968 *Eden Prairie*. New York: Trident Press.
1976a *Manly-Hearted Woman*. New York: Crown.
1976b *Milk of Wolves*. Boston: Avenue Victor Hugo.
1977 *Green Earth*. New York: Crown.
1979 *The Wind Blows Free*. Sioux Falls, S. Dak.: Center for Western Studies.
1980 *Sons of Adam*. New York: Crown.

Peter De Vries

1954 *The Tunnel of Love*. Boston: Little, Brown, and Company. [All De Vries's novels
     are published by this house.]
1956 *Comfort Me With Apples*
1958 *The Mackerel Plaza*
1959 *The Tents of Wickedness*
1961 *Through Fields of Clover*
1962 *The Blood of the Lamb*

1964 *Reuben, Reuben*
1965 *Let Me Count the Ways*
1967 *The Vale of Laughter*
1968 *The Cat's Pajamas & Witch's Milk*
1970 *Mrs. Wallop*
1971 *Into Your Tent I'll Creep*
1973 *Forever Panting*
1974 *The Glory of the Hummingbird*
1976 *I Hear America Swinging*
1977 *Madder Music*
1980 *Consenting Adults; or, The Duchess Will Be Furious*
1981 *Sauce for the Goose*
1983 *Slouching Towards Kalamazoo*

Interviews and Critical Studies

Davies, Douglas M. "An Interview with Peter DeVries." *College English* 28(April 1967): 524–28.
Flora, Joseph M. *Frederick Manfred*. Boise: Boise State University, 1974.
Fowlie, Wallace. "The Cogent Land." Review of *Across the Board: Poems*, by David C. DeJong. *Poetry* 62 (June 1943): 170–72.
Jellema, Roderick. *Peter DeVries*. Contemporary Writers in Christian Perspective Series. Grand Rapids: Wm. B. Eerdmans Publishing Co., 1966.
Manfred, Frederick F. "West of the Mississippi: Interview with Frederick Manfred." *Critique* 2(Winter 1959): 35–56.
Milton, John R., moderator. *Conversations with Frederick Manfred*. Salt Lake City: University of Utah Press, 1974.
    Transcript of television interviews with Manfred some ten years earlier.
———. "Frederick Feikema Manfred." *Western Review* 27(Spring 1958): 181–99.
Roth, Russell. "The Inception of a Saga: Frederick Manfred's 'Buckskin Man.'" *South Dakota Review* 7(Winter 1969–70): 87–97.
Ter Maat, Cornelius. "Three Novelists and a Community: A Study of American Novelists with Dutch Calvinist Origins." Ed.D. diss., University of Michigan, 1963.
Wright, Robert C. *Frederick Manfred*. Twayne United States Authors Series, no. 336. Boston: Twayne Publishers, 1979.

PART SIX: AT HOME AND UNEASY, 1948–1970s

Chapter 12: Americanization Again, 1948–1963

Bast, Henry. *An Appeal to the Ministers and Laymen of the Chicago and Iowa Synods*. Grand Rapids: Don Van Ostenburg, [1946].
———. "The Authority of the Bible." Grand Rapids: Society for Reformed Publications, 1951.
———. *The Lord's Prayer*. Grand Rapids: The Church Press, 1957.
———. "The Ordination Vows of Ministers and Elders." Grand Rapids: Evangelical Fund, 1947.
Berkhof, Louis. *The Kingdom of God: The Development of the Idea of the Kingdom, Especially Since the Eighteenth Century*. Grand Rapids: Wm. B. Eerdmans Publishing Co., 1951.

Boer, Harry R. *Pentecost and Missions*. Grand Rapids: Wm. B. Eerdmans Publishing Co., 1961.

———. *That My House May Be Filled*. Grand Rapids: Wm. B. Eerdmans Publishing Co., 1957.

Buis, Harry. *The Doctrine of Eternal Punishment*. Philadelphia: Presbyterian and Reformed Publishing Company, 1957.

Calvinistic Action Committee. *God-Centered Living; or, Calvinism in Action*. Grand Rapids: Baker Book House, 1951.

Daane, James. *A Theology of Grace*. Grand Rapids: Wm. B. Eerdmans Publishing Co., 1954.

———. *The Freedom of God: A Study of Election and Pulpit*. Grand Rapids: Wm. B. Eerdmans Publishing Co., 1973.

De Jong, Alexander C. *The Well-Meant Gospel Offer: The Views of K. Schilder and H. Hoeksema*. Franeker: T. Wever, 1954.

De Koster, Lester. *All Ye That Labor: An Essay on Christianity, Communism, and the Problem of Evil*. Grand Rapids: Wm. B. Eerdmans Publishing Co., 1956.

Geehan, E. R., ed. *Jerusalem and Athens: Critical Discussions on the Theology and Apologetics of Cornelius Van Til*. Nutley, N.J.: Presbyterian and Reformed Publishing Co., 1971.

Girod, Gordon. *The Deeper Faith*. Grand Rapids: Reformed Publications, 1958.

Kik, Henry. "The Federal Council of Churches and the Reformed Faith." N.p., n.d.

Klooster, Fred. *The Significance of Barth's Theology: An Appraisal*. Grand Rapids: Baker Book House, 1961.

Kraay, John, and Anthony Tol, eds. *Hearing and Doing: Philosophical Essays Dedicated to H. Evan Runner*. Toronto: Wedge Publishing Foundation, 1979.

Kuiper, Rienck Bouke. *God-Centered Evangelism*. Grand Rapids: Baker Book House, 1961.

———. *For Whom Did Christ Die?* Grand Rapids: Wm. B. Eerdmans Publishing Co., 1959.

———. *To Be or Not To Be Reformed: Whither the Christian Reformed Church?* Grand Rapids: Zondervan Publishing Co., 1959.

Masselink, William. *General Revelation and Common Grace*. Grand Rapids: Wm. B. Eerdmans Publishing Co., 1953.

Osterman, Gordon, et al. *To Find a Better Life: Aspects of Dutch Immigration to Canada . . . 1920–1970*. Grand Rapids: National Union of Christian Schools, 1975.

Runner, H. Evan. *The Relation of the Bible to Learning*. 3d ed. Toronto: Wedge Publishing Foundation, 1970.

———. *Scriptural Religion and the Political Task*. 3d ed. Toronto: Wedge Publishing Foundation, 1974.

Stob, Henry. *The Christian Conception of Freedom*. Grand Rapids: Grand Rapids International Publications, 1957.

Van Til, Cornelius. *Common Grace*. Philadelphia: Presbyterian and Reformed Publishing Co., 1947.

Van Til, Henry R. *The Calvinistic Concept of Culture*. Grand Rapids: Baker Book House, 1959.

Vander Goot, Henry, ed. *Life is Religion: Essays in Honor of H. Evan Runner*. St. Catharines, Ontario: Paideia Press, 1981.

Verduin, Leonard. *The Reformers and Their Stepchildren*. Grand Rapids: Wm. B. Eerdmans Publishing Co., 1964.

White, William, Jr. *Van Til: Defender of the Faith: An Authorized Biography*. Nashville: Thomas Nelson Publishers, 1979.

Youth and Calvinism Group. *Youth Speaks on Calvinism*. Grand Rapids: Baker Book House, 1948.
————. *Youth Speaks on Christianity and Civilization*. Grand Rapids: Piet Hein Publishers, 1950.
Zylstra, Henry. *Testament of Vision*. Grand Rapids: Wm. B. Eerdmans Publishing Co., 1958.

Chapter 13: Evangelical and Ethnic, 1964–1970s

Berkouwer, Gerrit C. *A Half Century of Theology*. Trans. Lewis B. Smedes. Grand Rapids: Wm. B. Eerdmans Publishing Co., 1977.
Bril, K. A., Hendrik Hart, and Jacob Klapwijk, eds. *The Idea of a Christian Philosophy: Essays in Honor of H. Th. Vollenhoven*. Toronto: Wedge Publishing Foundation, 1973.
Boer, Harry R. *Above the Battle? The Bible and Its Critics*. Grand Rapids: Wm. B. Eerdmans Publishing Co., 1977.
Bruggink, Donald. *Christ and Architecture: Building Presbyterian/Reformed Churches*. Grand Rapids: Wm. B. Eerdmans Publishing Co., 1963.
————. *When Faith Takes Form*. Grand Rapids: Wm. B. Eerdmans Publishing Co., 1971.
————, ed. *Guilt, Grace, and Gratitude: A Commentary on the Heidelberg Catechism*. New York: Half Moon Press, 1963.
Buning, Sietze [Stanley Wiersma]. *Purpaleanie and Other Permutations*. Orange City, Ia.: Middleburg Press, 1978.
De Jong, Peter Y. *The Church's Witness to the World*. Grand Rapids: Baker Book House, 1960.
————. *Crisis in the Reformed Churches: Essays in Commemoration of the Great Synod of Dort, 1618–1619*. Grand Rapids: Reformed Fellowship, 1968.
De Vos, Richard M. *Believe!* Old Tappan, N.J.: Revell, 1975.
Hageman, Howard. *Pulpit and Table: Some Chapters in the History of Worship in the Reformed Churches*. Richmond: John Knox Press, 1962.
Heideman, Eugene P. *Our Song of Hope: A Provisional Confession of Faith of the Reformed Church in America*. Grand Rapids: Wm. B. Eerdmans Publishing Co., 1975.
Hoekema, Anthony. *The Christian Looks at Himself*. Grand Rapids: Wm. B. Eerdmans Publishing Co., 1975.
————. *Holy Spirit Baptism*. Grand Rapids: Wm. B. Eerdmans Publishing Co., 1972.
Holwerda, David. *Neo-Pentecostalism Hits the Church*. Grand Rapids: Christian Reformed Board of Publications, 1974.
Jellema, Roderick. *The Lost Faces*. Washington: Dryad Press, 1979.
————. *Something Tugging at the Line*. Washington: Dryad Press, 1974.
Kalsbeek, L. *Contours of a Christian Philosophy*. Toronto: Wedge Publishing Foundation, 1975.
Kistemaker, Simon. *Interpreting God's Word Today*. Grand Rapids: Baker Book House, 1970.
Mouw, Richard J. *Called to Holy Worldliness*. Philadelphia: Fortress Press, 1980.
————. *Political Evangelism*. Grand Rapids: Wm. B. Eerdmans Publishing Co., 1974.
————. *Politics and the Biblical Drama*. Grand Rapids: Wm. B. Eerdmans Publishing Co., 1976.
Olthuis, John A., et al. *Out of Concern for the Church*. Toronto: Wedge Publishing Foundation, 1970.
Osterhaven, M. Eugene. *The Faith of the Church*. Grand Rapids: Wm. B. Eerdmans Publishing Co., 1971.

————. *The Spirit of the Reformed Tradition*. Grand Rapids: Wm. B. Eerdmans Publishing Co., 1982.

Smedes, Lewis B. *All Things Made New: A Theology of Man's Union with Christ*. Grand Rapids: Wm. B. Eerdmans Publishing Co., 1970.

————. *Love within Limits: A Realist's View of I Corinthians 13*. Grand Rapids: Wm. B. Eerdmans Publishing Co., 1978.

Wells, Ronald, ed. *The Wars of America: Eight Christian Views*. Grand Rapids: Wm. B. Eerdmans Publishing Co., 1981.

Wolterstorff, Nicholas. *Reason Within the Bounds of Religion*. Grand Rapids: Wm. B. Eerdmans Publishing Co., 1976.

Index

Americanization: B. K. Kuiper on, 41, 52, 78; F. M. Ten Hoor on, 50, 52, 58, 271n.18; and 1920s controversies, 98–99, 101, 104, 109, 113–19, 160; pre–World War I formulas for, 40, 43, 54, 56, 63; reflections on in 1970s, 213–14, 219–20; and World War I, 84, 89–90, 92; after World War II, 187, 202, 208

Anabaptism, 97, 100, 108, 110, 112–13, 201

Anti-Revolutionary: Dutch political party, 15, 24, 26, 30, 150; socio-political theory, 26–27, 71, 77. See also Neo-Calvinism

Antithesis: Abraham Kuyper's conception of, 18–20; in interwar period, 124, 126, 131, 156; Klaas Schoolland's conception of, 50, 71; in 1950s controversies, 191–93, 196; in 1920s controversies, 100–101, 103, 110–11, 113, 115

Antithetical Calvinism: as Dutch-American mentality, 47, 50–53, 194–96; in 1920s controversies, 96, 98–101, 103–4, 108, 110, 112, 118; socio-cultural commentary of, after World War II, 200, 209–10, 216; socio-cultural commentary of, before World War I, 61, 63, 72, 74–78; and World War I, 86, 88, 90

Arminianism: and American religion, 59, 132–33, 215, 217; in Dutch-American controversies, 39, 106–7, 114; in the Netherlands, 4, 22

Barth, Karl, 131, 190–91, 197, 213

Bavinck, Herman: career and thought of, 30–31; Dutch-American influence of, 99, 101, 135, 142, 212–14; in 1920s controversies, 97, 107, 110, 112, 115

Beets, Henry: on America, 56, 61, 65, 72, 74, 78; career of, 52–53, 118; piety and ethics of, 53, 64, 71, 117, 136; and positive Calvinism, 47, 52–53; and World War I, 85–86, 89, 91

Benes, Louis H., 130, 155, 189, 198–99, 209

Berger, Peter, 211, 251n.30, 254n.47

Berkhof, Louis: career of, 54, 188, 195; and Reformed doctrine, 60, 134–36, 207; socio-political commentary of, 71–72, 75, 77; and theological controversies, 97, 109, 123, 129, 207

Berkouwer, Gerrit C., 213–14

Biblical infallibility, 106, 134, 207

Blekkink, Evert J., 44–45, 47, 69, 73, 136

Blocker, Simon, 129, 136–37

Boer, Harry, 188, 190, 192, 201

Bouma, Clarence, 131, 134, 287n.12; in 1950s controversies, 188, 190, 192; socio-political commentary of, 90, 149–50, 152, 189; and World War II, 152–55

Bultema, Harry, 95–96, 99, 102, 104–6, 132, 286n.46

Calvin College: and Dutch-American novelists, 160, 163, 170–71, 176; faculty of after World War II, 189, 191, 194, 196, 200, 216; faculty of before World War II, 50, 142, 145, 150; and World Wars, 87, 154

Calvin Theological Seminary: and 1920s controversies, 105, 109, 118; and post–World War II controversies, 187–88, 190–91, 194, 203, 207; before World War I, 48, 54, 77

Capitalism, 25, 29, 75, 119, 148, 150, 190

Catholicism: Abraham Kuyper on, 22, 25, 29, 32, 213; Dutch-Americans on, 44, 49, 116, 199, 285n.37; German-American strain compared to

Dutch Calvinism, 259n.26, 270n.11, 280n.40, 286n.45. *See also* Kennedy, John Fitzgerald
Christian Reformed Church Synod, official actions of: in 1918, 90–91, 97, 102; in 1920s, 105, 109–10, 113–18, 139; before World War I, 47, 78; after World War II, 187, 190, 207–8, 215
Common grace, 53, 71, 124, 126; in the Netherlands, 19–20, 31; in 1950s controversies, 187, 191, 193, 196; in 1920s controversies, 101, 103, 105, 108, 110, 112–15
Communism, 88, 102, 116, 148, 188–90, 198, 201–2. *See also* Socialism
Confessionalism: and American evangelicalism, 215–17; as Dutch-American mentality, 40, 47, 50, 52, 54, 78, 126, 136; in 1920s controversies, 97–99, 106–8, 110, 112–16; in post–World War II controversies, 188, 190–91, 194–95, 197, 199, 203, 207; socio-political attitudes of, 63, 72–75, 90, 93, 208, 210, 271n.19. *See also* Kuiper, Henry J.; Pietism: socio-cultural commentary of; Ten Hoor, F. M.
Conventicles, 3, 6–7, 116

Daane, James, 193, 200, 207
Danhof, Henry, 103, 108–14, 118
De Boer, Cecil, 138, 146, 150, 155, 192
De Cock, Hendrik, 6–7, 47
De Jong, David Cornel, 159, 163–69, 176, 181
De Jong, Ymen P., 93–94, 97, 108
Dekker, Harold, 207–8
De Koster, Lester, 189–90, 200–202, 210
Depression (of 1930s), 123–24, 129, 141, 147, 149–51
De Vries, Peter, 159, 169–70, 176–83, 187, 311n.22, 311n.23
Diekema, Gerrit John, 69–70, 88
Dooyeweerd, Herman, 213–14, 319n.33
Dort, Synod of (1618–19), 4, 6, 46, 200
Douglas, Mary, 309n.7, 323n.51
Dutch immigration: to Canada, 195, 198, 312n.29; to U.S., 14, 37–39, 42, 123, 248n.1, 255n.1, 258n.19, 287n.1; and Secession of 1834, 3, 7–9, 29, 38–40, 245n.28, 246n.29, 246n.34

Enlightenment, 11–12, 18, 31, 149, 196, 200
Evangelicalism, 59, 133, 211, 216–21, 266n.14; and NAE, 133, 200. *See also* Fundamentalism; Methodism
Evolution, theory of, 21–22, 171, 215

Fas et Jus, 64, 72, 78
Federal Council of Churches, 62, 90, 114, 125, 133, 197, 214
Free University. *See* Vrije Universiteit
Fundamentalism: and Dutch-American controversies, 96, 106, 116, 127–28, 200; and Dutch Reformed character, 131–34, 142, 153, 200, 216, 220, 293n.47. *See also* Evangelicalism; Machen, J. Gresham; Presbyterianism: and Orthodox Presbyterian Church

Geerlings, Henry, 47, 62, 67–68, 84, 93, 102, 116, 147
Geldersche school. *See* Secession of 1834
Grand Rapids politics, 64–65, 69, 73, 188, 196, 201. *See also* "Home Front"
Groen van Prinsterer, Guilliaume, 11–12, 20–21, 30, 51, 196
Groen, Johannes, 140; in 1920s controversies, 103, 105, 109, 118–19; as positive Calvinist, 47, 52–54; socio-political commentary of, 76–78

Hageman, Howard, 214–15
Hays, Samuel P., 243n.2, 258n.19, 269n.42
Hervormde Kerk. *See* Nederlandse Hervormde Kerk
Hoeksema, Herman: as Antithetical Calvinist, 102–4, 193; in 1920s controversies, 107–14, 118–19; in World War I, 88–89. *See also* Antithetical Calvinism
"Home Front," 188, 192, 196. *See also* Grand Rapids politics
Hope College, 44–45, 67, 69, 99, 143, 159–160
Hulst, Lammert J., 47–49

Idealism, philosophical, 17, 21, 191, 194, 211, 214
Immigration. *See* Dutch immigration

Janssen, Ralph, 105–10, 112, 114, 119, 125, 131, 262n.51, 286n.46
Jellema, William Harry, 142, 189, 191

Kampen Seminary, 7, 47–48, 196
Kennedy, John Fitzgerald, 202–4, 208
Kolyn, Matthew, 44, 84, 91
Kromminga, Dietrich H., 102, 132, 292n.41
Kruithof, Bastian, 142–43
Kuiper, Barend Klaas: and Americanization, 41, 57, 78, 90, 101; demise of, 118–19, 125, 286n.44, 298n.25; as positive Calvinist, 47, 52–53, 60–61, 99–100, 109
Kuiper, Henry J.: on American religion, 131–33, 136, 199–200; character and career of, 124–26, 195, 208, 286n.46, 390n.7; in 1920s controversies, 108, 118–19; socio-political commentary of, 147–50, 152–55, 189–90, 298n.25; on worldliness, 118–19, 138–39, 190, 202
Kuiper, Rienck Bouke: and post–World War II controversies, 194–95, 207–8; and Westminster Theological Seminary, 128; and World War I–era controversies, 83, 94, 98, 119
Kuizema, Dorr, 65, 76
Kuizenga, John: and 1920s controversies, 99–101, 110; and Reformed doctrine, 128, 131, 134; socio-political commentary of, 143, 154
Kuyper, Abraham: character and career of, 14–17, 19, 28–29, 31–32; cultural critique of, 18, 21–22, 32, 212; in Dutch-American 1920s controversies, 97, 101, 107, 112–15; influence of on cultural critique in Dutch-America, 126, 143–44, 146, 209, 211–12; religious influence in Dutch-America, 46, 48–50, 52–53, 60, 128–30, 135–36, 289n.22; religious principles of, 15–20, 251n.30; socio-political influence of in Dutch America, 55, 62, 70, 87, 141, 149–50, 202; socio-political thought of, 23–30, 32, 251n.30, 254n.47; successors of in Netherlands, 213–14. *See also* Antithetical Calvinism; Kuyperianism; Neo-Calvinism; Positive Calvinism
Kuyperianism: and cultural critique, 54,

142–43, 145, 156, 194, 210–11, 213; and Dutch-American mentalities, 48, 126, 161, 199–201; and Dutch-American theology, 96, 99, 105, 193; and political commentary, 70–71, 74, 149. *See also* Kuyper, Abraham; Neo-Calvinism

Labor question: Abraham Kuyper on, 24–25, 28–30; in Dutch America after World War I, 150, 155, 196, 200–201; in Dutch America before World War I, 74–76, 78, 119
Leader circle. *See* Progressives, RCA

Machen, J. Gresham, 128, 190, 192, 289n.22
McKinley, William, 55–56, 69–70, 78
Manfred, Frederick, 159, 169–76, 181, 296n.2
Masonry, 39, 48, 257n.13
Methodism, 59–61, 97, 127, 129, 217, 266n.14, 322n.50. *See also* Evangelicalism
Modernism: Abraham Kuyper on, 21–22, 211; Dutch-American religious critique of, 54, 127–31, 133–34, 137, 139, 182, 220, 293n.47; Dutch-American socio-cultural critique of, 141–44, 147, 189; in 1920s controversies, 94, 106, 115–16; and World War II, 153–55. *See also* Protestant liberalism
Mulder, Arnold, 159–63, 176
Mulder, Bernard, 136, 151, 153

National Church in the Netherlands. *See* Nederlandse Hervormde Kerk
National Council of Churches. *See* Federal Council of Churches
National Reformed Church. *See* Nederlandse Hervormde Kerk
Nederlandse Hervormde Kerk: and Dutch dissenters, 3, 6–7, 14–15, 29; history of, 4–5, 12, 31, 244n.10; influence in Dutch America, 9, 38–40, 44, 197, 214
Netherlands Reformed Church. *See* Nederlandse Hervormde Kerk
Niebuhr, H. Richard, 131, 212
Niebuhr, Reinhold, 131, 197, 212, 280n.40, 300n.33
Neo-Calvinism: and Dutch-American

cultural critique, 59–60, 145, 213; and Dutch-American mentalities, 47–50, 53–54, 109, 126; and Dutch-American socio-political commentary, 70, 86–87, 142, 147–50, 154; and Dutch-American theology, 43, 47–50, 135–36; in the Netherlands, 14–19, 30–32, 38, 126, 195, 202; in Reformed Church in America, 46, 73. See also Anti-Revolutionary: socio-political theory; Kuyper, Abraham; Kuyperianism

Neo-orthodoxy, 131, 142, 191, 193, 197–98

New Brunswick Theological Seminary, 44, 214

New Deal, 148–49, 151, 201. See also Roosevelt, Franklin Delano

Northern school. See Secession of 1834

Peale, Norman Vincent, 136, 199, 322n.50

Pietism: Dutch-American critique of, 62, 99–100, 110, 193, 215; and Dutch-American devotional, 42; as Dutch-American mentality, 47, 50, 96, 104, 126, 161; Neo-Calvinist critique of, 16, 25, 28, 31, 212; in the Netherlands, 3–4, 38; RCA type of, 44–46, 72, 125, 136–37, 140, 147, 197–99, 209; socio-cultural commentary of after World War I, 140–41, 144, 147, 201, 208–9; socio-cultural commentary of during World War I, 74, 90, 93–94, 271n.19. See also Secession of 1834; Confessionalism

Piety, Dutch-American, 42–43, 45, 58, 133–37, 169, 209, 218

Positive Calvinism: and Americanization, 55, 57, 63, 201, 216–17; as Dutch-American mentality after World War I, 126, 142, 190, 211–12, 216–17, 220; as Dutch-American mentality before World War I, 47, 50, 52, 72–73, 76, 78; in 1950s controversies, 190, 192, 194; in 1920s controversies, 94, 96, 98–99, 101, 105, 112–18; and World War I, 89–90. See also Progressives, CRC

Premillennialism: and Bultema case, 95–98, 103–4; and Dutch-American ac-

culturation, 96, 98, 275n.15, 280n.40; vis à vis Reformed orthodoxy, 132–33, 143. See also Bultema, Harry; Fundamentalism; Kromminga, Dietrich H.

Presbyterianism: and Dutch-American doctrinal controversies, 128, 216, 281n.5, 290n.32; and Orthodox Presbyterian Church, 128, 191, 216; and proposed RCA mergers, 125, 136, 197. See also Machen, J. Gresham

Presuppositionalism, 126, 129, 194, 210. See also Principialism

Princeton Theological Seminary, 54, 107, 128, 190, 193, 288n.21

Principialism: and Abraham Kuyper, 17–19, 21; and American Neo-Calvinism, 50, 53, 63, 70, 131, 156, 211; Dutch-American critique of, 76, 98, 100. See also Presuppositionalism

Progressives, CRC: and Dutch-American mentality after World War II, 190, 192, 200–201, 208, 210; in 1920s controversies, 78, 102, 109, 114, 117–18. See also Positive Calvinism

Progressives, RCA: and Dutch-American mentality, 43–44, 47, 124–25; in 1920s, 98, 102, 115; socio-cultural commentary of, 53, 57, 61, 63, 67, 73, 78; and World War I, 84–86, 92

Progressivism (U.S. political movement, 1895–1920): and Arnold Mulder, 161, 163; and Dutch Americans, 64–67, 119, 269n.42, 273n.35; and World War I, 83, 92, 98, 276n.15

Prohibition, 73–74, 78, 102, 116, 119, 147, 199, 272n.23. See also Temperance

Protestant liberalism: Abraham Kuyper on, 15, 18, 21; Dutch-American critique of, 128–29, 131, 135, 179; and 1920s controversies, 107, 115; and World War I, 94–95, 275n.15. See also Modernism

RCA optimists. See Progressives, RCA

Reformed Church in America General Synod, 39, 205

Reformed Confessions, 46, 91, 132; and Confessionalist party, 48–49, 52, 57, 72; in the Netherlands, 6, 20, 29, 40; in 1920s controversies, 98, 101, 107, 110, 112, 114

Remonstrantism. *See* Arminianism
Reveil, 10–14, 20, 29, 31, 44
Revolution: 5, 11–12, 24; Abraham Kuyper on, 21, 23–26, 143; in Dutch-American commentary, 46, 54–55, 67, 75, 77, 124, 145, 149
Roosevelt, Franklin Delano, 148–50, 298n.25. *See also* New Deal
Runner, H. Evan, 196, 200
Ryskamp, Henry J., 150–51, 189

Scholte, Hendrik Pieter, 7, 10–11, 40
Schoolland, Klass: and Antithetical Calvinism, 47, 50–51, 100, 102; sociopolitical commentary of, 61, 65, 70–71, 74–77; and World War I, 85–86, 90
Schuller, Robert, 136, 198, 221
Schultze, Henry, 145, 155, 188
Seceders. *See* Secession of 1834
Secession of 1834: and Dutch-American controversies, 39–40, 44, 46–49, 197–98, 206; and Geldersche school, 7, 38, 44, 206; in the Netherlands, 3, 6–7, 10–15, 19, 29–31, 135, 244n.19; and Northern school, 7, 40, 206; and U.S. immigration, 7–10, 38–40, 53, 245n.28, 246n.34. *See also* Confessionalism; Pietism
Smedes, Lewis, 212, 216–17, 319n.34
Social question. *See* Labor question
Socialism, 24, 74, 148–50. *See also* Communism
Steffens, Nicholas M., 46, 60
Stob, George, 188, 190, 192, 201
Synod of Dort (1618–19), 4, 6, 46, 200

Tanis, Edward J., 55, 78, 90, 126, 149–50, 153, 155, 189
Temperance, 69, 73, 272n.22. *See also* Prohibition
Ten Hoor, Foppe M.: on America, 57–61, 90; and Confessionalism, 47–50, 52, 72, 126, 208; in 1920s controversies, 105–6, 108, 118

Theological School at Grand Rapids. *See* Calvin Theological Seminary

Van Andel, Henry J., 99–101, 110, 119, 142, 145, 149
Van Baalen, Jan Karel, 110–13, 119, 136, 142–43
Vander Ploeg, John, 154, 199, 208, 215–16
Van Lonkhuyzen, John: on America, 61, 77, 97; and Antithetical Calvinism, 47, 50, 52, 100; in 1920s controversies, 97, 109–10, 118; and World War I, 83–85
Van Raalte, Albertus C., 7, 10; and immigration, 38–40, 257n.10; relatives of, 110, 160; settlements of, 56, 62, 67, 140
Van Ruler, A. A., 214, 319n.34
Van Til, Cornelius, 128, 131, 190–93, 195–96
Van Til, Henry R., 191, 194–95, 208
Verduin, Leonard, 201, 210, 297n.8
Vos, Geerhardus, 107, 190, 262n.46, 264n.72
Vrije Universiteit, 14, 19, 30, 48, 105, 196, 213, 215

Westminster Theological Seminary, 128, 191, 196
Western Theological Seminary, 44, 46, 99, 197
Wilson, Woodrow, 83–84, 90, 102
World War I: and Americanization, 41, 57, 90–91; Dutch-American assessments of, 84–86, 89–95, 119; Dutch-American experience in, 83–84, 86–90; later influence of, 151, 154–55, 194
World War II, 123, 130, 141, 153–56, 187–88
Worldliness: and Americanization, 63, 116–17, 125; and Dutch-American novelists, 170, 179; and Netherlandic Calvinism, 4, 15; and pietistic ethic, 137–39, 143, 190, 199, 201